Course	Introduction to Sociology
Course Number	**SOC 101**
	Dr. Nick McRee
	The University of Portland
	Sociology

http://create.mheducation.com

ISBN-10: 1121597548   ISBN-13: 9781121597549

Contents

Credits

CHAPTER

2

The Sociological Eye

Modern sociologists continue to be inspired by two important qualities stressed by early sociologists: (1) the focus on the social and (2) skepticism.

The Focus on the Social

For American sociologist C. Wright Mills (1916–1962), the key to the sociological imagination was the ability to distinguish between personal troubles and social issues.

It is the focus on the social that allows sociologists to see much that escapes the notice of other observers; it is what makes sociology unique. But, I should warn you, this focus on the social makes sociology difficult for newcomers to the discipline because most of them have been taught to view the world in ways that are distinctly nonsociological.

Let me explain: People in modern Western societies have been taught to embrace the principle of *individualism*. Individualism is the idea that in life people pursue their own ends, that people follow their own ideas. Why does Mary get better grades than Johnny? It must be that Mary is smarter, or works harder, than Johnny. Why does Chris get drunk every weekend? Well, frankly, Chris just doesn't make good choices.

You might be thinking—of course we focus on individuals! How else can it be? The fact is, in other cultures (and even in our own in earlier times) individuals are hardly noticeable, but are treated as extensions of their family, clan, or tribe. If one person does something heroic, the group receives the credit; likewise, if one person does something wrong, it is the group that is shamed. How unlike our own society. Imagine the day when you graduate from college: Your parents will be proud, but they will be proud of

28

your accomplishments. The diploma will have your name on it; all of the congratulations (and gifts) will be bestowed on you.

Sociologists have taught themselves not to be satisfied with explanations that focus on individuals, but to look at the social environment and the ways in which it affects people. What is it about the social context in which some people grow up and live that facilitates academic achievement? In what ways do particular social circumstances encourage some people to drink to excess?

More generally, sociologists understand that individuals make choices about how they will act, that they do have "free will," but sociologists know that it is the social environment that makes some choices easier and others harder.

Consider the case of the motorist who arrives at an intersection: Will she go right, left, or continue on? The naive observer might say that we cannot predict her next move, that it's *her choice*. Yet we can be confident that she will not shift into reverse and back up; neither will she choose to remain in the intersection for more than a few moments. Even if she doesn't want to go right, left, or ahead, the social circumstances (the rules of the road, not to mention the line of impatient drivers in the cars behind her) will push her to do so (McIntyre 2005, 19).

Why are sociologists unsatisfied with individualistic explanations for behavior? Allan G. Johnson, who has written a number of books for sociology students, explains it this way: *"the individualistic perspective that dominates current thinking about social life doesn't work"*:

> Nothing we do or experience takes place in a vacuum; everything is always related to a [social] context of some kind. When a wife and husband argue abut who'll clean the bathroom, for example, or who'll take care of a sick child when they both work outside the home, the issue is never simply abut the two of them even though it may seem that way at the time. We have to ask about the larger context in which this takes place. We might ask how this instance is related to living in a society organized in ways that privilege men over women, in part by not making men feel obliged to share equally in domestic work except when they choose to "help out." On an individual level, he may think she's being a nag; she may think he's being a jerk; but it's never as simple as that. What both may miss is that in a different kind of society, they might not be having this argument in the first place because both might feel obliged to take care of the home and children. In similar ways, when we see ourself as a unique result of the family we came from, we overlook how each family is connected to larger patterns. The emotional problems we struggle with as individuals aren't due simply to what kind of parents we had, for their participation in social system — at work, in the community, in society as a whole — shaped them as people, including their roles as mothers and fathers.

> An individualistic model is misleading because it encourages us to explain human behavior and experience from a perspective that's so narrow it misses most of what's going on (Johnson 1997, 20-21).

This is not to say that sociologists are uninterested in the behavior of individuals. Many of us (myself included) are just as interested in the goings-on of the people we encounter as you are; many of us (myself included) watch and wonder about the antics of our neighbors, colleagues (and yes, our students) and seek explanations for what we see. What makes sociologists different from other people is the conviction that our ability to understand and explain what we observe will be enhanced if we look past the individuals involved to examine the impact of their social context.

The American sociologist C. Wright Mills sharpened the sociological perspective with his concept of the *sociological imagination*. The defining quality of the sociological imagination, Mills said, is the ability to look beyond what he called the *personal troubles* of individuals to see the *public issues of social structure*—that is, the social forces operating in the larger society.

> The first fruit of this imagination—and the lesson of the social science that embodies it—is the idea that the individual can understand his own experience and gauge his own fate only by locating himself within his period, that he can know his own chances in life only by becoming aware of those of all individuals in his circumstances. (1959, 5)

Mills observed that people in our society "often feel that their private lives are a series of traps. They sense that within their everyday worlds, they cannot overcome their troubles." In other words, people feel unable to alter their circumstances. And, Mills suggested, in this feeling of being trapped and impotent, people "are often quite correct."

Mills suggests that people often misunderstand their own circumstances because they have an individualistic bias. The individualistic bias leads people to think that their own situations are wholly a result of their own behavior. They don't notice that there are larger entities, including social institutions, that shape their behaviors.

Without guidance from the sociological imagination, our individualistic bias leads us to treat individuals as the source of problems. Of course, people frequently do make bad choices. But the individualistic bias prevents us from discovering that some of our worst problems are the result of *social forces*.

Consider John and Jill who, after nine years of marriage, have just divorced. Jill is feeling like a failure. When she vowed "'til death do us part," she meant it! Where did she go wrong? Her own parents are still married after 32 years! John, too, is at a loss.

Jill doesn't seem at all like the woman he fell in love with; she's changed. The passion is gone and they've grown apart.

John and Jill entered marriage with the understanding that it was up to them to make the union a success. As a result, as Mills would say, John and Jill regard the failure of their marriage as purely a *personal trouble;* a result of something they did or did not do.

Mills would understand Johns and Jill's point of view, but suggest it might be misguided. He pointed out that "inside a marriage a man and a woman may experience personal troubles," but when the divorce rate escalates, "this is an indication of a structural issue having to do with the institutions of marriage and the family and other institutions that bear upon them." John and Jill experience their divorce as a personal trouble, but current social arrangements (such as an economy that requires families to have two wage-earners and forces employees to work lots of overtime) has made marriage more difficult. Under such circumstances, Mills points out, "the problem of a satisfactory marriage remains incapable of purely private solution."

Here is the crucial sociological punch line: If people in society are concerned about the divorce rate and want to fix it, they must not focus on individuals; they must focus on the *social* structures and *social* arrangements that make marriage difficult.

Mills argued that most individuals feel trapped by the problems they encounter—and that their sense of entrapment comes from believing that their personal troubles are necessarily of their own making. Mills believed that the sociological imagination can help rescue people from such traps.

Without guidance from the sociological imagination, we are tempted to attack all problems by treating individuals. Again, this is because of our individualistic bias, which makes it hard for us to see beyond our own personal and immediate circumstances. With such a limited perspective, it's hard to see that some of our worst problems are a result of *social forces*.

The advantage of the sociological imagination or perspective, then, as Mills discovered, is that it opens up new resources for problem solving. Many of the most serious problems experienced by individuals, such as unemployment, have *social* causes, so it is futile to try to remedy or fix them at the individual level.

> When, in a city of 100,000, only one man is unemployed, that is his personal trouble, and for its relief we properly look to the character of the man, his skills, and his immediate opportunities. But when in a nation of 50 million employees, 15 million men are unemployed, that is a [social] issue, and we may not hope to find its solution within the range of opportunities open to any one individual. . . . Both the correct statement of the problem and the range of possible solutions require us

to consider the economic and political institutions of society, and not merely the personal situation and character of a scatter of individuals. (1959, 9)

As mentioned briefly in chapter 1, the French sociologist Émile Durkheim applied the sociological perspective to the problem of suicide. To most of Durkheim's colleagues, the decision to kill oneself seemed to be the most personal and individual of decisions. But, said Durkheim, *suicide is also a social issue.* From studying the differences in suicide statistics across different European countries, Durkheim found that the rate of suicide tended to vary with the degree of *social integration* in a particular society. In other words, *the rate of suicide varies with the degree to which people have strong ties to their social groups.*

More specifically, Durkheim found that people with weaker or fewer ties to their social groups were more likely to commit suicide. This finding helped to explain the fact that single people had higher rates of suicide than married people. Likewise, understanding the relationship between suicide and social integration helped to explain why Protestants (who are encouraged by their religion to be independent) had higher suicide rates than Catholics.

The sociological perspective of Durkheim, or what Mills later called the sociological imagination, suggested that suicide is not simply an individual problem, or personal trouble. Durkheim himself argued that the rate of suicide would decrease if more emphasis were placed on integrating people into society. To put it another way, according to Durkheim, the rate of suicide would drop if people were given more opportunities to bond with one another.

It is easy to find examples of situations in which the sociological imagination or perspective adds to our understanding. Sociologists who study organizations, for example, have discovered that working in a bureaucracy can have a tremendous impact on people's behavior. Regardless of how warm and caring people are *off* the job, their "on-the-job personalities" can be rigid, authoritarian, and uncaring—because that is how the structure of the organization forces them to be. People who work in bureaucracies have to follow the rules and act without regard for differences among individual clients. (Just remember this the next time you visit the registrar's office! If you want to make the system work for you, you need to take into account the ways in which the person across the counter is constrained by his or her position.)

Likewise, sociologists who study social inequality have examined the fact that people of different races are treated differently in most societies. This inequity should come as no surprise to you. But what may surprise you is that racial discrimination is not merely a matter of individuals being nasty to one another. Frequently, racism is a result of factors built into social systems. Because of this *institutional racism*, individuals may get locked into a larger pattern of racist behavior, perhaps without even being aware of it, let alone being able to resist it. The admissions officer at the exclusive private university who is told to give preference to the children of alumni is perpetuating racist admissions policies (because most of the alumni are white), even though he or she may personally abhor racism. The loan officer at the bank who is told not to approve loans for homes in certain parts of the city (populated mainly by African Americans) may not be racist, but her institution forces her to act as if she is. This does not, of course, excuse racist activities, but it does suggest that the fight against racism has to involve more than educating individuals. We have to treat this problem (or, as Mills would say, this *social issue*) at a higher level.

2.1 Describe the difference between crime as a personal trouble and crime as a public/social issue.

Skepticism

Like their nineteenth-century predecessors, contemporary sociologists are skeptical of commonly accepted explanations of things. Indeed, skepticism is an important foundation of scientific curiosity. If one accepts everyday explanations for things, there is no reason to inquire further. For example, in years past, only those who were skeptical of the commonly accepted "fact" that humans could not fly attempted to build "aeroplanes." Similarly, in the early nineteenth century, engineers believed that buildings could not be constructed more than a few stories high. But the skeptics among them, working with technology and the laws of physics, designed the immense structures that dominate the skylines of modern cities.

Sociologists are especially skeptical about the impact of social things. As an outgrowth of his skepticism, American sociologist Robert K. Merton provided us with an important research technique. Merton said that really understanding social things involves identifying both their *manifest* (intended and obvious) and *latent* (unintended and frequently hidden) consequences. Merton called these consequences *functions*.

One of the most obvious examples of the importance of latent consequences involves the modern experience with prisons. The manifest function of the prison system is to protect society by locking up dangerous criminals. As many researchers have found,

however, one of the latent functions of the prison system is the production of more knowledgeable criminals—that is, convicts learn
from one another in prison about how to commit crimes!

Here are two more examples of manifest versus latent functions.
The first has to do with medicine.

> In the nineteenth century there were hundreds of medical schools
> throughout the United States. The quality of these schools was
> uneven: Some offered hands-on training while others stressed only
> theory. Some required three years of study after four years of college,
> while others required three years of medical study but no college
> degree. Some taught traditional ("allopathic") medicine, while others
> pursued more novel approaches (such as homeopathy, osteopathy,
> chiropractic, and botanical medicine). Some had well-endowed labo-
> ratories and libraries, while others did not.
>
> In the early twentieth century, some members of the American
> medical profession believed that society would be better off if its
> physicians were trained in a more scientific manner. In 1910 the
> American Medical Association (AMA) commissioned one of its
> members, Abraham Flexner, to conduct a study of medical schools
> throughout the country. As he would report to the AMA, Flexner
> was appalled at the variety of training methods he encountered.
> Citing the Flexner Report as evidence, the AMA lobbied government
> officials to clamp down on schools that did not offer a specific sort
> of training. As a result, hundreds of medical schools were forced to
> close their doors.
>
> The manifest, or intended, consequence of tightening regulations
> for medical schools was to produce better-trained physicians. But this
> change in regulations had several latent consequences as well. One
> latent consequence was that practitioners who could not afford the
> more expensive training offered by traditional schools or who did
> not agree with traditional notions of medicine were forced out of
> the profession.[1] Tightened regulations also forced medical schools
> that trained women and African Americans to close their doors
> because they could not afford the expensive laboratory equipment
> and libraries that the AMA rules required. (Note that Flexner pre-
> sented no evidence that the patients of physicians trained in alterna-
> tive schools without laboratories and libraries were worse off than the

---

[1] It is important to point out that even in the early twentieth century, regular (allo-
pathic) medical practitioners could not successfully treat diseases like tuberculosis,
syphilis, and polio. Nor were such things as the importance of wearing rubber gloves
universally accepted among medical personnel (many hospitals did not provide gloves
for surgeons, and most surgeons did not want the added expense of purchasing their
own). Furthermore, regular medical treatments frequently did more harm than good.
For example, during the nineteenth century, many people died from being "bled" by
their physicians, who had hoped to drain out "bad humors" from the body. Some treatments even called for the letting of more blood than we now know exists in the entire
body (George Washington was said to have met his death this way). In contrast, alternative medical approaches generally took a less invasive, more supportive approach.
Thus, ironically, one was generally safer *not* being treated by regular medical personnel.

Nail down that distinction between manifest and latent functions!

University Education

Manifest function: Educate young adults.

Latent function: Keep young adults out of the job market, thereby easing competition for older adults.

Mother's Day and Father's Day

Manifest function: Provide an opportunity to express gratitude to one's parents.

Latent function: Help greeting card companies boost sales in the spring and summer months.

Carrying a Briefcase

Manifest function: Carry one's stuff.

Latent function: Indicate one's occupational status (for example, demonstrate that one is employed doing nonmanual labor).

---

patients of physicians who had trained at, say, Harvard.) And finally, doctors trained in the traditional manner no longer had to compete with the oftentimes more popular nontraditional practitioners.

Here is an example of how unintended or latent functions may have an impact on one aspect of *your* life.

New college professors generally must endure a six-year probationary period. At the end of this time, the quality of the professor's teaching, research, and service work is evaluated by senior colleagues. If the accomplishments of the probationary professor are deemed acceptable, they will grant him or her *tenure*. But if he or she has not lived up to expectations, the professor is denied tenure and forced to leave the university.

In the past few decades, most universities and colleges have tightened up their tenure requirements. Fifty years ago, tenure was practically a given. Today, things are different; most junior professors[2] spend their first years working like crazy to fulfill tenure requirements. One of the most important requirements is to conduct research and publish the results. As a rule of thumb, if you don't publish a fair amount, you will be denied tenure (hence the so-called publish-or-perish rule).

---

[2] Untenured professors typically are called assistant professors. Among the senior professors who have tenure, there are two ranks: associate professor and full professor.

36   CHAPTER 2   THE SOCIOLOGICAL EYE

The manifest function, or intended consequence, of emphasizing the importance of research for tenure is to produce more knowledge of the natural and social world. Universities do not want professors who simply sit around doing nothing. Professors should be out there, studying and making scholarly contributions. The latent function or consequence, however, is that some professors neglect their teaching responsibilities to do their research.[3]

This is not to say that all latent functions or consequences have a negative impact on society's usual functioning or are, as sociologists would put it, *dysfunctional*.[4] The unintended consequence of an action can be positive, or *functional*. For example, the manifest function of a neighborhood party is to have fun; a latent function can be to bring neighbors together or promote crime fighting. The manifest function of riding bicycles to work is to increase riders' fitness; a latent function can be fewer cars on the road or less air pollution.

Merton's distinction between manifest and latent functions is important. It reminds us to look beyond the obvious — frequently, the least obvious consequences are the most important ones.

STOP & REVIEW

2.2 For each of these common social events, list as many manifest and latent functions as you can:
   a. college athletics
   b. attending church
   c. attending sociology class

Chapter Review

1. Make a list of the sociological concepts that you learned in this chapter. Define each term. (*Hint:* You will learn the most from this exercise if, in addition to defining each concept, you create an example of it in your own words.)

2. Sociologists often have a difficult time persuading lay people that there is something to be gained by looking at divorce,

---

[3] Fortunately, as we begin the twenty-first century, university officials seem to be backtracking a bit and are once again beginning to emphasize the importance of teaching. At my own university, for example, candidates for tenure and promotion are required to show a measure of success in both teaching and research.

[4] Notice the spelling of *dysfunctional*. The *dys* prefix, which has its roots in the Greek language, suggests that something is defective, difficult, or painful. This prefix is frequently encountered in medicine — for example, *dysentery* ("painful intestine"), *dyspeptic* ("painful digestion"), or *dystrophy* ("abnormal growth"). On the other hand, the *dis* prefix, which is derived from Latin, tends to mean "apart," "asunder," or "deprived of" — for example, *dissemble, disable,* or *disrespect.* So, although the two prefixes are pronounced the same in English, they carry different meanings.

racism, or poverty (or anything else, for that matter) as a social issue rather than just a personal trouble. In your considered judgment, why might this be so?

3. What is a possible benefit of looking for latent as well as manifest functions of things in the social world?

Answers and Discussion

2.1 According to Mills's perspective, crime as a personal trouble involves the circumstances and problems of the people who are directly touched by the crime. For example, Joe Student was arrested for breaking and entering. Why on earth did Joe do such a thing (seeking the cause of the crime in Joe's personal circumstances)?

Crime as a social issue involves looking at the larger aspects of crime and the ways these are affected by historical and social circumstances. For example, the rate of burglaries is on the increase. What is happening in the rest of society (perhaps in the economic arena) that might be influencing this?

2.2

    a. Manifest functions of college athletics include enhancing school spirit, helping students develop physical as well as mental skills, and increasing the fame of the college or university. Latent functions include helping students who otherwise would not be able to attend college (because of poverty, for example) to do so by winning athletic scholarships, acting as a training ground for future professional athletes, and exploiting the talents of athletes from underprivileged backgrounds without actually having to provide a real education for them. (That's pretty cynical, isn't it? That last one might be a dysfunction of college athletics.)

    b. Manifest functions of church attendance include worshiping and joining with others to celebrate important beliefs. Latent functions include having an opportunity to dress up and see what other people are wearing and how their children behave.

    c. Manifest functions of attending class regularly include learning the assigned material more thoroughly and having the opportunity to hear brilliant lectures by your professors. Latent functions include impressing your professors with the sincerity of your quest for knowledge and having more opportunities to make friends with other students, or even having a quiet time to write a letter.

4

Who's Afraid of Sociology?

Once, on about the third day of the semester, a student in my introductory sociology class walked up to me and said, "Sociology is the work of the devil." Then he left.

I never saw that student again. But had he given me the chance, I would have told him that I disagreed with his assessment. In fact, I am sure that the devil hates sociology more than most things.

It is true that sociology emerged at a time in history when many individuals (including some sociologists) were questioning the authority of religious leaders. It is likewise true that a few of those early sociologists even thought that sociology might someday replace religion. But there is nothing inherently antireligious about sociology. Of course, the skepticism and questioning attitude of sociologists does threaten some people in authority. (Whether that is a bad thing is for you to judge. In any case, as I will discuss shortly, whether something is good or bad is *not* a proper sociological question.)

As much as sociology may threaten religious leaders, it is not really a threat to the social institution of religion—and certainly it is no threat to God (just imagine!). Sociologists are concerned with issues of *observable facts.* In other words, sociologists (like other scientists) tend to be preoccupied with the *empirical* world.

The Empirical World and Inconvenient Facts

This concept of empirical is an important one in science. *Empirical* refers to things that can be observed through the use of one's physical senses—sight, hearing, touch, taste, and smell. If a thing cannot be seen, heard, touched, tasted, or smelled—or, more specifically, if it is not *observable*—it is of little interest to sociologists.

For example, a sociologist doing research might well ask, "Do people in a particular society believe in God?" or, "What impact do religious beliefs have on a person's behavior?" or, "What are the manifest and latent functions of religion in society?" But no working sociologist would ask, "Is there a God?" or, "Is God more fond of Buddhists, Catholics, Muslims, Jews, or Protestants?" or, "Is religion X more correct in its beliefs and practices than religion Y?" These are *not* sociological questions.

Admittedly, anyone who preaches unquestioned obedience to authority will be troubled by sociology. This is well evidenced by the fact that in the twentieth century, whenever a dictator came into power, one of his first acts was to reassign or fire all the sociologists—anything to keep them from making trouble by asking questions. Obviously, you cannot have a successful dictatorship as long as people are questioning authority and being skeptical about its claims. Sociology can flourish only in a free society.

I remember that *my* first sociology course was quite an awakening. Like my classmates, I frequently was appalled to learn some of the stuff that sociologists have uncovered about society. Still, that was in 1972, and in those days we were just learning not to be shocked when we found out that there is a dysfunctional underside to society.

As a sociology professor, I have observed that some students become uncomfortable when they encounter the results of sociological research. I guess that even now it can be shocking to discover that many of the things you always accepted as true are, in fact, false.

Max Weber had a term for those pieces of evidence that contradict what you have always believed and/or want to believe about the social world; he called them *inconvenient facts*. As far as Weber was concerned, it was the sociologist's duty to deal with inconvenient facts. Indeed, Weber argued that one of the best things a sociology teacher could do

> is to teach his students to recognize inconvenient facts—I mean facts that are inconvenient for their party [that is, political] opinions. And for every party opinion there are facts that are extremely inconvenient, for my own opinion no less than for others. I believe the teacher accomplishes more than a mere intellectual task if he compels his audience to accustom itself to the existence of such facts. (Weber 1918/1958, 147)

Here are some empirical facts that have upset some beginning sociology students; in the Weberian sense, these are examples of inconvenient facts. Keep in mind that each of these facts about life in the United States has been validated by a great deal of research.

Even when they do the exact same jobs and have the exact same educational background, men tend to earn more money than women, and whites tend to earn more than African Americans. (See, for example, chapter 14 of this book.)

The majority of adults who sexually abuse children are heterosexual. (See Greenberg 1988; Sullivan 1995.)

Whether students get into college has more to do with their parents' socioeconomic standing than with their own intelligence or high school grades. (See chapters 12 and 13 of this book.)

Friendships between people of different races are as stable as friendships between people of the same race. (See Hallinan and Williams 1987.)

When they hear such things in lectures or read them in articles or books assigned in sociology classes, some students react as if the professor (me) is trying to pull a fast one: How can it be true that there is still salary discrimination based on gender and race? How can it be true that most child molesters are heterosexual? How can it be that money and status will get you into college over brains and knowledge? How can such things happen in a society that promotes equality, or in which the supposed corrupting influence of homosexuals is so feared, or in which people are supposed to succeed on their own merit?

Our society, like all societies, aspires to many things. But, as with all societies, there can be discrepancies between the ideal world and the real world. It may be disturbing to learn of these discrepancies, but hiding from them will not make the world a better place.

It is important to remember that the goal of sociology is not to undermine society or people's beliefs. Still, I can assure you of one thing: Any belief that can't stand up to objective scrutiny is hardly worth having. Sociologists cultivate the skill of examining beliefs about the nature of the social world and seeing which ones stand up to the evidence.

4.1 What did Weber mean by the term *inconvenient fact*?

Ethnocentrism

The most difficult thing about doing sociology is examining people whose customs and traditions differ from our own. Each of us likes to believe that his or her own people's customs and traditions are best. And when we encounter people whose ways of life are different, our tendency is to make a value judgment. More specifically, we generally do not see difference as merely difference, but as an indication of inferiority.

50   CHAPTER 4   WHO'S AFRAID OF SOCIOLOGY?

The human tendency to judge others as inferior is very much evident in the written records of those who were the first to explore other countries and to encounter "foreigners." When Europeans first met Africans, for example, they found African customs so different from European ones that they doubted that the Africans were even human. It seems likely that the Africans' first responses to the Europeans were similar.

To the ancient Greeks, the language of foreigners sounded like nonsensical stammering, like "bar-bar-bar." Because of this, the ancient Greeks came to call all foreigners "barbarians." Similarly, the Aztec peoples called their own language *nahuatl,* meaning "pleasant sounding," but called other people's languages *nonotl,* meaning "stammering." Modern languages reflect a similarly near-universal disdain for foreign peoples:

> In Japanese, the word for foreigner means "stinking of foreign hair."[1] To the Czechs a Hungarian is "a pimple." Germans call cockroaches "Frenchmen," while the French call lice "Spaniards." We in the English-speaking world take French leave, but Italians and Norwegians talk about departing like an Englishman, and Germans talk of running like a Dutchman. Italians call syphilis "the French disease," while both French and Italians call con games "American swindle." Belgian taxi drivers call a poor tipper "un Anglais." (Bryson 1990, 17)

This process of judging other peoples and their customs and norms as inferior to one's own people, customs, and norms is called *ethnocentrism.* Table 4.1 lists common ethnocentric attitudes toward one's own group and toward outsiders.

The positive side of ethnocentrism is that it brings together people and builds solidarity within a particular society. It is similar to believing that your team is the best team. Much as believing that one's team is the best helps to unite students and boost school spirit, believing that one's culture is the best helps to unite people in society. To use Durkheim's phrasing, ethnocentrism promotes social solidarity.

The negative (or dysfunctional) side of ethnocentrism is that it can lead to nasty consequences: prejudice, discrimination, even genocide or "ethnic cleansing."[2] For example, in 1619, a group of

"[Ethnocentrism is the view] of things in which one's own group is the center of everything and all others are scaled and rated with references to it. . . . Each group nourishes its own pride and vanity, boasts itself superior, exalts its own divinities, and looks with contempt on outsiders."

—William G. Sumner (1906)

---

[1] A close reader of the first edition of this book told me that the Japanese word for foreigner is *gaikokujin,* or more frequently *gaigin,* "which translates to 'foreigner' or 'outsider.'" But, according to my reader, either word is "pejorative, and no one would use it in public except children who haven't been socialized not to repeat in public what their parents say in the home." I confess that my knowledge of Japanese is very limited; but I did quiz more than a dozen of my students who are from Japan. When I asked, "What word do the Japanese people use to refer to people from other countries?" each one told me *gaigin.* I am still investigating this matter!

[2] The term *genocide* was introduced by Raphael Lemkin. In 1944, in his study of the Axis (German–Italian) rule of occupied Europe during World War II, Lemkin proposed the term to denote the destruction of a nation or an ethnic group. He coined the word by joining the ancient Greek word *genos* ("race, tribe") with the Latin term *cide* ("killing").

Table 4.1 Ethnocentric Attitudes—Toward One's Own Group and Toward Outsiders

Toward Own Group	Toward Outsiders
See members as virtuous and superior	See outsiders as contemptible, immoral, and inferior
See own values as universal and intrinsically true	See outsiders' values as false (where they differ from own group's values)
See own customs as original and centrally human, as reflecting true "human nature"	See outsiders' customs as suspicious, ignorant, and lacking in humanity

For an excellent introduction to the issue of ethnocentrism, see Levine and Campbell 1972.

religious dissidents in England sought a place where they could have religious freedom. These Pilgrims chose North America. Why? Because no "people" lived there! Here's how one of their leaders, William Bradford, explained the Pilgrims' rationale:

> The place [the Pilgrims] had their thoughts on was some of those vast and unpeopled countries of America, which are fruitful and fit for habitation, being devoid of all civil inhabitants, where there are only savage and brutish men which range up and down, little otherwise than the wild beasts of the same. (Quoted in Holmes 1891, 36)

Because the native inhabitants of North America had different customs and lifestyles, they were seen by these English as less than human and more like "wild beasts." This sort of reasoning allowed many European settlers (and their descendants) to believe that they were as justified in killing Native Americans as they were in killing any dangerous animal.

In my own experience, many people who live in the United States are ethnocentric about being ethnocentric! What I mean is that people in our society seem to think that we are the only ones who are ethnocentric—implying, perhaps, that we are the only ones who have any right to feel superior.

It comes as a shock to many North Americans to find, for example, that we smell bad to many Asians (it's because of all the dairy products we consume). Likewise, when the Thonga people of Africa first saw visiting Europeans kissing, they reacted with horror and disgust: What sort of people would engage in "eating each other's saliva and dirt" (Hyde 1979, 18)?

For sociologists, ethnocentrism is especially dangerous because it gets in the way of understanding. If we really want to understand why people in society X act the way they do, how their institutions work, and what their customs are, we have to see them in the context of *their* society. Ethnocentrism hinders such understanding because it means we are viewing society X in terms of our own society.

52   CHAPTER 4   WHO'S AFRAID OF SOCIOLOGY?

Avoiding Ethnocentrism Can Be Difficult

Even when we tell ourselves sternly that we must be objective, that we must examine the people of other cultures in terms of their cultures, it is difficult. Anthropologist Napoleon Chagnon gives a startling example of how difficult it can be to avoid being ethnocentric. Chagnon studied the Yanomamö Indians of South America by living among them for more than a year. Here's part of what he wrote about his first day in the field. Imagine yourself in his shoes: Could you have remained "objective?"

Encounters with different cultures challenge one's taken-for-granted assumptions about the way things are and ought to be. Social scientists refer to the resulting feeling of disorientation as culture shock.

My first day in the field illustrated to me what my teachers meant when they spoke of "culture shock." . . .

We arrived at the village, Biaasi-teri, about 2:00 P.M. and docked the boat along the muddy bank at the terminus of the path used by the Indians to fetch their drinking water. It was hot and muggy, and my clothing was soaked with perspiration. . . .

I looked up and gasped when I saw a dozen burly, naked, filthy, hideous men staring at us down the shafts of their drawn arrows! Immense wads of green tobacco were stuck between their lower teeth and lips making them look even more hideous, and strands of dark-green slime dripped or hung from their noses. We arrived at the village while the men were blowing a hallucinogenic drug up their noses. One of the side effects of the drug is a runny nose. The mucus is always saturated with green powder and the Indians usually let it run freely from their nostrils. My next discovery was that there were a dozen or so vicious, underfed dogs snapping at my legs, circling me as if I were going to be their next meal. I just stood there holding my notebook, helpless and pathetic. Then the stench of the decaying vegetation and filth struck me and I almost got sick. I was horrified. . . .

The whole situation was depressing, and I wondered why I ever decided to switch from civil engineering to anthropology in the first place. I had not eaten all day, I was soaking wet from perspiration, the gnats were biting me, and I was covered with red pigment, the result of a dozen or so complete examinations I had been given by as many burly Indians. These examinations capped an otherwise grim day. The Indians would blow their noses into their hands, flick as much of the mucus off that would separate in a snap of the wrist, wipe the residue into their hair, and then carefully examine my face, arms, legs, hair, and the contents of my pockets. I asked Mr. Barker [a local missionary and Chagnon's temporary guide] how to say "Your hands are dirty"; my comments were met by the Indians in the following way: They would "clean" their hands by spitting a quantity of slimy tobacco juice into them, rub them together, and then proceed with the examination. (Chagnon 1977, 4–7)

Our initial reaction to the Yanomamö likely would be one of horror and disgust—just as it was Chagnon's reaction. In time, however, if we tried to keep an open mind, we too could become accustomed to the Yanomamö's ways—once we saw these in the context of their entire living situation.

> Mr. Barker and I crossed the river and slung our hammocks. When he pulled his hammock out of a rubber bag, a heavy, disagreeable odor of mildewed cotton came with it. "Even the missionaries are filthy," I thought to myself. Within two weeks everything I owned smelled the same way, and I lived with the odor for the remainder of the field work. My own habits of personal cleanliness reached such levels that I didn't even mind being examined by the Indians, as I was not much cleaner than they were after I had adjusted to the circumstances. . . .
>
> I discovered that it was an enormously time-consuming task to maintain my own body in the manner to which it had grown accustomed in the relatively antiseptic environment of the northern United States. Either I could be relatively well fed and relatively comfortable in a fresh change of clothes and do very little fieldwork, or, I could do considerably more fieldwork and be less well fed and less comfortable. (Chagnon 1977, 4–7)

It could certainly be argued that Chagnon's experiences were extreme, that most social scientists do not venture into such exotic locales. But one does not have to go very far to experience the shock of cultural differences. Probably, even in your own city or town, there are groups of people who live their lives very differently than you do. Quite possibly, you experienced a bit of culture shock when you first arrived at college!

When one encounters cultural strangers, one's first reaction is likely to be the same as Chagnon's when he met the Yanomamö. Ethnocentrism is normal. However, because it gets in the way of understanding, social scientists work to overcome it.

"Culture shock refers to the whole set of feelings about being in an alien setting, and the resulting reactions. It is a chilly, creepy feeling of alienation, of being without some of the most ordinary, trivial—and therefore basic—cues of one's culture of origin."

—Conrad P. Kottak (1992)

4.2 What does it mean to be ethnocentric? What's an example of ethnocentrism?

4.3 What is culture shock? What's an example of culture shock?

STOP & REVIEW

Cultural Relativism

Sociologists work to overcome their ethnocentrism by practicing something called *cultural relativism*. Cultural relativism is *the belief that other people and their ways of doing things can be understood only in terms of the cultural context of those people.* This is based on the assumption that if our goal is to truly understand people's behavior, we have to look for clues in *their* culture.

Some people have misunderstood this notion of cultural relativity. They suspect that it implies that any one way of doing things is as good as any other way. As far as sociologists are concerned,

54   CHAPTER 4   WHO'S AFRAID OF SOCIOLOGY?

Ethnocentrism can lead to shocking cases of ignorance. During a debate over the merits of bilingual education, for example, one congressman quite seriously said to Dr. David Edwards (head of the Joint National Committee on Languages):

"If English was good enough for Jesus Christ, it's good enough for me."

—Quoted by Bill Bryson (1990)

however, cultural relativity has nothing to do with assessing which ways of doing things are better or worse. Remember, "Which way is better or worse?" is *not* a legitimate sociological question.

For sociologists, cultural relativity means being objective enough to understand people's behaviors in terms of their culture and social situation. Sociology does not agree or disagree with, or approve or disapprove of, behavior; sociology seeks to understand and explain behavior. And understanding and explaining is difficult to do unless one is willing to look at things in their own context.

Chapter Review

1. Make a list of the sociological concepts that you learned in this chapter. Define each term. (*Hint:* You will learn the most from this exercise if, in addition to defining each concept, you create an example of it in your own words.)

2. What is cultural relativism? Why is it considered crucial for sociologists?

Answers and Discussion

4.1 Weber used the term inconvenient facts to refer to facts or data that go against one's social and political beliefs. For example, suppose you are very much in favor of imposing the death penalty on convicted murderers. If that were the case, the following facts might be inconvenient for you:

   a. There is no evidence that the threat of the death penalty has any appreciable effect on a country's murder rate.

   b. In the United States, it costs more to put a person to death than to keep him or her in prison for life.

By the way, it is amazingly difficult to think of examples of inconvenient facts. That is not because they aren't there, but because it is easier to try to ignore them.

4.2 Your definition of ethnocentrism should include the ideas that it occurs when we judge other people's customs and behaviors against the standards of our own culture. Asking a kilted Scotsman why he is dressed like a woman is ethnocentric.

4.3 Culture shock is that feeling of disorientation and even squeamishness that one feels when plunked down into a different culture. Chagnon felt this as he stood there and let the Yanomamö examine him.

MODULE 13 | The Role of Socialization

Sociologists are interested in the process of **socialization,** through which people learn the attitudes, values, and behaviors appropriate for members of their culture. Socialization occurs through human interactions that begin in infancy and continue throughout life. We learn a great deal from those people who are most important in our lives—immediate family members, best friends, and teachers. But we also learn from people we see on the street, on television, on the Internet, and in films and magazines. From a microsociological perspective, socialization helps us discover how to behave "properly" and what to expect from others if we follow (or challenge) society's norms and values. From a macrosociological perspective, socialization provides for the transmission of a culture from one generation to the next and thereby for the long-term continuance of society.

Socialization also shapes our self-images. For example, in the United States, a person who is viewed as "too heavy" or "too short" does not conform to the ideal cultural standard of physical attractiveness. This kind of unfavorable evaluation can significantly influence the person's self-esteem. In this sense, socialization experiences can help shape our personalities. In everyday speech, the term **personality** refers to a person's typical patterns of attitudes, needs, characteristics, and behavior.

How much of a person's personality is shaped by culture, as opposed to inborn traits? In other words, what makes us who we are? Is it the genes we are born with, or the environment in which we grow up? Researchers have traditionally clashed over the relative importance of biological inheritance and environmental factors in human development—a conflict called the *nature versus nurture* (or *heredity versus environment*) debate. Today, most social scientists have moved beyond this debate, acknowledging instead the *interaction* of these variables in shaping human development. We can best appreciate how heredity and environmental factors interact and influence the socialization process if we first examine situations in which one factor operates almost entirely without the other (Homans 1979).

● Social Environment: The Impact of Isolation

In the 1994 movie *Nell,* Jodie Foster played a young woman hidden from birth by her mother in a backwoods cabin. Raised without normal human contact, Nell crouches like an animal, screams wildly, and speaks or sings in a language all her own. This movie was drawn from the actual account of an emaciated 16-year-old boy who appeared mysteriously in 1828 in the town square of Nuremberg, Germany (Lipson 1994).

Isabelle and Genie: Two Cases

Some viewers may have found the story of Nell difficult to believe, but the painful childhood of Isabelle was all too real. For the first six years of her life, Isabelle lived in almost total seclusion in a darkened room. She had little contact with other people, with the exception of her mother, who could neither speak nor hear. Isabelle's mother's parents had been so deeply ashamed of Isabelle's illegitimate birth that they kept her hidden away from the world. Ohio authorities finally discovered the child in 1938, when Isabelle's mother escaped from her parents' home, taking her daughter with her.

When she was discovered at age six, Isabelle could not speak; she could merely make various croaking sounds. Her only communications with her mother were simple gestures. Isabelle had been largely deprived of the typical interactions and socialization experiences of childhood. Since she had seen few people, she showed a strong fear of strangers and reacted almost like a wild animal when confronted with an unfamiliar person. As she became accustomed to seeing certain individuals, her reaction changed to one of extreme apathy. At first, observers believed that Isabelle was deaf, but she soon began to react to nearby sounds. On tests of maturity, she scored at the level of an infant rather than a six-year-old.

Specialists developed a systematic training program to help Isabelle adapt to human relationships and socialization. After a few days of training, she made her first attempt to verbalize. Although she started slowly, Isabelle quickly passed through six years of development. In a little over two months she was speaking in complete sentences. Nine months later she could identify both words and sentences. Before Isabelle reached age 9, she was ready to attend school with other children. By age 14 she was in sixth grade, doing well in school, and emotionally well adjusted.

Yet without an opportunity to experience socialization in her first six years, Isabelle had been hardly human in the social sense when she was first discovered. Her inability to communicate at the time of her discovery—despite her physical and cognitive potential to learn—and her remarkable progress over the next few years underscore the impact of socialization on human development (K. Davis 1940, 1947).

FIGURE 13-1 Genie's Sketch

This sketch was made in 1975 by Genie—a girl who had been isolated for most of her 14 years, until she was discovered by authorities in 1970. In her drawing, her linguist friend (on the left) plays the piano while Genie listens. Genie was 18 when she drew this picture.
Source: Curtiss 1977:274.

Unfortunately, other children who have been locked away or severely neglected have not fared so well as Isabelle. In many instances, the consequences of social isolation have proved much more damaging. For example, in 1970 a 14-year-old Californian named Genie was discovered in a room where she had been confined since age 20 months. During her years of isolation, no family member had spoken to her, nor could she hear anything other than swearing. Since there was no television or radio in her home, she had never heard the sounds of normal human speech. One year after beginning extensive therapy, Genie's grammar resembled that of a typical 18-month-old. Though she made further advances with continued therapy, she never achieved full language ability. Today Genie, now in her mid-50s, lives in a home for developmentally disabled adults. Figure 13-1 shows a sketch Genie made of her teacher five years after she was discovered (Curtiss 1977, 1985; Rymer 1993).

Isabelle's and Genie's experiences are important to researchers because there are only a few cases of children reared in total isolation. Unfortunately, however, there are many cases of children raised in extremely neglectful social circumstances. In the 1990s, public attention focused on infants and young children from orphanages in the formerly communist countries of Eastern Europe. In Romanian orphanages, babies once lay in their cribs for 18 to 20 hours a day, curled against their feeding bottles and receiving little adult care. Such minimal attention continued for the first five years of their lives. Many of them were fearful of human contact and prone to unpredictable anti-social behavior.

This situation came to light as families in North America and Europe began adopting thousands of the children. The adjustment problems for about 20 percent of them were often so dramatic that the adopting families suffered guilty fears of being ill-fit adoptive parents. Many of them have asked for assistance in dealing with the children. Slowly, efforts are being made to introduce the deprived youngsters to feelings of attachment that they have never experienced before (Groza et al. 1999; Craig Smith 2006).

Increasingly, researchers are emphasizing the importance of the earliest socialization experiences for children who grow up in more normal environments. We now know that it is not enough to care for an infant's physical needs; parents must also concern themselves with children's social development. If, for example, children are discouraged from having friends even as toddlers, they will miss out on social interactions with peers that are critical for emotional growth.

Primate Studies

Studies of animals raised in isolation also support the importance of socialization in development. Harry Harlow (1971), a researcher at the primate laboratory of the University of Wisconsin, conducted tests with rhesus monkeys that had been raised away from their mothers and away from contact with other monkeys. As was the case with Isabelle, the rhesus monkeys raised in isolation were fearful and easily frightened. They did not mate, and the females who were artificially inseminated became abusive mothers. Apparently, isolation had had a damaging effect on the monkeys.

A creative aspect of Harlow's experimentation was his use of "artificial mothers." In one such experiment, Harlow presented monkeys raised in isolation with two substitute mothers—one cloth-covered replica and one covered with wire that had the ability to offer milk. Monkey after monkey went to the wire mother for the life-giving milk, yet spent much more time clinging to the more motherlike cloth model. It appears that the infant monkeys developed greater social attachments from their need for warmth, comfort, and intimacy than from their need for milk.

While the isolation studies just discussed may seem to suggest that heredity can be dismissed as a factor in the social development of humans and animals, studies of twins provide insight into a fascinating interplay between hereditary and environmental factors.

 use your **sociological imagination**

What events in your life have had a strong influence on who you are?

trend|spotting

Multiple Births

The birth of identical twins or triplets is a rare event, only about 1 in every 250 births. Recently, however, multiple births have increased dramatically. There is some evidence that fertility treatments such as in-vitro fertilization may be contributing to the increase, as it did with Kate and Jon Gosselin's sextuplets, born in 2004, and the Suleman octuplets, born in 2009. However, multiple births in general seem to be on the rise. Over the quarter century from 1980 to 2006, the birth rate for triplets and other multiples, identical or not, increased more than fourfold, from 37 to 153 of every 100,000 births.

wire-rimmed glasses and mustaches. They both liked spicy foods and sweet liqueurs, were absent-minded, flushed the toilet before using it, stored rubber bands on their wrists, and dipped buttered toast in their coffee (Holden 1980).

The twins also differed in many important respects: Jack was a workaholic; Oskar enjoyed leisure-time activities. Oskar was a traditionalist who was domineering toward women; Jack was a political liberal who was much more accepting of feminism. Finally, Jack was extremely proud of being Jewish, while Oskar never mentioned his Jewish heritage (Holden 1987).

Oskar and Jack are prime examples of the interplay of heredity and environment. For a number of years, the Minnesota Twin Family Study has been following pairs of identical twins reared apart to determine what similarities, if any, they show in personality traits, behavior, and intelligence. Preliminary results from the available twin studies indicate that *both* genetic factors *and* socialization experiences are influential in human development. Certain characteristics, such as temperaments, voice patterns, and nervous habits, appear to be strikingly similar even in twins reared apart, suggesting that these qualities may be linked to hereditary causes. However, identical twins reared apart differ far more in their attitudes, values, chosen mates, and even drinking habits; these qualities, it would seem, are influenced by environmental factors. In examining clusters of personality traits among such twins, researchers have found marked similarities in their tendency toward leadership or dominance, but significant differences in their need for intimacy, comfort, and assistance.

Researchers have also been impressed with the similar scores on intelligence tests of twins reared apart in *roughly similar* social

● The Influence of Heredity

Identical twins Oskar Stohr and Jack Yufe were separated soon after their birth and raised on different continents, in very different cultural settings. Oskar was reared as a strict Catholic by his maternal grandmother in the Sudetenland of Czechoslovakia. As a member of the Hitler Youth movement in Nazi Germany, he learned to hate Jews. In contrast, his brother Jack was reared in Trinidad by the twins' Jewish father. Jack joined an Israeli kibbutz (a collective settlement) at age 17 and later served in the Israeli army. When the twins were reunited in middle age, however, some startling similarities emerged: They both wore

on intelligence tests—a finding that supports the impact of socialization on human development (Joseph 2004; Kronstadt 2008a; McGue and Bouchard 1998; Minnesota Center for Twin and Family Research 2010).

We need to be cautious in reviewing studies of twin pairs and other relevant research. Widely broadcast findings have often been based on preliminary analysis of extremely small samples. For example, one study (not involving twin pairs) was frequently cited as confirming genetic links with behavior. Yet the researchers had to retract their conclusions after they increased the sample and reclassified two of the original cases. After those changes, the initial findings were no longer valid.

Critics add that studies of twin pairs have not provided satisfactory information concerning the extent to which separated identical twins may have had contact with each other, even though they were raised apart. Such interactions—especially if they were extensive—could call into question the validity of the twin studies. As this debate continues, we can certainly anticipate numerous efforts to replicate the research and clarify the interplay between heredity and environmental factors in human development (Horgan 1993; Plomin 1989).

Despite the striking physical resemblance between these identical twins, there are undoubtedly many differences. Research points to some behavioral similarities between twins, but little beyond the likenesses found among nontwin siblings.

settings. Most of the identical twins register scores even closer than those that would be expected if the same person took a test twice. At the same time, however, identical twins brought up in *dramatically different* social environments score quite differently

MODULE 13 | Recap and Review

Summary

Socialization is the process through which people learn the attitudes, values, and actions appropriate for members of a particular culture.

1. Socialization affects the overall cultural practices of a society; it also shapes the images we hold of ourselves.
2. Heredity and environmental factors interact in influencing the socialization process.

Thinking Critically

1. What might be some ethical concerns regarding research on the influences of heredity and environment?

2. What are some social policy implications of research on the effects of early socialization experiences?

Key Terms

Personality
Socialization

We all have various perceptions, feelings, and beliefs about who we are and what we are like. How do we come to develop them? Do they change as we age?

We were not born with these understandings. Building on the work of George Herbert Mead (1964b), sociologists recognize that our concept of who we are, the *self*, emerges as we interact with others. The **self** is a distinct identity that sets us apart from others. It is not a static phenomenon, but continues to develop and change throughout our lives.

Sociologists and psychologists alike have expressed interest in how the individual develops and modifies the sense of self as a result of social interaction. The work of sociologists Charles Horton Cooley and George Herbert Mead, pioneers of the interactionist approach, has been especially useful in furthering our understanding of these important issues.

Sociological Approaches to the Self

Cooley: Looking-Glass Self

In the early 1900s, Charles Horton Cooley advanced the belief that we learn who we are by interacting with others. Our view of ourselves, then, comes not only from direct contemplation of our personal qualities but also from our impressions of how others perceive us. Cooley used the phrase **looking-glass self** to emphasize that the self is the product of our social interactions.

The process of developing a self-identity or self-concept has three phases. First, we imagine how we present ourselves to others—to relatives, friends, even strangers on the street. Then we imagine how others evaluate us (attractive, intelligent, shy, or strange). Finally, we develop some sort of feeling about ourselves, such as respect or shame, as a result of these impressions (Cooley 1902; M. Howard 1989).

A subtle but critical aspect of Cooley's looking-glass self is that the self results from an individual's "imagination" of how others view him or her. As a result, we can develop self-identities based on *incorrect* perceptions of how others see us. A student may react strongly to a teacher's criticism and decide (wrongly) that the instructor views the student as stupid. This misperception may be converted into a negative self-identity through the following process: (1) the teacher criticized me, (2) the teacher must think that I'm stupid, (3) I *am* stupid. Yet self-identities are also subject to change. If the student receives an A at the end of the course, he or she will probably no longer feel stupid.

Mead: Stages of the Self

George Herbert Mead continued Cooley's exploration of interactionist theory. Mead (1934, 1964a) developed a useful model of the process by which the self emerges, defined by three distinct stages: the preparatory stage, the play stage, and the game stage.

The Preparatory Stage   During the *preparatory stage,* children merely imitate the people around them, especially family members with whom they continually interact. Thus, a small child will bang on a piece of wood while a parent is engaged in carpentry work, or will try to throw a ball if an older sibling is doing so nearby.

As they grow older, children become more adept at using symbols, including the gestures and words that form the basis of human communication. By interacting with relatives and friends, as well as by watching cartoons on television and looking at picture books, children in the preparatory stage begin to understand symbols. They will continue to use this form of communication throughout their lives.

Like spoken languages, symbols vary from culture to culture, and even from one subculture to

Children imitate the people around them, especially family members they continually interact with, during the *preparatory stage* described by George Herbert Mead.

Table **14-1** Mead's Stages of the Self

Stage	Self Present?	Definition	Example
Preparation	No	Child imitates the actions of others.	When adults laugh and smile, child laughs and smiles.
Play	Developing	Child takes the role of a single other, as if he or she were the other.	Child first takes the role of doctor, then the role of patient.
Game	Yes	Child considers the roles of two or more others simultaneously.	In game of hide-and-seek, child takes into account the roles of both hider and seeker.

another. In North America, raising one's eyebrows may communicate astonishment or doubt. In Peru, the same gesture means "money" or "pay me," and may constitute an unspoken request for a bribe. In the Pacific island nation of Tonga, raised eyebrows mean "yes" or "I agree" (Axtell 1990).

The Play Stage Mead was among the first to analyze the relationship of symbols to socialization. As children develop skill in communicating through symbols, they gradually become more aware of social relationships. As a result, during the *play stage,* they begin to pretend to be other people. Just as an actor "becomes" a character, a child becomes a doctor, parent, superhero, or ship captain.

Mead, in fact, noted that an important aspect of the play stage is role-playing. **Role taking** is the process of mentally assuming the perspective of another and responding from that imagined viewpoint. For example, through this process a young child will gradually learn when it is best to ask a parent for favors. If the parent usually comes home from work in a bad mood, the child will wait until after dinner, when the parent is more relaxed and approachable.

The Game Stage In Mead's third stage, the *game stage,* the child of about age eight or nine no longer just plays roles but begins to consider several tasks and relationships simultaneously. At this point in development, children grasp not only their own social positions but also those of others around them—just as in a football game the players must understand their own and everyone else's positions. Consider a girl or boy who is part of a scout troop out on a weekend hike in the mountains. The child must understand what he or she is expected to do but must also recognize the responsibilities of other scouts as well as the leaders. This is the final stage of development under Mead's model; the child can now respond to numerous members of the social environment.

Mead uses the term **generalized other** to refer to the attitudes, viewpoints, and expectations of society as a whole that a child takes into account in his or her behavior. Simply put, this concept suggests that when an individual acts, he or she takes into account an entire group of people. For example, a child will not act courteously merely to please a particular parent. Rather, the child comes to understand that courtesy is a widespread social value endorsed by parents, teachers, and religious leaders.

At the game stage, children can take a more sophisticated view of people and the social environment. They now understand what specific occupations and social positions are and no longer equate Mr. Williams only with the role of "librarian" or Ms. Sanchez only with "principal." It has become clear to the child that Mr. Williams can be a librarian, a parent, and a marathon runner at the same time and that Ms. Sanchez is one of many principals in our society. Thus, the child has reached a new level of sophistication in observations of individuals and institutions.

Table 14-1 summarizes the three stages of self outlined by George Herbert Mead.

Mead: Theory of the Self

Mead is best known for his theory of the self. According to Mead (1964b), the self begins at a privileged, central position in a person's world. Young children picture themselves as the focus of everything around them and find it difficult to consider the perspectives of others. For example, when shown a mountain scene and asked to describe what an observer on the opposite side of the mountain might see (such as a lake or hikers), young children describe only objects visible from their own vantage point. This childhood tendency to place ourselves at the center of events never entirely disappears. Many people with a fear of flying automatically assume that if any plane goes down, it will be the one they are on. And who reads the horoscope section in the paper without looking at their horoscope first? Why else do we buy lottery tickets, if we do not imagine ourselves winning?

Nonetheless, as people mature, the self changes and begins to reflect greater concern about the reactions of others. Parents, friends, co-workers, coaches, and teachers are often among those who play a major role in shaping a person's self. The term **significant others** is used to refer to those individuals who are most important in the development of the self. Many young people, for example, find themselves drawn to the same kind of work their parents engage in (H. Sullivan [1953] 1968).

In some instances, studies of significant others have generated controversy among researchers. For example, some researchers have contended that Black adolescents are more "peer-oriented" than their White counterparts because of presumed weaknesses in Black families. However, investigations indicate that these hasty conclusions were based on limited studies focusing on less affluent Blacks. In fact, there appears to be little difference in who Blacks and Whites from similar economic backgrounds regard as their significant others (Giordano et al. 1993; Juhasz 1989).

use your **sociological imagination**

How do you view yourself as you interact with others around you? How do you think you formed this view of yourself?

Goffman: Presentation of the Self

How do we manage our "self"? How do we display to others who we are? Erving Goffman, a sociologist associated with the interactionist perspective, suggested that many of our daily activities involve attempts to convey impressions of who we are. His observations help us to understand the sometimes subtle yet critical ways in which we learn to present ourselves socially. They also offer concrete examples of this aspect of socialization.

Early in life, the individual learns to slant his or her presentation of the self in order to create distinctive appearances and satisfy particular audiences. Goffman (1959) referred to this altering of the presentation of the self as **impression management.** The Sociology on Campus box describes an everyday example of this concept—the way students behave after receiving their exam grades.

In analyzing such everyday social interactions, Goffman makes so many explicit parallels to the theater that his view has been termed the **dramaturgical approach.** According to this perspective, people resemble performers in action. For example, a clerk may try to appear busier than he or she actually is if a supervisor happens to be watching. A customer in a singles' bar may try to look as if he or she is waiting for a particular person to arrive.

Goffman (1959) also drew attention to another aspect of the self—**face-work.** How often do you initiate some kind of face-saving behavior when you feel embarrassed or rejected? In response to a rejection at the singles' bar, a person may engage in face-work by saying, "There really isn't an interesting per-

son in this entire crowd." We feel the need to maintain a proper image of the self if we are to continue social interaction.

Face-work is a necessity for those who are unemployed. In an economic downturn like the recent recession, unemployment affects people of all social classes, many of whom are unaccustomed to being jobless. A recent ethnographic study found the newly unemployed redefining what it means to be out of work. They were focusing more than in the past on what they were accomplishing, and had begun to value volunteer work more since they had become volunteers themselves. Participants in this study engaged in both impression management and face-work (Garrett-Peters 2009).

In some cultures, people engage in elaborate deceptions to avoid losing face. In Japan, for example, where lifetime employment has until recently been the norm, *company men* thrown out of work by a deep economic recession may feign employment, rising as usual in the morning, donning suit and tie, and heading for the business district. But instead of going to the office, they congregate at places such as Tokyo's Hibiya Library, where they pass the time by reading before returning home at the usual hour. Many of these men are trying to protect family members, who would be shamed if neighbors discovered the family breadwinner was unemployed. Others are deceiving their wives and families as well (French 2000).

Goffman's work on the self represents a logical progression of sociological studies begun by Cooley and Mead on how personality is acquired through socialization and how we manage the presentation of the self to others. Cooley stressed the process by which we create a self; Mead focused on how the self develops as we learn to interact with others; Goffman emphasized the ways in which we consciously create images of ourselves for others.

Psychological Approaches to the Self

Psychologists have shared the interest of Cooley, Mead, and other sociologists in the development of the self. Early work in psychology, such as that of Sigmund Freud (1856–1939), stressed the role of inborn drives—among them the drive for sexual gratification—in channeling human behavior. More recently, psychologists such as Jean Piaget have emphasized the stages through which human beings progress as the self develops.

Like Charles Horton Cooley and George Herbert Mead, Freud believed that the self is a social product, and that aspects of one's personality are influenced by other people (especially one's parents). However, unlike Cooley and Mead, he suggested that the self has components that work in opposition to each other. According to Freud, our natural impulsive instincts are in constant conflict with societal constraints. Part of us seeks limitless

A prospective employer reviews an applicant's qualifications for the job. To present themselves in a positive manner, both interviewer and applicant may resort to *impression management* and *face-work*, two tactics described by the interactionist Erving Goffman.

Sociology on Campus

Impression Management by Students

When you and fellow classmates get an exam back, you probably react differently depending on the grades that you and they earned. This distinction is part of *impression management*, as sociologists Daniel Albas and Cheryl Albas have demonstrated. The two explored the strategies college students use to create desired appearances after receiving their grades on exams. Albas and Albas divided these encounters into three categories: those between students who have all received high grades (Ace–Ace encounters); those between students who have received high grades and those who have received low or even failing grades (Ace–Bomber encounters); and those between students who have all received low grades (Bomber–Bomber encounters).

Ace–Ace encounters occur in a rather open atmosphere, because there is comfort in sharing a high mark with another high achiever. It is even acceptable to violate the norm of modesty and brag when among other Aces, since as one student admitted, "It's much easier to admit a high mark to someone who has done better than you, or at least as well."

Ace–Bomber encounters are often sensitive. Bombers generally attempt to avoid such exchanges, because "you . . . emerge looking like the dumb one" or "feel like you are lazy or unreliable." When forced into interactions with Aces, Bombers work to appear gracious and congratulatory. For their part, Aces offer sympathy and support to the dissatisfied Bombers

and even rationalize their own "lucky" high scores. To help Bombers save face, Aces may emphasize the difficulty and unfairness of the examination.

> When forced into interactions with Aces, Bombers work to appear gracious and congratulatory.

Bomber–Bomber encounters tend to be closed, reflecting the group effort to wall off the feared disdain of others. Yet, within the safety of these encounters, Bombers openly share their disappointment and engage in expressions of mutual self-pity that they themselves call "pity parties." They devise face-saving excuses for their poor performance, such as "I wasn't feeling well all week" or "I had four exams and two papers due that week." If the grade distribution in a class includes particularly low scores, Bombers may blame the professor, attacking him or her as a sadist, a slave driver, or simply an incompetent.

As is evident from these descriptions, students' impression management strategies conform to society's informal norms regarding modesty and consideration for less successful peers. In classroom settings, as in the

workplace and in other types of human interaction, efforts at impression management are most intense when status differentials are pronounced, as in encounters between the high-scoring Aces and the low-scoring Bombers.

Of course, grade comparisons are not the only occasion when students engage in impression management. Another study has shown that students' perceptions of how often fellow students work out can also influence their social encounters. In athletic terms, a bomber would be someone who doesn't work out; an ace would be someone who works hard at physical fitness. At the student lounge, then, Bomber–Bomber encounters might involve nonathletic students belittling those who spend a lot of time working out. At the recreation center, Ace–Ace encounters might involve student athletes sharing training tips.

LET'S DISCUSS

1. How do you react to those who have received higher or lower grades than you? Do you engage in impression management? How would you like others to react to your grade?

2. What social norms govern students' impression management strategies?

Sources: Albas and Albas 1988, 1996; M. Mack 2003.

---

pleasure, while another part favors rational behavior. By interacting with others, we learn the expectations of society and then select behavior most appropriate to our culture. (Of course, as Freud was well aware, we sometimes distort reality and behave irrationally.)

Research on newborn babies by the Swiss child psychologist Jean Piaget (1896–1980) has underscored the importance of social interactions in developing a sense of self. Piaget found that newborns have no self in the sense of a looking-glass image. Ironically, though, they are quite self-centered; they demand that all attention be directed toward them. Newborns have not yet separated themselves from the universe of which they are a part. For these babies, the phrase "you and me" has no meaning; they understand only "me." However, as they mature, children are gradually socialized into social relationships, even within their rather self-centered world.

In his well-known **cognitive theory of development,** Piaget (1954) identified four stages in the development of children's thought processes. In the first, or *sensorimotor,* stage, young children use their senses to make discoveries. For example, through touching they discover that their hands are actually a part of themselves. During the second, or *pre-operational,* stage, children begin to use words and symbols to distinguish objects and ideas. The milestone in the third, or

concrete operational, stage is that children engage in more logical thinking. They learn that even when a formless lump of clay is shaped into a snake, it is still the same clay. In the fourth, or *formal operational,* stage, adolescents become capable of sophisticated abstract thought and can deal with ideas and values in a logical manner.

Piaget suggested that moral development becomes an important part of socialization as children develop the ability to think more abstractly. When children learn the rules of a game such as checkers or jacks, they are learning to obey societal norms. Those under age eight display a rather basic level of morality: rules are rules, and there is no concept of "extenuating circumstances." As they mature, children become capable of greater autonomy and begin to experience moral dilemmas and doubts as to what constitutes proper behavior.

According to Jean Piaget, social interaction is the key to development. As children grow older, they pay increasing attention to how other people think and why they act in particular ways. In order to develop a distinct personality, each of us needs opportunities to interact with others. As we saw earlier, Isabelle was deprived of the chance for normal social interactions, and the consequences were severe (Kitchener 1991).

Table **14-2**   Theoretical Approaches to Development of the Self

Scholar	Key Concepts and Contributions	Major Points of Theory
Charles Horton Cooley 1864–1929 sociologist (USA)	Looking-glass self	Stages of development not distinct; feelings toward ourselves developed through interaction with others
George Herbert Mead 1863–1931 sociologist (USA)	The self Generalized other	Three distinct stages of development; self develops as children grasp the roles of others in their lives
Erving Goffman 1922–1982 sociologist (USA)	Impression management Dramaturgical approach Face-work	Self developed through the impressions we convey to others and to groups
Sigmund Freud 1856–1939 psychotherapist (Austria)	Psychoanalysis	Self influenced by parents and by inborn drives, such as the drive for sexual gratification
Jean Piaget 1896–1980 child psychologist (Switzerland)	Cognitive theory of development	Four stages of cognitive development; moral development linked to socialization

We have seen that a number of thinkers considered social interaction the key to the development of an individual's sense of self. As is generally true, we can best understand this topic by drawing on a variety of theory and research. Table 14-2 summarizes the rich literature, both sociological and psychological, on the development of the self.

● Socialization throughout the Life Course

The Life Course

Among the Kota people of the Congo in Africa, adolescents paint themselves blue. Mexican American girls go on a daylong religious retreat before dancing the night away. Egyptian mothers step over their newborn infants seven times, and graduating students at the Naval Academy throw their hats in the air. These are all ways of celebrating **rites of passage,** a means of dramatizing and validating changes in a person's status. Rites of passage can mark a separation, as in a graduation ceremony, or an incorporation, as in an initiation into an organization (Van Gennep [1909] 1960).

Rites of passage are a worldwide social phenomenon. The Kota rite marks the passage to adulthood. The color blue, viewed as the color of death, symbolizes the death of childhood. Hispanic girls celebrate reaching womanhood with a *quinceañera* ceremony at age 15. In the Cuban American community of Miami, the popularity of the *quinceañera* supports a network of party planners, caterers, dress designers, and the Miss Quinceañera Latina pageant. For thousands of years, Egyptian mothers have welcomed their newborns to the world in the Soboa ceremony by stepping over the seven-day-old infant seven times. And Naval Academy seniors celebrate their graduation from college by hurling their hats skyward.

These specific ceremonies mark stages of development in the life course. They indicate that the process of socialization continues through all stages of the life cycle. In fact, some researchers have chosen to concentrate on socialization as a lifelong process. Sociologists and other social scientists who take such a **life course approach** look closely at the social factors that influence people throughout their lives, from birth to death, including gender and income. They recognize that biological changes mold but do not dictate human behavior.

Several life events mark the passage to adulthood. Of course, these turning points vary from one society and even one generation to the next. In the United States, the key event seems to be the completion of formal schooling (see Table 14-3). On average, Americans expect this milestone to occur by a person's 23rd birthday. Other major events in the life course, such as getting married or becoming a parent, are expected to follow three or four years later. Interestingly, comparatively few survey respondents identified marriage and parenthood as important milestones (S. Furstenberg et al. 2004).

One result of these staggered steps to independence is that in the United States, unlike some other societies, there is no clear dividing line between adolescence and adulthood. Nowadays, few young people finish school, get married, and leave home at

A young Apache woman undergoes a mudding ceremony traditionally used in rites of passage such as puberty and in some cases weddings.

Table **14-3**   Milestones in the Transition to Adulthood

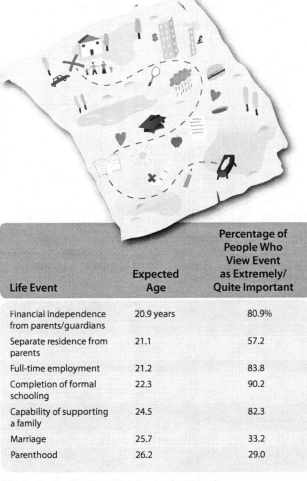

Life Event	Expected Age	Percentage of People Who View Event as Extremely/ Quite Important
Financial independence from parents/guardians	20.9 years	80.9%
Separate residence from parents	21.1	57.2
Full-time employment	21.2	83.8
Completion of formal schooling	22.3	90.2
Capability of supporting a family	24.5	82.3
Marriage	25.7	33.2
Parenthood	26.2	29.0

Note: Based on the 2002 General Social Survey of 1,398 people.
Source: T. Smith 2003.

Think about It

Why did so few respondents consider marriage and parenthood to be important milestones? Which milestones do you think are most important?

about the same age, clearly establishing their transition to adulthood. The terms *youthhood* and *emerging adulthood* have been coined to describe the prolonged ambiguous status that young people in their 20s experience (Côté 2000; Christian Smith 2007).

We encounter some of the most difficult socialization challenges (and rites of passage) in the later years of life. Assessing one's accomplishments, coping with declining physical abilities, experiencing retirement, and facing the inevitability of death may lead to painful adjustments. Old age is further complicated by the negative way that many societies, including the United States, view and treat the elderly. The common stereotypes of the elderly

as helpless and dependent may well weaken an older person's self-image. However, many older people continue to lead active, productive, fulfilled lives, whether still in the paid labor force or as retirees.

Anticipatory Socialization and Resocialization

The development of a social self is literally a lifelong transformation that begins in the crib and continues as one prepares for death. Two types of socialization occur at many points throughout the life course: anticipatory socialization and resocialization.

Anticipatory socialization refers to processes of socialization in which a person rehearses for future positions, occupations, and social relationships. A culture can function more efficiently and smoothly if members become acquainted with the norms, values, and behavior associated with a social position before actually assuming that status. Preparation for many aspects of adult life begins with anticipatory socialization during childhood and adolescence, and continues throughout our lives as we prepare for new responsibilities.

You can see the process of anticipatory socialization take place when high school students start to consider what colleges they may attend. Traditionally, this task meant looking at publications received in the mail or making campus visits. However, with new technology, more and more students are using the Web to begin their college experience. Colleges are investing more time and money in developing attractive Web sites through which students can take virtual campus tours and hear audio clips of everything from the college anthem to a sample zoology lecture.

Occasionally, assuming a new social or occupational position requires us to *unlearn* an established orientation. **Resocialization** refers to the process of discarding former behavior patterns and accepting new ones as part of a transition in one's life. Often resocialization occurs during an explicit effort to transform an individual, as happens in reform schools, therapy groups, prisons, religious conversion settings, and political indoctrination camps. The process of resocialization typically involves considerable stress for the individual—much more so than socialization in general, or even anticipatory socialization (Gecas 2004).

Resocialization is particularly effective when it occurs within a total institution. Erving Goffman (1961) coined the term **total institution** to refer to an institution that regulates all aspects of a person's life under a single authority, such as a prison, the military, a mental hospital, or a convent. Because the total institution is generally cut off from the rest of society, it provides for all the needs of its members. Quite literally, the crew of a merchant vessel at sea becomes part of a total institution. So elaborate are its requirements, so all-encompassing its activities, a total institution often represents a miniature society.

Goffman (1961) identified four common traits of total institutions:

- All aspects of life are conducted in the same place under the control of a single authority.

- Any activities within the institution are conducted in the company of others in the same circumstances—for example, army recruits or novices in a convent.

Prisons are centers of resocialization, where people are placed under pressure to discard old behavior patterns and accept new ones. These prisoners are learning to use weights to release tension and exert their strength—a socially acceptable method of handling antisocial impulses.

- The authorities devise rules and schedule activities without consulting the participants.

- All aspects of life within a total institution are designed to fulfill the purpose of the organization. Thus, all activities in a monastery might be centered on prayer and communion with God. (Davies 1989; P. Rose et al. 1979)

People often lose their individuality within total institutions. For example, a person entering prison may experience the humiliation of a **degradation ceremony** as he or she is stripped of clothing, jewelry, and other personal possessions. From this point on, scheduled daily routines allow for little or no personal initiative. The individual becomes secondary and rather invisible in the overbearing social environment (Garfinkel 1956).

MODULE 14 | Recap and Review

Summary

This module examines sociological and psychological views of the development of the **self.**

1. In the early 1900s, Charles Horton Cooley advanced the belief that we learn who we are by interacting with others, a phenomenon he called the **looking-glass self.**

2. George Herbert Mead, best known for his theory of the self, proposed that as people mature, their selves begin to reflect their concern about reactions from others, both **generalized others** and **significant others.**

3. Erving Goffman has shown that in many of our daily activities, we try to convey distinct impressions of who we are, a process he called **impression management.**

4. According to Jean Piaget's **cognitive theory of development,** social interaction is the key to psychological development.

5. Socialization proceeds throughout the life course. Some societies mark stages of development with formal **rites of passage.** In the culture of the United States, significant events such as marriage and parenthood serve to change a person's status.

Thinking Critically

1. Use Erving Goffman's dramaturgical approach to describe impression management among members of one of the following groups: athletes, college instructors, parents, physicians, or politicians.

2. What are some similarities between Mead's stages of the self and Piaget's cognitive development stages? What are some differences?

Key Terms

Anticipatory socialization

Cognitive theory of development

Degradation ceremony

Dramaturgical approach

Face-work

Generalized other

Impression management

Life course approach

Looking-glass self

Resocialization

Rite of passage

Role taking

Self

Significant other

Total institution

MODULE 15 | Agents of Socialization

As we have seen, the culture of the United States is defined by rather gradual movements from one stage of socialization to the next. The continuing and lifelong socialization process involves many different social forces that influence our lives and alter our self-images.

The family is the most important agent of socialization in the United States, especially for children. In this module, we'll also discuss six other agents of socialization: the school, the peer group, the mass media and technology, the workplace, religion, and the state. We'll explore the role of religion in socializing young people into society's norms and values more fully in Module 45.

● Family

The lifelong process of learning begins shortly after birth. Since newborns can hear, see, smell, taste, and feel heat, cold, and pain, they are constantly orienting themselves to the surrounding world. Human beings, especially family members, constitute an important part of their social environment. People minister to the baby's needs by feeding, cleaning, carrying, and comforting the baby.

All families engage in socialization, but the way that Amish families encourage their children to accept their community's subculture is particularly striking. The Research Today box describes their tolerance for the period of rebellion known as *rum springa,* during which Amish children flirt with the adolescent subculture of mainstream American society.

Cultural Influences

As both Charles Horton Cooley and George Herbert Mead noted, the development of the self is a critical aspect of the early years of one's life. How children develop this sense of self can vary from one society to another, however. For example, most parents in the United States do not send six-year-olds to school unsupervised. But that is the norm in Japan, where parents push their children to commute to school on their own from an early age. In cities like Tokyo, first graders must learn to negotiate buses, subways, and long walks. To ensure their safety, parents carefully lay out rules: never talk to strangers; check with a station attendant if you get off at the wrong stop; if you miss your stop stay on to the end of the line, then call; take stairs, not escalators; don't fall asleep. Some parents equip the children with cell phones or pagers. One parent acknowledges that she worries, "but after they are six, children are supposed to start being independent from the mother. If you're still taking your child to school after the first

On a busy commercial street in Bangalore, India, pedestrians dressed in traditional garb stroll past a shop and billboard advertising Western fashions. Socialization comes from cultural influences as well as from family and friends. In today's globalized world, Western media expose children to cultural values that their parents and other authorities may not embrace.

month, everyone looks at you funny" (Tolbert 2000:17).

As we consider the family's role in socialization, we need to remember that children do not play a passive role. They are active agents, influencing and altering the families, schools, and communities of which they are a part.

The Impact of Race and Gender

In the United States, social development includes exposure to cultural assumptions regarding gender and race. Black parents, for example, have learned that children as young as age two can absorb negative messages about Blacks in children's books,

Research Today

Rum Springa: Raising Children Amish Style

All families face challenges raising their children, but what if your parents expected you not to dance, listen to music, watch television, or access the Internet? This is the challenge faced by Amish teens and their parents, who embrace a lifestyle of the mid-1800s. Amish youths—boys in particular—often rebel against their parents' strict morals by getting drunk, behaving disrespectfully, and indulging in "worldly" activities, such as buying a car. At times even the girls may become involved, to their families' dismay. As one scholar puts it, "The rowdiness of Amish youth is an embarrassment to church leaders and a stigma in the larger community" (Kraybill 2001, 138).

> All families face challenges raising their children, but what if your parents expected you not to dance, listen to music, watch television, or access the Internet?

Yet the strong pull of mainstream American culture has led Amish parents to routinize, almost to accept, some of their children's worldly activities. They expect adolescents to test their subculture's boundaries during a period of discovery called *rum springa,* a German term meaning "running around." A common occurrence during which young people attend barn dances and break social norms that forbid drinking, smoking, and driving cars, *rum springa* is definitely not supported by the Amish religion.

A typical *rum springa* begins when Amish boys signal the Amish girls to come out with a flashlight:

> Once the young ladies hit the cars, and the cars have pulled away from the homestead,

appearances and behaviors begin to change. While riding along, each Amish girl performs at least one of many actions that have been forbidden to her throughout her childhood: lights up a cigarette, grabs a beer, switches on the rock and rap music on the car radio or CD player, converses loudly and in a flirtatious manner with members of the opposite sex (Shachtman 2006:6).

[Shortly the car full of adolescents makes its way to a truck stop.] When the girls emerge from the bathrooms, only two of the eight still look Amish; the other six have been transformed. They wear jeans, T-shirts, and other mainstream American teenage outfits, some revealing their navels. Hair coverings have been removed, and a few have also let down their hair, uncut since childhood. "Ready to party" one lady avows. "Cruisin' and boozin'," another responds. The counter clerk, an older woman . . . seems unabashed by the changes in attire (Shachtman 2006:7).

Parents often react to these escapades by looking the other way, sometimes literally. If they hear radio music coming from the barn, or a motorcycle driving onto their property in the middle of the night, they don't retaliate by punishing their offspring. Instead, they pretend not to notice, secure in the knowledge that Amish children almost always return to the community's traditional values. Indeed, despite the flirtation with popular culture and modern technology that is common during the *rum springa,* the vast majority of Amish youths do return to the Amish community and become baptized. Scholars report that 85 to 90 percent of Amish children accept the faith as young adults.

To mainstream Americans, this little known and understood subculture recently became a source of entertainment. In 2004, UPN aired a 10-week reality program called *Amish in the City.* In the series, five Amish youths allegedly on *rum springa* moved in with six worldly wise young adults in Los Angeles. On behalf of the Amish community, some critics called the series exploitative, a sign of how vulnerable the Amish are. No similar series would be developed on the rebellion of Muslim or Orthodox Jewish youths, they charged.

LET'S DISCUSS

1. Do you or anyone you know come from a subculture that rejects mainstream American culture? If so, describe the community's norms and values. How do they resemble and how do they differ from Amish norms and values?

2. Why do you think so many Amish youths return to their families' way of life after rebelling against it?

Sources: Kraybill 2001; Shachtman 2006; Stevick 2007; Weinraub 2004.

toys, and television shows—all of which are designed primarily for White consumers. At the same time, Black children are exposed more often than others to the inner-city youth gang culture. Because most Blacks, even those who are middle class, live near very poor neighborhoods, children such as Charisse (see the chapter-opening excerpt) are susceptible to these influences, despite their parents' strong family values (Linn and Poussaint 1999; Pattillo-McCoy 1999).

The term **gender role** refers to expectations regarding the proper behavior, attitudes, and activities of males and females. For example, we traditionally think of "toughness" as masculine—and desirable only in men—while we view "tenderness" as feminine. As we will see in Module 34, other cultures do not necessarily assign these qualities to each gender in the way that, our culture does. The existence of gender roles does not imply that, inevitably, males and females will assume certain

Taking Sociology to Work

Rakefet Avramovitz, *Program Administrator, Child Care Law Center*

Rakefet Avramovitz has been working at the Child Care Law Center in San Francisco since 2003. The center uses legal tools to foster the development of quality, affordable child care, with the goal of expanding child care options, particularly for low-income families. As a support person for the center's attorneys, Avramovitz manages grants, oversees the center's publications, and sets up conferences and training sessions. One of her most important tasks has been to organize a working group that brings together people from all parts of the child care community. "The documents that come out of this forum inform the organization's work for the year," she explains.

Avramovitz graduated from Dickinson College in 2000. She first became interested in sociology when she took a social analysis course. Though she enjoyed her qualitative courses most, she found her quantitative courses fun, "in that we got to do surveys of people on campus. I've always enjoyed fieldwork," she notes. Avramovitz's most memorable course was one that gave her the opportunity to interact with migrant farmworkers for an entire semester. "I learned ethnography and how to work with people of different cultures. It changed my life," she says.

Avramovitz finds that the skills she learned in her sociology courses are a great help to her on the job. "Sociology taught me how to work with people . . . and how to think critically. It taught me how to listen and find the stories that people are telling," she explains. Before joining the Child Care Law Center, Avramovitz worked as a counselor for women who were facing difficult issues. "My background in ethnography helped me to talk to these women

and listen effectively," she notes. "I was able to help many women by understanding and being able to express their needs to the attorneys we worked with."

Avramovitz is enthusiastic about her work and her ability to make a difference in other people's lives. Maybe that is why she looks forward to summer at the center, when the staff welcomes several law students as interns. "It is really neat to see people learn and get jazzed about child care issues," she says.

LET'S DISCUSS

1. What might be some of the broad, long-term effects of the center's work to expand child care options? Explain.

2. Besides the law, what other professions might benefit from the skills a sociology major has to offer?

---

roles, nor does it imply that those roles are quite distinct from one another. Rather, gender roles emphasize the fact that males and females are not genetically predetermined to occupy certain roles.

As the primary agents of childhood socialization, parents play a critical role in guiding children into those gender roles deemed appropriate in a society. Other adults, older siblings, the mass media, and religious and educational institutions also have a noticeable impact on a child's socialization into feminine and masculine norms. A culture or subculture may require that one sex or the other take primary responsibility for the socialization of children, economic support of the family, or religious or intellectual leadership. In some societies, girls are socialized mainly by their mothers and boys by their fathers—an arrangement that may prevent girls from learning critical survival skills. In South Asia, fathers teach their sons to swim to prepare them for a life as fishermen; girls typically do not learn to swim. When a deadly tsunami hit the coast of South Asia in 2004, many more men survived than women.

Interactionists remind us that socialization concerning not only masculinity and femininity but also marriage and parenthood begins in childhood as a part of family life. Children observe their parents as they express affection, deal with finances, quarrel, complain about in-laws, and so forth. Their learning represents an informal process of anticipatory socialization in which they develop a tentative model of what being married and being a parent are like. (We will explore socialization for marriage and parenthood more fully in Module 40.)

School

Where did you learn the national anthem? Who taught you about the heroes of the American Revolution? Where were you first tested on your knowledge of your culture? Like the family, schools have an explicit mandate to socialize people in the United States—especially children—into the norms and values of our culture.

As conflict theorists Samuel Bowles and Herbert Gintis (1976) have observed, schools in this country foster competition through built-in systems of reward and punishment, such as grades and evaluations by teachers. Consequently, a child who is experiencing difficulty trying to learn a new skill can sometimes come to feel stupid and unsuccessful. However, as the self matures, children become capable of increasingly realistic assessments of their intellectual, physical, and social abilities.

Functionalists point out that schools, as agents of socialization, fulfill the function of teaching children the values and customs of the larger society. Conflict theorists agree, but add that schools can reinforce the divisive aspects of society, especially those of social class. For example, higher education in the United States is costly despite the existence of financial aid programs. Students from affluent backgrounds therefore have an advantage in gaining access to universities and professional training. At the same time, less affluent young people may never receive the preparation that would qualify them for the best-paying and most prestigious jobs. The contrast between the functionalist and conflict views of education will be discussed in more detail in Module 43.

Table **15-1** High School Popularity

What makes high school girls popular?		What makes high school boys popular?	
According to college men:	**According to college women:**	**According to college men:**	**According to college women:**
1. Physical attractiveness	1. Grades/intelligence	1. Participation in sports	1. Participation in sports
2. Grades/intelligence	2. Participation in sports	2. Grades/intelligence	2. Grades/intelligence
3. Participation in sports	3. General sociability	3. Popularity with girls	3. General sociability
4. General sociability	4. Physical attractiveness	4. General sociability	4. Physical attractiveness
5. Popularity with boys	5. Clothes	5. Car	5. School clubs/government

Note: Students at the following universities were asked in which ways adolescents in their high schools had gained prestige with their peers: Cornell University, Louisiana State University, Southeastern Louisiana University, State University of New York at Albany, State University of New York at Stony Brook, University of Georgia, and University of New Hampshire.
Source: Suitor et al. 2001:445.

In other cultures as well, schools serve socialization functions. Until the overthrow of Saddam Hussein in 2003, the sixth-grade textbooks used in Iraqi schools concentrated almost entirely on the military and its values of loyalty, honor, and sacrifice.

Children were taught that their enemies were Iran, the United States, Israel and its supporters, and NATO, the European military alliance. Within months of the regime's fall, the curriculum had been rewritten to remove indoctrination on behalf of Hussein, his army, and his Baath Socialist Party (Marr 2003).

Peer Group

Ask 13-year-olds who matters most in their lives and they are likely to answer "friends." As a child grows older, the family becomes somewhat less important in social development. Instead, peer groups increasingly assume the role of Mead's significant others. Within the peer group, young people associate with others who are approximately their age, and who often enjoy a similar social status (Giordano 2003).

We can see how important peer groups are to young people when their social lives are strained by war or disaster. In Baghdad, the overthrow of Saddam Hussein has profoundly changed teenagers' worlds, casting doubt on their future. Some young people have lost relatives or friends; others have become involved with fundamentalist groups or fled with their families to safer countries. Those youths who are left behind can suffer intense loneliness and boredom. Confined to their homes by crime and terrorism, those fortunate enough to have computers turn to Internet chat rooms or immerse themselves in their studies. Through e-mail, they struggle to maintain old friendships interrupted by wartime dislocation (Sanders 2004).

Gender differences are noteworthy among adolescents. Boys and girls are socialized by their parents, peers, and the media to identify many of the same paths to popularity, but to different degrees. Table 15-1 compares male and female college students' reports of how girls and boys they knew became popular in high school. The two groups named many of the same paths to popularity but gave them a different order of importance. While neither men nor women named sexual activity, drug use, or alcohol use as one of the top five paths, college men were much more likely than women to mention those behaviors as a means to becoming popular, for both boys and girls.

A young girl from Michigan displays Razanne, a modestly dressed doll made especially for Muslim children. Because girls learn about themselves and their social roles by playing with dolls, having a doll that represents their own heritage is important to them.

Mass Media and Technology

In the past 80 years, media innovations—radio, motion pictures, recorded music, television, and the Internet—have become important agents of socialization. Television, and increasingly the Internet, are critical forces in the socialization of children in the United States. One national survey indicates that 68 percent of U.S. children have a television in their bedroom, and nearly 50 percent of all youths ages 8 to 18 use the Internet every day (see Figure 15-1).

These media, however, are not always a negative socializing influence. Television programs and even commercials can introduce young people to unfamiliar lifestyles and cultures. Not only do children in the United States learn about life in "faraway lands," but inner-city children learn about the lives of farm children, and vice versa. The same thing happens in other countries.

Sociologists and other social scientists have begun to consider the impact of technology on socialization. They are particularly interested in the online friendship networks, like Facebook. Does this way of communicating resemble face-to-face interaction, or does it represent a new form of social interaction? The Research Today box explores the significance of this social phenomenon.

Not just in industrial nations, but in Africa and other developing areas, people have been socialized into relying on new communications technologies. Not long ago, if Zadhe Iyombe wanted to talk to his mother, he had to make an eight-day trip from the capital city of Kinshasa up the Congo River by boat to the rural town where he was born. Now both he and his mother have access to a cell phone, and they send text messages to each other daily. Iyombe and his mother are not atypical. Although cell phones aren't cheap, 1.4 billion owners in developing countries have come to consider them a necessity. Today, there are more cell phones in developing nations than in industrial nations—the first time in history that developing nations have outpaced the developed world in the adoption of a telecommunications technology (K. Sullivan 2006).

Workplace

Learning to behave appropriately in an occupation is a fundamental aspect of human socialization. In the United States, working full-time confirms adult status; it indicates that one has passed out of adolescence. In a sense, socialization into an occupation can represent both a harsh reality ("I have to work in order to buy food and pay the rent") and the realization of an ambition ("I've always wanted to be an airline pilot") (W. Moore 1968:862).

It used to be that going to work began with the end of our formal schooling, but that is no longer the case, at least not in

the United States. More and more young people work today, and not just for a parent or relative. Adolescents generally seek jobs in order to make spending money; 80 percent of high school seniors say that little or none of what they earn goes to family expenses. These teens rarely look on their employment as a means of exploring vocational interests or getting on-the-job training.

Some observers feel that the increasing number of teenagers who are working earlier in life and for longer hours are finding the workplace almost as important an agent of socialization as school. In fact, a number of educators complain that student time at work is adversely affecting schoolwork. The level of teenage employment in the United States is the highest among industrial countries, which may provide one explanation for why U.S. high school students lag behind those in other countries on international achievement tests.

Socialization in the workplace changes when it involves a more permanent shift from an after-school job to full-time employment. Occupational socialization can be most intense during the transition from school to job, but it continues throughout one's work history. Technological advances may alter the requirements of the position and necessitate some degree of resocialization. Today, men and women change occupations, employers, or places of work many times during

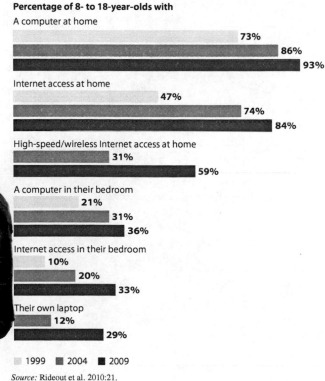

FIGURE 15-1 The New Normal: Internet at Home

Percentage of 8- to 18-year-olds with

A computer at home
73%
86%
93%

Internet access at home
47%
74%
84%

High-speed/wireless Internet access at home
31%
59%

A computer in their bedroom
21%
31%
36%

Internet access in their bedroom
10%
20%
33%

Their own laptop
12%
29%

■ 1999 ■ 2004 ■ 2009

Source: Rideout et al. 2010:21.

their adult years. Occupational socialization continues, then, throughout a person's years in the labor market.

College students today recognize that occupational socialization is not socialization into one lifetime occupation. They anticipate going through a number of jobs. The Bureau of Labor Statistics (2008) has found that from ages 18 to 42, the typical person has held 11 jobs. This high rate of turnover in employment applies to both men and women, and to those with a college degree as well as those with a high school diploma.

 Research Today

Online Socializing: A New Agent of Socialization

Membership in the online social networks Facebook, Friendster, and MySpace has grown exponentially in recent years. At first, young adults monopolized these social networks. Indeed, Facebook was created in 2004 as a way for students on a single campus to become acquainted with one another before actually

> Online networks—especially those that indicate how many "friends" an individual has—can also be seen in terms of social capital.

meeting. Now there are well over 150 million profiles online, more than 70 percent of them from outside the United States. Sociologists are interested in these new social networks not because of the sophisticated technology that supports them, but because of their social significance. Much like face-to-face encounters with schoolmates or fellow workers, online social encounters serve as an agent of socialization. They affect both the development of the self and the identification of significant others, especially among youths, for whom online social networks are a particularly dominant agent of socialization.

Even in the brief history of online networking, sociologists can see social trends. For example, older people are now creating profiles on these sites. As Figure A shows, there is still a clear

correlation between age and online profiles: in a national survey of community college students, younger people were much more likely than older people to be online. However, the fastest-growing age groups are now those over 30, including those who are much older. As a result, online socializing is becoming much less age-specific—more like socializing in the real world. Moreover, this new agent of socialization can continue to influence people throughout the life course. Twitter is largely the exception to this trend; it is still a very age-specific method of social interaction, as Figure B shows.

Online networks—especially those that indicate how many "friends" an individual has—can also be seen in terms of social capital. In fact, "friending" is one, if not the, main activity on some online sites. Often the number of friends a person socializes with becomes the subject of boasting. By extension, individuals may use these sites to search for "friends" who may prove helpful to them in future endeavors. Becoming aware of new opportunities, either social or economic, through friends is a significant benefit of social capital.

Researchers have looked at the relationship between the display of friends online and the number of real-world friends people socialize with, and have proposed two competing hypotheses. According to the social enhancement hypothesis ("the rich get richer"), those who are popular offline further increase

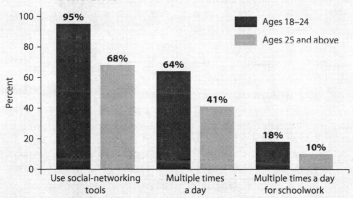

FIGURE A **Staying Connected: Community College Students**

Legend: Ages 18–24 (dark), Ages 25 and above (light)

- Use social-networking tools: 95%, 68%
- Multiple times a day: 64%, 41%
- Multiple times a day for schoolwork: 18%, 10%

Note: Question asked was "How often do you use social networking tools, such as instant messaging, text messaging, MySpace and/or Facebook, Twitter, etc., for any purpose? (This does not include e-mail.)"
Source: Center for Community College Student Engagement 2009:8.

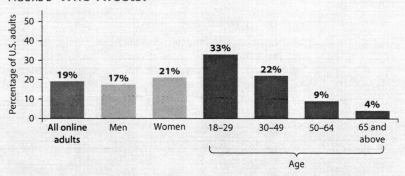

FIGURE B **Who Tweets?**

- All online adults: 19%
- Men: 17%
- Women: 21%
- 18–29: 33%
- 30–49: 22%
- 50–64: 9%
- 65 and above: 4%

Age

Note: Data collected in September 2009 and limited to adult respondents because of ethical guidelines governing survey research. Includes other update services in addition to Twitter.
Source: Fox et al. 2009:4.

their popularity through online networking sites. According to the social compensation hypothesis ("the poor get richer"), however, social network users try to increase their popularity online to compensate for inadequate popularity offline. The social compensation hypothesis, if correct, would be an example of impression management. Research to date supports elements of both hypotheses; neither hypothesis fully defines the participants in online networking sites.

Another means of social networking, Twitter, emerged recently. A way of tracking people online, Twitter allows members to receive very brief instant messages from friends and acquaintances, who may signal their whereabouts or remark on what they are doing or seeing. This form of networking is even more passive than the original social networking sites. Once a member agrees to accept a tweet from someone, the alerts keep coming.

Viewed from a societal perspective, socializing online can have both positive and negative functions. For members of some marginalized populations, it is a way to socialize with like-minded people. For example, Muslims in Great Britain connect with friends online to learn how to navigate through a society in which they form a distinct minority. For other people, such as members of the Nazis in Germany and the Mafia in Italy, online networking is a way to proclaim allegiance to socially objectionable organizations. Governments frown on such online organizing, seeing it as dysfunctional, and periodically monitor these sites to see whether any laws have been violated.

LET'S DISCUSS

1. Do you list your "friends" on an online social networking site? If so, what is your motivation for doing so? How much social capital do you think your list represents?

2. Do you think the advantages of online social networking outweigh the disadvantages?

Sources: Donadio 2009; N. Ellison et al. 2007; Facebook 2009; Gentile 2009; Hundley and Ramirez 2008; Lenhart 2009; Miyata and Kobayashi 2008; Zywica and Danowski 2008.

Religion and the State

Increasingly, social scientists are recognizing the importance of both religion and government ("the state") as agents of socialization, because of their impact on the life course. Traditionally, family members have served as the primary caregivers in our culture, but in the 20th century, the family's protective function was steadily transferred to outside agencies such as hospitals, mental health clinics, and child care centers. Many of these agencies are run by groups affiliated with certain religions or by the state.

Both organized religion and government have impacted the life course by reinstituting some of the rites of passage once observed in agricultural communities and early industrial societies.

For example, religious organizations stipulate certain traditional rites that may bring together all the members of an extended family, even if they never meet for any other reason. And government regulations stipulate the ages at which a person may drive a car, drink alcohol, vote in elections, marry without parental permission, work overtime, and retire. These regulations do not constitute strict rites of passage: most 18-year-olds choose not to vote, and most people choose their age of retirement without reference to government dictates.

In the Social Policy section at the end of this module, we will see that government is under pressure to become a provider of child care, which would give it a new and direct role in the socialization of infants and young children.

social policy and Socialization

Child Care around the World

In Israel, Aisheh and Eliza run a nursery for 29 Israeli and Palestinian children, ages four to six. Aisheh, who is Palestinian, speaks to the children in Arabic. Eliza, who is Jewish, speaks to them in Hebrew. The result: a bilingual, binational classroom that supports both Arab and Jewish culture—a first for Israel.

This unusual educational setting underscores the importance of early childhood socialization outside the home. Child care programs are not just babysitting services; they have an enormous influence on the development of young children—an influence that has been growing with the movement of more and more women into the paid labor force. The rise in single-parent families, increased job opportunities for women, and the need for additional family income have all propelled mothers of young children into the working world. Who should care for the children of working mothers during working hours?

Looking at the Issue

Preschoolers typically are not cared for by their parents. Seventy-three percent of employed mothers depend on others to care for their children, and 30 percent of mothers who aren't employed have regular care arrangements. In fact, children under age five are more likely to be cared for on a daily basis by their grandparents than by their parents. Over a third of them are cared for by nonrelatives in nursery schools, Head Start programs, day care centers, family day care, and other arrangements (Bureau of the Census 2008c).

Researchers have found that high-quality child care centers do not adversely affect the socialization of children; in fact, good day care benefits children. The value of preschool programs was documented in a series of studies conducted in the United States. Researchers found no significant differences in infants who had received extensive nonmaternal care compared with those who had been cared for solely by their mothers. They also reported that more and more infants in the United States are being placed in child care outside the home, and that, overall, the quality of those arrangements is better than has been found in previous studies. It is difficult, however, to generalize about child care, since there is so much variability among day care providers, and even among government policies from one state to another (Loeb et al. 2004; Ludwig and Sawhill 2007; NICHD 2007).

Few people in the United States or elsewhere can afford the luxury of having a parent stay at home, or of paying for high-quality live-in child care. For millions of mothers and fathers, finding the right kind of child care is a challenge both to parenting and to the pocketbook. At present, the federal government supports child care through subsidized programs, which target low-income families, and income tax credits, which benefit families with more moderate incomes. The annual expenditure to assist low-income parents is about $12 billion; the expenditure to support more affluent parents is $58 billion (Cushing-Daniels and Zedlewski 2008).

Applying Sociology

Studies that assess the quality of child care outside the home reflect the micro level of analysis and the interest of interactionists in the impact of face-to-face interaction. These studies also explore macro-level implications for the functioning of social institutions like the family. But some of the issues surrounding day care have also been of interest to those who take the conflict perspective.

Children play at the Communicare day care center in Perth, Australia. The Australian government subsidizes children's attendance at day care and after-school programs from birth to age 12.

In the United States, high-quality day care is not equally available to all families. Parents in wealthy communities have an easier time finding day care than those in poor or working-class communities. Finding *affordable* child care is also a problem. Viewed from a conflict perspective, child care costs are an especially serious burden for lower-class families. The poorest families spend 25 percent of their income for preschool child care, while families who are *not* poor pay only 6 percent or less of their income.

Feminist theorists echo the concern of conflict theorists that high-quality child care receives little government support because it is regarded as "merely a way to let women work." Nearly all child care workers (97 percent) are women; many find themselves in low-status, minimum-wage jobs. Typically, food servers, messengers, and gas station attendants make more money than the 1.2 million child care workers in the United States, who averaged $9.43 per hour in 2008. Not surprisingly, turnover among employees in child care centers runs at 25 to 40 percent per year (Bureau of the Census 2009a:Table 596; NACCRRA 2010).

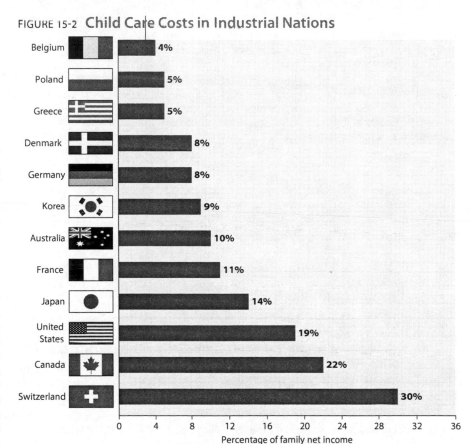

FIGURE 15-2 **Child Care Costs in Industrial Nations**

Note: Out-of-pocket expenses for two children in full-time care, less cash benefits and tax concessions.
Source: Organisation for Economic Co-operation and Development (OECD) 2007b:3.

Initiating Policy

Policies regarding child care outside the home vary throughout the world. As Figure 15-2 shows, the cost of child care as a proportion of one's income can vary dramatically, but at least it is available in industrial nations. Most developing nations do not have the economic base to provide subsidized child care. Thus, working mothers rely largely on relatives or take their children to work. In the comparatively wealthy industrialized countries of western Europe, government provides child care as a basic service, at little or no expense to parents. But even those countries with tax-subsidized programs occasionally fall short of the need for high-quality child care.

When policymakers decide that child care is desirable, they must determine the degree to which taxpayers should subsidize it. In Sweden and Denmark, one-half to two-thirds of preschoolers were in government-subsidized child care full-time in 2003. In the United States, annual fees for full-time child care of a four-year-old range from an average of $3,900 in Mississippi to an average of $11,678 in Massachusetts (Immervoll and Barber 2005; NACCRRA 2010).

We have a long way to go in making high-quality child care more affordable and accessible, not just in the United States but throughout the world. In an attempt to reduce

(continued)

government spending, France is considering cutting back the budgets of subsidized nurseries, even though waiting lists exist and the French public heartily disapproves of cutbacks. In Germany, reunification has reduced the options previously open to East German mothers, who had become accustomed to government-supported child care. Experts in child development view such reports as a vivid reminder of the need for greater government and private-sector support for child care (Hank 2001; L. King 1998).

1. Were you ever in a day care program? Do you recall the experience as good or bad? In general, do you think it is desirable to expose young children to the socializing influence of day care?

2. In the view of conflict theorists, child care receives little government support because it is "merely a way to let women work." Can you think of other explanations?

3. Should the costs of day care programs be paid by government, by the private sector, or entirely by parents?

MODULE 15 | Recap and Review

Summary

Important agents of socialization include the family, schools, peer groups, the mass media, the workplace, religious institutions, and the state.

1. As the primary agents of socialization, parents play a critical role in guiding children into those **gender roles** deemed appropriate in a society.

2. Like the family, schools in the United States have an explicit mandate to socialize people—especially children—into the norms and values of our culture.

3. Peer groups and the mass media, especially television and the Internet, are important agents of socialization for adolescents.

4. Socialization in the workplace begins with part-time employment while we are in school and continues as we work full-time and change jobs throughout our lives.

5. Religion and the state shape the socialization process by regulating the life course and influencing our views of appropriate behaviors at particular ages.

6. As more and more mothers of young children have entered the labor market, the demand for child care has increased dramatically, posing policy questions for many nations around the world.

Thinking Critically

1. How would functionalist and conflict theorists differ in their analysis of socialization by the mass media?

2. What sanctions limit participation in social networking? Describe the rules you have observed that limit the way people access and use online social networks. What are the purposes of such sanctions?

Key Term

Gender role

CHAPTER 8

Gender Inequality

Gender Stratification

Sexism and Patriarchy
Gender Inequality Around the World
Gender Inequality in the United States

Sources of Gender Differences

Gender and Biology
Gender and Culture
Gender Identities

Sociological Perspectives on Gender Stratification

The Functionalist Perspective
The Conflict Perspective
The Interactionist Perspective
The Feminist Perspective

BOX 8.1 **Social Inequalities: For Gender Equality, It Matters Where You Live**

BOX 8.2 **Doing Social Research: How Many People Get Raped?**

BOX 8.3 **Students Doing Sociology: Gender Expectations: Cigars, Tupperware, and Condoms**

What do *Black Beauty, Finding Nemo, Chicken Run, Babe, Toy Story, The Lion King, The Princess Diaries,* and *Monsters, Inc.* have in common?

(a) They are top box-office grossing films.

(b) They are rated G.

(c) They have mostly male characters.

(d) They are watched by kids, in theaters and on video, over and over again.

(e) All of the above.

Did you guess e? You're right. These and 94 other top box-office-grossing, G-rated, live-action and animated films—all released between 1990 and 2005—were analyzed by University of Southern California researchers for gender balance (Kelly and Smith, 2006). Of a total of 4,249 speaking characters in the 101 films, 28 percent are female. Only a quarter of all the characters (speaking and nonspeaking) are female, and only 17 percent of the characters in crowd scenes are female. Even the narration is male dominated, with 83 percent of narrators being male.

Does it matter? Clearly, women have come a long way since the beginning of the 20th century, when many of them were farm wives slaving over hot stoves or were urban workers confined to low-paying occupations such as seamstress, laundry worker, or maid. Today, women in the United States can vote, run for office, control their own finances, and work outside the home in professional occupations. They now are more likely than men to earn bachelor's, master's, and doctoral degrees, and they are increasingly likely to do work previously thought of as "men's work."

At the same time, women still make up only a small proportion of our elected leaders, for the most part are passed over when top executives are being selected, are mostly excluded from a

248   Chapter 8 *Gender Inequality*

wide variety of male-dominated occupations and careers, are portrayed and treated as sex objects in many ways, and, when they work, often carry the burden of two full-time jobs, one in the paid workforce and one as an unpaid housekeeper and child care worker in the family.

Patterns of gender representation in G-rated movies both reflect and help to perpetuate such gender disparities. These movies teach and reinforce the belief that activities of men are at the center of what is important, that men have the initiative and presence of mind to solve problems, and that men are the ones who have the authority, intelligence, and background to tell us what is worth knowing about the unfolding of events.

Of course, many factors go into producing gender inequality, and imagery that reinforces inequality in the media, including movies, is only one piece of the puzzle.

Just as our society structures inequalities based on race and ethnic membership, so it institutionalizes inequalities based on gender (Martin, 2004). Men and women differ in their access to privilege, prestige, and power. Despite advances in the United States and elsewhere, the distribution problem of who gets what, when, and how has nearly always been answered in favor of males.

In Chapter 6 we examined stratification by class, and in Chapter 7 we looked at the role race and ethnicity play in stratification. In this chapter we examine inequalities based on gender. As we saw, class, race, and ethnicity can result in segregation in residence, education, employment, and other areas of life. Gender stratification differs from other systems of stratification in that, for the most part, males and females work, live, go to school, and otherwise interact together on a daily basis. Nevertheless, inequalities exist. We begin our chapter by considering sex, gender, sexism, and patriarchy. We then take a closer look at the status of women in society, both in the United States and around the world. We will discuss the acquisition of gender

identities, looking at the parts played by biology, culture, and socialization. Finally, we will examine the functionalist, conflict, interactionist, and feminist perspectives on gender stratification.

Gender Stratification

Throughout the world, human activities, practices, and institutional structures are organized with respect to the social distinction people make between men and women—in brief, by gender. For the most part the state, the law, politics, religion, higher education, and the economy are institutions that historically have been developed by men, are currently dominated by men, and are symbolically interpreted from the standpoint of men. As such they are "gendered institutions." The only major institution in which women have had a central, defining role, although a subordinate one, has been the family (Acker, 1992).

Before we continue our discussion of gender stratification, we need to define some basic terms. **Sex** refers to whether one is genetically male or female and determines the biological role that one will play in reproduction. **Gender,** on the other hand, is a form of social differentiation; it refers to the sociocultural distinction between males and females. While sex is given in nature, gender is a socially constructed framework that human beings have created to make sense of and deal with the sex difference.

Gender identities are the conceptions we have of ourselves as being male or female. One's gender identity is part of one's self-concept and consequently is a product of social interaction (see Chapter 3, p. 80). Our gender identity emerges as we enact gender roles and are reacted to by others as being either male or female.

Gender roles are sets of cultural expectations that define the ways in which the members of each sex should behave. Gender roles influence a wide range of human behaviors, including how people speak, dress, walk, engage in courtship, get angry, play sports, deal with distress, and choose a career.

The gender roles defined by a society have profound consequences for the lives of its men and women. They constitute master statuses that carry primary weight in people's interactions and relationships with others (see Chapter 2, p. 56). In doing so they place men and women in the social structure, establishing where and what they are in social terms. Thus, gender roles establish the framework within which men and women gain their identities, formulate their goals, and carry out their training. Gender roles are a major source of social inequality.

In this section we will consider sexism and patriarchy. We will then take a closer look at women's roles and gender inequality in society both around the world and in the United States.

Sexism and Patriarchy

Gender inequality is perpetuated by a set of complex processes referred to as **sexism.** Like racism, sexism operates at two levels. At the *individual level,* sexism is the belief that one sex is superior to the other. This form of sexism involves two basic ideas: (1) that because of inherent biological differences, men and women are naturally suited to different roles and (2) that this is the primary cause of the differential distribution of status, power, and income by gender. At the *institutional level,* sexism involves policies, procedures, and practices that produce unequal outcomes for men and women. In principle, sexism refers to disadvantages that may be experienced by either sex. In reality, the patterns of gender inequality in history and throughout the world today generally involve disadvantages for women and advantages for men. What we usually mean by sexism, then, is a set of cultural and social processes that justify and promote disadvantage for women.

Do Women Constitute a Minority Group?

Sexism operates against women the way racism operates against persons of minority racial backgrounds. However, although they are similar to a minority group, women are clearly not in the minority in most societies. Given higher mortality rates for men, as men and women age, there are increasingly more women than there are men. But as we noted in the previous chapter, being a minority group does not require relatively low numbers. The key characteristic of a minority group is that it *lacks power* relative to a dominant group. And this is true of the situation of women in virtually every society.

Let's look again at the five properties of a *minority group* we considered in Chapter 7 (pp. 214–215), this time with women in mind.

1. Historically, women have encountered *prejudice and discrimination* and have not had access to the institutionalized power needed to readily change this situation.

2. Women possess *physical and cultural traits* that distinguish them from men, the dominant group.

3. Through the efforts of the women's liberation movement and consciousness-raising groups, women have increasingly become a *self-conscious social group* characterized by an awareness of oneness.

4. *Membership is involuntary* since gender is an ascribed status that is assigned to a person at birth.

5. Only the fifth characteristic, endogamy, does not apply to women, because, of course, women are not required to marry women.

The existence of sexism not only disadvantages women but also has a wide-ranging impact on how we think about our lives and the places of women and men in them. As sociologist

250   Chapter 8 *Gender Inequality*

Gender inequality exists in every society around the world, but recent changes have moved many women who traditionally did only unpaid domestic labor into the paid labor force.

Jessie Bernard put it in a discussion of the impact of sexism on women:

[Sexism is] the unconscious, taken-for-granted, assumed, unquestioned, unexamined, unchallenged acceptance of the belief that the world as it looks to men is the only world, that the way of dealing with it which men have created is the only way, that the values which men have evolved are the only ones, that the way sex looks to men is the only way it can look to anyone, that what men think about what women are like is the only way to think about what women are like. (Quoted in Gornick and Moran, 1971:xxv)

Patriarchy

The most pervasive form of institutional sexism is **patriarchy,** a system of social organization in which men have a disproportionate share of power. Patriarchy is rooted in cultural and legal systems that historically gave fathers authority in family and clan matters, made wives and children dependent on husbands and fathers, and organized descent and inheritance through the male line. Sociologist Judith Lorber (1994) believes that early societies may have been egalitarian for thousands of years, and Jeannine Davis-Kimball (1997) cites archaeological evidence of female military and social power. One possibility is that patriarchy emerged gradually as the economic arrangements of societies became more complicated (Barber, 1994; Ortner, 1996). Most sociologists believe that patriarchal systems serve the interests of men at the expense of women, and nearly all societies around the world today are patriarchal.

Although in some societies political change has undermined the legal basis of patriarchy, and attitudinal change has undermined its cultural power, modern societies include many patriarchal elements. An obvious one is the practice of women and children taking the last name of the husband and father; in the United States, only about 10 percent of all married women have not adopted their husbands' names (Golden and Shim, 2004). More importantly, men have more social, economic, and political power than women in societies around the world, the topic of our next section.

Gender Inequality Around the World

In their book *Half the Sky,* Nicholas D. Kristof and Sheryl WuDunn describe the problems faced by women in countries in which men are valued more highly than women (2009:xvi–xvii):

In the wealthy countries of the West, discrimination is usually a matter of unequal pay or underfunded sports teams or unwanted touching from a boss. In contrast, in much of the world discrimination is lethal . . . The global statistics on the abuse of girls are numbing. It appears that more girls have been killed in the last fifty years, precisely because they were girls, than men were killed in all the battles of the twentieth century.

Sex-selective abortions, neglect of female infants, more food and better health care for boys and men, and other forms of discrimination have resulted in higher survival rates for males than for females in China, India, Pakistan, and other countries. How much higher? Researchers estimate that at least 2 million girls per year die and that between 60 million and 101 million women are missing from the world's population because of gender discrimination (Kristof and WuDunn, 2009).

The U.S. State Department's 2009 human rights report, which included information from 194 countries, presented evidence of "continuing and escalating discrimination and persecution" of women around the world (Eisenbraun, 2010). In Ghana, Bangladesh, and many other countries, the trafficking of women and children for the sex trade and for forced labor remains a significant problem. Underage prostitution, sex tourism, and the sexual abuse of children also are listed in the human rights reports of many countries. Overall, one in three women has experienced violent victimization (Garcia-Moreno et al., 2005). The governments of many countries turn a blind eye to the abuse of women, and in many nations the state is a major institutional source of discrimination. In the Middle East and Northern Africa, for example, the legal system often excuses a man for killing his wife for alleged immoral acts—an "honor killing."

Maternal mortality is a major cause of death in many parts of the world. In 2008, an estimated 350,000 women died during pregnancy, childbirth, or the first six weeks after delivery (Hogan et al., 2010). Although women's ability to control their fertility has improved significantly, around the world, more than a quarter of the babies born are unwanted or unplanned. In less-developed countries, the percentage of women using contraception increased from 9 percent in 1960 to 51 percent in 2007 (Population Reference Bureau, 2007).

Women are sexually victimized throughout the world. One form of victimization is the traditional ethnic practice of female genital mutilation; another is the transmission of HIV to young women and girls by older men. Half of the world's HIV-infected population is now female, and in sub-Saharan Africa, 15- to 24-year-old women are three times more likely to be HIV-positive than men of the same age (Lamptey, Johnson, and Khan, 2006; Quinn and Overbaugh, 2005). Mass rape and sexual sadism in war are still common around the world, often accompanying the collapse of social order that occurs during war.

Two-thirds of the world's illiterates are female, and worldwide there are approximately 60 million girls not in primary school (Lewis and Lockheed, 2006; UNESCO, 2006). The education gender gap is closing, however, with primary school enrollments high in most countries and increasing numbers of women participating in secondary and higher education. Worldwide, women are making significant gains in higher education (United Nations, 2003). Women account for an increasing share of the labor force, although they still are concentrated in just a few occupations, have little or no authority on the job, and receive less pay than men.

Women around the world do considerably better than U.S. women in some areas. More than 160 countries provide paid maternity leave by law; the United States does not (Heymann et al., 2004; see Table 8.1). A number of nations have had a woman prime minister or president, including Great Britain, Canada, Ireland, Norway, Germany, Finland, Portugal, Iceland, the Philippines, Argentina, Bolivia, Chile, Nicaragua, Poland, Israel, Turkey, India, Pakistan,

252   Chapter 8   *Gender Inequality*

Table 8.1	Maternity Benefits, Selected Countries	
Country	Weeks of Leave Provided	Percentage of Pay
Belarus	18	100
Portugal	17	100
Austria	16	100
Netherlands	16	100
Poland	16	100
Spain	16	100
Congo	15	100
Gabon	14	100
Germany	14	100
China	13	100
Mexico	12	100
Zambia	12	100
Sweden*	68	80
Italy	20	80
Ireland	18	70
Czech Republic	28	69
Japan	14	60
Australia	52	0
Swaziland	12	0
United States	12	0

Sweden provides 390 days at 80 percent pay and 90 days at a flat rate.

Source: United Nations statistics and indicators on women and men (Table 5C). Available at http://unstats.un.org/unsd/demographic/products/indwm/ww2005/tab5c.htm.

Bangladesh, Sri Lanka, Haiti, Netherlands Antilles, and Dominica (Reel, 2007; Lewis, 2006). For the first time, a country—Rwanda—has achieved equal representation of men and women in its legislature, and the world average for the percentage of women in the national parliaments has risen to 18.9. Many countries now have 30–40 percent of their legislatures composed of women, far ahead of the United States

at 16.8 percent (see Figure 8.1). Changes for women also can be seen in other aspects of their lives, including national strategies for increasing the proportions of women in scientific and engineering fields (Normile, 2002; Dewandre, 2002), increased attention to prostitute and sex slave trafficking, the disappearance of foot binding in China, and increases in education and employment opportunities for women in many countries. Analyses of test scores show that achievement gaps between boys and girls have been closing around the world, with no differences and even reversals of the gap in countries whose cultures are more gender-equal (Machin and Pekkarinen, 2008). The percentage of women in the industrial research workforce is higher in Ireland, Greece, Portugal, France, Denmark, and Spain than it is in the United States, although it does not exceed 30 percent in any industrialized nation and stands at under 10 percent in some (Holden, 2003).

Gender Inequality in the United States

Social scientists have long noted many similarities between the status of African Americans and that of women within the United States (Myrdal, 1944; Hacker, 1951, 1974; Smith and Steward, 1983). Look, for example, at racist and sexist stereotypes. Both African Americans and women have been portrayed as intellectually inferior, emotional, irresponsible, dependent, and childlike. Both groups lack power, and the rationalization for their subordination has been similar—the myth of "contented African Americans who know their place" and the notion that "women's place is in the home." Recent generations of both African Americans and women have challenged those stereotypes by participating in social movements for equal rights.

How disadvantaged are women in U.S. society? That varies from state to state (see Box 8.1). In this section we look at the division of labor in the family, gender stratification in the

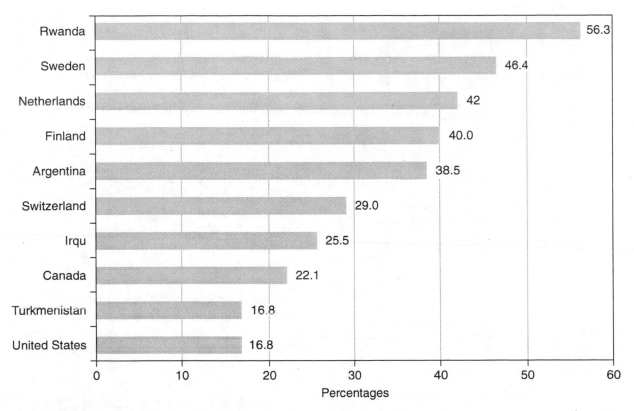

Figure 8.1 Women Legislators Around the World, 2010

More than 50 percent of Rwanda's legislators are women, the highest proportion in the world. Seventy-three other countries are ahead of the United States, where 16.8 percent of legislators are female. A number of countries have no women legislators whatsoever, including Micronesia, Oman, the Solomon Islands, Saudi Arabia, and Belize.

Source: Figure generated by the authors using data for the lower, or single, House of each country; data from the Inter-Parliamentary Union's website, www.ipu.org.

workplace, the "glass ceiling," disparities in pay, career patterns, sexual harassment and rape, politics and government, and the women's movement.

Dividing Labor in the Family

Sexual inequality historically has been sustained by assigning the economic-provider role to men and the child-rearing role to women. Labor in the public sphere has been rewarded by money, prestige, and power, whereas labor in the domestic sphere typically has been isolated and undervalued (Crittenden, 2001; Daniels, 1987; Ferree, 1990; Kessler-Harris, 1990). Gender

stereotypes arise in response to a gender division of labor and then serve to rationalize it by attributing to the sexes substantially different personality characteristics and traits (Hoffman and Hurst, 1990).

Across the years the gender division of labor has operated to bind women to their reproductive function. Women were viewed as providing men with sexual and domestic services in exchange for financial support. Within this arrangement a sexual double standard prevailed that permitted men, but not women, considerable sexual freedom. Until the 20th century, English and American common law viewed

254   Chapter 8 *Gender Inequality*

Since 1950 the number of American mothers who work outside the home has tripled, but most of them still do most of the household and child care work as well.

women as undergoing "civil death" upon marriage. Women lost their legal identity when they married and, in the eyes of the law, became "incorporated and consolidated" with their husbands. A wife could not own property in her own right or sign a contract. And a husband could require his wife to live wherever he chose and to submit to sexual intercourse against her will—a practice we now call rape.

Today marriage and family have become less of an organizing force in the lives of contemporary American women. In 2005, more than half of American women were living without a spouse (Roberts, 2007). Although they still place a high value on marriage and the family, younger women are now more likely to delay

marriage and childbearing (Gregory, 2007) (see Chapter 10, pp. 328–329). The nearly half who are married, however, can expect a lot more help from their husbands than women received in the past. Over the last four decades, fathers have more than doubled the amount of time they spend doing housework and almost tripled the amount of time they spend caring for their children (Bianchi, Robinson, and Milkie, 2006). In time diary studies, in which participants keep detailed accounts of their daily activities, researchers at the University of Maryland found that the total workloads of all married mothers and fathers were about the same. Paid work, child care, and housework added up to an average 65 hours per week for mothers and 64 hours per week for fathers, although mothers employed outside the home put in about 5 more hours of work per week than employed fathers (Bianchi, Robinson, and Milkie, 2006).

Despite the increased contribution from fathers, women still carry most of the child care and housework burden in families. The time diary studies showed that mothers spend, on average, 14 hours per week on primary child care (time when a child is the primary focus of a parent's attention), compared to 7 hours for fathers. Similarly, married mothers spend 19.4 hours per week on housework compared to the 9.6 hours contributed by married fathers (Bianchi, Robinson, and Milkie, 2006). This unequal involvement of working mothers and wives in household work was labeled "the second shift" nearly two decades ago, reflecting the idea that working women start a second shift of work when they get home from their paid work (Hochschild, 1990). Recent research shows that the total workload of a mother employed full-time is greater than a working father's by about a week and a half per year (Milkie, Raley, and Bianchi, 2009).

Despite their greater household responsibilities, women allocate just as much effort on paid jobs as men—indeed, some research suggests that they work harder in the workplace

8.1 Social Inequalities

For Gender Equality, It Matters Where You Live

The quality of people's lives has much to do with individual choices, abilities, and aspirations. But social institutions also affect quality of life. Women's vastly different experiences in different societies illustrate the importance of social institutions for gender equality and women's quality of life.

Women's experiences differ within the United States, too. In fact, women's political participation, employment and earnings, social and economic autonomy, reproductive rights, and health and well-being vary substantially from state to state. These factors have been assessed in an ongoing research project, *The Status of Women in the States,* conducted by the Institute for Women's Policy Research (Werschkul and Williams, 2004).

So—if you're a woman or a man interested in gender equality and better outcomes for women—where should you live? In 2004, the best states for women to live in were Vermont, Connecticut, Minnesota, and Washington. The worst state was Mississippi, followed by South Carolina, Kentucky, Arkansas and Oklahoma (tied), Tennessee, and Texas. How does the IWPR decide? The top states must rank in the top 10 of all the states in at least one of the factors listed above and must *not* appear in the bottom half of all states in any of the factors. In contrast, the worst states are identified as those that rank in the bottom 10 for at least one factor and in the bottom half for all factors.

How different are the differences? Let's look at political partici-

pation and representation as an example. In Hawaii only 51 percent of the state's women are registered to vote, while in North Dakota the comparable figure is 91 percent. In state legislatures, the proportion of women ranges from 9.4 percent (South Carolina) to 36.7 percent (Washington). Four states have had two female U.S. senators at the same time; five states have never had a woman elected to either the Senate or the House.

A more recent IWPR assessment of state economies found favorable business climates for women in Maryland, New Mexico, and the District of Columbia, where more than 30 percent of businesses are owned by women (Hartmann et al., 2006). Women's wages have risen in all states over the past 25 years, with women earning the most in Maryland, the District of Columbia, and New Jersey.

While some of the states are "all good" or "all bad," others are strange mixes of benefits and problems for women. Women in the District of Columbia, for example, had the highest earnings in the nation in 2004, the least difference in pay between men and women, and the highest proportion of women in management and professional occupations (Werschkul and Williams, 2004). On the other hand, District women have the worst overall health status, high rates of poverty, and low rates of health insurance coverage.

Some general findings have emerged from the research. Racial and ethnic disparities in women's

health status are wide in every state. The significantly higher probability that African American women will die of heart disease or breast cancer or will have AIDS is among the specific findings on health status. Another general finding is that a small wage gap, high earnings, and high representation in professional and managerial occupations co-occur in many states.

The IWPR research also identifies general patterns of progress and lack thereof for American women. Among the disappointing findings they list are an increase in women's poverty in 15 states and only a very small decrease in 15 others (Hartmann et al., 2006), a decrease in reproductive health services in a number of states, and only a very small increase in the proportion of women state legislators (Werschkul and Williams, 2004).

Questions for Discussion

1. How do you think your home state measures up in terms of women's rights? Go to www.iwpr.org/states and find data for your state. What institutional factors (e.g., law, economy, politics, education, health care, religion) do you think determine the position of your state in the ranking?

2. One route to gender equality is to promote policies that lead to changes in social structure. How might the factors assessed by the IWPR be linked through this idea?

256   Chapter 8   *Gender Inequality*

(Bielby and Bielby, 1988). Not surprisingly, when women assume overwhelming responsibility for household duties, they suffer stress and overload (Moen and Yu, 2000). Their dissatisfaction with the division of household work also can affect their marital happiness. One researcher found that women who expect to do all the housework (and do) have relatively happy marriages, while women who think that men should contribute to the maintenance of a home (and they don't) have unhappier marriages (Greenstein, 1996). Men's attitudes play a part. Another study found that women perceive their situations as less unfair when husbands believe that housework should be shared—even if the husbands are not really doing much of the work (DeMaris and Longmore, 1996).

Sociologists find that women who work outside the home decrease their housework as their earnings increase (Bittman et al., 2003). Likewise, as men's contributions to family income decrease from all to half the total family earnings, their time spent on housework increases (Greenstein, 2000).

Gender Stratification in the Workplace

In 2007, the labor-force participation rate for U.S. women 16 and older was 59 percent (U.S. Department of Labor, 2008). Almost half—46 percent—of all U.S. workers are women. Have American women always worked outside the home? The labor-force participation of married women in the United States over the past 200 years is represented by a U-shaped curve, with relatively high participation rates in the 1790s, declining rates accompanying industrialization during the 19th century, and rising rates after the beginning of the 20th century—and mounting substantially after 1960. Although the participation of married women in the labor force fell during the 19th century, single women entered the labor force in increasing numbers throughout that period. In recent decades, lower fertility and changing social attitudes contributed to the jump in the labor-force participation of women, while higher rates of divorce

impelled more women to join the workforce. African American women have always worked for pay in larger proportions than white women (Herring and Wilson-Sadberry, 1993).

In the United States, 65 percent of single and 61 percent of married women 16 and older are now in the paid labor force, compared with 70 percent of single and 77 percent of married men (U.S. Census Bureau, 2009); see Figure 8.2 for a comparison with other countries. Since 1950, the number of American mothers employed outside the home has tripled. In 71 percent of the families with children under age 18, the mother is employed. (U.S. Department of Labor, 2008). Mothers with older children are more likely to work than those with very young children.

Women have gained ground by entering college in higher numbers than men (U.S. Census Bureau, 2009) and now earn more high school diplomas (Bergman, 2003) and more bachelor's, master's, and doctoral degrees than men and about the same number of medical and law degrees as men (Snyder, Dillow, and Hoffman, 2009). Women also have been moving into higher-paying fields traditionally dominated by men. For example, between 1980 and 2004, the percentage of women lawyers rose from 14 percent to 29 percent (U.S. Census Bureau, 2006). In the same time period, the proportion of female doctors increased from 13 percent to 27 percent, and half the entering medical students for the 2003–2004 school year were women (Association of American Medical Colleges, 2003).

Despite these changes many of the current figures on the employment of women bear a striking resemblance to those of previous decades. There was little substantial change in the gender segregation of occupations between 1900 and 1970. Levels of segregation did decline in the 1980s and 1990s, but 40 percent of women and 44 percent of men continue to work in what we might think of as sex-segregated occupations (Hegewisch and Liepmann, 2010). The stereotypes many of us hold are based on fact: 96.9 percent of all secretaries and administrative assistants are female, 92.2 percent of registered

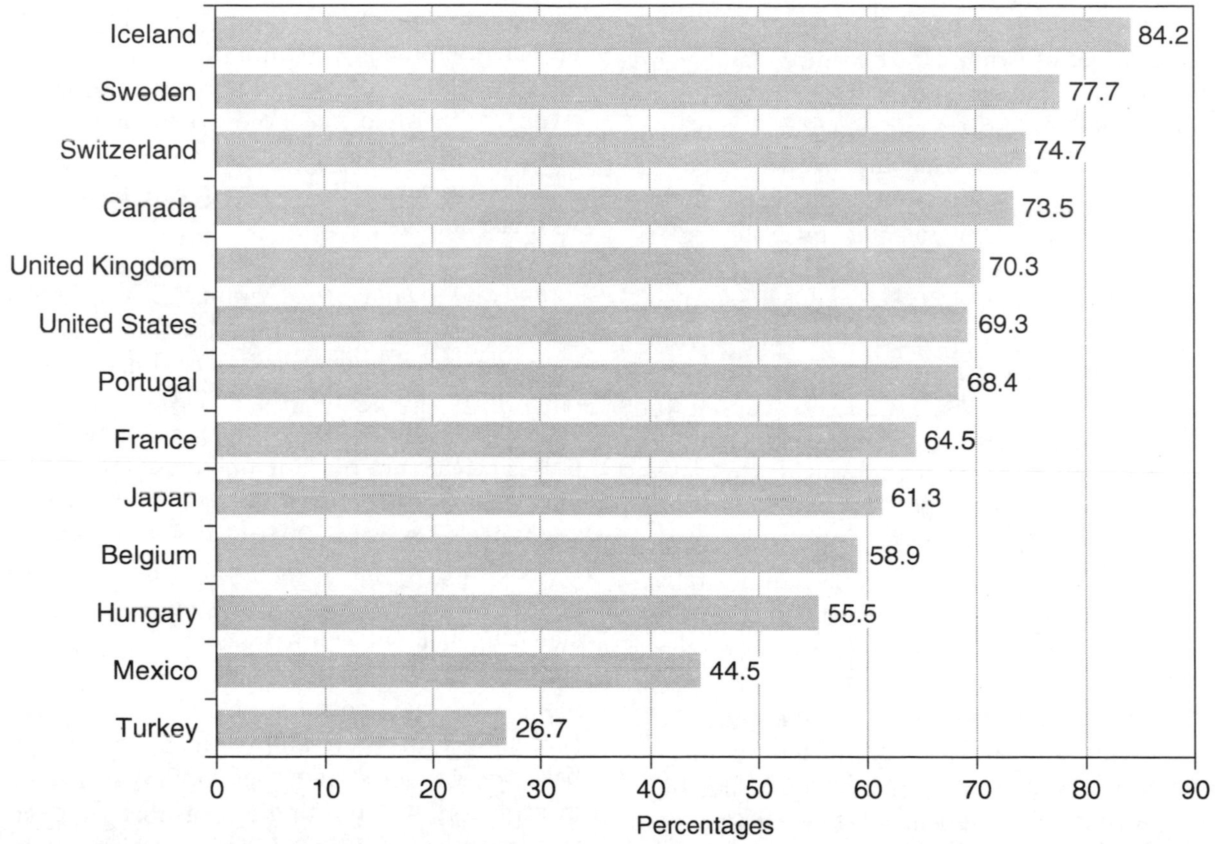

Country	Percentage
Iceland	84.2
Sweden	77.7
Switzerland	74.7
Canada	73.5
United Kingdom	70.3
United States	69.3
Portugal	68.4
France	64.5
Japan	61.3
Belgium	58.9
Hungary	55.5
Mexico	44.5
Turkey	26.7

Percentages

Figure 8.2 **Women's Labor-Force Participation Rates for Selected Countries, 2006**
The participation of women in the paid labor force in the United States is not the highest in the world, but neither is it the lowest.

Source: Figure generated by the authors using data from the U.S. Bureau of Labor Statistics, International Comparisons of Annual Labor Force Statistics, 10 Countries, 1960–2007, published October 2008. See also: http://www.bls.gov/fls/flscomparelf.htm.

nurses are female, 91.5 percent of all hairdressers and cosmetologists are women, and 81.3 percent of elementary and middle-school teachers are female (U.S. Census Bureau, 2006). On the other hand, only about 30 percent of lawyers, physicians, and surgeons were women in 2004; 20 percent of detectives, criminal investigators, and farm and ranch managers were women, about 5 percent of pilots and firefighters were female, and there is a sizable list of occupations with no women employees whatsoever.

Men and women sort into occupational categories in some general ways: 59 percent of men work in precision production, craft, and repair jobs; executive, administrative, and managerial positions; professional specialty; and sales, while 73 percent of women work in administrative support, professional specialty, and service work, and hold executive, administrative, and managerial positions (Spraggins, 2003). The increase in female employment has come largely through the displacement of men by women in some low-paying categories and through the rapid expansion of "pink-collar" occupations such as secretary, bookkeeper, and receptionist.

The "sticky floor" is an apt metaphor for the occupational frustrations experienced by most U.S. working women in low-paying, dead-end jobs.

258   Chapter 8   *Gender Inequality*

The Glass Ceiling

The number of women top executives and board directors has increased over the years, but positions at the top still elude women. Women in business crash into what has been labeled the "glass ceiling," a set of invisible barriers that prevent women from advancing. When glass ceilings do not stop women, glass walls do; these are barriers that prevent women from moving laterally in corporations and thereby gaining the experience they need to advance vertically (Lopez, 1992). A 2003 survey showed that both male CEOs and female executives say a major obstacle for women is insufficient work experience (Catalyst, 2003).

At the beginning of this century, 45 percent of the jobs classified as executive, administrative, and managerial were held by women (U.S. Census Bureau, 2003). But in 2007, very few of these women were at the very top: Only 14.8 percent of Fortune 500 companies' board seats were held by women, only 15.4 percent of their corporate officer positions were filled by women, and only 6.7 percent of the country's top earners were female (Catalyst, 2008). Further, the number of companies with no women corporate officers at all had increased by 15.6 percent since the previous year. A closer look at specific companies shows that women corporate officers are doing best in traditionally "feminine" work, such as apparel, publishing, and soaps and cosmetics. Avon, for example, has more women in management positions than any other company, with a female CEO and half its board positions filled by women (Catalyst, 2003).

Women who make it to the top get there differently. One analysis of women CEOs showed that at least half were "imported" from outside the company, while male CEOs almost always come from the inside (Reed, 2005). The 2007 census of Fortune 500 companies showed that only 27.2 percent of "line positions," those that may lead to top jobs, were held by women, a slight decrease from 2006 (Catalyst, 2008).

Getting more women into top executive positions will require active steps to eradicate stereotypes about women, according to a 2005 study (Catalyst, 2006). This survey of both male and female corporate leaders showed that perceptions of men and women leaders are based on gender stereotypes, not on fact-based information. A major finding was that men consider women to be less skilled at problem solving than men are. With men far outnumbering women in top management positions, this idea "dominates current corporate thinking" and

Although some women face a "glass ceiling" in their careers, most women are limited by a "sticky floor"—women are concentrated in low-paying service, support, and nurturance occupations.

SIX CHIX by Margaret Shulock. Reprinted with permission of King Features Syndicate.

prevents women from advancing. The report recommends that companies educate managers and executives about stereotyping and ways to overcome it and that the achievements of women leaders be showcased. Another Catalyst study found that the top career advancement strategies used by women were "consistently exceeding performance expectations and developing a style with which male managers are comfortable" (Catalyst, 2003).

Disparities in Pay

Women earn less than men. On average, women employed full-time in 2009 earned 80.2 cents for each dollar earned by males, up from 60.7 cents per dollar in 1960 (Hegewisch

and Liepmann, 2010). The disparity is even greater when the analysis accounts for time taken off to perform family work, including bearing and raising children; a long-term study showed that over 15 years women earned only 38 cents for every dollar earned by men (Rose and Hartmann, 2004). More women than men have low incomes and live below the poverty level, and more men than women earn over $75,000 a year (DeNavas-Walt, Proctor, and Smith, 2009). Although the wage gap has closed over the past several decades, the rate of decrease has slowed (IWPR, 2008) and significant disparities remain overall (see Figure 8.3a) as well as within occupational categories (see Figure 8.3b). Though the education

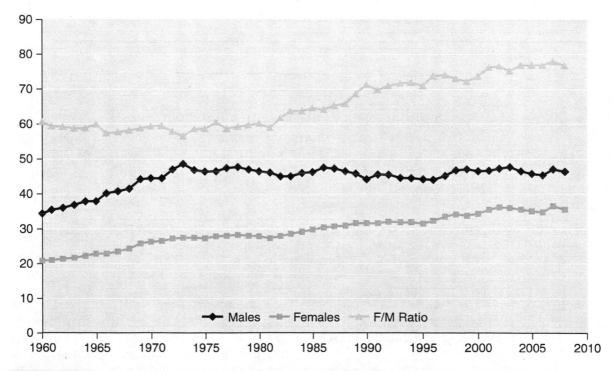

Figure 8.3a **Disparities in Earnings Remain Significant**
Median yearly earnings in thousands of dollars of full-time, year-round workers in the United States by gender, in constant 2008 dollars, 1955–2008; ratio of median female earnings to median male earnings. Recent gains by women in terms of the ratio of their earnings to those of men are due both to a decrease in earnings of men and to an increase in earnings of women.

Source: Figure generated by the authors from data in DeNavas-Walt, Proctor, and Smith, 2009.

260   Chapter 8   *Gender Inequality*

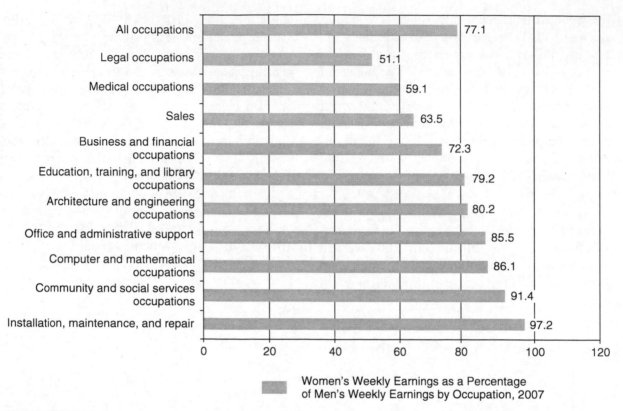

Women's Weekly Earnings as a Percentage
of Men's Weekly Earnings by Occupation, 2007

Figure 8.3*b* ## Disparities in Earnings Remain significant (*continued*)

Women's weekly earnings as a percentage of men's weekly earnings for full-time wage and salary workers by occupation in the United States, 2007. In all occupations, women earned an average of 77 cents for every dollar earned by men. The ratio of female-to-male median weekly earnings for full-time wage and salary workers in the United States is especially low in sales occupations and especially high in installation, maintenance, and repair.

Source: Calculated by the authors from data in Alemayehu Bishaw and Jessica Smega, 2008, "Income, Earnings, and Poverty Data from the 2007 American Community Survey." U.S. Census Bureau, American Community Survey Reports, ACS-09. Washington, DC: U.S. Government Printing Office. Available at http://www.census.gov/prod/2008pubs/acs-09.pdf.

gap between men and women has closed, there is a sharp disparity in earnings between men and women at all levels of education (see Figure 8.3c).

Paying a woman less to do the same job a man does is illegal. What, then, explains the pay gap? It is affected by many factors. Sociologist Paula England (1993b) suggested three major explanations. First, discrimination in hiring and placement reduces women's chances for high-paying jobs in occupations dominated by men, such as management, craft occupations, and some professions. Second, jobs that are occupied mostly by women provide lower wages than jobs that are dominated by men. In one analysis, it was found that nurses were paid less than fire truck mechanics, and librarians were paid less than custodians. Pay differentials for gendered occupations account for much, but not all, of the earnings gap (Boraas and Rodgers, 2003). Third, women often have less job experience than men because they interrupt their

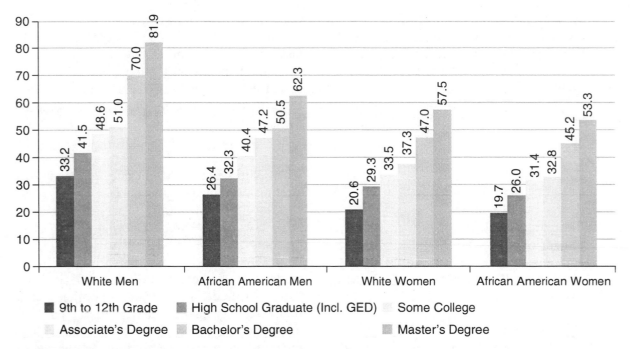

Figure 8.3c **Disparities in Earnings Remain Significant (*continued*)**
Yearly earnings in thousands of dollars of full-time, year-round workers 25 years and older, by gender, race, and education, 2008. Black and white women earn less in every educational category than black and white men.

Source: Figure generated by the authors using data from the U.S. Census Bureau, Current Population Survey, Annual Social and Economic Supplement, 2009. Available at http://www.census.gov/hhes/www/cpstables/032009/perinc/new03_000.htm.

careers to care for children. This "motherhood penalty" has been found to be 5 percent per child even after the cost of lost experience is accounted for, a penalty the researchers attributed to discrimination by employers against mothers and/or the effect of motherhood on productivity at work (Budig and England, 2001).

Other related factors also contribute to the pay gap. For example, on average, women work fewer hours than men and are less likely to work full-time, but this fact and other factors do not completely explain the gender gap in pay. A study of graduates of the University of Michigan law school found that men's salaries were 52 percent higher than women's salaries. The researchers looked at hours worked, law school grades, marital status, number of children, number of

years practicing law, and type of legal practice and found that 23 percent of women's salary disadvantage remained unexplained by these factors (Noonan, Corcoran, and Courant, 2005). For all college graduates, the portion of the pay gap that remains unexplained after accounting for experience, training, education, personal characteristics, and college major is 5 percent one year after graduation and 12 percent 10 years after graduation, evidence of discrimination against women (Dey and Hill, 2007).

Differences in earnings vary by race and ethnicity, with Hispanic and African American women earning even less than white women compared to white men, and wage disparity continues to disadvantage women into retirement. In 2008, men receiving Social Security

262 Chapter 8 *Gender Inequality*

benefits were getting an average of $1,299 per month, while women were getting an average of $1,001 per month (Social Security Administration, 2010). Because benefits are based primarily on years worked and wages earned, women's lower wages and time out of the workforce for reproductive responsibilities result in smaller retirement benefits.

Career Patterns: Out of Sync with Family Life

Overall, the career patterns of women can be quite different from those of men. The economic advancement of women is complicated by the social organization of child care. Economist Sylvia Ann Hewlett observed (quoted in Castro, 1991:10):

[W]e have confused equal rights with identical treatment, ignoring the realities of family life. After all, only women can bear children. And in this country, women must still carry most of the burden of raising them. We think that we are being fair to everyone by stressing identical opportunities, but in fact we are punishing women and children.

Women who have children encounter substantial career disadvantages (Crittenden, 2001; Desai and Waite, 1991; Glass and Camarigg, 1992; Tilghman, 1993). The years between ages 25 and 35 are critical in the development of a career. Yet these are the years when women are most likely to have children. If they leave the labor force to do so, they suffer in their ability to acquire critical skills and to achieve promotions. Very often they also suffer a complete loss of income for the time they are away from work, and they may also leave with no guarantee that they can return; the United States is one of only three industrialized nations that do not provide paid maternity leave by law (see Table 8.1). New mothers who return to work within a few months may find themselves shunted from a career track to a "mommy track"; male managers conclude that the women are no longer free to take on time-consuming tasks or as motivated to get ahead and fail to consider them for promotion (Wadman, 1992). Increased awareness of the problems women face, however, has resulted in corporations increasing efforts to retain employees. PricewaterhouseCoopers, for example, has a director of gender retention and advancement, whose job it is to persuade women to return to work after maternity leave (Joyce, 2007).

Nevertheless, family issues continue to impede women's careers (Dey and Hill, 2007). Sociologist Arlie Russell Hochschild (1997) spent three years doing research on family and work at a midwestern Fortune 500 company that promoted family-friendly policies. She found that executives demanded increasingly longer hours of work from employees without regard to the impact on families. In one family Hochschild followed, the husband took a short paternity leave, but both he and his wife felt that the company was not ready to have employees who wanted to spend time with their families.

Equal opportunity for women in public spheres remains substantially frustrated by gender-role differentiation within the family. Sociologist Mirra Komarovsky (1991:23) observed:

[I]n order to provide real options for men and women we shall have to reorganize economic and other institutions in a profound way, more profound in my opinion, than would be necessary, for example, to solve the problems of the black minority in the United States. . . . Social investments in child care, maternity and paternity leaves, flexible work hours, job sharing, and other changes will be required to balance the private and public worlds for both men and women.

We will further address child care and other problems related to women in the paid labor force in Chapter 10 (pp. 324–325).

Sexual Harassment and Rape

The Equal Employment Opportunity Commission defines **sexual harassment** as "unwelcome" sexual attention, whether verbal or physical, that affects an employee's job conditions or creates a "hostile" working environment (Adler, 1991). Examples of sexual harassment include unsolicited and unwelcome flirtations, advances, or propositions; graphic or degrading comments about an employee's appearance, dress, or anatomy; the display of sexually suggestive objects or pictures; ill-received sexual jokes and offensive gestures; sexual or intrusive questions about an employee's personal life; explicit descriptions of a male's own sexual experiences; abuse of familiarities such as "honey," "baby," and "dear"; unnecessary, unwanted physical contact such as touching, hugging, pinching, patting, or kissing; whistling and catcalls; and leering. In 2004, violations of sexual harassment law resulted in awards and settlements of $35.5 million (Graff, 2005).

Explanations of sexual harassment include societal-, organizational-, and individual-level approaches (Welsh, 1999). Researchers who have studied sexual harassment on the job find that women are much more likely to be harassed than men, and that important factors affecting sexual harassment in the workplace are power differences (financially vulnerable people are more likely to be harassed) and masculinity (Uggen and Blackstone, 2004).

Sexual harassment is not limited to the workplace. Half of all female college students who participated in a nationwide survey reported having been subjected to sexist remarks, catcalls, and whistles. In addition, 15.5 percent reported sexual victimizations other than rape, 13.1 reported having been stalked, 20 percent reported getting obscene phone calls, and 10 percent had had false rumors spread about their sex lives (Fisher, Cullen, and Turner, 2000).

Rape is the most violent form of sexual victimization, and it is a form of sexual violence that victimizes women much more than it does men (Kessler et al., 1995). The legal definition of forcible rape varies across states in the United States, but it is generally defined as forcing persons to engage in sexual intercourse against their will. It can also include forcing a person to engage in oral sex and other sex acts. Defined in this way, rape of men by women is extremely rare (Thio, 2010). But rape of women by men is anything but rare: Reasonable estimates of the percentage of women in the United States who have been raped by men sometime in their lifetimes range from 10 to 25 percent (see Box 8.2).

Why do men rape women? Most rapists are *not* psychologically disturbed, sexually inadequate, or unable to relate to women in a normal way. Because psychological explanations at the individual level leave so much unexplained, sociologists have turned to explanations that emphasize culture, socialization, and social structure.

Culture can create a context in which rapes are more likely to occur. It does this through the creation and dissemination of norms, values, and ways of thinking that encourage and justify rape. Examples are music videos, movies, television shows, magazine displays, and pornography that portray women as sex objects, always being ready for sex, and being coerced or forced into sexual activity, perhaps even "enjoying it." Masculine culture among young men often involves patterns of discussion, joking, and banter that treat women primarily as objects of sexual desire and as legitimate targets in sexual pursuits (Fields, 1993; Thio, 2010). This may not directly cause rape, but it creates a normative environment that makes the world safer for rape and rapists (Martin and Hummer, 1995). Studies show that campus athletes, perhaps the group most heavily influenced by the culture of masculinity, are more likely to exhibit sexual aggression than other college men (Koss and Gaines, 1993; Nelson, 1994; Crosset et al., 1996).

Cultural factors might not be such important factors in rape and sexual harassment if it

8.2 Doing Social Research

How Many People Get Raped?

Researcher Mary Koss made headlines—and drew heavy criticism—when she published her findings that more than a quarter of all college women have experienced an act that met the legal definition of rape (Koss, Gidycz, and Wisniewski, 1987). Her estimate was 10–15 times higher than comparable rates reported by the Bureau of Justice Statistics in their National Crime Victimization Survey (NCVS). Why are the numbers so different?

Rape may be the crime for which it is most difficult to get reliable numbers, and it seems that how the data are gathered is critical. The Uniform Crime Reports (UCR) data, measured by the FBI Index of Crime, are based on police reports of crime. Before a rape appears in the UCR, it must be reported to the police, and the police must be satisfied that "a man must have had (1) carnal knowledge of a woman, (2) forcibly, and (3) against her will" (Gove, Hughes, and Geerken, 1985).

While the NCVS typically uncovers higher rates of rape than appear in the UCR, the questions used to determine these rates do not

actually ask a woman if she has ever been raped. A woman must tell the interviewer that she has been raped in response to general questions about whether she has ever been attacked or threatened. Rape itself is never mentioned; it is up to the person being questioned to volunteer the information (Gove, Hughes, and Geerken, 1985).

An obvious way to get more information is to ask people directly whether they have been raped. A national survey that asked this question of both men and women found that 9.2 percent of women and less than 1.0 percent of men had ever been raped (Kessler et al., 1995). Both numbers are significantly higher than those that appear in either the NCVS or the UCR.

Even higher rates are obtained when the question is phrased in a different way. When respondents were asked if anyone had ever forced them to do something sexual, 22 percent of women and 4 percent of men responded yes (Laumann et al., 1994; Michael et al., 1994). A study of nearly 5,000 women attending U.S. colleges and universities also found that what is asked makes

a big difference (Fisher, Cullen, and Turner, 2000). This study included a comparison component that used methods similar to those in the NCVS. The main study, which included extremely detailed questions about "unwanted sexual experiences," found rates of rape and attempted rape that were 11 and 6 times higher, respectively, than the rates found by the comparison study.

The rates reported by Bonnie Fisher and her colleagues (2000) are in line with those reported by Mary Koss (1987) for college women and by others for the general population. Fisher's survey responses showed that 1.7 percent of the college women had experienced a rape and 1.1 percent an attempted rape during an average period of about seven months. What does such a rate mean? For a school with 10,000 female students, more than 350 of them experience rape or attempted rape in a single academic year. Projected over the five years that most students now spend getting an undergraduate degree, one-fifth to one-quarter of all college women would experience a rape or attempted rape.

were not for gender inequality. Because of gender inequality, women lack the power to respond forcefully and effectively to prevent harassment and rape and to deal with situations leading to them. In addition, some social scientists argue that sexual harassment, sexual aggression, and rape are methods men use to intimidate women, keeping them dependent, powerless, and out of male-dominated jobs (Graff, 2005; Peterson, 1992).

Culture and gender inequality combine to powerfully influence the prevalence of rape and sexual aggression. Sanday's (1981) study of

small societies showed that societies with high rates of rape were those where males were heavily dominant and in which sexual aggression was a symbol of masculinity and of men's control and mastery of women, while those with little rape were those that discouraged sexual aggression. Sanday (1996) and other researchers (Schwartz and DeKeseredy, 1997; Martin and Hummer, 1995; Schwartz, 1995) have found that college campuses with low rates of rape are those in which the culture of masculinity is not strong and where sexual assault and rape are taken seriously and severely

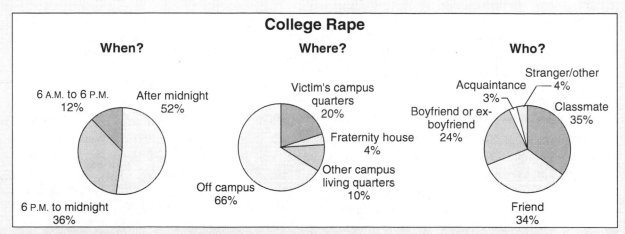

College Rape

When?

6 A.M. to 6 P.M.
12%

After midnight
52%

6 P.M. to midnight
36%

Where?

Victim's campus quarters
20%

Fraternity house
4%

Other campus living quarters
10%

Off campus
66%

Who?

Stranger/other
4%

Acquaintance
3%

Boyfriend or ex-boyfriend
24%

Classmate
35%

Friend
34%

It would appear that rape is not primarily a problem of public life. These data for college women apply to the general population. Rapists are not likely to be lurking in dark alleys; they are likely to be sitting in your living room or next to you in a car. Rape is primarily a problem of private life, and rapists are most likely to be people with whom the rape victim has a personal relationship.

Source: Figure generated by the authors using data from Fisher, Cullen, and Turner, 2000.

How many rapes we believe occur seems to depend primarily on how victims are asked about their experiences. Fisher and her colleagues concluded, "The use of graphically worded screen questions . . . likely prompted more women who had experienced a sexual victimization to report this fact to the interviewer" (Fisher, Cullen, and Turner, 2000:14).

Questions for Discussion

1. If you were researching rape, what problems would you face in determining the number of rapes that occur in a given time period?

2. The data on college rape show that rapists are most likely to be someone the victim knows, perhaps intimately. Why do rapes occur in such situations? What strategies would help prevent such rapes?

punished. Those with high rates of rape are those where the student culture values heavy drinking, male dominance, and traditional masculine values.

Politics and Government

The number of women in politics in the United States has increased in recent years, and Hillary Clinton's bid for the Democratic Party presidential nomination drew the country's attention to a variety of gender issues. Although 27 states have never had a female governor, the others have, and six women were serving terms in 2010; in all, 32 women have governed a U.S. state. The U.S. Senate had 18 women serving in 2010, and 67 representatives were women. And women have turned out in greater numbers than men to vote in recent elections. Thousands of women have entered politics at the local and state levels over the last several decades, enlarging the pool of candidates for higher office.

But political success has not come easily to American women (Witt, Paget, and Matthews, 1993), and it is not proceeding at a steady pace. Although the number of women in the U.S. House

266 Chapter 8 *Gender Inequality*

and Senate has increased, the proportion—16 percent—has grown only slightly in recent years (Werschkul and Williams, 2004), and the proportion of women legislators is much smaller in the United States than in many other countries (see Figure 8.1). If the United States adds women to Congress at the rate it did during the past decade, we will have equal numbers of male and female senators and representatives in about 100 years (Werschkul and Williams, 2004).

Three sets of factors play a part in women's representation in politics (Paxton and Kunovich, 2003). Structural factors include the low "supply" of women candidates, as political candidates tend to come from the law and other professions in which women have been underrepresented. Political factors include the low "demand" for women candidates. Ideological beliefs were assessed in a cross-national study to determine a national "climate" measure, based on responses to questions about women's place in politics, education, and the labor force. The researchers found that ideology played a more important role than politics in predicting women's political representation in a country, affecting both supply and demand (Paxton and Kunovich, 2003).

Does having women in positions of leadership make a difference? A study of state supreme court judges found that female judges voted more liberally than males in the cases studied—death penalty and obscenity cases (Songer and Crews-Meyer, 2000). The researchers also found that male judges were more likely to support liberal positions when there was a woman among their ranks. And researchers have found that in sex discrimination cases female judges are more likely than males to rule in favor of the victim, and male judges are more likely to rule in favor of the victim when female judges are serving with them (Boyd and Epstein, 2009).

Perhaps more important is the potential for women in positions of power to make real social structural changes. For example, it is unlikely to be mere coincidence that in Sweden, with one

of the highest proportions of women legislators in the world, maternity benefits also are among the best in the world (see Table 8.1).

The Women's Movement

Over the past 40 years, no social movement has had a more substantial impact on the way Americans think and act than the women's movement. In the 1960s the women's movement built upon earlier movements while gaining new impetus from the involvement of women in the civil rights movement (Taylor, 1989; Buechler, 1990; Simon and Danziger, 1991). Cross-national research suggests that the "first wave" (1800–1950) of women's movements focused primarily on legal equality, including the pursuit of suffrage, or the right to vote; the "second wave" (since the 1960s) has centered primarily on social equality, particularly in jobs and education (Chafetz and Dworkin, 1986; Schnittker, Freese, and Powell, 2003).

Increasing numbers of women are achieving positions of leadership and authority. Shown here is Ruth J. Simmons, president of Brown University. The presidents of Harvard and MIT also are women.

The revival of feminist activity in the 1960s was spearheaded by a variety of groups. Some, such as the National Organization for Women (NOW), were organized at the national level by well-known women. Others were grassroots groups that engaged in campaigns for abortion reform or welfare rights, consciousness-raising discussion sessions, or promotion of the interests of professional or lesbian women.

Sources of Gender Differences

We have been focusing on gender inequality with respect to the macrostructural features of society. What about more micro- or individual-level explanations for gender differences? In this section we will look at gender differences and biology, culture, and identity.

Gender and Biology

The biological aspects of gender consist of the physical differences between men and women: Women have the capacity to ovulate, carry a fetus until delivery, and provide it with milk after birth; men have the ability to produce and transmit sperm. Women and men also differ in their responses to drugs and other medical interventions as well as in their susceptibilities to many illnesses (Greenberger, 2008; Simon, 2005).

The role biology plays in producing behavioral differences between men and women is far less clear than the role it plays in physical differences. A review of research published in the 1970s concluded that there were four fairly well established differences between girls and boys, including greater verbal ability among girls and greater visual-spatial and mathematical abilities and higher aggression among boys (Maccoby and Jacklin, 1974). However, recent research casts these findings in a new light. We now know that the vast majority of gender differences

reported in studies have been small or essentially negligible. Janet Shibley Hyde (2005) reviewed 46 *meta-analyses* , in which researchers combine and summarize research findings from many studies of the same question. The 46 papers Hyde reviewed all were meta-analyses of gender difference studies, and they included a wide variety of specific topics: verbal skills, mathematical skills, physical strength, reading comprehension, spatial visualization, aggression, helping behaviors, sexuality, leadership abilities, self-esteem, depression, cheating, moral reasoning, and many more.

Hyde found that 78 percent of the gender differences in these meta-analyses were small or close to zero—in other words, hardly differences at all. Gender differences in most aspects of communication are small, as are gender differences in moral reasoning and moral orientation. Males and females differ very little in their life satisfaction, happiness, self-esteem, attitudes about work, approaches to leadership, reading and mathematics abilities, and many other variables.

Do men and women differ at all? Some gender differences were found to be large and reasonably stable, showing up in a variety of studies. Hyde's review of gender difference studies showed that the largest differences are in motor performance, especially after puberty, when male bone size and muscle mass begin to exceed that of females. Specifically, males are, on average, able to throw faster and farther than females. There also are moderate differences for other measures of motor performance, with men having a stronger grip and being able to sprint faster.

Some of the measures of sexuality also showed large gender differences; males are more likely than females to masturbate frequently and to have a positive attitude about sex in casual and uncommitted relationships. A moderate gender difference was found for aggression, with men and boys more likely than women and girls to engage in physical aggression.

268   Chapter 8   *Gender Inequality*

What about Maccoby and Jacklin's (1974) findings on verbal, mathematical, and visual-spatial abilities? Hyde's (2005) review found gender differences ranging in size from very small to moderate for cognitive variables. Two exceptions were moderate-to-large differences favoring males in mechanical reasoning and mental rotation. A study of public school children in grades 2 to 11 reported no gender differences in math skills (Hyde et al., 2008). Only very small differences have been found in language skills, and studies contradicted one another, with girls ahead of boys in vocabulary in one study but behind in another (Hyde, 2005).

Hyde's (2005) review of the information gathered in many studies also showed that some gender differences change with growth and development. Others depend on social context, with differences in aggression, smiling, interrupting, mathematical performance, and helping behaviors changing and even reversing under different circumstances.

In spite of arguments that deemphasize biology in gendered behavior, this issue is far from settled. Recently, some sociologists have proposed formally integrating social and biological factors in a single framework, and have argued that the effect of gender socialization depends on biological factors and vice versa. For example, Udry (2000) showed that prenatal exposure to testosterone (a male hormone that is found in both sexes) in females reduces the effects of gender socialization on adult gendered behavior. Udry concluded that biological and socialization factors work together in generating gendered behavior but that biology also sets individual limits on gender socialization and additional limits to the macroconstruction

"I broncobust *and* I Dust-Bust. You got a problem with that?"

of gender. Udry's findings and conclusions are controversial and have generated debate, making it clear that more research will be needed before we can arrive at firm conclusions in this area (Kennelly, Merz, and Lorber, 2001; Miller and Costello, 2001; Risman, 2001; Udry, 2001).

Gender and Culture

Despite the very few gender differences identified by researchers, all societies assign gender roles—the sets of cultural expectations that define the ways in which the members of each sex should behave. Anthropological evidence suggests that gender roles probably represent the earliest division of labor among human beings. Consequently, we are all born into societies with well-established cultural guidelines for the behavior of men and women (see Box 8.3).

That these cultural expectations are based on any "real" gender differences is cast into doubt by the results of a survey of 224 societies (Murdock, 1935). Anthropologist George P. Murdock found in his cross-cultural survey that vast differences exist in the social definitions of what constitutes appropriate masculine and feminine behavior. Indeed, as shown in Table 8.2, the allocation of duties often differs sharply from that of our own society. For example, for generations, U.S. communities have had laws restricting the weights that a working woman is permitted to lift. Yet the Arapesh of New Guinea assigned women the task of carrying heavy loads because their heads were believed to be harder and stronger than those of men. Among the Tasmanians of the South Pacific, the most dangerous type of hunting—swimming out to remote rocks in the sea to stalk and club sea otters—was assigned to women. Moreover, women formed the bodyguard of Dahomeyan kings because they were deemed to be particularly fierce fighters. And although most peoples believe that men should take the initiative in sexual matters, the Maori of New Zealand and the Trobriand Islanders (near New Guinea) give this prerogative to women (Ford and Beach, 1951).

The great variation in the gender roles of men and women from one society to another points to a social foundation for most of these differences (Bernard, 1987; South and Trent, 1988; Intons-Peterson, 1988). So do the changes observed from one time to another in sex-linked behavior patterns within the same society, such as hair length and style and clothing fashions. All this suggests that gender roles are largely a matter of social definition and socially constructed meanings.

Gender Identities

Gender identities are the conceptions we have of ourselves as being male or female. Most people have a good fit between their anatomy and their gender identity. Boys generally come to behave in ways their culture labels "masculine," and girls learn to be "feminine."

But there are some individuals for whom this is not the case. The most striking examples are *transsexuals*—individuals who have normal sexual organs but who psychologically feel like members of the opposite sex. Transsexuality should not be confused with homosexuality. Homosexuality is a sexual orientation, not a confused gender identity; lesbians have a strong sense of themselves as females, and they are sexually attracted to other females. In some cases of transsexuality, medical science has found a way to modify the person's anatomy to conform with the person's gender identity.

How do individuals develop gender identities? In this section we will examine three explanations.

Cultural Transmission Theory

Cultural transmission theorists contend that the acquisition of gender identities and behaviors is a gradual process of learning that begins in infancy (Bandura, 1971, 1973; Fagot, Leinbach, and O'Boyle, 1992). They suggest that parents, teachers, and other adults shape a child's behavior by reinforcing responses that

8.3 Students Doing Sociology

Gender Expectations: Cigars, Tupperware, and Condoms

Many—perhaps most—college students today believe that gender inequality is pretty much a thing of the past. Because they grew up in a time when women could vote, go to college, work outside the home, run for office, and the like, some students find feminist ideology—well, extreme. So complacent are many students that they are quick to reject arguments of feminist sociologists that our culture promotes gender inequality through its "compulsory heterosexuality." But the results of more than 650 field observations recorded by sociology students over a 15-year period offer substantial evidence that compulsory heterosexuality is deeply embedded in American culture (Nielsen, Walden, and Kunkel, 2000).

Students were assigned to think up some way to violate a gender norm and to record what happened as a result of their violation. They were to choose and perform in public some act typically associated with the opposite sex and record both the reactions of others and their own feelings. Over the years, students came up with more than one hundred different "gender transgressions." Male students crocheted in

public, bought sanitary napkins, wore women's clothes or shoes, cried, carried purses, tried out "women's occupations," painted their fingernails, and read romance novels. One even threw a Tupperware party. Female students opened doors for men, smoked cigars and pipes, chewed tobacco, sent men flowers, went shirtless while doing sports activities, bought condoms, and read *Playgirl*. Some displayed knowledge about "guy stuff," such as cars and sports.

And what were the reactions to these norm violations? Surprisingly, especially given the wide variety of projects, the reactions were easily categorized—and completely different depending on whether the norm violator was a woman or a man. Men were labeled homosexual or potentially homosexual, and women were considered either to be sexually aggressive and promiscuous or of dubious attractiveness to men. Comments heard by the male gender-norm violators included "We gotta sweet fella here," "What a fag!" and "Fairies aren't allowed in here." Comments recorded by female gender-norm violators included "It's a good thing she's married because she

probably wouldn't get any dates," "Is this any way for two pretty young girls to behave?" and "There's a totally cute girl smoking a———ing cigar!"

The experiences of the hundreds of students involved in this study clearly demonstrate the power of gender expectations. Gender-role norms function as a signal of the willingness of those adhering to them to be part of the heterosexual world, and they provide sanctions for those who would violate them. Feminist sociologists argue that compulsory heterosexuality is deeply embedded in our culture and in the demands it makes on us in our everyday lives. This study supports that argument.

Questions for Discussion

1. Have you ever knowingly or unknowingly violated a gender norm? What did you do? What was the reaction of those around you?

2. How do you feel when you see men dressed as women? Or women with men's haircuts, no makeup, and men's clothes? Explain your reaction.

---

are deemed appropriate to the child's gender role and discouraging inappropriate ones. Moreover, children are motivated to attend to, learn from, and imitate same-sex models because they think of same-sex models as more like themselves (Mischel, 1970). Children are given cues to their gender roles in a great variety of ways, from how their rooms are decorated to what toys they are given to play with and clothes they are given to wear.

Cognitive Development Theory

Cultural transmission theory portrays children as passive individuals who are programmed for behavior by adults. *Cognitive development theory* calls our attention to the fact that children actively seek to acquire gender identities and roles.

According to cognitive development theory as discussed in Chapter 3 (p. 71) (Kohlberg, 1966, 1969; Kohlberg and Ullian, 1974),

Table 8.2   The Division of Labor by Sex in 224 Societies

	Number of Societies and Sex of Person by Whom the Activity Is Performed				
Activity	Men Always	Men Usually	Either Sex	Women Usually	Women Always
Hunting	166	13	0	0	0
Trapping small animals	128	13	4	1	2
Herding	38	8	4	0	5
Fishing	98	34	19	3	4
Clearing agricultural land	73	22	17	5	13
Dairy operations	17	4	3	1	13
Preparing and planting soil	31	23	33	20	37
Erecting and dismantling shelter	14	2	5	6	22
Tending and harvesting crops	10	15	35	39	44
Bearing burdens	12	6	35	20	57
Cooking	5	1	9	28	158
Metalworking	78	0	0	0	0
Boat building	91	4	4	0	1
Working in stone	68	3	2	0	2
Basket making	25	3	10	6	82
Weaving	19	2	2	6	67
Manufacturing and repairing of clothing	12	3	8	9	95

Source: Reprinted by permission from *Social Forces,* May 15, 1937. "Comparative Data on the Division of Labor by Sex," by George P. Murdock. Copyright © The University of North Carolina Press.

children come to label themselves as "boys" or "girls" when they are between 18 months and three years of age. Once they have identified themselves as males or females, they want to adopt behaviors consistent with their newly discovered status. This process is called *self-socialization.* According to Kohlberg, children form a stereotyped conception of maleness and femaleness—an oversimplified, exaggerated, cartoonlike image. Then they use this stereotyped image to organize behavior and cultivate the attitudes and actions associated with being

a boy or a girl. Neuroscientist Lise Eliot points out that very small cognitive gaps can grow because of positive feedback loops (Eliot, 2009).

Both the cultural transmission and cognitive-development theories of gender-role learning have received research support (Maccoby and Jacklin, 1974; Bem, 1981; Serbin and Sprafkin, 1986; Martin and Little, 1990). Social and behavioral scientists increasingly see gender-role acquisition as being explained by elements from both theoretical approaches.

272 Chapter 8 *Gender Inequality*

Self-Construals and Gender

In Chapter 3 (p. 80) we discussed self-conception and identity. Psychologists Susan Cross and Laura Madson used differences in self-construal, which is essentially synonymous with our term *self-conception,* to explain gender differences in the United States (Cross and Madson, 1997). Individuals in some societies develop a sense of self that is highly interdependent; in East Asian cultures, for example, self-definition is based primarily on relationships and group memberships. Maintaining harmonious relationships with others is extremely important. Such a definition of self is referred to by psychologists as an *interdependent self-construal.* In contrast, many Western societies are individualistic, and self-definition is based on individualism: One's unique attributes and the importance of an individual distinguishing him- or herself from others are key to developing a sense of self. This definition of self has been called an *independent self-construal.*

Cross and Madson, with other researchers, pointed out that the independent self-construal model describes men better than it does women in the United States and that most U.S. women can probably be best described by the interdependent self-construal model. Many social influences in the United States promote independent ways of behaving, feeling, and thinking for men; for women, relational ways of behaving, feeling, and thinking are more likely to be promoted. This major difference in self-construal between men and women in the United States, Cross and Madson argued, has important consequences in terms of gender differences, including those in cognition, motivation, emotion, and social behavior. For example, they found that women are more willing to express most emotions, while men are more willing to express anger. Women are also more likely to be sensitive to the emotions of others and to base their own emotions on those.

Sociological Perspectives on Gender Stratification

As noted in Chapter 1 (p. 16) the roles, contributions, and experiences of women were not a major part of theory and social research for most of the history of sociology. Well into the 20th century, female social scientists, who were most likely to make contributions in this area, were marginalized and never able to establish themselves in academic sociology. As a result, traditional theories included little that was relevant to the issue of gender inequality. Perhaps the first work to attempt a systematic understanding of the differentiation of gender roles was Parsons and Bales' (1955) study of the family from the functionalist perspective. But as we will see, many sociologists view this work as both an attempt to explain gender roles *and* as a justification of prevailing gender inequalities.

Since the 1960s, however, sociologists have been heavily influenced by feminist thinking (see Chapter 1, p. 16). And while neither the conflict nor the interactionist perspective includes an organized theory of gender inequality, feminists and contemporary sociologists have drawn upon the insights of the conflict and interactionist perspectives to develop an understanding of the nature of gender inequality and the sociocultural forces that perpetuate it.

As you will see, the functionalist, conflict, and interactionist perspectives offer interpretations of gender stratification that resemble and parallel their positions on class and racial or ethnic stratification. We will look more closely at each in this section, as well as discuss the feminist perspective on gender inequality.

The Functionalist Perspective

Functionalists suggest that a division of labor originally arose between men and women because of the woman's role in reproduction. Because women were often pregnant or nursing, preindustrial societies assigned domestic and child-rearing tasks to them. In contrast, men were assigned hunting and defense tasks because of their larger size and greater muscular strength. Functionalists contend that a gender division of labor promoted the survival of the species and therefore was retained.

Sociologists Talcott Parsons and Robert Bales (1955) built upon principles derived from the study of the dynamics of small groups in refining their functionalist position. They argued that two types of leaders are essential if a small group is to function effectively (see Chapter 4, pp. 103–105). *Instrumental leaders* (task specialists) devote their attention to appraising the problem at hand and organizing people's activity to deal with it. *Expressive leaders* (social-emotional specialists) focus on overcoming interpersonal problems in the group, defusing tensions, and promoting solidarity. Parsons and Bales suggested that families are also organized along instrumental-expressive lines. Men specialize in instrumental tasks, particularly roles associated with having a job and making money, and women in expressive tasks, supporting their husbands, doing household labor, and caring for children.

Essentially, Parsons and Bales were arguing that it was functional and beneficial for the society, for families, and for individuals if males play instrumental, goal-oriented roles and females play expressive roles, supporting husbands and nurturing children. Through the 1960s, 1970s, and 1980s, many sociologists attacked this position as taking an idealized family form from the United States in the 1950s and claiming that it was the uniquely superior model for gender and family relations in industrial societies. Other patterns exist and meet the needs of individuals, families, and the society—for example, the household where both wife and husband work and the household headed by a single parent with resources that allow access to high-quality child care. Critics of the functionalist approach also pointed out that this idealized structure makes men the more powerful actors and women relatively powerless and dependent on men. By arguing that this arrangement is necessary, functionalism becomes a powerful justification for the existence of gender inequality.

The Conflict Perspective

Much of the critique of functionalism from the 1950s to the 1980s came from conflict theorists who rejected functionalist arguments as simply offering a rationale for male dominance. They contended that a sexual division of labor is a social vehicle devised by men to ensure for themselves privilege, prestige, and power in their relationships with women. Gender inequality exists because it benefits men, who use the power it gives them to ensure its perpetuation. By relegating women to the home, men have been able to deny women those resources they need to succeed in the larger world. More particularly, conflict theorists have advanced a number of explanations for gender stratification (Collins, 1975; Vogel, 1983; Collier, 1988; Bradley, 1989; Chafetz, 1990). Some argue that the motivation for gender stratification derives from the economic exploitation of women's labor. Others say that the fundamental motive is men's desire to have women readily available for sexual gratification. Still others emphasize that the appropriation of women is not for copulation but for procreation, especially to produce male heirs and daughters who can be used as exchanges in cementing political and economic alliances with other families.

Sociologist Joan Acker (1992) suggested that in industrial capitalist societies, production is valued over reproduction. Whereas business, commerce, and industry are viewed as an essential source of well-being and wealth, child rearing, child care, and elder care are seen as secondary and wealth-consuming. Although "the family" is enshrined and idealized, reproduction (the domain of women) is shrouded in societal shadows and devalued.

274   Chapter 8 *Gender Inequality*

The Interactionist Perspective

Interactionism has had a very important impact on the thinking of sociologists about gender inequality. If meanings form the basis of social life, then as meanings change, patterns of social interaction can change, thus altering the nature of social structure. Sociologists also have made use of the interactionist idea that we experience the world as a constructed reality. They developed the idea that while sex is given in nature, gender is socially constructed; it is a product of sociocultural processes involving symbols and meanings. Interactionists argue that cultural meanings, including those that give rise to gender inequality, are continuously emerging and changing through social interaction. If so, then people can intentionally change the structure of gender differentiation and inequality by changing the meanings that underlie them. For example, when men define themselves in traditional masculine terms, value male dominance, and view women primarily as objects of sexual pleasure, rape and sexual harassment are more likely to occur. When we replace these meanings with those that value gender equality and view women as complete human beings, the rates of rape and sexual harassment decline.

Another example of how interactionism has influenced specific ideas about gender inequality can be seen in the study of gender stereotyping in everyday language. Our use of language can imply that women are secondary to men, in less powerful positions than men, or less competent than men, all of which thus encourages us to think about women in ways that perpetuate inequality. This happens when we use words like "men" and "he" to refer to both men and women, when we refer to presidents and doctors as "he" but to secretaries and teachers as "she," and when we refer to adult women as "girls" but refrain from calling adult men "boys." Use of such a symbolic framework encourages people to think of women stereotypically as less suited for powerful instrumental roles, to behave toward them accordingly, and to limit the options available for women's self-definition (Richardson, 1987). Interactionist theorists argue that by influencing people's identities in this way, everyday sexist language helps to perpetuate gender inequality, and that changing our language patterns can help to eliminate it.

The Feminist Perspective

As we pointed out in Chapter 1 (p. 16), feminism is not a single theory but an evolving set of theoretical perspectives. Just as conditions for women may not change rapidly until some critical number of women attain positions of economic, social, and political power, so sociological research focused on women's experiences and activities has increased as a function of women becoming research sociologists. Feminist critique of or addition to other perspectives on gender inequality has emerged in recent decades. For example, Miriam Johnson (1993) argued that serving the expressive function in family and society need not lead to disadvantage for women but that it has led to disadvantage because it exists in the context of a patriarchal culture that values men's instrumentality over women's expressiveness. Changing the patriarchal normative order instead of changing patterns of role differentiation, then, is a more effective way to reduce gender inequality. However, this cultural change has so far eluded us, and we are left with the question of how patriarchal structures can be functional (Lengermann and Niebrugge, 2008a). If they are, it would appear that they are primarily functional for men.

Myra Marx Ferree and Elaine J. Hall (2000) provide another critique of functionalism. While functionalists see group differences as beneficial, they explain, feminists "see this grouping process as a socially costly repression of individual variation and potential." Ferree and Hall argue that inequality does not arise from individual differences between people. Rather, their

The Chapter in Brief **275**

gender-relations model of inequality posits that social structures produce inequality and gender differences follow from them:

Gender is organized through micro-, meso-, and macro-level processes that apply gender labels to jobs, skills, institutions, and organizations as well as to people and that use these labels to produce, express, and legitimate inequality. . . . When gender itself operates in and through macro-social institutions, what it produces is not just differences . . . , but inequality. (2000:476)

Sociologists Cecilia Ridgeway and Lynn Smith-Lovin (1999) point out that gender is significantly different from other forms of social inequality. Unlike racial and ethnic inequality or class stratification, the key players in gender inequality—men and women—interact extensively at home, at work, at church, and in a variety of role relationships. These everyday interactions, they contend, re-create the gender system. Such interactions would act to undermine the gender system only in two cases: (1) if the interactions feature women with status or power advantages over men or (2) if they are peer interactions not driven by cultural beliefs about the competence of males and females.

Feminist research has added substantially to our knowledge of women's experiential,

subjective, and emotional lives. Though a variety of perspectives make up the "feminist perspective," they are unified in the effort to develop understandings of gender inequality that can be used to transform society and women's lives.

 What Can Sociology Do for You?

This chapter presented information about the challenges facing and opportunities available to women in contemporary U.S. society. Male or female, if you are concerned about gender equity in the United States, you may be interested in pursuing a career in policy, research, diversity training, employee retention, or the prevention of sexual harassment. Business and Professional Women/USA promotes workplace equity for women and is a leading advocate for working women; check out its website at **http://careers.bpwusa.org.** Another website of interest might be **www.womensleadershipexchange.com.** For more information about how your choice of major affects your long-term earnings, see the American Association of University Women's 2007 study "Behind the Pay Gap" at **www.aauw.org/research/behindPayGap.cfm.**

If the issues raised in Chapter 8 were of interest to you, you may want to take upper-level sociology courses in gender or sexuality.

The Chapter in Brief: *Gender Inequality*

Gender Stratification

Men and women differ in their access to privilege, prestige, and power. The distribution problem of who gets what, when, and how has traditionally been answered in favor of males. **Sex** is a biologically determined characteristic; **gender** is a socially constructed characteristic. All societies use anatomical differences to assign **gender roles. Gender identities** are the conceptions we have of ourselves as being male or female.

■ **Sexism and Patriarchy** Sexism operates at both an individual level and an institutional level. The most pervasive form of institutional sexism is **patriarchy.** Women exhibit four of the five properties associated with a *minority group*.

■ **Gender Inequality Around the World** No nation treats its women as well as its men. Women in many countries suffer discrimination and abuse, yet women around the world do considerably better than U.S. women in some areas.

276   Chapter 8 *Gender Inequality*

■ **Gender Inequality in the United States**   U.S. women have made substantial gains over the past decades but continue to do most of the household work and child rearing. Despite increasing involvement in the paid workforce, women continue to be excluded from top jobs and to earn less than men. **Sexual harassment** remains a common workplace hazard for women, and somewhere between 10 and 25 percent of women have been raped. Men still dominate U.S. political life.

Sources of Gender Differences

Gender roles can be seen as arising from biological development or cultural contributions.

■ **Gender and Biology**   The biological aspects of gender consist of the physical differences between men and women, but the role biology plays in producing behavioral differences between men and women is shrouded in controversy.

■ **Gender and Culture**   Gender roles probably represent the earliest division of labor among humans. Various societies have specific social definitions of appropriate behavior for males and females.

■ **Gender Identities**   Gender identities are the concepts we have of ourselves as being male or female. Theories of the acquisition of gender identities include cultural transmission, cognitive development, and self-construals.

Sociological Perspectives on Gender Stratification

The major sociological perspectives offer interpretations of gender stratification that resemble and parallel their positions on class and racial or ethnic stratification.

■ **The Functionalist Perspective**   Functionalists suggest that families are organized along instrumental-expressive lines, with men specializing in instrumental tasks and women in expressive tasks.

■ **The Conflict Perspective**   Conflict theorists contend that a sexual division of labor is a social vehicle devised by men to ensure themselves of privilege, prestige, and power in their relationships with women.

■ **The Interactionist Perspective**   Interactionists argue that gender inequality persists because of the way we define men and women and their appropriate roles in society. Language helps perpetuate inequality.

■ **The Feminist Perspective**   Feminism is not a single theory but an evolving set of theoretical perspectives. Feminists argue that women are disadvantaged because society is patriarchal; the assignment of group differences is socially costly and repressive. Everyday interactions between men and women re-create and support the gender system.

Glossary

gender   The sociocultural distinction between males and females.

gender identities   The conceptions we have of ourselves as being male or female.

gender roles   Sets of cultural expectations that define the ways in which the members of each sex should behave.

patriarchy   A system of social organization in which men have a disproportionate share of power.

sex   A reference to whether one is genetically male or female; determines the biological role that one will play in reproduction.

sexism   The set of cultural and social processes that justify and promote disadvantage for women.

sexual harassment   Unwelcome sexual attention, whether verbal or physical, that affects an employee's job conditions or creates a hostile working environment.

Review Questions

1. Define sex and gender.

2. How do the terms *gender role* and *gender identity* differ?

3. What is patriarchy?

4. Briefly summarize the variability in quality of life experienced by women around the world.

5. How do U.S. women compare with U.S. men in terms of occupations, employment, earnings, and representation in politics?

6. Compare and contrast biological and cultural bases for gender differences.

7. Briefly describe the theories of gender identity acquisition.

8. How do the functionalist, conflict, interactionist, and feminist perspectives explain gender inequalities?

 ## Internet Connection   www.mhhe.com/hughes10e

The most powerful political positions in most societies have almost always been held by men. Until recently, women's involvement in the formal operations of political institutions has been minimal. Go to the website of the Inter-Parliamentary Union, **http://www.ipu.org/.** Explore this site for information about women's involvement in political institutions in societies around the world. Using this information, and other information in the current chapter, write a short report about the nature of gender inequality in politics and the efforts of governments and political organizations and associations to promote change.

5

Power

looking AHEAD

What is **power** and how does it affect your life?

Why do you have more **power** than you might realize?

How is understanding **power** essential for understanding inequality?

Two decades ago, Munni Akter could barely afford enough food to survive. "I was lost and had no skill to earn," Munni recalls. That's when she managed to get a microloan—just $40—from the Bangladesh Rural Advancement Committee (BRAC). The loan enabled her to begin selling food on the street at a profit. Over the years her business grew. Today Munni runs a small food factory that employs twenty-six workers. She is out of poverty and proudly independent.

Munni Akter is just one of nearly 11 million Bangladeshis who have benefited from microloans, and BRAC is the world's largest nongovernment organization working to reduce poverty. But BRAC is much more than a microlender. The group organizes recipients of microloans into small groups of twenty to thirty people. Group members guarantee each other's loans, provide mutual assistance, and often operate as a springboard for other improvements in their lives. BRAC also operates health care and education programs and teaches women about gender equality and the law so that they can speak up for their rights and resist exploitation.

To spread the message of empowerment, BRAC trains some women as paralegals, or *shebikas* ("helpers" in Sanskrit). These women learn how to handle crises such as rape or domestic abuse as well as to provide other legal services. Over 11,000 *shebikas* now share their knowledge and support with others.

By helping individual women to become empowered and by developing a long-term organizational structure to train a growing number of educators and advocates, the women in these various programs have increased their collective power. That has always been the goal of BRAC's founder and chairperson, Fazle Hasan Abed, who observes, "Poor people are poor because they are powerless. We must organise people for power" (BRAC 2010a, 2010b; Changemakers 2009; Haq 2011). ▪

Power is a fundamental sociological concept, affecting every level of society and influencing our daily lives in countless ways. Because power pervades social life, to understand how society works we must consider its role in various social contexts. As noted political philosopher and social critic Bertrand Russell (1938/2004, 4) put it, "the fundamental concept in social science is Power, in the same way in which Energy is the fundamental concept in physics." Power, like energy, takes many forms and is essential in understanding why things happen as they do in society.

The amount of power that we have heavily influences what we can accomplish in life, whether at home, at work, or in our community. People with more resources typically have more power, and those with power can use it to obtain more resources. Power, therefore, is closely linked to social inequality, another fundamental feature of society. Inequality can be based on many different characteristics, including class, race, gender, ethnicity, nationality, sexual orientation, and religious affiliation. But these different forms of inequality have something in common: power and its influence.

In this chapter, we define and examine power and its various characteristics. We look at examples of power in daily life as well as how differences in power affect inequality, and we explore how different types of inequality interact. We conclude by noting how economic power is increasingly translated into political influence through campaign contributions.

Understanding Forms of Power

You know that the United States is a powerful nation and that your boss has more power than you do. But what is "power," exactly? And how can this concept be applied to such different settings as international relations and the workplace? Different approaches to understanding power highlight different aspects of this important concept (Blalock 1989; Gaventa 1982; Lukes 2005; Mann 1986; Poggi 2001; Sharp 1973; Smith 1990; Wartenberg 1990; Wrong 1979).

Defining Power

The word *power* is derived from a Latin word, *potere*, which means "to be able." Max Weber (1922/1978, 926) viewed **power** as *the ability to bring about an intended outcome, even when opposed by others.* Two key components of this definition are the basis for an important distinction: Some sociologists focus on the "ability to bring about an intended outcome," or

the "power to" approach, so called because it highlights the capacity to accomplish something. Others focus on the ability to overcome opposition, or the "power over" approach, so called because it highlights the capacity to dominate others (Ng and Bradac 1993). These two aspects of power are not mutually exclusive, and feminist scholars, especially, have worked to integrate both approaches into a comprehensive analysis of power (Allen 2008). Let's consider these aspects of power more closely.

Empowerment: "Power To"

As noted, the "power to" approach emphasizes *the ability to bring about an intended outcome,* highlighting the positive and constructive aspects of power. **Empowerment,** which *increases people's capacity to bring about an intended outcome,* is the focus of much feminist scholarship on power. Social philosopher Virginia Held (1993), for example, argues that power is the capacity to change and empower oneself and others. According to political scientist Nancy Hartsock (1983, 226), the "feminist theory of power" views power as a competence and ability, rather than a form of dominance. Sociologist Patricia Hill Collins (2000) highlights the use of power to resist oppression.

People often discuss power and empowerment in terms of individual effort and achievement. If your goal is to find an interesting, decent-paying job, then acquiring appropriate education and experience can help give you the "power to" accomplish your objective. Empowerment often involves individual enhancement and self-improvement. Individual self-empowerment is the theme of popular self-help books with titles such as *Empowerment: The Art of Creating Your Life as You Want It.*

SPOTLIGHT on social theory

Feminist theories point out that power can involve competence and empowerment, rather than just the domination of others. Have you experienced empowerment in your own life in some way without diminishing the power of others?

Empowerment can also involve organizations, communities, and entire categories of people. International development agencies, for example, try to empower poor people by increasing their capacity to care for themselves and their families (Alsop and Heinsohn 2005). The Bangladesh Rural Advancement Committee mentioned at the beginning of this chapter, for example, seeks to empower an oppressed group through a combination of economic assistance and educational programs. Other programs and organizations have also used this combination to produce promising results worldwide. A program in South Africa, for instance, has empowered women to reduce by half the incidence of physical and sexual violence in their community (Kim et al. 2007). Similarly, the women's movement in the United States has helped to empower women, enabling them to gain greater equality in the workplace, more options in their roles at home, better medical care, more equitable access to education, and greater participation in sports. As women have become empowered, they have accomplished these gains without dominating men, making their achievements examples of the "power to" act rather than "power over" others.

The "power to" approach can also apply to social systems such as schools, governments, or even entire societies. American sociologist Talcott Parsons (1960) saw power as the capacity of a social system to achieve collective goals. In the tradition of structural functionalism, Parsons was most interested in the overall operation of societies as social systems. According to his framework, a society is powerful to the extent that it can accomplish its goals. Doing so requires access to resources, among them money and knowledge. Wealthy societies have more resources—and thus are more powerful—than poorer societies (one way that power and inequality are often connected). Powerful societies can maintain a high standard of living for their citizens, ensure self-defense, advance scientific and technological frontiers, and achieve other collective goals. By all these measures, the United States and other wealthy nations are powerful societies, whereas impoverished countries are much less powerful.

SPOTLIGHT on social theory

Functionalist theories of power focus on the capacity of social systems to achieve collective goals. What is an example of a social system that you are a part of, and what collective goals does it attempt to achieve?

Strategies of Empowerment: Educate, Organize, Network

The old saying, "Give a man a fish and you feed him for a day; teach a man to fish and you feed him for a lifetime" expresses the difference between charity and empowerment. A gift provides only temporary relief and fosters a relationship of dependency; a person who is empowered develops an enduring capacity and independence. Whether adopted by an individual, a small group, or a national or an international organization, strategies to increase empowerment generally involve a combination of education, organization, and networking (Dugan 2003).

- *Education* is probably the best-known approach to empowerment. Some teaching philosophies, for example, focus heavily on empowering students rather than simply transmitting facts (Freire 1970). To achieve their goal, people or groups must understand their situation, have a vision of what needs to be done, and obtain the training and skills they need to reach their goal. For some people, a college education can be an important means of learning about their situation and developing the skills necessary for rewarding employment and a more fulfilling life.

- *Organization* involves bringing people together to identify common goals and work to achieve them. Smoothly operating workplaces are well organized, for example, with employees and management cooperating to achieve organizational goals. When communities of disempowered people organize, the neighborhood associations, labor unions, and advocacy groups that result can serve as megaphones

to amplify the concerns of group members and help them to stand up more powerfully to adversaries. The *shebikas* organized through BRAC's Human Rights and Legal Education program, discussed in our chapter opening, show how organization can empower people. As one guide to community organizing notes, "Building a strong, lasting, and staffed organization alters the relations of power. . . . When the organization is strong enough, it will have to be consulted about decisions that affect its members" (Bobo, Kendall, and Max 2001, 12).

- *Networking* involves reaching outside your immediate circle of contacts to find allies. Professional associations in many fields hold conferences and social events to facilitate networking to search for employment or to advance careers. Organizations also network by forming coalitions and other collaborative efforts. In this way, they pool their resources to achieve goals they would be unlikely to accomplish on their own.

Domination: "Power Over"

At all levels of social life, people disagree. For example, a parent grounds a teenager but the teenager resists; a corporation wants to build a toxic waste incinerator near a neighborhood, but the residents object; or one political party proposes legislation that another party opposes. In all these cases, the effort to accomplish something meets opposition and produces conflict. That's why the second part of our definition of power includes the idea of conflict: "the ability to bring about an intended outcome, *even when opposed by others.*" This emphasis is called the "power over" approach, since it focuses on overcoming oppo-

This classic graphic illustrates the idea that through organization weaker parties can join forces to take on a more powerful adversary.

sition or dominating others. In one classic definition from political scientist Robert Dahl (1957), power is seen exclusively in terms of domination: "A has power over B to the extent that he can get B to do something that B would not otherwise do" (p. 202).

Domination can occur at any level of society. Forcing children to be brides, as is done in some cultures, reflects both domination at the individual level (the future of a specific young woman is determined by her extended family) as well as inequalities at the societal level (women in such societies lack power in social life). Often macrolevel inequalities in power trickle down to affect people's daily lives. At the same time, the personal choices people make have a cumulative impact on broader dynamics of social power, a process captured neatly by the feminist slogan "The personal is political."

The most obvious use of power as a means of domination is in political and economic conflicts, as powerful elites attempt to maintain their advantages over others. We examine such situations more closely later in the chapter, when we explore systems of social inequality.

Strategies to Overcome Opposition: Persuade, Reward, Coerce

Imagine that someone you live with—your roommate, partner, or spouse—has a much lower standard of cleanliness than you do. He or she leaves the sink full of dirty dishes and leaves clothes, papers, and half-eaten food lying around. If you want this person to be neater, you have three options. First, you could try persuasion, which would involve convincing the person to clean up out of fairness, because of health concerns, or to eliminate the growing stench that is putting a damper on your social life. If persuasion didn't work, you could try offering a reward: "If you do your share of the cleaning for a month, I'll pay for us to go out to see a movie." Finally, if all else fails, you could try a threat: "If you don't keep up with your share of the cleaning, you can't live here anymore."

Participants in any conflict, whether minor or serious, have these same three basic options: persuade, reward, or coerce others to get them to comply (Kriesberg 1982, 115).

■ To **persuade** is *to get people's compliance by convincing them of the correctness of your position and goals.* An organization dedicated to combating sexually transmitted diseases, for example, might launch a campaign to educate people about the importance of condoms. Over time, as people hear this message repeatedly, some might begin to alter their behavior. The group has power—it is able to achieve

PLS DNT TXT + DRIVE

A Public Service Announcement
brought to you by your school + other drivers

◄ Public service announcements, such as this one discouraging texting while driving, are an example of trying to persuade people to act—or not act—in a certain way.

its goals—to the extent that it can reach and influence people through education. However, this type of power is limited, since it usually cannot overcome stubborn opposition. Also, the use of persuasion is not always forthright or honest. Some actors manipulate, distort, or withhold information to convince others to act in a desired way, such as authoritarian governments that control the media. Citizens in such societies may voluntarily comply with the government's wishes, but the rulers have obtained this compliance by using false, incomplete, or misleading information. Even in open societies, misleading propaganda efforts by governments and powerful corporations can shape the terms of debate about many issues, thereby achieving compliance under false pretenses (Chomsky 1989).

■ A second strategy to overcome opposition is to offer a reward. To **reward** is *to encourage people's compliance by offering a positive incentive.* Rewarding a child with words

PROCLAMATION
$5,000.00
REWARD
FOR EACH of SEVEN ROBBERS of THE TRAIN at WINSTON, MO., JULY 15, 1881, and THE MURDER of CONDUCTER WESTFALL

$ 5,000.00
ADDITIONAL for ARREST or CAPTURE

DEAD OR ALIVE
OF JESSE OR FRANK JAMES
THIS NOTICE TAKES the PLACE of ALL PREVIOUS REWARD NOTICES.
CONTACT SHERIFF, DAVIESS COUNTY, MISSOURI IMMEDIATELY
T. T. CRITTENDEN, GOVERNOR
STATE OF MISSOURI
JULY 26, 1881

◄ Rewarding others is one way to achieve compliance. Why are rewards often used to capture criminals? What rewards—other than cash—can be useful in daily life?

Understanding Forms of Power

of praise, an athlete with a trophy, or a country with economic or military assistance are all ways to encourage or reinforce desirable behavior.

■ To **coerce** is *to force compliance by threatening, intimidating, pressuring, or harming someone.* Drivers generally obey the speed limit (or something close to it) because they know a speeding ticket can be very expensive. Therefore, the threat of possible punishment has a coercive effect on their behavior. In this case, compliance is a result of *systemic* coercion in which social structures—not just individuals—are in place to deliver a threat.

Reward and coercion are sometimes two sides of the same coin. As a student you may work hard in school, even when you do not enjoy it, because you have been taught that your chances for good employment—with all the accompanying rewards—will be improved significantly if you have a college degree. You also know that receiving failing grades is likely to harm your prospects for graduation and employment—an implicit coercion.

In many cases, coercion is much more sinister, involving threats to people's livelihood, freedom, or physical well-being. In some repressive societies, people who fail to comply with authority can lose their jobs, while those who obey are allowed to pursue successful careers. In the most authoritarian societies, those with power use the most sinister forms of coercion: imprisoning, beating, or killing people who refuse to comply. Because these techniques are inefficient, they are typically used as a last resort. However, through the force of their example, they can have a coercive effect on large numbers of citizens. (Nations, too, use such coercion against their enemies.) Ultimately, though, because force is expensive and can create opposition, people in power cannot rely for long on coercion alone. It is more efficient to have people control their own behavior.

Egyptian police use violence to disperse pro-democracy demonstrators in the country's 2011 revolution. Physical force is typically the last resort in obtaining compliance. As a type of coercion, it is expensive, inefficient, and often ineffective in the long run because it generates anger and resentment.

Power operates in all levels of social life. Many everyday interactions involve power. In this soccer match, a referee uses his authority to intervene in a dispute.

Power in Everyday Life

Power is an essential part of social relationships at every level of social life, including your relationships with your family and friends, your professor, your boss, the police, and the government. Many sociologists, including Max Weber and Karl Marx, focused much of their attention on the operation of power at the macro level of society, examining governmental and economic power. We explore these ideas in more detail later in the chapter.

However, power is also involved in social interactions at the micro level. For example, intimate partner violence is a serious social issue, and rates of physical and sexual abuse are especially high among high school and college students (Straus 2004). Women, in particular, suffer the consequences of this abuse. Intimate partner violence produces a sense of powerlessness in the victim, often leading to depression. A survey of undergraduate women found that the more violence they experience in their relationships, the less powerful and the more depressed they feel (Filson et al. 2010). Perpetrators use violence to assert control and gain power over their partners.

In between macro- and micro-level interactions are the meso-level organizations to which we all belong. Studying power can also help us to understand how such organizations operate.

Power in Small Groups and Organizations

Sociologists who study power in small groups and organizations examine how such groups operate and what roles their leaders play. Many of their insights can be applied to friendship circles, families, and clubs as well as to more formal settings such as schools and workplaces.

thinking about power
How do those who have **power** over your actions and decisions maintain their control?

In one classic formulation, John French and Bertram Raven identified six bases of power in small groups and organizations (French and Raven 1959/2001; Raven 1965). Notice how these power bases overlap with the broader strategies for overcoming opposition we discussed earlier:

- *Reward power* is the control one party has over valued resources that can be used to provide positive incentives. By offering children a weekly allowance, parents can gain power over their behavior.

- *Coercive power* is the ability to punish—for example, by withholding valued resources or by inflicting verbal or physical harm. Police officers can usually generate compliance because they can issue citations, arrest people, or even shoot them if necessary.

- *Legitimate power* is exercised by those who invoke a feeling of obligation; one "ought" to obey, perhaps as a result of shared cultural values or out of respect for someone's formal rank or position in the social structure. You are likely to carry out a boss's order to do a routine task at work; you would ignore a similar order about your private home life.

- *Referent power* is based on feelings of identification, affection, and respect for another person, even if that person does not seek influence over others. A popular colleague in a workplace might have referent power because others look up to her and view her as a model.

- *Expert power* arises from the perception that a person has superior knowledge in a particular area. A lawyer has expert power in legal matters in relation to a client. Expert power is about the perception of knowledge, not necessarily actual knowledge. Someone seen as an authority carries expert power whether or not he has actual expertise. Conversely, a real authority on some topic may not have expert power if others do not recognize that expertise.

- *Informational power* is based on a person's use of facts, data, or other evidence to argue rationally or persuade. A project manager has informational power when she convinces her boss to approve a new product. Those with information can increase their influence by sharing it, withholding it, organizing it effectively, or even manipulating or falsifying it.

These categories can overlap—a leader can withhold a reward as a type of coercion—but the distinctions help us to recognize different sources of power. Also, a person's use of one type of power can affect another. For example, when a manager gives an employee a bad evaluation—a use of coercive power—that action is likely to undermine his or her referent power with that person.

Sociologists and social psychologists have done a great deal of research on the dynamics of small groups, including those associated with power (Forsythe 2010). Researchers have shown that when authorities rely on reward or coercive power, their influence weakens if the amount of resources they control is reduced. However, authorities who have earned respect and are seen as legitimate enjoy group members' loyalty regardless of their ability to reward or coerce. Such loyalty can evaporate, however, if the person in authority acts in ways that group members consider unfair, unethical, or disrespectful (Lammers et al. 2008; Tyler 2005; Tyler and Blader 2003).

Compared to powerful people, those who feel relatively powerless are more likely to use coercion, because they think they have no other means of achieving their aims. Some parents and teachers feel relatively powerless when children seem out of control. These adults are more likely to use coercive threats and punishment than are parents and teachers who feel empowered (Bugental and Lewis 1999).

Authorities generally prefer rewards over coercion because they worry about retaliation (Molm 1997). However, group members often tolerate a coercive leader if the group is successful in achieving its goals (Michener and Lawler 1975), or if they trust the leader (Friedland 1976). If a leader lacks referent power, uses coercion, and asks group members to carry out unpleasant tasks, though, group members are more likely to resist his or her authority (Yukl, Kim, and Falbe 1996). People are also more likely to oppose authorities if they perceive their actions as unjust, view fellow group members as comrades, learn to act together as a group, and believe they have group support when speaking out (Gamson, Fireman, and Rytina 1982).

Power Tactics

How do you try to get your way when dealing with your friends or your boss? **Power tactics** are *the specific strategies people use to influence others in everyday life*. These familiar strategies involve power, though we often do not think of them in those terms. (See Table 5.1.) A child who persists in yelling, "I want it! I want it!" in a store is using a power tactic. A worker who ridicules his or her colleague is using a power tactic. Power tactics vary along three key dimensions (Forsythe 2010, 228):

- *Hard and soft.* Hard tactics are forceful, direct, or harsh. People employing them use economic rewards and other tangible outcomes, and even threats. A cash rebate or a threat to repossess your car is a hard tactic. Soft tactics focus on relationships. People employing soft tactics make use of collaboration and friendship to achieve an aim. A friendly reminder that you need to do some task is a soft tactic.

Power in Everyday Life

TABLE 5.1   POWER TACTICS USED TO INFLUENCE OTHERS IN EVERYDAY SITUATIONS

Tactic	Examples
Appeal	Beg for help; plead with someone to play fair
Bully	Yell; push someone around
Collaborate	Invite someone to help; provide assistance as needed
Complain	Protest to a store manager about poor service; grumble to a professor about an assignment
Criticize	Point out the limitations in a plan; find fault with someone's work
Demand	Ask for a refund; insist on speaking to a supervisor
Discuss	Talk over a situation in a group; come up with a plan of action
Disengage	Walk out in the middle of the argument; give someone the cold shoulder
Evade	Change the subject; don't return phone calls
Inform	Point out the advantages of a plan; note the personal benefits someone will receive
Ingratiate	Flatter; compliment
Inspire	Appeal to a person's loyalty; cheer someone on
Join forces	Find allies to help fight an opponent; agree to approach the boss as a group
Joke	Use humor to help others relax; ridicule opponents
Manipulate	Lie; leave out important details in a report
Negotiate	Offer a deal; offer to compromise
Persist	Refuse to take no for an answer; keep trying
Persuade	Convince someone of the wisdom of a position
Promise	Assure someone that you will follow through with a plan
Punish	Fire someone; ground a child for the week
Put down	Insult someone; disparage a person's abilities
Request	Ask for a favor
Reward	Take someone to lunch as thanks; give someone a promotion
Socialize	Ask about the family; make small talk
Threaten	Warn about taking legal action; warn that you will divulge embarrassing information

Source: Adapted from Forsythe (2010).

■ *Rational and nonrational.* Rational tactics appeal to logic and include bargaining and rational persuasion. Many newspaper editorials use rational tactics. Nonrational tactics include emotional appeals, such as when television commercials imply that driving a particular type of car will make you sexy.

■ *Unilateral and bilateral.* Unilateral tactics do not require cooperation to initiate; they include demands, orders, or disengagement. Military leaders employ unilateral tactics when they issue orders. Bilateral tactics involve give-and-take, as in negotiations and discussions. When a homeowner and a prospective buyer negotiate a sale price for a house, they use bilateral tactics.

The way power and inequality operate within broader society can influence the dynamics of small groups. For example, women have higher levels of referent power than men

THROUGH A SOCIOLOGICAL LENS

Foucault's Distinctive View of Power

Did you ever think school was like a prison? If so, French sociologist Michel Foucault (1926–1984) would have agreed with you. In *Discipline and Punish* (1975/1995) Foucault explained how modern prisons emerged in the eighteenth century as a humane way of treating criminals, rather than torturing or killing them. Advocates of prison reform argued they would deter crime by more effectively controlling criminals. As it turns out, prisons didn't deter crime, but they did demonstrate a new form of power and social control that involved detailed time schedules, restricting prisoners' physical movement, and observing and evaluating their behavior. These features of prisons were adapted and applied to other new social institutions, including factories, psychiatric hospitals, and modern schools. (We revisit these developments in Chapter 8, on social control.)

Foucault's study of prisons made use of his unique view of power, which has influenced many scholars. Foucault argued that although power can be oppressive and dominating, it can also have a positive effect. He wrote, "We must cease once and for all to describe the effects of power in negative terms: it 'excludes,' it 'represses,' it 'censors,' it 'abstracts,' it 'masks,' it 'conceals.' In fact power produces; it produces reality . . ." (Foucault 1975/1995, 194).

For Foucault, power "produces reality" because it is made up of systems of knowledge that organize, label, and measure the world in distinct ways. For example, science, religion, and business each have an internal logic, unique assumptions, distinct vocabulary, and central ideas. Because a minister or priest views the world in terms of "grace," a scientist in terms of "empirical evidence," or an executive in terms of "profit," each understands the world differently. Each person's ideas and beliefs influence his or her behavior by encouraging some actions and discouraging others.

As knowledge systems—faith in a God, science, or capitalism— become accepted, they become taken-for-granted assumptions about the world and therefore assume enormous power and influence. Those who question or challenge such dominant systems of knowledge are marginalized, ostracized, and even punished. In the end, such systems of knowledge help to control behavior and are therefore forms of power in themselves.

Foucault coined the term *power/knowledge* to show that how we understand and interpret the world both enlightens and restricts us. That's because systems of knowledge order, rank, and

make visible various aspects of the world, enabling it to be controlled more effectively. When applied to people, such systems of knowledge serve as mechanisms of social control. New ways of thinking—like the idea for creating the modern prison—are developed into real-world social institutions in which certain types of actions are allowed and encouraged and others are prohibited and discouraged, though resistance is always possible.

Although some people benefit from certain forms of knowledge—clergy have considerable legal power in religiously based societies whereas psychiatrists are influential within our own society—they don't necessarily control the use of that knowledge. That is, individuals don't wield power; instead they navigate through a system of knowledge. In fact, Foucault argued that, rather than people using power, power helps form our sense of self; we are the product of power.

Foucault saw power as dispersed throughout society, rather than being centralized in the hands of small groups or individuals. "Power is everywhere," he wrote (Foucault 1978/1980, 93), "not because it embraces everything but because it comes from everywhere." Power relationships play out in countless local "fields," such as the family, prison, the workplace, a doctor's office, a classroom, and a church. As a consequence, power is fragmented into many different forms. This is why much of Foucault's work was organized around particular subjects, such as prison, sexuality, and madness. Each of these fields has its own power dynamics.

Most powerful of all are the systems of knowledge that cause people to change their behavior willingly, by monitoring their own actions to conform to expectations. Susan Bartky (1990) argues that because of such self-surveillance, many women closely regulate their own bodies through constant dieting, "proper" hair removal, and wearing make-up and fashionable clothing. When carried to extremes, the impact of such disciplinary power can produce eating disorders and other unhealthy behaviors— another form of prison.

think about it

1. *Do you agree with Foucault that power/knowledge helps to control people's behavior? Why or why not?*

2. *Can you think of examples to illustrate Foucault's idea that we regulate ourselves by conforming to social expectations?*

do; people typically evaluate women more favorably than men and like them more (Carli 1999). But women who use a direct leadership style are judged more harshly than men, and they have to outperform men to be seen as equally competent. Men have more expert power, and because people generally believe men are more competent than women, men can draw upon

this perception as a source of influence. Gender differences are affected by a person's position within the social structure, however; people who are relatively powerful—women or men— report using more direct strategies to influence others than do less powerful individuals. (For a very different take on power, consider the Through a Sociological Lens box.)

The Economic, Political, and Cultural Uses of Power

Think of the people and institutions that have power in our society. What do they do with it? Power is used in many ways, but three of the most important purposes to which it is applied are economic, political, and cultural.

Economic Power: Allocating Resources

Within any group or society, power determines who will receive important resources and how those resources will be used. Within a family, the person who controls spending wields considerable power over other family members, deciding in many cases what food or clothes will be bought, how leisure time will be spent, and where the family will live. Business executives have the power to open new stores, offices, or factories in one place and close them in others. They have the power to hire and lay off workers and to determine their salaries, decisions that can have a profound impact on employees' lives and communities.

Governments at all levels have the power to allocate resources, generating revenue by collecting taxes and fees and then distributing that money through public projects, social programs, military spending, and other policies. Within particular agencies or departments, officials wield power by exercising control over budgets and supplies.

Political Power: Making Rules and Decisions

Power can also be used for political purposes, enabling some people to set the conditions under which others are expected to live. Parents typically set the rules for how a household will function and how children should behave. In a workplace or school, the managers or administrators establish how the group will operate. Setting the rules for how the entire society will operate is the role of government. Politicians and government officials pass laws and establish regulations that organize many aspects of our daily lives. Those with power set the rules, and those without power are expected to follow them.

Cultural Power: Defining Reality

To prepare others to comply with their agenda, those with power define social reality in a particular way and encourage others to agree with their interpretation. Parents, for example, steer their children toward or away from certain types of books, entertainment, or religious instruction. By doing so, they are trying to shape how their children understand and define social reality by influencing their children's values and worldviews. If children internalize their parents' beliefs and values, they are unlikely to challenge or violate the rules set down by parents.

A similar process operates in society at large, as the media and schools shape our worldview. By selecting certain news stories and sources, the news media teach us to view certain topics and people as important and worthy of consideration (local crime stories or celebrities), while marginalizing or ignoring others who are not given routine coverage (advocates for the poor) (Croteau and Hoynes 1994b). Influencing the stories people read, the ideas they consider, and the perspectives to which they are regularly exposed is one way of exercising power in a society (Herman and Chomsky 1988/2002).

Schools exert power by including certain topics and excluding others. Until the middle of the twentieth century, history courses at all levels—elementary school to college—taught American history almost exclusively from the perspective of white, wealthy, straight men. Indeed, U.S. history was virtually equated with this group, since they were the ones who held positions of power in the government, military, and economy. Women of all classes, people of color, the working class, gays

Schools of all sorts shape how children understand the world. Here, boys study in an Islamic religious school or *madrassa*. How did your education help shape your worldview?

and lesbians—the vast majority of the population—were nearly invisible. As these groups have gained power in society, school curriculums have changed, and they now provide a more diverse view of history.

Italian Marxist activist-scholar Antonio Gramsci (1891–1937) argued that the class in power maintains its dominance not simply through the use of force, which is the job of the state's police and military forces, but also through the manipulation of ideas, which it accomplishes primarily through its control of cultural institutions such as the mass media, research and policy institutes ("think-tanks"), and universities. Gramsci (1929–1935/1971) applied the word *hegemony* to this situation. **Hegemony** *exists when those in power have successfully spread their ideas—and marginalized alternative viewpoints—so that their perspectives and interests are accepted widely as being universal and true.* By manipulating ideas, those in power can often manufacture the consent of others. For example, political leaders typically demonize foreign enemies in rallying citizen support for a war. Gramsci argued that hegemony is a tenuous condition that must be actively maintained in the face of constant challenges.

As we see later in this chapter, systems of social inequality are also reinforced by a justifying ideology that oppressed people themselves sometimes internalize. Cultural norms, the legal system, schools, the media, and other social institutions may all play a role in creating and maintaining this ideology.

Economic, political, and cultural powers are based in real-world social institutions, including businesses, government, and religions. At different points in history, each of these has been more influential than the other two. In the West, the power of religious institutions was most important in shaping daily life in the medieval period. By the eighteenth and nineteenth centuries, the rise of the secular nation-state signaled the growing influence of military and political power. In recent decades, economic power, in the form of transnational corporations, has become the most influential, in many cases eclipsing the influence of government (Mann 1986; Poggi 2001).

Power and Social Relationships

Power at all levels of society is rooted in social relationships, and it is limited by the relationships on which it is based. In this section we explore various aspects of these social re-

lationships, including the role of compliance in relationships of power and the importance of disobedience as a strategy for resisting power.

Types of Authority: Traditional, Rational-Legal, and Charismatic

Max Weber (1915/1946b) made an important distinction between legitimate and illegitimate power. **Legitimate power** is *voluntarily accepted by those who are affected.* Weber's idea of legitimate power is sometimes translated as "authority." A religious congregation, for example, might recognize and accept its spiritual leader's right to issue instructions and therefore voluntarily follow his or her wishes. **Illegitimate power** *relies on force or coercion to generate obedience.* A kidnapper or military dictator may be able to cause others to obey orders, but they do not obey willingly. Instead, they comply only because of the threat of violence if they disobey.

Weber (1915/1946b) further specified three types of legitimate power, or authority. The first, **traditional authority,** *has legitimacy because of compliance with well-established cultural practices.* These practices can vary widely, but from Europe's medieval nobility to modern chieftains in countless tribal societies around the globe, traditional leaders are widely perceived as legitimate because they derive their power from longstanding cultural customs that are usually not questioned. The child of a king becomes the next ruler for life because that is the way royalty works; people believe in the tradition. Often religious beliefs help to justify and support traditional authority.

By contrast, **rational-legal authority** *has legitimacy because it is based on established laws, rules, and procedures.* A president or prime minister is elected for a set term through an established process. A university president is hired after the school conducts a formal search and a series of interviews. These individuals gain legitimacy because they were selected through an agreed-upon procedure.

In the classic British movie *Monty Python and the Holy Grail*, an amusing scene sums up the difference between traditional and rational-legal authority. In the scene, Britain's legendary King Arthur encounters some peasants who challenge his legitimacy. The king appeals to traditional authority whereas the peasants insist on a rational-legal process for choosing a leader.

ARTHUR: I am your king!

PEASANT WOMAN: Well, I didn't vote for you.

ARTHUR: You don't vote for kings.

---

thinking about power

How were you socialized to view those who hold **power** in government?

Those who wield corporate **power**?

PEASANT WOMAN: Well, how did you become king then?

ARTHUR: The Lady of the Lake . . . held aloft [the sword] Excalibur from the bosom of the water signifying by Divine Providence that I, Arthur, was to carry Excalibur. That is why I am your king!

PEASANT MAN: Listen—strange women lying in ponds distributing swords is no basis for a system of government. Supreme executive power derives from a mandate from the masses, not from some farcical aquatic ceremony.

ARTHUR: Be quiet!

As these peasants recognize, a rational-legal process requires some transparency and logical justification, whereas tradition is, in effect, self-justifying. Weber argued that with the rise of science, industrialization, and democratic processes, rational-legal forms of authority rapidly replaced traditional ones. The contemporary spread of democratic forms of government around the world continues this trend.

Weber also described a third form of legitimate power. **Charismatic authority** is *power whose legitimacy is derived from the extraordinary personal characteristics of an individual leader, which inspire loyalty and devotion.* Charismatic leadership is usually not transferable. Therefore, this form of authority is typically short lived and episodic. Charismatic leaders can inspire groups of people to act, even though such leaders may possess no formal institutional power. Examples of charismatic leaders include compelling politicians, a motivating team coach or captain, a dynamic celebrity activist, or an inspirational spiritual leader.

The Role of Compliance

Weber based his distinctions between legitimate and illegitimate power on the perceptions of the people obeying the orders, but he did not address *how* those perceptions are created

and, therefore, how different types of leaders sustain their power by maintaining their followers' compliance. To take an extreme example, long-term hostages sometimes identify with their captors and voluntarily follow their wishes, an effect called the *Stockholm Syndrome.* This phenomenon, however, does not transform the abductor's power from illegitimate to legitimate. Instead, it shows compliance is more complicated than it may at first appear.

Power is limited by the social relationships on which it is based. The president of the United States, for example, is powerful only as long as others agree to carry out his commands. If the president orders a military attack or initiates a relief effort, many other people must carry out the commands for these goals to be accomplished. Authoritarian regimes can collapse when a large enough number of citizens refuse to obey their leaders and demonstrate for change—a situation that has occurred many times in history.

On a more mundane level, those with power in everyday life also depend on compliance to maintain their position. Students must agree to complete the paper assigned by their teacher, workers usually comply with the boss's rules, and children consent to their parent's request to finish their chores. In other words, people are not passive objects of the demands of those in power; they can react in a variety of ways, from complying voluntarily to resisting and thereby undermining authority.

The degree of compliance in a social situation is often not apparent at first glance. It takes a sociological understanding of power to see that simmering conflict can lurk just beneath the apparently calm, orderly surface of societies. When compliance is withdrawn, conflict may seem to erupt suddenly and dramatically. For example, in 2011 a series of revolutions and uprisings swept northern Africa and the Middle East in what became known as the Arab Spring. Protests, riots, strikes, and other disruptions can start small and spread rapidly as people decide that they will no longer comply. This type of rebellion is itself another form of power: the power of disobedience.

The three types of authority outlined by Weber can be found in contemporary life. The Pope relies on traditional authority to gain the allegiance of the world's Catholics. A police officer relies on rational-legal authority to carry out her duties. Although she no longer holds public office, Sarah Palin has had a significant impact on U.S. politics through her charismatic authority. What other examples of each type of authority can you think of?

SOCIOLOGY Matters

Promoting the Power of Nonviolence

One of the core sociological insights about power is that it depends on compliance. Consequently, those with little apparent power can use noncompliance, or disobedience, to great effect in bringing about social change. Since this insight comes from sociology, it is no surprise that three of the people most closely associated with the power of disobedience studied sociology in college.

Martin Luther King, Jr. (1929–1968) was a sociology major as an undergraduate. His later activism showed his understanding of how power operates in social relationships and how those who appear powerless can organize to effect change. King's well-known role as a charismatic leader in the civil rights movement began during the bus boycott in Montgomery, Alabama, in 1955–1956, a campaign that relied on disobedience. By refusing to ride the city's buses for over a year and setting up an alternative system of transportation, thousands of African Americans helped end segregation on public transportation. King went on to aid other rights campaigns that relied heavily on *civil disobedience:* nonviolent direct action that violates unjust laws. Using this strategy, activists successfully challenged segregation at lunch counters, department stores, public swimming pools, and many other facilities, and their efforts helped achieve access to voting rights that had previously been denied to African Americans throughout the South.

Although not as well known as Dr. King, Saul Alinsky (1909–1972), who studied sociology as a graduate student, was also highly influential. Among activists he is recognized as the creator of what is often called "Alinsky-style" community organizing. Alinsky transformed his sociological understanding of power into practical applications on behalf of low-income citizens. In Alinsky-style organizing, trained organizers identify and coordinate the efforts of existing neighborhood leaders, who in turn mobilize fellow residents to work on issues they identify as priorities, such as better housing, safer neighborhoods, and stronger schools. In addition to emphasizing the importance of creating strong organizations, Alinsky advocated the use of creative confrontational tactics that rely on disobedience to apply pressure on those in power. He emphasized the importance of operating outside of the experience of your opponent: for example, he organized fun public demonstrations, street theater, and other actions in which community residents could participate, rather than closed-door meetings that those in authority could domi-

nate. In 2008, Alinsky-style community organizing received some unusual popular attention when a one-time community organizer named Barack Obama was elected president.

King and Alinksy focused on developing tactics for civil disobedience in the United States, whereas Gene Sharp (b. 1928) studies and writes about the power of nonviolent social action to bring about change in the face of dictatorship, war, and oppression around the world. Sharp's academic training includes a master's degree in sociology. His classic three-volume work, *The Politics of Nonviolent Action,* sketches out a theory of power based on sociological principles and describes the strategic uses of disobedience. Volume Two chronicles hundreds of nonviolent protest actions, including many forms of communication (petitions, marches, teach-ins), noncooperation (boycotts and strikes), and nonviolent interventions (sit-ins, land seizures, and disclosure of secret information). One little-known action: in 1942, when the German army occupying Poland posted "For Germans Only" signs at cafes and hotels in Warsaw, Polish youth stole the signs and defiantly placed them on the lampposts and trees where Germans had hanged Polish patriots. Sharp's work, now outlined in *From Dictatorship to Democracy* (1993/2010), has been translated into more than thirty languages and made available for free download on the Internet.

Sharp has irritated authoritarian regimes and influenced activists around the globe. As part of an effort to counter calls for more liberal reform and democracy, the Iranian Information Ministry in 2008 began airing a television propaganda message that condemned Sharp as a "theoretician of civil disobedience and velvet revolutions." That was a reference to the fact that many democracy movements in Eastern Europe during the 1980s and 1990s used ideas and tactics found in Sharp's work. The young people who led the Egyptian revolution in 2011 were also influenced by his work, leading the *New York Times* to comment, "For the world's despots, [Sharp's] ideas can be fatal" (Stohlberg 2011).

think about it

1. *How does the concept of power relate to the work of the three people featured in this box?*

2. *Can you think of other situations in which disobedience can be a source of power? If disobedience is so powerful, why isn't it used more often?*

The Power of Disobedience

Since power operates within social relationships, one of the great ironies of social life is that those who think they are powerless often have a great deal of power. History is filled with examples of ordinary people who united and toppled powerful opponents. (The Sociology Matters box discusses

several key figures associated with the strategic application of disobedience.)

Workers have united to gain concessions from employers, and women have united to achieve changes in the law and in male-dominated institutions. The nonviolent strategies of the U.S. civil rights movement during the 1950s and 1960s inspired many social movements to fight for the rights of other oppressed groups. The people behind all these movements started out with little or no apparent power to effect change. In the end, however, their collective efforts generated enough power to overcome their oppressors.

Everyone has some power. At a minimum, you always have power over your own actions. James Scott (1987) found that peasants in a Malaysian community could exert some influence over public policies by using "weapons of the weak," including gossip about those in authority, foot-dragging, noncompliance, pilfering, and sabotage. None of these were organized or formal protests, but they enabled relatively powerless peasants to resist domination.

Though it may appear that college students are another group with little power within the institutions they attend, successful student activism has led to changes in college policies and regulations and created new academic programs. During the 1980s, for example, student activism caused many institutions to withdraw their investments in apartheid South Africa. Later, student efforts on behalf of living-wage and anti-sweatshop campaigns led to policy changes regarding pay for campus staff and the way in which schools license and acquire athletic wear. In recent years, students have protested tuition hikes and cuts in funding for education. The success of these efforts demonstrates that students have more power than they often realize.

The success of efforts on behalf of oppressed groups, as well as student activism, demonstrates two simple truths about power. First, when people work together, they increase their own power as individuals to effect change. Second, disobedience is a powerful weapon for those who struggle to effect change. Since power is a social relationship, people ultimately have the power to refuse to comply. They rarely use this power, often out of fear of coercion or force. But when people unite in an act of civil disobedience, they can instigate enormous change. This insight has been a powerful tool for many social movements, which we explore in Chapter 17. Those in power typically resist change promoted by oppressed groups because it threatens the privileges they hold, a topic we turn to now.

In recent years, a variety of "Tea Party" efforts have protested healthcare reform and what they see as high taxes and excessive government spending. What issues related to power are likely to produce national protests in the coming years?

Power and Privilege

As we cautioned in Chapter 1, viewing the world from a sociological perspective can sometimes make people uncomfortable. Nowhere is that more true than in dealing with the issues of power and privilege, topics that cut across race, class, gender, and other social differences (Johnson 2001). Our interests and perspectives—our existing power relations—affect how we think about power (Lukes 2005). When we learn about the unequal power various groups possess, we realize that, compared to many other people in the world, we enjoy a considerable amount of power and privilege. **Privilege** is *a special advantage or benefit that not everyone enjoys.* The fact that most people go about their daily lives unaware of the privileges they enjoy is, in itself, an indicator of that power.

For example, heterosexuals need not concern themselves with their sexual orientation, since our society's norms, laws, and institutional practices have long been organized to accommodate them. Straight people can get married, obtain employment benefits for their spouses, adopt children, talk openly about their relationships without fear of negative consequences—they can go about their daily lives without thinking about being heterosexual. These are privileges that gays and lesbians often do not have. At the same time, a gay man might be acutely aware of discrimination based on sexual orientation while being unaware of his position of privilege as a white, upper-middle-class male. It is easier to recognize disadvantage than privilege.

The point of recognizing privilege is not to make people feel guilty. Rather, doing so allows us to understand society more accurately by removing the blinders that block our ability to see how power operates. In one way or another, we are all involved in power relations. In our society "race," "gender," "class," and "sexuality" tend to conjure up images of Blacks and Latinos, women, working class and poor people, and lesbians and gays. But studying these topics is not just about studying those with less power. Instead, we study subjects such as gender and sexual orientation to determine how *everyone* in a society is connected through relations of power. In addition, understanding privilege can help us to identify the resources we have available to empower ourselves, assist others, and perhaps reduce inequality.

To understand dynamics of power and privilege, it is often useful to consider the situation of those with less power. Dorothy Smith (1987, 1990) developed **standpoint theory,** which *questions taken-for-granted assumptions about society by looking at it from multiple viewpoints, especially from the perspective of people in subordinate positions.* A "standpoint" is the place from which a person views the world. A person's standpoint is structured by his or her social location, which includes race, class, gender, and sexual orientation.

People with different standpoints see and understand the world differently. For example, when Hurricane Katrina and the subsequent flooding from a faulty levy destroyed large sections of New Orleans and the Gulf Coast in 2005, the federal government's inadequate emergency response efforts left the poor and mostly black residents of this city abandoned (Squires and Hartman 2006). Two-thirds of Blacks believed the government response would have been faster if most of the victims had been white. More than three-quarters of Whites, though, disagreed (Pew Research Center 2005). To varying degrees, we can find similar differences in the perspectives of different groups (men and women, members of different classes) on a variety of issues.

In societies with deep inequalities, groups have differing perspectives. Each of these perspectives is necessarily partial. As a result, considering multiple standpoints, especially of those who have less power, is crucial to gaining a more complete understanding of social life.

Power and Inequality

As we have seen, different groups have varying degrees of power within a society, a situation that inevitably produces **inequality,** *the unequal distribution of resources among groups of people.* All societies have some form of inequality, but its nature and extent vary significantly, because patterns of unequal distribution are not natural, inevitable, or the product of chance. Instead, inequality is socially constructed; it varies according to the culture and social structure of a society.

Social inequality is multidimensional: in other words, different forms of inequality coexist within a society. Max Weber (1915/1946b) argued that society is stratified in terms of class, status, and political power.

Class: Economic Conditions

Everyone has dreamed of winning the lottery at some point because we all know that obtaining a large amount of money can transform a person's life. With it you can buy a beautiful home, a fancy car, premium health care, travel, and other luxury items. You might also use your winnings to buy leisure time, quitting your job and hiring others to cook your meals, clean your home, handle your finances, and so on. Some people have, in effect, already won the lottery simply by being born into wealth. Clearly, one major type of inequality in society is the uneven distribution of money and other economic resources.

A **class** is *a group of people who share a roughly similar economic position and lifestyle.* Karl Marx's analysis of the importance of class was especially influential. As we discussed in Chapter 1, Marx focused on economic inequality and considered how the different classes in capitalist societies relate to each other as they participate in the process of economic production. Marx highlighted the world of work and analyzed classes as groups of people who share a common relationship to the means of production.

In many ways, Max Weber—whose ideas are also discussed in Chapter 1—agreed with Marx that economics is a key to understanding inequality. However, whereas Marx examined the concept of class in terms of work, Weber looked at class in terms of **life chances,** *the opportunities offered by a person's economic position.* For Weber, a class is a group of people who have a similar capacity to earn money, and who consequently share a similar lifestyle. We consider class-based systems of inequality later in this chapter. In Chapter 9, we explore the importance of class in more detail and examine further the differences between Marx's and Weber's approach to this topic. For now, it is enough to know that class is one major type of inequality.

SPOTLIGHT on social theory

Marx and Weber both formulated **conflict theories** that address power and economic inequality. Whereas Marx emphasized class differences among workers, Weber focused on lifestyle differences among consumers. Which do you think is more important in understanding inequality today? Are these approaches compatible?

Housing is one of the clearest examples of economic inequality in the United States. Neighborhoods tend to be segregated based on income levels. As children grow up, they tend to accept the economic standards of their neighborhood as the norm.

CORE CONCEPTS CHALLENGE

What did your neighborhood look like when you were growing up? What would pictures of your street suggest about the class composition of your neighborhood and the relative power of the members of your community?

Status: Prestige

Although Weber and Marx agreed on the importance of class, Weber differed from Marx by arguing that status and political power—two noneconomic factors—were also key to understanding inequality. To Weber, both status and political power could be sources of power independent of a person's class.

Adherents of traditional Marxist thought treated class as the single most important source of inequality, supported by other types of inequality such as those based on race and gender. Weber, though, argued that a person's status—based on his or her social characteristics, such as race, ethnicity, or gender—could have an impact independent of class and therefore should be considered as a distinct form of inequality, not merely a secondary feature of economic inequality.

As we noted in Chapter 4, *status* is a person's position in a social system; it is also the prestige attributed to that individual. Depending on the context, then, status can have two meanings—the position itself or the prestige associated with it. People in their fourth year of high school have the status of a senior, a social position. In addition, seniors enjoy the prestige afforded that social position. A person has a given status because he or she belongs to a community of people who have the same lifestyle, ethnicity, race, ancestry, gender, sexual orientation, education, or occupation. Membership in a status group is usually not formal. Instead, members define some shared feature as important or valuable. Status is, in effect, self-perpetuating. Status groups develop formal and informal rules that designate who belongs. Those who belong may socialize with one another, live in the same neighborhoods, join the same organizations, send their children to the same schools, and marry others within the group.

The members of a status group can sometimes use their membership to gain power over nonmembers. **Social closure** is *the process whereby a status group maximizes its own advantages by restricting access to rewards only to members of the group.* This process can involve subtle or blatant **discrimination,** *treating others unequally based on their background or other personal characteristics.* The white populations in the southern states of the United States before the civil rights era and in South Africa before the 1990s both engaged in social closure to exclude other racial groups from access to voting, education, and other rights and opportunities.

In our society, status and class are often linked; people who belong to higher classes disproportionately come from groups with higher status. However, sometimes people of relatively modest means—respected religious leaders, influential politicians, or admired artists—gain access to high-status communities, even though they have relatively modest incomes. Conversely, people with considerable economic resources sometimes face discrimination and other hurdles because of their status. Middle-class African Americans can face both subtle and blatant harassment and discrimination because of their race (Cose 1995; Feagin and Sikes 1994). This situation

has improved significantly in recent years, but in many racially diverse communities, high-status organizations and social circles still tend to be all, or nearly all, white.

Ethnicity and religion, too, have long divided status groups in the United States. At one time, people of Irish ancestry, Jews, and Catholics faced discrimination and were excluded, by rule or by custom, from some neighborhoods, jobs, social clubs, civic associations, and schools. In the nineteenth century, for example, employment ads sometimes specified, "No Irish need apply." For the most part, these groups no longer face such discrimination, but Latinos, Muslims, and other ethnic and religious groups continue to experience discrimination today. Gender and sexual orientation, too, continue to present powerful barriers.

Political Power: Strength Through Organization

In addition to class and status, Weber argued that society is stratified in terms of political power. Weber saw that by creating organizations to advance particular goals, people working together could influence society. He referred to these organizations as "parties," meaning a broad range of political groups, including what we would today call social movements, advocacy groups, and citizens' organizations. As we saw earlier, organizing such groups is one form of empowerment.

Weber saw political power as potentially independent of class and status. For example, lesbian and gay people in the United States who faced status-based discrimination due to their sexual orientation have been able to organize themselves into an influential political force over the past few decades. Although not particularly rich and subject to intense social discrimination, this group has been able to develop political power to improve policies and laws affecting its members' lives. Political organization, then, can serve as a source of power independent of class or status and, as we have seen, can accomplish social change through collective action. But like class and status, political power is distributed unequally in society.

The Intersections of Race, Class, and Gender

As we have seen, Weber argued that social inequality involves class, status, and political power. Similarly, in his work analyzing the black community, sociologist W.E.B. Du Bois, writing early in the twentieth century, highlighted issues of race, class, and nationality. These early works suggested that we should consider many aspects of social life when examining power and inequality.

In recent years, some feminist scholars, including Patricia Hill Collins (2000), have built on this tradition through **intersectionality theory,** which *highlights the connections and interactions between various forms of inequality, especially race, class,*

---

thinking about power

What status groups do you belong to? Do the members of those groups use **power**
to maximize their advantages over others?

 A woman points approvingly to a racist sign in this photograph from the early 1920s. Although this woman faced the disadvantages of gender inequality, her status as a white person afforded privileges not available to Japanese Americans of either gender.

CORE CONCEPTS CHALLENGE

How does this photograph illustrate the fact that inequality is multidimensional? How does a person's **culture** *teach the kind of attitudes shown in this photo?*

and gender. These theorists recognize the different dimensions of inequality and highlight the interactions that take place between these dimensions. For example, white people as a group enjoy privileges in our society because of their race, but white families trapped in poverty face hurdles because of their class. Meanwhile, within the context of poor white families, men are likely to enjoy privileges not afforded to women.

Focusing on the interaction between power and inequality can help us to gain a deeper understanding of social life in several ways:

- It gives us a more accurate reflection of how we experience the social world. Any person's identity is multifaceted, including his or her race, class, gender, ethnicity, sexual orientation, and nationality. Taking into account all these aspects of identity gives us a better understanding of our own social location.

- Once we recognize that these factors intersect, we can acknowledge that the relative importance of different types of inequality varies depending on the social context and circumstances. Although a Latino man living in poverty may enjoy privileges within his family because of traditional gender inequality, he also faces many disadvantages because he occupies a low position on the class hierarchy and belongs to an ethnic minority.

- We can also see that intersections involve more than simply "adding up" different identities. One aspect of identity can change another. Being wealthy or poor, for example, can change what it means to be male or female.

- When we recognize that race, class, and gender interact, we are better able to avoid overgeneralizing about any one group of people. Patricia Hill Collins (2000, 5–6) notes, "Theories advanced as being universally applicable to women as a group upon closer examination appear greatly limited by the white, middle-class and Western origins of their proponents." For example, the idea that the women's movement of the 1960s and 1970s opened the way for women's participation in the paid workforce needs to be qualified, because significant percentages of poor and working-class women in the United States—especially

women of color—were already part of the workforce. By viewing women's increased participation in the paid labor force solely through the lens of gender, we miss the important impact of class and race.

Collins (2000) coined the phrase **matrix of domination** to indicate *the interlocking systems of oppression associated with race, class, and gender.* The metaphor of a matrix suggests more than one dimension and allows for the idea that people can be privileged in some ways and oppressed in others. When one group believes it is superior to another, has the right to dominate the other, and is able to do so, oppression results. Her framework highlights the active domination of weaker groups by those with more power at the individual, group, and institutional levels. Reflecting the core concept of structure, as well as the capacity people have for action, Collins recognizes that these various levels of oppression are also sites for resistance as people use their collective power to achieve autonomy and promote equality.

Collins's matrix approach shows that there are few pure oppressors or victims in society. Most people are privileged on some dimension of inequality and disadvantaged on some other. This is true across different types of stratification systems, which we consider next.

Structured Inequality: Stratification Systems

Societies formalize and institutionalize inequality—including the unequal distribution of power—by developing social structures that perpetuate stratification. **Stratification systems** are made up of *social structures and cultural norms that create and maintain inequality by ranking people into a hierarchy of groups that receive unequal resources.* Over the centuries, various societies have created different types of stratification systems. All stratification systems, however, share three key elements:

1. The unequal distribution of valued *resources*
2. Distinct *groups* that make up society's strata (layers)
3. An *ideology* that explains and justifies inequality

The particular form these elements take in any given society determines the dominant type of stratification system and the distribution of power within the society. We will take a closer look at the elements shared by all stratification systems before we consider some examples.

Unequal Resources

The first element of all stratification systems is the unequal distribution of valued resources. These may include (Grusky 2001, 4):

- *Economic* resources, including money, property, and land
- *Human* resources, such as education, training, and specialized skills
- *Cultural* resources that aid in achieving success, such as knowledge and skills learned through socialization
- *Social* resources, including access to important networks of people
- *Honorific* resources, involving the acquisition of prestige and status
- *Civil* resources, including legal rights involving property, contracts, voting, and speech
- *Political* resources, involving authority in the home, workplace, political arena, or social life

In any stratification system, some resources are distributed more evenly than others. For example, in the United States all citizens have similar legal rights based on the principle of equality under the law, but there are stark differences between rich and poor in terms of economic and human resources. In addition, if a resource is available more readily to one group than to another, that discrepancy can have an impact on another resource. Because the affluent can afford better legal counsel than the poor, the apparent equality of the legal system can be compromised.

Stratified Groups

The second element of all stratification systems is the groups that make up the various strata in society. Stratification based on class, race, and gender is especially widespread and significant, which is why sociologists pay especially close attention to them. However, stratification can also be based on ethnicity, age, religious affiliation, sexual orientation, and disability, among other factors.

The groups within systems of stratification can be based on either an ascribed or an achieved status. As noted in Chapter 4, an *ascribed status* is a position an individual has been assigned in life, regardless of his or her wishes or abilities. Race and sex are examples of ascribed statuses. Stratification systems based primarily on ascribed statuses are said to be closed: they are rigid and impermeable, making it virtually impossible for an individual to move from one stratum to another.

An *achieved status* is a position an individual attains voluntarily, to a considerable degree, as the result of his or her own effort and abilities. College graduates, for example, attain their status due largely to their own efforts. Stratification systems based primarily on achieved statuses are said to be open: it is possible for an individual within such a system to achieve **social mobility,** *movement from one stratum of a stratification system to another.* In systems of class stratification, for example, a person's class status can change as a result of structural changes in the economy, individual ability, education, effort, luck, or other factors. However, a person's achieved statuses are still influenced to varying degrees by social factors beyond his or her control. For example, the family into which you are born can significantly influence your class status.

The various social categories associated with inequality—such as races, ethnicities, classes, and genders—are not natural, inevitable, or biologically based. Instead, the meaning and significance of each category is determined by its cultural context and the social structure—in other words, these categories are socially constructed. They change over time, and they are continually contested, revised, and reinvented. We learn the meaning and significance of these categories for our time and our culture through the socialization process, which we discuss in Chapter 6.

Ideologies That Justify Inequality

The third element of all stratification systems is a related *ideology,* a system of beliefs that helps define and explain the world and justifies the existence of inequality. Those in power produce and promote these ideas to maintain the stratification system, but others sometimes internalize them, as well. In fact, the most efficient way to maintain a system of inequality is to convince most people that the system is fair, inevitable, or both. If the groups within a society believe in the ideology that justifies a stratification system, or if they are cynical about any possibility of changing the system, they are unlikely to challenge it. Consequently, those who struggle to reduce inequality must often debate the ideology that supports it. For example, women's rights advocates have long had to debunk myths about women's biological inferiority.

The three key elements that all stratification systems have in common—unequal resources, distinct groups, and a justifying ideology—vary within different stratification systems. We now take a brief look at several examples of such systems.

Caste Systems: India, Feudal Estates, and Racial Segregation

A **caste system** features *stratification based on various ascribed characteristics determined at birth.* The social stratum—or caste—into which people are born largely determines their life chances, typically affecting their access to education, their work options, where they can live, and whom they can marry. Many agrarian societies have some type of closed caste system, but the best known, by far, is the one found in India, which was outlawed in 1952 but which continues to be practiced informally.

INDIA'S CASTE SYSTEM India's stratification system is traditionally based on the unequal distribution of social honor or respect associated with four major castes, known as *varnas:*

- *Brahmins,* the highest caste, are priests, scholars, and teachers.
- *Kshatriyas,* the second caste, are kings, warriors, and political leaders.
- *Vaisyas,* the third caste, constitute a broad group that includes landowners, merchants, and skilled craftspeople.
- *Sudras,* the fourth caste, includes peasants, servants, and laborers.

Rounding out this complex system are hundreds of sub-caste groups, or *jatis,* typically organized around a single occupation, such as carpenters or barbers and often situated in a particular village or region.

At the lowest stratum of Indian society is a group that exists outside of the *varna* system. Physical contact with members of this lowest grouping is thought to pollute anyone of higher status, so they are often referred to as "untouchables," but they call themselves *Dalits* ("downtrodden"). *Dalits* are often uneducated and typically perform the lowest and least desirable types of labor, such as cleaning public toilets. In addition, *Dalits* are social outcasts who are banned from worshiping with members of the four *varnas.* Consequently, *Dalits* have little power in society.

Membership in a particular caste is determined at birth and cannot be changed. The justifying ideology, derived from both tradition and Hindu religious doctrine, emphasizes the maintenance of caste purity by restricting social contact to members of one's own caste. People are expected to marry within their own caste.

Throughout India's history, the caste system helped maintain social order by clearly defining the rights and responsibilities of those who belonged to various castes. However, resistance and opposition to this system date back thousands of years. After India gained independence from British rule in the mid-twentieth century, it adopted a constitution that eventually outlawed discrimination based on caste. Today the caste system plays only a limited role in India's modern urban life. However, in the country's more traditional rural areas and small towns, the influence of castes remains significant.

FEUDAL ESTATE SYSTEMS During the Middle Ages, European societies were stratified into a castelike system that regulated economic, political, and social life based primarily on the unequal distribution of land. Feudalism, as this system is now known, varied but commonly featured three *estates* that comprised a society's major strata:

- *The nobility.* The nobility, the dominant estate, owned the vast tracts of land upon which the agricultural economy—and their power—was based. Wealthy and powerful nobles lived lives of relative luxury, reaping the benefits of others' labor. An elaborate system of honorific titles, such as *king, queen, duke, earl,* and *baron,* indicated the relative rank

Because of the family into which she was born, this Indian woman is a *Dalit,* or "untouchable." The man in the portrait behind her is Bhimrao Ramiji Amdedkar, a scholar and activist who founded the movement for civil rights for Untouchables, which challenges the ideology underlying this caste system.

and power of each individual within this estate. A person's rank was inherited, and marriage was typically restricted to other members of the nobility. Typically, only the eldest son of a noble could inherit land, so other male children served as military officers, judges, government administrators, or high-ranking members of the Church.

- *The Christian clergy.* As the second estate, the clergy largely served the nobles but had some independence due to their claim of religious authority. They were generally well educated and were themselves divided into an elaborate hierarchy made up of the pope, cardinals, bishops, priests, and other positions. An important role of the clergy was to articulate and enforce the ideology that justified the feudal system. The Church taught that inequality was the will of God and that the poor would receive their reward in heaven rather than on earth. To question inequality, therefore, was to question God's will.
- *Commoners.* The commoners made up the bulk of the population. Typically illiterate, they did not own land but instead lived on and worked the land owned by the nobles. The commoners' labor enriched the nobles but left them living in poor and difficult conditions.

Commoners repeatedly challenged the harsh conditions of the estate system by staging peasant uprisings. Eventually, the power of nobles was curbed with the advent of more democratic political systems and less-rigid class-based economic systems in the eighteenth and nineteenth centuries, as we saw in Chapter 1.

RACIAL SEGREGATION IN THE UNITED STATES The system of racial segregation in the United States, which evolved between the Civil War and the 1960s, can be considered a caste-based stratification system. (It influenced South Africa's apartheid, another caste-based stratification system, beginning in 1948.) The division between Blacks

Though it is primarily associated with the southern states, where it was most comprehensive and brutally enforced, racial segregation existed throughout the United States. Blacks faced the most formal and broadest oppression, dating back to a race-based system of slavery. However, other races, ethnicities, and nationalities—most notably Mexican and Chinese Americans—also faced segregation. Whites excluded minorities from many types of employment, and laws restricted their access to education, public transportation, theaters, restaurants, voting, and seats in public office. The legal system supported this unequal treatment. For example, in many communities, deeds to white-owned homes stipulated that they could not be sold to Blacks.

Blacks and other minorities long resisted racial discrimination. The civil rights movement of the 1950s and 1960s successfully challenged the legal foundation for racial segregation. Since then, advocates for social justice have reduced the economic and social impact of racial discrimination, though its impact continues, and informal segregation is still a social reality. We examine various aspects of race and ethnicity in more detail in Chapter 10.

Class Systems: Capitalist and Socialist

Unlike a caste system, in which a person's position is determined by birth, a **class system** features *stratification determined by economic position, which results from a combination of individual achievement and family of birth.* Class systems are more flexible than caste systems and offer more opportunities for social mobility. They are still stratification systems, however; they organize the unequal distribution of resources among distinct groups and are supported by a justifying ideology. We examine classes more closely in Chapter 9. This brief

CLASS

SEGREGATION AND CHANGE

Many forms of public accommodation and transportation are segregated by class. In an earlier era, luxury ocean liners, such as the one illustrated here, served wealthy clientele. In today's faster-paced society, first-class luxury is more likely to be found on private jets, such as the one shown here. Most Americans today are appalled by the racial segregation that once existed in public facilities. Why then is class-based segregation still taken for granted?

and Whites was based on birth and could not be changed. The ideology that justified racial segregation was racism, which those in power supported by invoking tradition, Christian teachings, and pseudo-science. Racial inequality was said to be the foundation of the traditional "southern way of life." Bible stories and passages were used selectively to justify slavery, including the tale that descendents of Noah's son, Ham, were cursed to be slaves (Genesis 9:18–27) and St. Paul's advice that servants accept their lot and obey their masters (Ephesians 6:5–9). So-called scientific classifications of races, based on racist assumptions, also justified racial inequality, as we examine in Chapter 10.

Whites used their power in the United States to create caste-like divisions between Whites and Blacks. Such inequality was challenged successfully when Blacks organized in the civil rights movement to maximize their power.

CHAPTER 5   Power

preview sketches out some of the features of class systems in the two major types of economies, capitalist and socialist.

CLASS IN CAPITALIST SYSTEMS In the United States and other contemporary capitalist societies, considerable affluence is accompanied by significant class inequality. Economic resources such as income, stocks, real estate, and other forms of property are distributed unevenly, as are education and training. A small upper class of capitalist investors owns a substantial amount of the wealth and thereby wields enormous power. A broad middle class of relatively well-educated workers is employed in jobs that require considerable knowledge and skill and that pay well enough to afford a comfortable existence. A large working class is employed in modest-to-low-paying jobs that require less training and formal education. Those working for low wages and those unable to secure steady employment often live in poverty.

In capitalist class systems, the ideology emphasizes individualism—the idea that success is based on merit, not inherited advantage. The popular idea that "With hard work and determination, you can accomplish whatever you want" is an implicit explanation for inequality: those at the bottom do not work hard, while those at the top do. Inequality is seen as good because it motivates people to work hard to achieve economic success, thereby contributing to the overall affluence of society. As we see in Chapter 9, however, structural factors and barriers beyond an individual's control have a considerable impact on economic success or failure.

Throughout modern history, those below the capitalist class have often resisted inequality; in particular, workers in various countries have organized themselves into labor unions to gain more power and improve their working conditions. As a result, today's capitalist societies vary substantially in the degree to which they are unequal.

CLASS IN SOCIALIST SYSTEMS The major difference between capitalist and socialist class systems is the nature and degree of government intervention in the economy, a topic we examine in Chapter 16. Capitalist ideology suggests that people should compete in the marketplace free of government interference. In contrast, socialist ideology emphasizes the collective good and economic equality as coordinated by the government. In a socialist system, the government typically owns major industries and taxes wealthy citizens heavily to pay for free or subsidized social programs such as education, health care, housing, and daycare.

Because the state plays such a central role, economic stratification varies across socialist societies, depending on the type of government. State socialism—as found most notably in the former Soviet Union and other communist countries of Eastern Europe before 1991—is characterized by totalitarian governments that typically downplay the existence of inequality. In such systems, political dissent was not tolerated, and those who held political positions (in other words, those who had access to political resources)—especially membership in the Communist Party and authority in the workplace—were at the highest levels of the stratification system. Thus Communist Party officials had the most power. The key divisions in society were between party leaders, workplace managers, and ordinary workers.

The politically oppressive nature of state socialism, coupled with its inefficiency as an economic system, helped lead to its demise. Today's major socialist societies are quite different. In China, for example, the Communist Party has adopted flexible economic policies, but the central authority still rigidly controls the government-owned companies that carry them out. The party also controls government bodies at all levels of society, including the military, the courts, the media, universities, and religious organizations (McGregor 2010). As a result, China continues to suppress political freedom while incorporating aspects of capitalism into its economy and harboring stark inequalities.

In contrast to state socialism, democratic socialism combines a government accountable to the electorate with an economy that includes considerable state intervention. Found most notably in some Scandinavian countries today, democratic socialism has produced some of the world's most affluent and least unequal countries. These societies tend to cultivate an ideology that values equality and the common good, even if it means putting strict limits on the income and wealth of the country's richest citizens.

Patriarchy

Another type of systemic stratification is based on gender. Women have long been subjected to **patriarchy,** *male domination through social institutions and cultural practices.* Patriarchy can be thought of as a system of stratification since it emphasizes separate and unequal groups (men and women), distributes resources unequally, and justifies this inequality with an ideology that assumes the superiority of men.

Patriarchal arrangements of power are built into many aspects of social life, including the cultural norm that a man should be the "head of household," the idea in some religions that women should play secondary roles, and the continuing underrepresentation of women in positions of political and economic power. Many feminist sociologists focus on understanding women's oppression, how sexism operates, and how women's subordination intersects with other forms of inequality. Consequently, power is an important concept in feminist theory and research (Allen 2000, 2005, 2008; Hartsock 1996; Yeatmann 1997; Young 1992).

As we explore further in Chapter 11, feminist scholars have developed a variety of approaches to understanding the relationships among gender, inequality, and power (Connell 1991; Davis, Leijenaar, and Oldersma 1991; Radtke and Stam 1994). Some argue that women's oppression resulted from the power men had over them and that the liberation of women will challenge and break this power. Socialist-feminists argue that women's oppression was a result of capitalism; women were

Structured Inequality: Stratification Systems

---

thinking about power
Do you think success is based on individualism and merit, or are other factors involved?
How does a person's **power** or lack of power fit into the equation?

SOCIOLOGY WORKS

Kiya Stokes and the Service Workers' Union

When Kiya Stokes enrolled in a sociology course on class and inequality, he had no idea that a few years later he would be on the front lines of the struggle for economic justice. As he studied the sociological perspective, learned about stratification, and read about the contemporary labor movement, he started thinking that maybe he could become a part of the effort to improve workers' lives.

"As an African-American man, I was well aware of the various forms of racial discrimination and oppression that I witnessed and endured," Stokes notes. "Sociology helped broaden my perspectives and showed me in a scientific way that there were other groups within our society that were also victims of various forms of oppression." Learning about the intersections of inequality was not always easy. Stokes admits, "The process was slightly traumatic as I learned not only that there were other oppressed people here but that in different ways I had benefited and participated in their oppression. After I moved past the shame, and empathy, I decided that I needed to do something to make the world a better place."

At the suggestion of his sociology professor, Stokes enrolled in a short training program run by a labor union, and he was hooked. He went on to earn a master's degree in labor studies and then went to work for the Service Employees International Union (SEIU), the nation's largest labor union. After working in Atlanta and Washington, D.C., Stokes is now a research analyst for the union in Los Angeles. He says, "The work that I do helps support campaigns that are designed to increase worker wages, to improve safety standards, and to eventually stamp out poverty."

Reflecting back, Stokes says, "In sociology class I learned a new way to view the world. I learned that we were not just one big happy family here with a predestined lot in life. I saw that

Kiya Stokes

many people *do* work hard and do *not* get adequately compensated for that labor. Others do not do a bit of work but have wealth beyond our wildest imagination. I started questioning other premises and assumptions about the state of the world that most people take for granted. In the end I am certain that without the critical thinking and analytical skills that I learned in sociology class I would not be fighting for working people today."

Through his work, Stokes has seen firsthand that when people organize and work together for collective change, they can realize their own power and help promote economic justice. This approach is neatly summed up in the two-word motto of his union: "Stronger Together."

> "Sociology helped broaden my perspectives and showed me in a scientific way that there were other groups within our society that were also victims of various forms of oppression."

think about it

1. *How are the sociological concepts and ideas introduced in this chapter reflected in Kiya Stokes's story?*

2. *What did Stokes mean by saying that seriously considering inequality was "a slightly traumatic experience" for him? Do you feel the same way about your study of power and social inequality? Why or why not?*

---

exploited as cheap labor in the paid labor force and as unpaid labor at home, helping to sustain male workers. This argument links class and gender inequality.

These examples of stratification systems illustrate some of the many ways that inequality is structured. Although each form of stratification has distinct features, by viewing all of them through the lens of power, we can see many similarities.

Can Inequality Be Reduced?

If all societies have inequality, can it be reduced? The simple answer is yes, although some forms of inequality are easier

to combat than others. Interestingly, equality is a fairly new value in human history. Only since the Enlightenment of the eighteenth century has inequality been seen as undesirable. Before that time, it was considered inevitable and often a part of God's will. However, sociology teaches us that inequality is socially constructed and, thus, its nature and extent are neither inevitable nor foreordained. Human action produces inequality, and people can organize to empower themselves and reduce inequality. (The profile in the Sociology Works box illustrates how sociological insights helped to shape one person's decision to fight against economic inequality.)

In Transition

MONEY, POWER, AND POLITICS

Supreme Court Justice Louis Brandeis famously commented, "We may have democracy, or we may have wealth concentrated in the hands of a few, but we can't have both" (in Lonergan 1941, 42). Brandeis's concern that concentrated economic power can be converted unfairly into political power has resurfaced in recent years as economic inequality has grown (a topic we explore in Chapter 9) and as money has come to play an increasing role in politics. These concerns cut across party lines. As former senators Bob Kerrey (a Nebraska Democrat) and Larry Pressler (a South Dakota Republican) argue, in this age of "wealthy interests" and "big money givers," "confidence in Congress has reached an all-time low in part because Americans perceive that their representatives are primarily accountable to those who fund their campaigns" (Kerrey and Pressler 2010).

Political participation in the United States is unequal and influenced heavily by class, with those at the top having the greatest voice and influence (Schlozman et al. 2005). This disparity is especially true of campaign contributions, which have always played a role in politics. But because of two recent developments, wealthy people have more ability than ever before to translate their economic power into political power, renewing concerns about the danger of which Justice Brandeis warned.

First, the amount of money involved in political campaigns has grown dramatically, making wealthy donors all the more important. For example, after holding steady for decades, the amount candidates spent on presidential campaigns increased dramatically from about $661 million in 2000 to $1.75 billion in 2008 (in 2008 dollars) mostly due to increased reliance on media advertising and sophisticated polling (Figure 5.1). To fund their campaigns, candidates rely primarily on big donors, with less than 1 percent of Americans providing 80 percent of the total funding for the 2008 presidential election (Americans for Campaign Reform 2010). Nearly half (47 percent) of contributions to the 2008 Obama campaign came from just 13,000 donors, each of whom contributed $1,000 or more, whereas only 26 percent came from donors who gave $200 or less. Obama's opponent, John McCain, received an even higher percentage of his contributions (59 percent) from donors giving $1,000

Total contributions (millions of 2008 dollars)

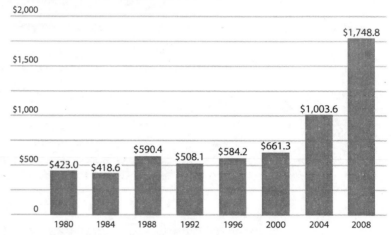

FIGURE 5.1 | TOTAL CONTRIBUTIONS TO PRESIDENTIAL CANDIDATES, 1980–2008 (MILLIONS OF 2008 DOLLARS)
After remaining relatively stable for a quarter-century, the amount of money spent on presidential campaigns has skyrocketed in recent years, with total contributions topping $1.7 billion in 2008. *Source:* Center for Responsive Politics: OpenSecrets.org. Adjusted for inflation by authors.

or more (Malbin 2008). Not surprisingly, large donors come from wealthy households. In 2000, 95 percent of large donors ($1,000 or more) came from the wealthiest 12 percent of households (Schlozman et al. 2005).

Second, much of the money that influences elections does not go directly to campaigns but is instead spent on independent advertising to support or oppose candidates. The potential influence of this kind of indirect funding was exacerbated in 2010 when a divided Supreme Court, citing First Amendment "free speech" concerns, issued a controversial ruling (*Citizens United v. the Federal Election Commission*) that swept away limits on corporate spending in political elections (Liptak 2010). As a result of this decision, a flood of new money entered the process—outside groups spent nearly four times as much on the midterm elections in 2010 than they had in 2006. Led by the biggest contributor, the business community's U.S. Chamber of Commerce, the bulk of this money appears to have come from corporations and their allies, but because such indirect spending does not have to comply with campaign disclosure laws, the source of about half this money was hidden from public view. For example, the second biggest contributor, American Crossroads, was set up by Republican political operatives but is funded primarily by anonymous donors (American Crossroads 2011; Public Citizen 2011; SourceWatch 2011). Thus, although more money is flowing into the electoral process, transparency regarding the source of these funds has declined.

Will citizens organize to curb the power of money in politics? Or, as Justice Brandeis warned, will concentrated economic power erode the health of our democracy? Those questions remain to be answered.

THINKING SOCIOLOGICALLY ABOUT . . .

Power

- **Power** is the capacity to bring about a desired outcome as well as to overcome resistance by others. It operates at all levels of society.

- **Power** can be used to allocate resources (economic), make rules and decisions (political), and help to define reality (cultural).

- **Power** is based on social relationships and requires compliance. Disobedience can be a form of power, since it denies the compliance being sought.

REVIEW, REFLECT, AND APPLY

Looking Back

1. Power includes the ability to bring about a desired outcome ("power to"), as well as the capacity to overcome resistance ("power over"). Education, organization, and networking contribute to empowerment. Compliance may be obtained by persuasion, reward, or coercion.

2. Power operates at all levels of society and can be seen in both everyday situations as well as at the macro level. Power is commonly used to allocate resources (economic), make rules and decisions (political), and help to define reality (cultural)—and thus is closely tied to inequality.

3. Power can be legitimate, accepted voluntarily by those who are affected by it; or illegitimate, relying on coercion to generate obedience. Legitimate power can be based on traditional, rational-legal, or charismatic authority.

4. Power is based on social relationships and requires compliance from others. Disobedience, or noncompliance, can be a form of power, especially for those without access to other forms of power.

5. Considering power and inequality alerts us to the issue of privilege. Understanding relations of power involves understanding various perspectives, including those of people with little power.

6. Inequality is multidimensional and includes stratification based on class (economic conditions), status (prestige), and power (political organization). Intersectionality theory suggests that to understand inequality, we need to consider the ways in which race, class, and gender interact and form what is sometimes referred to as a matrix of domination.

7. All societies have some system of stratification, featuring unequally distributed resources, distinct groups that make up the strata, and an ideology that explains and justifies inequality. Major types of stratification systems include caste systems, class systems, and patriarchy.

8. Economic power can be translated into political power through financial contributions to election campaigns and related advertising efforts.

Critical Thinking: Questions and Activities

1. What are power and inequality, and how are these two concepts related?

2. Do you consider yourself powerful? If you answer yes, what is the source of your power? If your answer is no, what would have to change to increase your power?

3. Identify and describe a common situation in your daily life where you comply with power. Is this a case of legitimate or illegitimate power? Explain.

4. How do various types of inequality intersect in your life? In what ways are you relatively privileged? In what ways do you face disadvantages?

5. Make a list of three people or organizations that you consider to be powerful. Using what you have learned in this chapter, explain what makes each of them powerful. For each, explain how power is rooted in social relationships. Now do the same with three people or organizations that you think are relatively powerless.

Key Terms

caste system (p. 126) stratification based on various ascribed characteristics determined at birth.

charismatic authority (p. 120) power whose legitimacy is derived from the extraordinary personal characteristics of an individual leader, which inspire loyalty and devotion.

class (p. 123) a group of people who share a roughly similar economic position and lifestyle.

class system (p. 128) stratification determined by economic position, which results from a combination of individual achievement and family of birth.

coerce (p. 114) to force people's compliance by threatening, intimidating, pressuring, or harming them.

discrimination (p. 124) treating others unequally based on their background or other personal characteristics.

empowerment (p. 111) an increase in the capacity of people to bring about an intended outcome.

hegemony (p. 119) a condition that exists when those in power have successfully spread their ideas—and marginalized alternative viewpoints—so that their perspectives and interests are accepted widely as being universal and true.

illegitimate power (p. 119) a form of authority that relies on force or coercion to generate obedience.

inequality (p. 123) the unequal distribution of resources among groups of people.

intersectionality theory (p. 124) a perspective that highlights the connections and interactions between various forms of inequality, especially race, class, and gender.

legitimate power (p. 119) authority that is voluntarily accepted by those who are affected.

life chances (p. 123) the opportunities offered by a person's economic position.

matrix of domination (p. 125) the interlocking systems of oppression associated with race, class, and gender.

patriarchy (p. 129) male domination through social institutions and cultural practices.

persuade (p. 113) to obtain people's compliance by convincing them of the correctness of your position and goals.

power (p. 111) the ability to bring about an intended outcome, even when opposed by others.

power tactics (p. 115) the specific strategies people use to influence others in everyday life.

privilege (p. 122) a special advantage or benefit that is not enjoyed by everyone.

rational-legal authority (p. 119) power that has legitimacy because it is based on established laws, rules, and procedures.

reward (p. 113) to encourage people's compliance by offering some compensation as a positive incentive.

social closure (p. 124) the process whereby a status group maximizes its own advantages by restricting access to rewards only to members of the group.

social mobility (p. 126) movement from one stratum of a stratification system to another.

standpoint theory (p. 122) a theory that questions taken-for-granted assumptions about society by looking at it from multiple viewpoints, especially from the perspective of people in subordinate positions.

stratification systems (p. 125) social structures and cultural norms that create and maintain inequality by ranking people into a hierarchy of groups that receive unequal resources.

traditional authority (p. 119) power that has legitimacy because of compliance with well-established cultural practices.

MODULE 29 Stratification in the World System

The Global Divide

In some parts of the world, the people who have dedicated their lives to fighting starvation refer to what they call "coping mechanisms"—ways in which the desperately poor attempt to control their hunger. Eritrean women will strap flat stones to their stomachs to lessen their hunger pangs. In Mozambique, people eat the grasshoppers that have destroyed their crops, calling them "flying shrimp." Though dirt eating is considered a pathological condition (called *pica*) among the well-fed, the world's poor eat dirt to add minerals to their diet. And in many countries, mothers have been known to boil stones in water, to convince their hungry children that supper is almost ready. As they hover over the pot, these women hope that their malnourished children will fall asleep (McNeil 2004).

Around the world, inequality is a significant determinant of human behavior, opening doors of opportunity to some and closing them to others. Indeed, disparities in life chances are so extreme that in some places, the poorest of the poor may not be aware of them. Western media images may have circled the globe, but in extremely depressed rural areas, those at the bottom of society are not likely to see them.

A few centuries ago, such vast divides in global wealth did not exist. Except for a very few rulers and landowners, everyone in the world was poor. In much of Europe, life was as difficult as it was in Asia or South America. This was true until the Industrial Revolution and rising agricultural productivity produced explosive economic growth. The resulting rise in living standards was not evenly distributed across the world.

Figure 29-1 compares the industrial nations of the world to the developing nations. Using total population as a yardstick, we see that the developing countries have more than their fair share of rural population, as well as of total births, disease, and childhood deaths. At the same time, the industrial nations of the world, with a much smaller share of total population, have much more income and exports than the developing nations. Industrial

FIGURE 29-1 **Fundamental Global Inequality**

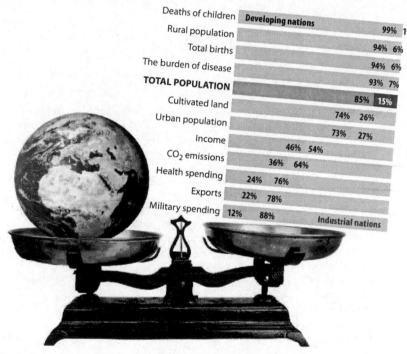

	Developing nations	Industrial nations
Deaths of children	99%	1%
Rural population	94%	6%
Total births	94%	6%
The burden of disease	93%	7%
TOTAL POPULATION	85%	15%
Cultivated land	74%	26%
Urban population	73%	27%
Income	46%	54%
CO$_2$ emissions	36%	64%
Health spending	24%	76%
Exports	22%	78%
Military spending	12%	88%

Note: In this comparison, industrial nations include the United States and Canada, Japan, western Europe, and Australasia. Developing nations include Africa, Asia (except for Japan), Latin America, eastern Europe, the Caribbean, and the Pacific. *Source:* Adapted from Sutcliffe 2002:18.

Think about It

What is the relationship between health spending, disease, and deaths of children? Between CO$_2$ emissions, income, and exports?

nations also spend more on health and the military than other nations, and they emit more carbon dioxide (CO$_2$; Sachs 2005; Sutcliffe 2002).

Although the divide between industrial and developing nations is sharp, sociologists recognize a continuum of nations, from the richest of the rich to the poorest of the poor. For example, in 2006, the average value of goods and services produced per citizen (or per capita gross national income) in the industrialized countries of the United States, Japan, Switzerland, Belgium, and Norway was more than $34,000. In at least 12 poorer countries, the value was just $900 or less. However, most countries fell somewhere between those extremes, as Figure 29-2 shows.

MAPPING LIFE WORLDWIDE

FIGURE 29-2 Gross National Income Per Capita

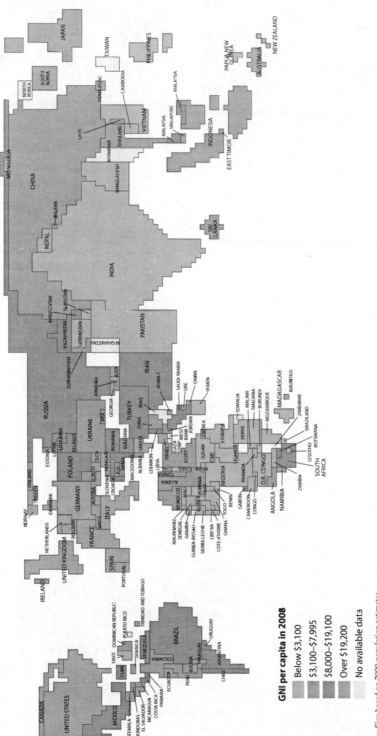

GNI per capita in 2008

- Below $3,100
- $3,100–$7,995
- $8,000–$19,100
- Over $19,200
- No available data

Note: Size based on 2000 population estimates.
Sources: Haub and Kent 2009; Weeks 2008:30–31.

This stylized map reflects the relative population sizes of the world's nations. The color for each country shows the 2008 estimated gross national income (the total value of goods and services produced by the nation in a given year) per capita. As the map shows, some of the world's most populous countries—such as Nigeria, Bangladesh, and Pakistan—are among the nations with the lowest standard of living, as measured by per capita gross national income.

What do we stand in line for? People's needs and desires differ dramatically depending on where they live. On the left, eager customers line up outside a store in New York City to purchase the newly released version of X-Box 360. On the right, residents of Ethiopia line up to receive water.

Still, the contrasts are stark. Three forces discussed here are particularly responsible for the domination of the world marketplace by a few nations: the legacy of colonialism, the advent of multinational corporations, and modernization.

● The Legacy of Colonialism

Colonialism occurs when a foreign power maintains political, social, economic, and cultural domination over a people for an extended period. In simple terms, it is rule by outsiders. The long reign of the British Empire over much of North America, parts of Africa, and India was an example of colonial domination. The same can be said of French rule over Algeria, Tunisia, and other parts of North Africa. Relations between the colonial nation and colonized people are similar to those between the dominant capitalist class and the proletariat, as described by Karl Marx.

By the 1980s, colonialism had largely disappeared. Most of the nations that were colonies before World War I had achieved political independence and established their own governments. However, for many of those countries, the transition to genuine self-rule was not yet complete. Colonial domination had established patterns of economic exploitation that continued even after nationhood was achieved—in part because former colonies were unable to develop their own industry and technology. Their dependence on more industrialized nations, including their former colonial masters, for managerial and technical expertise, investment capital, and manufactured goods kept former colonies in a subservient position. Such continuing dependence and foreign domination are referred to as **neocolonialism.**

The economic and political consequences of colonialism and neocolonialism are readily apparent. Drawing on the conflict perspective, sociologist Immanuel Wallerstein (1974, 1979a, 2000) views the global economic system as being divided between nations that control wealth and nations from which resources are taken. Through his **world systems analysis,** Wallerstein has described the unequal economic and political relationships in which certain industrialized nations (among them the United States, Japan, and Germany) and their global corporations dominate the *core* of this system (Figure 29-3). At the *semiperiphery*

of the system are countries with marginal economic status, such as Israel, Ireland, and South Korea. Wallerstein suggests that the poor developing countries of Asia, Africa, and Latin America are on the *periphery* of the world economic system. The key to Wallerstein's analysis is the exploitative relationship of *core* nations toward *noncore* nations. Core nations and their corporations control and exploit noncore nations' economies. Unlike other nations, they are relatively independent of outside control (Chase-Dunn and Grimes 1995).

The division between core and periphery nations is significant and remarkably stable. A study by the International Monetary Fund (2000) found little change over the course of the *past 100 years* for the 42 economies that were studied. The only changes were Japan's movement up into the group of core

FIGURE 29-3 World Systems Analysis at the Beginning of the 21st Century

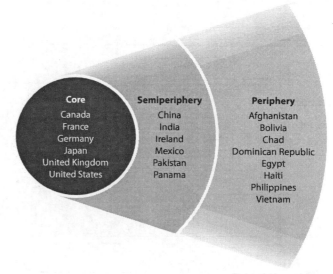

Core	Semiperiphery	Periphery
Canada	China	Afghanistan
France	India	Bolivia
Germany	Ireland	Chad
Japan	Mexico	Dominican Republic
United Kingdom	Pakistan	Egypt
United States	Panama	Haiti
		Philippines
		Vietnam

Note: Figure shows only a partial listing of countries, selected by the author.

nations and China's movement down toward the margins of the semiperiphery nations. Yet Immanuel Wallerstein (2000) speculates that the world system as we currently understand it may soon undergo unpredictable changes. The world is becoming increasingly urbanized, a trend that is gradually eliminating the large pools of low-cost workers in rural areas. In the future, core nations will have to find other ways to reduce their labor costs. Exhaustion of land and water resources through clear-cutting and pollution is also driving up the costs of production.

Wallerstein's world systems analysis is the most widely used version of **dependency theory.** According to this theory, even as developing countries make economic advances, they remain weak and subservient to core nations and corporations in an increasingly intertwined global economy. This interdependency allows industrialized nations to continue to exploit developing countries. In a sense, dependency theory applies the conflict perspective on a global scale.

In the view of world systems analysts and dependency theorists, a growing share of the human and natural resources of developing countries is being redistributed to the core industrialized nations. This redistribution happens in part because developing countries owe huge sums of money to industrialized nations as a result of foreign aid, loans, and trade deficits. The global debt crisis has intensified the Third World dependency begun under colonialism, neocolonialism, and multinational investment. International financial institutions are pressuring indebted countries to take severe measures to meet their interest payments. The result is that developing nations may be forced to devalue their currencies, freeze workers' wages, increase the privatization of industry, and reduce government services and employment.

Closely related to these problems is **globalization,** the worldwide integration of government policies, cultures, social movements, and financial markets through trade and the exchange of ideas. Because world financial markets transcend governance by conventional nation-states, international organizations such as the World Bank and the International Monetary Fund have emerged as major players in the global economy. The function of these institutions, which are heavily funded and influenced by core nations, is to encourage economic trade and development and to ensure the smooth operation of international financial markets. As such, they are seen as promoters of globalization and defenders primarily of the interests of core nations.

Critics call attention to a variety of issues, including violations of workers' rights, the destruction of the environment, the loss of cultural identity, and discrimination against minority groups in periphery nations. The impact of globalization appears to be most problematic for developing countries in Latin America and Africa. In Asia, developing nations seem to do better. Foreign investment there involves the high-tech sector, which produces more sustainable economic growth (Kerbo 2006).

Some observers see globalization and its effects as the natural result of advances in communications technology, particularly the

The pitfalls of globalization were brought home—literally—to U.S. consumers in 2007, when U.S. companies were forced to recall toys manufactured in China because they were finished with lead-based paint.

use your **sociological imagination**

You are traveling through a developing country. What evidence do you see of neocolonialism and globalization?

Internet and worldwide transmission of the mass media. Others view it more critically, as a process that allows multinational corporations to expand unchecked, as we will see in the next section (Chase-Dunn et al. 2000).

Multinational Corporations

Worldwide, corporate giants play a key role in neocolonialism. The term **multinational corporations** refers to commercial organizations that are headquartered in one country but do business throughout the world. Such private trade and lending relationships are not new; merchants have conducted business abroad for hundreds of years,

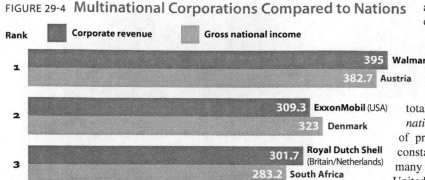

FIGURE 29-4 **Multinational Corporations Compared to Nations**

Rank ▮ Corporate revenue   ▮ Gross national income

Rank		
1	395 Walmart (USA)	382.7 Austria
2	309.3 ExxonMobil (USA)	323 Denmark
3	301.7 Royal Dutch Shell (Britain/Netherlands)	283.2 South Africa
4	266.3 BP British Petroleum (Britain)	257.9 Venezuela
5	203.8 Toyota (Japan)	207.9 Colombia
6	175 Chevron (USA)	170.4 Philippines
7	155.1 Volkswagen (Germany)	157.5 Chile
8	153.5 General Electric (USA)	157.3 Pakistan
9	150.2 Conoco Phillips (USA)	146.8 Egypt
10	123.1 AT&T (USA)	118.8 New Zealand

Sources: Ranking prepared by author. Revenue from corporate quarterly report statements (Q2 2009 through Q2 2010). GNI from World Bank 2010a:32–34.

Think about It

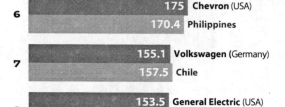

What happens to society when corporations grow richer than countries and spill across international borders?

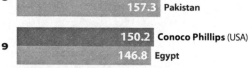
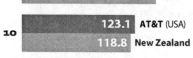

trading gems, spices, garments, and other goods. However, today's multinational giants are not merely buying and selling overseas; they are also *producing* goods all over the world (Wallerstein 1974).

Moreover, today's "global factories" (factories throughout the developing world that are run by multinational corporations) may soon have the "global office" sitting alongside them. Multinationals based in core countries are beginning to establish reservation services and centers for processing data and insurance claims in periphery nations. As service industries become a more important part of the international marketplace, many companies are concluding that the low costs of overseas operations more than offset the expense of transmitting information around the world.

Do not underestimate the size of these global corporations. As Figure 29-4 shows, the total revenues of multinational businesses are on a par with the total value of goods and services exchanged in *entire nations*. Foreign sales represent an important source of profit for multinational corporations, which are constantly seeking to expand into other countries (in many cases, developing nations). The economy of the United States depends heavily on foreign commerce, much of which is conducted by multinationals. Over 10 percent of all goods and services produced in the United States relates to the export of goods to foreign countries, which accounts for 20 percent of the nation's annual growth (U.S. Trade Representative 2007).

Functionalist View

Functionalists believe that multinational corporations can actually help the developing nations of the world. They bring jobs and industry to areas where subsistence agriculture once served as the only means of survival. Multinationals also promote rapid development through the diffusion of inventions and innovations from industrial nations. Viewed from a functionalist perspective, the combination of skilled technology and management provided by multinationals and the relatively cheap labor available in developing nations is ideal for a global enterprise. Multinationals can take maximum advantage of technology while reducing costs and boosting profits.

Through their international ties, multinational corporations also make the nations of the world more interdependent. These ties may prevent certain disputes from reaching the point of serious conflict. A country cannot afford to sever diplomatic relations or engage in warfare with a nation that is the headquarters for its main business suppliers or a key outlet for its exports.

Conflict View

Conflict theorists challenge this favorable evaluation of the impact of multinational corporations. They emphasize that multinationals exploit local workers to maximize profits. Starbucks—the international coffee retailer based in Seattle—gets some of its coffee from farms in Guatemala. But to earn enough money to buy a pound of Starbucks coffee, a Guatemalan farmworker would have to pick 500 pounds of beans, representing five days of work: see Sociology in the Global Community: Your Morning Cup of Coffee (Entine and Nichols 1996).

The pool of cheap labor in the developing world prompts multinationals to move factories out of core countries. An added bonus for the multinationals is that the developing world discourages strong trade unions. In industrialized countries, organized labor insists on decent wages and humane working conditions, but governments seeking to attract or keep multinationals may develop a "climate for investment" that includes repressive antilabor laws which restrict union activity and collective bargaining. If labor's demands become too threatening, the multinational firm will simply move its plant elsewhere, leaving a trail of unemployment behind. Nike, for example, moved its factories from the United States to Korea to Indonesia to Vietnam in search of the lowest labor costs. Conflict theorists conclude that, on the whole, multinational corporations have a negative social impact on workers in *both* industrialized and developing nations.

Workers in the United States and other core countries are beginning to recognize that their own interests are served by helping to organize workers in developing nations. As long as multinationals can exploit cheap labor abroad, they will be in a strong position to reduce wages and benefits in industrialized countries. With this in mind, in the 1990s, labor unions, religious organizations, campus groups, and other activists mounted public campaigns to pressure companies such as Nike, Starbucks, Reebok, Gap, and Walmart to improve wages and working conditions in their overseas operations (Global Alliance for Workers and Communities 2003; Gonzalez 2003).

Several sociologists who have surveyed the effects of foreign investment by multinationals conclude that although it may at first contribute to a host nation's wealth, it eventually increases economic inequality within developing nations. This conclusion holds true for both income and land ownership. The upper and middle classes benefit most from economic expansion; the lower classes benefit least. As conflict theorists point out, multinationals invest in limited economic sectors and restricted regions of a nation. Although certain sectors of the host nation's economy expand, such as hotels and expensive restaurants, their very expansion appears to retard growth in agriculture and other economic sectors. Moreover, multinational corporations often buy out or force out local entrepreneurs and companies, thereby increasing economic and cultural dependence (Chase-Dunn and Grimes 1995; Kerbo 2009; Wallerstein 1979b).

 use your sociological imagination

Think of something you bought recently that was made by a multinational corporation. How do you know the maker was a multinational?

Worldwide Poverty

In developing countries, any deterioration of the economic well-being of those who are least well off threatens their very survival. As we saw in Module 28 (see the Sociology in the Global Community box), even the wealthy in the developing world are poor by U.S. standards. Those who are poor in developing countries are truly destitute.

What would a map of the world look like if we drew it to a scale that reflects the number of *poor* people in each country

instead of the number of people, as in Figure 29-2? As Figure 29-5 shows, when we focus on the poverty level rather than the population, the world looks quite different. Note the huge areas of poverty in Africa and Asia, and the comparatively small areas of affluence in industrialized North America and Europe. Poverty is a worldwide problem that blights the lives of billions of people.

How do social scientists measure global poverty? As we saw in Module 28, there is significant disagreement over where to draw the poverty line in the United States. Adding the rest of the world to the equation further complicates the task. Individually, many developing nations define poverty based on the minimum income a person needs to survive—an amount that typically ranges from a low of $1 a day to a high of $2 a day. Zambia defines poverty in terms of the inability to afford specific foods in a subsistence diet (Chen and Ravallion 2008; *The Economist* 2008c).

In 2000 the United Nations launched the Millennium Project, whose objective is to eliminate extreme poverty worldwide by the year 2015 (Sociology in the Global Community: Cutting Poverty Worldwide). Although 15 years may seem a long time, the challenge is great. Today, almost 3 billion people subsist on $2 a day or less. To reach the project's goal, planners estimated that industrial nations must set aside 0.51 percent of their *gross national income*—that is, the total value of a nation's goods and services (GNP), plus or minus income received from and sent to other nations—to aid developing countries.

At the time the Millennium Project was launched, only five countries were giving at that target rate: Denmark, Luxembourg, the Netherlands, Norway, and Sweden. As of 2010, the United States would need to multiply its present aid level by 150 percent

trend|spotting

Urbanization and Its Costs

The 20th century brought rapid urbanization, not just to the United States, but to countries around the world. Globally, the proportion of the population that lives in cities increased from 13 percent in 1900 to 29 percent in 1950. By 2005, according to the United Nations, the proportion had reached 49 percent.

In developing countries, this rush toward urbanization is complicating government efforts to improve people's living conditions. Providing adequate food and water is more difficult in cities than it is in rural areas, where wells, garden plots, and farm animals are often enough to sustain residents. In cities, food must be trucked in from the countryside, and water must be purified and piped from one location to the next.

Somehow, rapidly expanding cities must find the resources to expand their infrastructures—a challenge considering the poverty of many residents. Compared to industrial countries, developing countries are urbanizing with a relatively lower per capita income. The United States did not reach 65 percent urbanization until 1950, when per capita income had risen to nearly $13,000 in today's dollars. In comparison, Nigeria, Pakistan, and the Philippines are approaching the same level of urbanization with just one-fifth of that per capita income. In these countries, the bright lights of the city—assuming that the power grid is working—may not herald such a bright future.

MAPPING LIFE WORLDWIDE

FIGURE 29-5 Poverty Worldwide

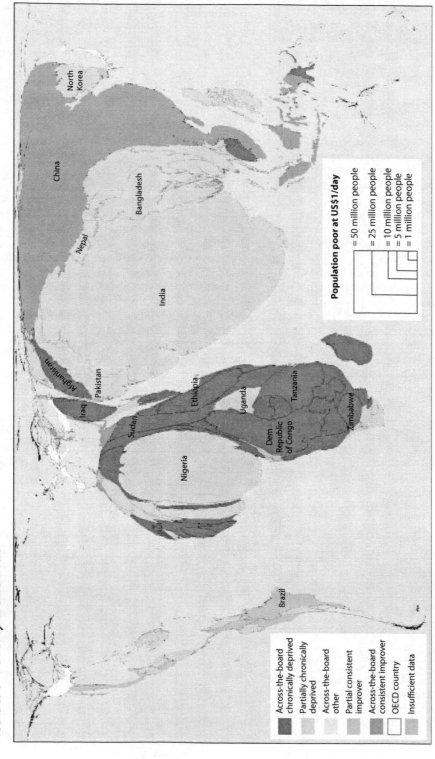

Legend:
- Across-the-board chronically deprived
- Partially chronically deprived
- Across-the-board other
- Partial consistent improver
- Across-the-board consistent improver
- OECD country
- Insufficient data

Population poor at US$1/day
- = 50 million people
- = 25 million people
- = 10 million people
- = 5 million people
- = 1 million people

Source: Chronic Poverty Research Centre 2009.

The scale of this map is based on the number of people in each region who are chronically poor. The colors represent the income levels of those who are poorest. In OECD countries—those that belong to the Organisation for Economic Co-Operation and Development (white)—chronic poverty is not a nationwide issue.

Think about It

To what degree does this map minimize those countries you have studied or might want to visit? To what degree does it emphasize parts of the world about which you know very little?

Sociology in the Global Community

Cutting Poverty Worldwide

The goal of the United Nations' Millennium Project is to cut the world's poverty level in half by 2015. The project has eight objectives:

1. *Eradicate extreme poverty and hunger.* Poverty rates are falling in many parts of the globe, particularly in Asia. But in sub-Saharan Africa, where the poor are hard-pressed, millions more have sunk deeper into poverty.
2. *Achieve universal primary education.* While many parts of the developing world are approaching universal school enrollment, in sub-Saharan Africa, only 30 percent of all children are enrolled in high school.
3. *Promote gender equality and empower women.* The gender gap in primary school enrollment that has characterized the developing world for so long is slowly closing. However, women still lack equal representation at the highest levels of government.

> Each year malaria and tuberculosis kill almost as many people as AIDS, severely draining the labor pool in many countries.

4. *Reduce child mortality.* Death rates among children under age 5 are dropping, but not nearly fast enough. In the least developed nations, about 85 of every 1,000 children die in the first year of life, compared to 6 of every 1,000 in the more developed nations. Sadly, evidence indicates that progress toward reducing child mortality has slowed in recent decades.
5. *Improve maternal health.* Each year more than half a million women die during pregnancy or childbirth. Progress has been made in reducing maternal death rates in some developing regions, but not in countries where the risk of giving birth is highest.
6. *Combat HIV/AIDS, malaria, and other diseases.* AIDS has become the leading cause of premature death in sub-Saharan Africa, where two-thirds of the world's AIDS patients reside.

Worldwide, the disease is the fourth most frequent killer. Though new drug treatments can prolong life, there is still no cure for this scourge. Moreover, each year malaria and tuberculosis kill almost as many people as AIDS, severely draining the labor pool in many countries.

7. *Ensure environmental sustainability.* Sufficient progress has not been made toward reversing the loss of the world's environmental resources through rampant clear-cutting of forests and other forms of environmental destruction. Even so, many developing countries lack the infrastructure needed to support public health. Though access to safe drinking water has increased, half the developing world lacks toilets and other forms of basic sanitation.
8. *Develop a global partnership for development.* The United Nations Millennium Declaration seeks a global social compact in which developing countries pledge to do more to ensure their own development, while developed countries support them through aid, debt relief, and improved trade opportunities.

What progress has been made in meeting these objectives? Despite the much-publicized Live 8 global benefit concerts, held in connection with a meeting of the world's eight major economies (Canada, France, Germany, Great Britain, Italy, Japan, Russia, and the United States), called the G8, in 2005, developed nations have fallen far short of the targets they set for themselves. By mid-2008, well before the global recession began, the G8 had contributed much less than their interim goals. The following year, at an even larger meeting, the economic superpowers pledged $1.1 trillion to help developing nations weather the worldwide economic crisis—which of course had not even been contemplated when the Millennium Project was conceived. In response, the watchdog Africa Progress Panel called on donor nations to consider establishing a tax or an international lottery to meet the Millennium Project's goals.

LET'S DISCUSS

1. Do you think the Millennium Project's objectives are realistic, given the enormity of the obstacles that must be overcome? Why do you think the project's founders gave themselves 15 years to accomplish their goal?

2. How are the project's eight objectives related to one another? Could some of the objectives be reached successfully without addressing the others? If you were a government planner with the resources to address just one objective, which would you pick, and why?

Sources: Annan 2009; Haub 2008; Katel 2005; Landler and Sanger 2009; Sachs 2005; United Nations 2005a; Weisbrot et al. 2005; World Bank 2006a, 2007:63, 80.

to match the Millennium target of 0.51 percent of gross national income. Although, in dollar terms, the U.S. government delivers far more aid to foreign countries and multinational organizations than any other nation, the amount is not impressive considering the nation's tremendous wealth relative to other countries. In terms of the percentage of gross national income, the United States' contribution is the lowest among the 22 most advanced industrial countries, on a par with Japan's and Italy's (Figure 29-6).

Direct government-to-government foreign aid is only one way of alleviating poverty, however. Although per capita aid from the U.S. government may not be strong, private spending by U.S. residents is. Individual charitable giving is much higher in the United States than in other industrial nations.

Privileged people in industrialized nations tend to assume that the world's poor lack significant assets. Yet again and again, observers from these countries have been startled to discover how far even a small amount of capital can go. Numerous microfinance programs, which involve relatively small grants or loans, have encouraged marginalized people to invest not in livestock, which may die, or jewelry, which may be stolen, but in technological improvements such as small stoves. We will discuss this topic in greater depth in Modules 48 through 51, on the government and the economy.

● Modernization

Around the world, millions of people are witnessing a revolutionary transformation of their day-to-day life. Contemporary social scientists use the term **modernization** to describe the far-reaching process by which periphery nations move from traditional or less developed institutions to those characteristic of more developed societies.

Wendell Bell (1981), whose definition of modernization we are using, notes that modern societies tend to be urban, literate, and industrial. These societies have sophisticated transportation and media systems. Their families tend to be organized within the nuclear family model rather than the extended-family model (see Module 40). Thus, members of societies that undergo modernization must shift their allegiance from traditional authorities, such as parents and priests, to newer authorities, such as government officials.

Many sociologists are quick to note that terms such as *modernization* and even *development* contain an ethnocentric bias. The unstated assumption behind these terms is that "they" (people living in developing nations) are struggling to become more like "us" (people in core industrialized nations). Viewed from a

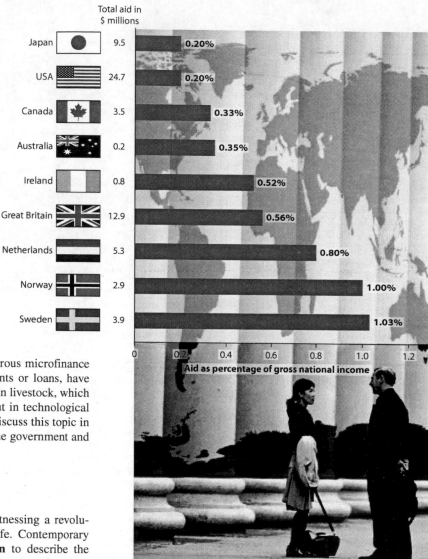

FIGURE 29-6 **Foreign Aid Per Capita in Nine Countries**

Total aid in $ millions

Country	Total aid in $ millions	Aid as percentage of gross national income
Japan	9.5	0.20%
USA	24.7	0.20%
Canada	3.5	0.33%
Australia	0.2	0.35%
Ireland	0.8	0.52%
Great Britain	12.9	0.56%
Netherlands	5.3	0.80%
Norway	2.9	1.00%
Sweden	3.9	1.03%

Note: Projected development assistance in 2010, released February 15, 2010.
Source: Organisation for Economic Co-operation and Development 2010.

conflict perspective, these terms perpetuate the dominant ideology of capitalist societies.

The term *modernization* also suggests positive change. Yet change, if it comes, often comes slowly, and when it does it tends to serve the affluent segments of industrial nations. This truism seems to apply to the spread of the latest electronic technologies to the developing world (Sociology in the Global Community: The Global Disconnect).

A similar criticism has been made of **modernization theory,** a functionalist approach that proposes that modernization and development will gradually improve the lives of people in developing nations. According to this theory, even though nations

Sociology in the Global Community

The Global Disconnect

Bogdan Ghirda, a Romanian, is paid 50 cents an hour to participate in multiplayer Internet games like City of Heroes and Star Wars. He is sitting in for someone in an industrialized country who does not want to spend days ascending to the highest levels of competition in order to compete with players who are already "well armed." This arrangement is not unusual. U.S.-based services can earn hundreds of dollars for recruiting someone in a less developed country, like Ghirda, to represent a single player in an affluent industrial country.

Meanwhile, villagers in Arumugam, India, are beginning to benefit from their new Knowledge Centre. The facility, funded by

> For developing nations, the consequences of the global disconnect are far more serious than an inability to surf the Net.

a nonprofit organization, contains five computers that offer Internet access—an amenity unknown until now to thousands of villagers.

These two situations illustrate the technological disconnect between the developing and industrial nations. Around the world, developing nations lag far behind industrial nations in their access to and use of new technologies. The

World Economic Forum's Networked Readiness Index (NRI), a ranking of 134 nations, shows the relative preparedness of individuals, businesses, and governments to benefit from information technologies. As the accompanying table shows, the haves of the world—countries like Singapore, the United States, and Denmark—are network ready; the have-nots—countries like Ethiopia, Chad, and Bolivia—are not.

For developing nations, the consequences of the global disconnect are far more serious than an inability to surf the Net. Thanks to the Internet, multinational organizations can now function as a single global unit, responding instantly in real time, 24 hours a day. This new capability has fostered the emergence of what sociologist Manuel Castells calls a "global economy." But if large numbers of people—indeed, entire nations—are disconnected from the new global economy, their economic growth will remain slow and the well-being of their people will remain retarded. Those citizens who are educated and skilled will immigrate to other labor markets, deepening the impoverishment of these nations on the periphery.

Remedying the global disconnect is not a simple matter. To gain access to new technologies, people in developing nations typically must serve the world's industrial giants, as Bogdan Ghirda does. Some may benefit from investment by nongovernmental organizations, as the villagers in India have. But progress to date has been slow. In 2005, in an effort to accelerate the diffusion of new technologies, the United Nations launched the Digital

Networked Readiness Index

Top 10 Countries	Bottom 10 Countries
1. Sweden	124. Nepal
2. Singapore	125. Nicaragua
3. Denmark	126. Suriname
4. Switzerland	127. Paraguay
5. United States	128. Cameroon
6. Finland	129. Burundi
7. Canada	130. Timor-Leste
8. Hong Kong	131. Bolivia
9. Netherlands	132. Zimbabwe
10. Norway	133. Chad

Solidarity Fund. The hope is that global information technology companies can be persuaded to set aside some of their profits to help developing nations connect to the Internet.

LET'S DISCUSS

1. For nations on the periphery, what are some of the social and economic consequences of the global disconnect?

2. What factors might complicate efforts to remedy the global disconnect in developing nations?

Sources: Castells 2010a; Dutta and Mia 2010; *The Economist* 2005c; Lim 2007; Tony Thompson 2005; United Nations 2005b; World Economic Forum 2009.

---

develop at uneven rates, the development of peripheral nations will be assisted by innovations transferred from the industrialized world. Critics of modernization theory, including dependency theorists, counter that any such technology transfer only increases the dominance of core nations over developing nations and facilitates further exploitation.

When we see all the Coca-Cola and IBM signs going up in developing nations, it is easy to assume that globalization and economic change are effecting cultural change. But that is not always the case, researchers note. Distinctive cultural traditions, such as a particular religious orientation or a nationalistic identity, often persist and can soften the impact of modernization on a developing nation. Some contemporary sociologists emphasize that both industrialized and developing countries are "modern." Increasingly, researchers gauge modernization using a series of social indicators—among them degree of

urbanization, energy use, literacy, political democracy, and use of birth control. Clearly, some of these are subjective indicators; even in industrialized nations, not everyone would agree that wider use of birth control represents an example of progress (Armer and Katsillis 1992; Hedley 1992; Inglehart and Baker 2000).

Current modernization studies generally take a convergence perspective. Using the indicators just noted, researchers focus on how societies are moving closer together, despite traditional differences. From a conflict perspective, the modernization of developing nations often perpetuates their dependence on and continued exploitation by more industrialized nations. Conflict theorists view such continuing dependence on foreign powers as an example of contemporary neocolonialism.

Table 29-1 summarizes the three major approaches to global inequality.

Table **29-1** Sociological Perspectives on Global Inequality

Approach	Sociological Perspective	Explanation
World systems analysis	Functionalist and conflict	Unequal economic and political relationships maintain sharp divisions between nations.
Dependency theory	Conflict	Industrial nations exploit developing nations through colonialism and multinational corporations.
Modernization theory	Functionalist	Developing nations move away from traditional cultures and toward the cultures of industrialized nations.

summing up

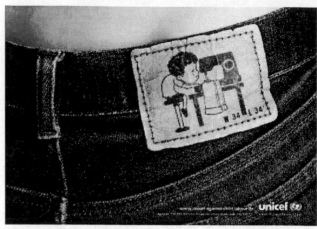

Where am I wearing? This UNICEF poster reminds affluent Western consumers that the brand-name jeans they wear may be produced by exploited workers in developing countries. In sweatshops throughout the developing world, nonunion garment workers—some of them children—labor long hours for what we would consider extremely low wages—even if for the workers in those semiperiphery countries, those wages are relatively high.

MODULE 29 | Recap and Review

Summary

Worldwide, stratification can be seen both in the gap between rich and poor nations and in the inequality within countries. This module examines the global divide and stratification within nations as well as the impact of **globalization, modernization,** and **multinational corporations** on developing countries.

1. Developing nations account for most of the world's population and most of its births, but they also bear the burden of most of its poverty, disease, and childhood deaths.

2. Former colonized nations are kept in a subservient position, subject to foreign domination, through the process of **neocolonialism.**

3. Drawing on the conflict perspective, Immanuel Wallerstein's **world systems analysis** views the global economic system as divided between nations that control wealth (core nations) and those from which capital is taken (periphery nations).

4. According to **dependency theory,** even as developing countries make economic advances, they remain weak and subservient to core nations and corporations in an increasingly integrated global economy.

5. **Globalization,** the worldwide integration of government policies, cultures, social movements, and financial markets through trade and the exchange of ideas, is a controversial trend that critics blame for contributing to the cultural domination of periphery nations by core nations.

6. **Multinational corporations** bring jobs and industry to developing nations, but they also tend to exploit workers in order to maximize profits.

7. Sociologists note that terms such as **modernization** and even *development* carry an ethnocentric bias. **Modernization theory** suggests that the development of periphery countries will be assisted by innovations transferred from the industrialized world.

Thinking Critically

1. Relate Durkheim's, Tönnies's, and Lenski's theories of social structure to the global divide that exists today. Could sociocultural evolution have something to do with the global divide?

2. Relate modernization theory to dependency theory. Do you agree with critics that modernization will increase the dominance of core nations? Why or why not?

Key Terms

Colonialism
Dependency theory
Globalization
Modernization
Modernization theory
Multinational corporation
Neocolonialism
World systems analysis

MODULE 27 | Stratification by Social Class

We continually assess how wealthy people are by looking at the cars they drive, the houses they live in, the clothes they wear, and so on. Yet it is not so easy to locate an individual within our social hierarchies as it would be in slavery or caste systems of stratification. To determine someone's class position, sociologists generally rely on the objective method.

Measuring Social Class

In the **objective method** of measuring social class, class is viewed largely as a statistical category. Researchers assign individuals to social classes on the basis of criteria such as occupation, education, income, and place of residence. The key to the objective method is that the *researcher,* rather than the person being classified, identifies an individual's class position.

The first step in using this method is to decide what indicators or causal factors will be measured objectively, whether wealth, income, education, or occupation. The prestige ranking of occupations has proved to be a useful indicator of a person's class position. For one thing, it is much easier to determine accurately than income or wealth. The term **prestige** refers to the respect and admiration that an occupation holds in a society. "My daughter, the physicist" connotes something very different from "my daughter, the waitress." Prestige is independent of the particular individual who occupies a job, a characteristic that distinguishes it from esteem. **Esteem** refers to the reputation that a specific person has earned within an occupation. Therefore, one can say that the position of president of the United States has high prestige, even though it has been occupied by people with varying degrees of esteem. A hairdresser may have the esteem of his clients, but he lacks the prestige of a corporate executive.

Table 27-1 ranks the prestige of a number of well-known occupations. In a series of national surveys, sociologists assigned prestige rankings to about 500 occupations, ranging from surgeon to panhandler. The highest possible prestige score was 100; the lowest was 0. Surgeon, physician, lawyer, dentist, and college professor were the most highly regarded occupations. Sociologists have used such data to assign prestige rankings to virtually all jobs and have found a stability in rankings from 1925 to the present. Similar studies in other countries have also developed useful prestige rankings of occupations (Nakao and Treas 1994).

Gender and Occupational Prestige

For many years, studies of social class tended to neglect the occupations and incomes of *women* as determinants of social rank.

With more than half of all married women now working outside the home (see Module 35), this approach seems outmoded. How should we judge class or status in dual-career families—by the occupation regarded as having greater prestige, the average, or some other combination of the two? Sociologists—in particular, feminist sociologists in Great Britain—are drawing on new approaches to assess women's social class standing. One approach is to focus on the individual (rather than the family or household) as the basis for categorizing a woman's class position. Thus, a woman would be classified according to her own occupational status rather than that of her spouse (O'Donnell 1992).

Another feminist effort to measure the contribution of women to the economy reflects a more clearly political agenda. International Women Count Network, a global grassroots feminist organization, has sought to give a monetary value to women's unpaid work. Besides providing symbolic recognition of women's role in labor, this value would also be used to calculate pension and other benefits that are usually based on wages received. The United Nations has placed an $11 trillion price tag on unpaid labor by women, largely in child care, housework, and agriculture. Whatever the figure, the continued undercounting of many workers' contributions to a family and to an entire economy means that virtually all measures of stratification are in need of reform (United Nations Development Programme 1995; Wages for Housework Campaign 1999).

Multiple Measures

Another complication in measuring social class is that advances in statistical methods and computer technology have multiplied the factors used to define class under the objective method. No longer are sociologists limited to annual income and education in evaluating a person's class position. Today, studies use as criteria the value of homes, sources of income, assets, years in present occupations, neighborhoods, and considerations regarding dual careers. Adding these variables will not necessarily paint a different picture of class differentiation in the United States, but it does allow sociologists to measure class in a more complex and multidimensional way. When researchers use multiple measures, they typically speak of **socioeconomic status (SES),** a measure of social class that is based on income, education, and occupation. To determine the socioeconomic status of a young person, such as a college student under age 25, they use *parental* income, education, and occupation.

Whatever the technique used to measure class, the sociologist is interested in real and often dramatic differences in power, privilege, and opportunity in a society. The study of stratification

Table **27-1**   Prestige Rankings of Occupations

Occupation	Score	Occupation	Score
Surgeon	87	Farm manager	48
Physician	86	Mail carrier	47
Lawyer	75	Secretary	46
Dentist	74	Insurance agent	45
College professor	74	Bank teller	43
Architect	73	Nurse's aide	42
Psychiatrist	72	Farmer	40
Clergy	69	Correctional officer	40
Pharmacist	68	Receptionist	39
Registered nurse	66	Carpenter	39
High school teacher	66	Barber	36
Accountant	65	Child care worker	35
Optician	65	Hotel clerk	32
Elementary school teacher	64	Bus driver	32
Banker	63	Auto body repairer	31
Veterinarian	62	Truck driver	30
Legislator	61	Salesworker (shoes)	28
Airline pilot	60	Garbage collector	28
Police officer or detective	60	Waiter and waitress	28
Prekindergarten teacher	55	Cook in a pizza shop	27
Librarian	54	Bartender	25
Firefighter	53	Farmworker	23
Social worker	52	Janitor	22
Dental hygienist	52	Newspaper vendor	19
Electrician	51	Prostitute	14
Funeral director	49	Panhandler	11

Note: 100 is the highest and 0 the lowest possible prestige score.
Source: J. Davis et al. 2009. See also Nakao and Treas 1994.

Think about It

Can you name what you think are two more high-prestige occupations? Two more low-prestige occupations?

is a study of inequality. Nowhere is the truth of that statement more evident than in the distribution of income and wealth.

● Income and Wealth

By all measures, in the United States **income,** a term that refers to salaries and wages, is distributed unevenly. Nobel Prize–winning economist Paul Samuelson has described the situation in the following words: "If we made an income pyramid out of building blocks, with each layer portraying $500 of income, the peak would be far higher than Mount Everest, but most people would be within a few feet of the ground" (Samuelson and Nordhaus 2011:324).

Recent data support Samuelson's analogy. In 2008 the median household income in the United States was $50,303. In other words, half of all households had higher incomes that year and half had lower incomes. However, this fact does not fully convey the income disparities in our society. We can get some sense of income inequality by contrasting this median (middle) income with the mean arithmetic average, which in 2008 was $68,424. The mean is so much higher than the median because some people make a lot more money than others, which draws the mean up. Thus, the mean is a less useful statistic than the median for describing the average, or typical, income (DeNavas-Walt et al. 2009:29).

We can gain additional insight into income inequality in the United States by looking at the relative placement of households within the income distribution. One of the most common ways of doing so is to line up all income-earning households from low to high and then break them into quintiles, or fifths. Because there are approximately 117 million households in the United States, each quintile includes an equal number of about 23.4 million households. This method gives us a sense of the average income within each quintile, along with the percentage of the nation's total income earned in each quintile.

As Figure 27-1 shows, looking at the population in this way reveals a significant degree of income inequality. The mean income for households in the lowest quintile is $11,656; in the top quintile, it is $171,057. Those households in the top 5 percent—the ones most responsible for bringing up the arithmetic mean—average a staggering $294,709 in annual income. If we were to move up even higher in the income distribution, we would find that the top 0.01 percent of taxpayers—about 15,000 households—make incomes of at least $11.5 million a year. Collectively, they control 6 percent of the nation's total income (Sloan 2009:27).

There has been a modest redistribution of income in the United States over the past 80 years, but not always to the benefit of the poor or even the middle class. From 1929 through 1970, the government's economic and tax policies shifted some income to the poor. However, in the past four decades—especially in the 1980s and in the decade from 2001 through 2010—federal tax policies have favored the affluent. Moreover, while the salaries of highly skilled workers and professionals have continued to rise, the wages of less skilled workers have *decreased* when controlled for inflation.

As a result, the Census Bureau and other researchers report that regardless of the measure that is used, income inequality rose substantially from 1967 through the end of the century. Former Federal Reserve Board Chairman Alan Greenspan was referring to this significant increase in income inequality when

trend|spotting

Women as Wage Earners

In 2010, for the first time, women outnumbered men in the U.S. workforce. The historic reversal was caused by long-term changes in women's roles that began four decades ago. In the 2008 recession, massive job losses among men tipped the balance.

This change in the trend reflects the growing importance of women as wage earners, although on average, women still work fewer hours than men. They also hold more part-time jobs than men, and they earn only 77 percent of what men make. And of course, men still dominate the higher-paying executive levels of the workforce.

Women's share of the once heavily male labor force has been growing for nearly a century. Big expansions occurred during the Great Depression, when payrolls were limited, and World War II, when millions of men left their jobs to join the service. In 2008, the boost to women's employment came from a severe economic slowdown that hit hard at male-dominated occupations, such as construction and manufacturing.

Although women's outnumbering of men in the labor force may be temporary—an artifact of the current recession—their transformation of the U.S. workplace is permanent. There are no signs of a countertrend to their participation in the workforce.

Careful economic analysis has shown that over the past 30 years, federal and state tax policies have tended to accentuate this trend toward income inequality. During one 25-year period, the top 1 percent of income earners *after taxes* saw their incomes rise 228 percent, compared to only 21 percent for households in the middle quintile. Little wonder that the middle class is shrinking (Billitteri 2009; Sherman 2007).

Finally, the impact of the recent recession is unlikely to be shared evenly among racial and ethnic groups.

FIGURE 27-1   **Mean Household Income by Quintile**

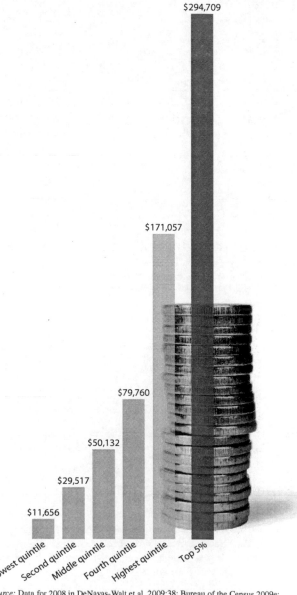

Source: Data for 2008 in DeNavas-Walt et al. 2009:38; Bureau of the Census 2009e: Table H-3.

he told Congress that the gap between the rich and the poor in the United States has become so wide that a democratic society must address it (Cushing-Daniels and Zedlewski 2008; Grier 2005; Neckerman and Torche 2007; Saez 2008).

Just how dramatic has this growth in inequality been? Consider the period between 1984 and 2008. In just 25 years, the following changes occurred in real household income (adjusted for inflation):

- For the lowest 20 percent of the population, income rose 9 percent.
- For the next lowest 20 percent of the population, income rose 10 percent.
- For the middle 20 percent of the population, income rose 13 percent.
- For the next highest 20 percent of the population, income rose 20 percent.
- For the top 20 percent of the population, income rose a whopping 40 percent.

The pattern is clear. Though everyone has done better, by far the biggest winners have been the affluent.

Has the recent economic slowdown reduced income inequality? Not really. A comparison of household incomes in 1999 (the peak before the 2001 recession) with the most recent income data shows that lower-income households' earnings have declined, while the higher-income households' earnings have held steady. By one measure, inequality between the top 10th and the bottom 10th of the income distribution has increased 9 percent (DeNavas-Walt et al. 2009:38–39).

FIGURE 27-2 Distribution of Wealth in the United States

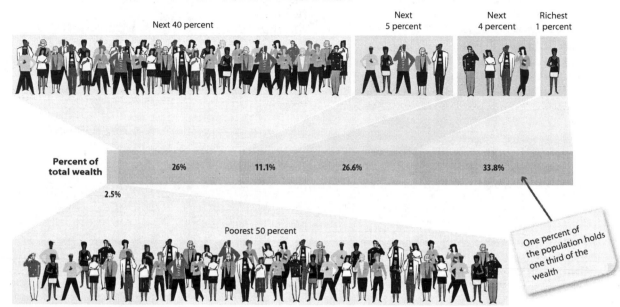

Source: Data for 2007, as reported in a 2009 Federal Reserve Bank study. See Kennickell 2009:35.

During the recession of 1999–2001, the median household wealth of Hispanic and Black Americans fell 27 percent. At the same time, White households' wealth grew 2 percent (D. Hamilton and Darity 2009).

Globalization is often blamed for this growing inequality, because it has forced less skilled workers to compete with lower-paid foreign-born workers. While that is true, research suggests that the number of displaced workers who are reemployed at similarly paid or even higher-paid jobs roughly equals the number of workers whose earnings drop (S. Zimmerman 2008a).

Americans often seem not to be seriously concerned about income and wealth inquality in the United States. In a comparison of opinions about social inequality in 27 different countries, respondents in the United States were less aware than those in other countries of the extent of inequality at the top of the income distribution. Americans would prefer to "level down" the top of the nation's earning distribution, but compared to

people in other countries, they are less concerned about reducing income differentials at the bottom of the distribution (Osberg and Smeeding 2006).

Wealth, an inclusive term encompassing all a person's material assets (including land, stocks, and other types of property), is distributed much more unevenly than income in the United States. A 2009 Federal Reserve Bank study showed that half the population controls 2.5 percent of the nation's wealth; the other half controls over 97 percent (Figure 27-2). Put another way, the wealth of the top 1 percent exceeds the collective wealth of the bottom 90 percent. Researchers have also found a dramatic disparity in wealth between African Americans and Whites. This disparity is evident even when educational backgrounds are held constant: the households of college-educated Whites have about three times as much wealth as the households of college-educated Blacks (Conley 2010; Kennickell 2009; Oliver and Shapiro 2006, 2008).

MODULE 27 | Recap and Review

Summary

One consequence of social class in the United States is that both **income** and **wealth** are distributed unevenly.

1. Sociologists use the **objective method** of measuring social class, which uses criteria such as occupation,

education, and income. **Socioeconomic status (SES)** is an objective measure based on these criteria.

2. Regardless of the measure used, income inequality rose from the late 1960s to the end of the 20th century.

Thinking Critically

1. To what degree are students motivated by the prestige of their future occupations?

2. What does the pattern of income distribution in the United States tell you about your own future income? How much can you expect it to grow over the years?

Key Terms

Esteem

Income

Objective method

Prestige

Socioeconomic status (SES)

Wealth

G. William Domhoff teaches at the University of California, Santa Cruz. He has a B.A. from Duke University, an M.A. from Kent State University, and a Ph.D. from the University of Miami. His many articles and books on power in the United States include *The Power Elite and the State* (1990), *State Autonomy or Class Dominance?* (1996), and *Who Rules America?* (1998).

essay

Who Rules America Today?

G. William Domhoff

Who has predominant power in the United States? The short answer is found in an adaptation of the well-known golden rule: Those who have the gold are the rulers. To be exact, the wealthy people who own income-producing property—corporations, real estate, and agribusinesses—set the rules within which policy battles are waged in this country.

The idea that a relatively fixed group of privileged people dominates the economy and government for its own benefit goes against the American grain and the founding principles of this country. "Class" and "power" are terms that make Americans uneasy, and concepts such as the "upper class" and the "power elite" put people on their guard. Americans may differ in social and income levels and some may have more influence than others, but it is felt that there can be no fixed power group when power is constitutionally lodged in all the people, when there is broad political participation through elections and lobbying, and when *social mobility*—the intergenerational rise or fall in income and occupation—is everywhere apparent.

There is a measure of truth to this generally held view. Highly trained professionals with an interest in environmental and consumer issues have been able to combine their technical expertise and understanding of the legislative and judicial processes with timely publicity and lawsuits to establish governmental restrictions on some corporate practices. When average wage earners are organized into unions or are disruptive, they sometimes gain concessions on wages, hours, or working conditions. In addition, voters have been able to restrain the actions of the wealthy under some circumstances, especially when there are disagreements within the higher circles of wealth and influence.

Despite these several qualifications, this essay demonstrates how rule by the wealthy few is possible in the context of free speech, regular elections, and organized opposition by a loosely knit liberal-environmental-labor coalition. It shows how "the rich" coalesce into a social upper class that has institutions through which the children of its members are socialized and newly wealthy people are assimilated. It explains how members of the upper class control corporations, and describes the network of nonprofit organizations through which members of the upper class and corporate leaders shape policy debates. It also shows how the wealthy few influence elections and describes the differences between power relationships at the national and community levels. Finally, this essay explains why the wealthy owners complain that they are powerless despite all objective evidence to the contrary, and why the opposition to rule by the wealthy few is so weak and disorganized.

No predictions are made about possible changes in the distribution of power in the future, but one major transformation of the past 50 years is discussed that could have implications for the success of the liberal-environmental-labor coalition. The Civil Rights Movement of the early 1960s and the Voting Rights Act of 1965, which gave African Americans the right to vote in the South, forced the wealthy whites out of the southern Democratic Party, making that party available as a potential expression of the liberal-environmental-labor coalition for the first time in American history.

▶ POWER AND POWER INDICATORS

"Power" is a word that is easy to understand but hard to define precisely. We know it means clout or juice or muscle or the ability to make things happen. We know it comes from words that imply the ability to act in a strong, compelling, and direct way, but we also know that power can be projected in a quiet and indirect manner.

For the purposes of this essay, power means "the capacity of some persons to produce intended and foreseen effects on others."[1] This is a very general definition that allows for many forms of power, such as economic, political, military, and intellectual (knowledge and expertise) power. It leaves open the question of whether force or coercion is a necessary aspect of the exercise of power. However, to define power in this manner does not mean that it is a simple matter to study the power of a group or social class. For one thing, a formal definition does not explain how a concept can be measured. Also, it is seldom possible to observe interactions that reveal the operation of power even in small groups, let alone to see one social class producing effects on another. It is therefore necessary to develop indicators of power.

For research purposes, power can be thought of as an underlying trait or property of a social group or social class. It can be measured by a series of signs, or indicators, that bear a probabilistic relationship to it. In other words, all the indicators do not necessarily appear every time power manifests itself. Research proceeds through a series of "if-then" statements: If a group or class is powerful, then it should be expected that certain indicators of that power will be present. It is important to have more than one indicator. Ideally, these indicators will be of very different types so that any irrelevant components will cancel each other out. When these multiple indicators point to the same group or class, we can be confident that the underlying concept has been measured correctly.

The three primary indicators of power can be summarized as follows: (1) Who benefits? (2) Who governs? and (3) Who wins? In every society certain experiences and material objects are highly valued. If it is assumed that everyone in a society wants to have as great a share as possible of these experiences and objects, the distribution of values in that society can be utilized as a power indicator. In American society, wealth and well-being are highly valued. People seek to own property, earn high incomes, have interesting and safe jobs, and live long and healthy lives. All these values are unequally distributed and may be used as power indicators.

Power also can be inferred by studying who occupies important institutional positions and takes part in important decision-making groups. If a group or class is highly overrepresented in relation to its proportion in the population, it can be considered powerful. For example, if a group makes up 10 percent of the population but has 50 percent of the seats in the main governing institutions, it has five times more governing positions than would be expected, so it must be exercising "power."

There are many policy issues over which groups or classes disagree. In the United States different policies are suggested by opposing groups in "issue areas" such as foreign policy, taxation, business regulation, and the environment. Power can be inferred on such issues by determining who initiates, modifies, or vetoes policy alternatives. By focusing on actions within the decision-making process, this indicator comes closest to approximating the process of power that is contained in the formal definition. However, the decisional (who wins) indicator is the most difficult to use accurately. It is hard to gain access to decision makers for an interview, much less observe them in action. Aspects of a decision-making process may remain hidden, informants may exaggerate or play down their roles, and people's memories about who did what often become cloudy shortly after the event.

All three of these indicators have strengths and weaknesses, but their weaknesses do not present a serious problem because each indicator involves different kinds of information drawn from different kinds of studies. The case for the power of a group or class should be considered convincing only if all three types of indicators "triangulate" on a particular group or social class.

▶ THE SOCIAL UPPER CLASS

A good starting point for the study of power in the United States focuses careful consideration on the small social upper class at the top of the ladders of wealth, income, and status because this social upper class is one of the most visible and accessible aspects of the power equation. A *social class* is a set of intermarrying and interacting families who see each other as equals, share a common lifestyle, and have a common world view. This general definition is accepted by most social scientists regardless of their views on the distribution of power. By the social upper class, or simply the upper class, we mean the social class that is commonly agreed to be the "top" or "exclusive" class. In various times and places Americans have called such people the "high hats," the "country club set," the "snobs," and the "rich." In turn, members of this class recognize themselves as distinctive, calling themselves "old families," "established families," and "community leaders."

The upper class probably makes up only a few tenths of 1 percent of the population. For the purposes of this essay, we estimate that it includes 0.5 percent to 1 percent of the population. Members of the upper class live in exclusive suburban neighborhoods, expensive downtown co-ops, and large country estates. They often have far-away summer and winter homes as well. They attend a system of private schools that extends from preschool to the university level; the best known of these schools are the "day" and "boarding" prep schools that take the place of public high schools for upper-class teenagers (Table 1). Adult members of the upper class socialize in expensive country clubs, downtown luncheon clubs, hunting clubs, and garden clubs. Young women of the upper class are "introduced" to high society through an elaborate series of debutante teas, parties, and balls. Upper-class women gain experience as volunteers through a nationwide organization known as the Junior League and then go on to serve as directors of cultural organizations, family service associations, and hospitals.

These social institutions create social cohesion and a sense of in-group

TABLE 1

Some Leading Coed Boarding Schools and Men's Clubs

Coed Boarding Schools	Men's Clubs
Choate (Wallingford, CT)	Bohemian Club (San Francisco)
Deerfield (Deerfield, MA)	Brook (New York)
Groton (Groton, MA)	California (Los Angeles)
Kent (Kent, CT)	Eagle Lake (Houston)
Kinkaid (Houston, TX)	Knickerbocker (New York)
Lawrenceville (Lawrenceville, NJ)	Piedmont Driving (Atlanta)
Middlesex (Concord, MA)	Rainier (Seattle)
Punahou (Honolulu, HI)	Rittenhouse (Philadephia)
St. Paul's (Concord, NH)	Rolling Rock (Pittsburgh)
Taft (Watertown, CT)	Saturn (Buffalo)
Thatcher (Ojai, CA)	St. Cecelia (Charlestown, SC)
Westminister (Atlanta, GA)	Somerset (Boston)

"we-ness." This sense of cohesion is heightened by the fact that people can be excluded from these organizations. Through these institutions, young members of the upper class and those who are new to wealth develop a shared understanding of how to be wealthy. Because these social settings are expensive and exclusive, members of the upper class usually think of themselves as special or superior. They think they are better than other people and certainly better able to lead and govern. Their self-confidence and social polish are useful in dealing with people from other social classes, who often admire them and defer to their judgment.

These social institutions provide a starting point for systematic studies of power. For example, class indicators allow us to determine which economic and political leaders are members of the upper class and which are not. Put another way, class indicators allow us to trace the paths of members of the upper class into the economic, political, and ideological power systems of the society.

Starting with these class indicators, it can be shown that the upper class is nationwide in scope because there is overlapping membership among the many social clubs around the country. People from Chicago, for example, may belong to clubs in New York, Boston, and San Francisco, implying that they interact with upper-class counterparts in all those cities. By comparing dozens of club membership lists, sociologists have been able to establish the "density" of this club network. Similarly, the alumni lists of exclusive private schools reveal that their students come from all over the country. The summer addresses of members of the upper class who are listed in in-group "blue books" and "social registers" show that people from all parts of the country mingle at secluded summer resorts that have been upper-class watering holes for generations.[2]

But here we must be cautious because these class indicators are not perfect. Some members of the upper class do not join clubs, nor list themselves in a social register, nor reveal their school affiliations in *Who's Who in America*. We cannot trace such people through the power system; they are counted as not being part of the upper class when they really are. By contrast, local or scholarship children at some prep schools and some honorary members of social clubs are not members of the upper class; they are counted as part of the upper class when they really are not. In large-scale studies, these two kinds of mistakes tend to cancel each other out, and so in general one can obtain an accurate picture. However, class indicators can be wrong in regard to specific individuals.

There can be no doubt that there is a nationwide upper class in the United States with its own distinctive social institutions, lifestyle, and outlook. There also can be no doubt that most of these people are active in business or the professions and that all of them are wealthy. Their great wealth is evident from the large sums it takes to maintain their homes and their style of life, but systematic studies also show that the wealthiest families are part of the social institutions of the upper class. If we combine our studies with findings on the wealth and income distributions, it is possible to say that the upper class, which accounts for at most 1 percent of the population, owns 37.2 percent of net worth (assets minus debts), 45.6 percent of financial wealth, and 15.7 percent of yearly income.[3] In short, the upper class scores very high on the "who benefits" power indicator.

The wealth and income of members of the upper class imply that the upper class is powerful, but they do not demonstrate how power operates. It is thus necessary to turn to studies of the economy to understand the American power structure, then to studies of how the political system operates.

► THE CORPORATE COMMUNITY

Economic power in the United States has been concentrated in an organizational and legal form known as the corporation since the last decades of the nineteenth century. Individual corporations have great power in this society. They can hire and fire workers, move their resources, and use their income in a variety of tax-deductible ways to influence schools, charities, and the government. The argument among scholars begins over whether large corporations are united enough to exert a common social power. It then moves to the question of whether these corporations are still controlled by members of the upper class.

The unity of corporations can be demonstrated in a number of ways. Corporations share a common interest in making a profit. They are often owned by the same families or financial institutions. Their executives have very similar educational and work experiences. Corporate leaders also see themselves as sharing common opponents in organized labor, environmentalists, consumer advocates, and government officials. A sense of togetherness is created by their use of the same legal, accounting, and consulting firms.

However, the best available way to demonstrate unity among corporations is through the study of *interlocking directors,* individuals who sit on two or more of the boards of directors that are in charge of the overall direction of corporations. Boards of directors usually include major owners, top executives from similar corporations, financial and legal advisers, and the three or four officers who run a corporation on a daily basis. Numerous studies show that the 15 to 20 percent of corporate directors who sit on two or more boards, who are called the *inner circle* of the corporate directorate, unite almost every major corporation in the United States into a well-connected corporate community.[4] This network is very dense in that there are many connections among its members (Table 2). Corporations with many connections tend to be the most central ones in the corporate community, and they are typically banks or very large manufacturing firms. The fact that there are so many connections among the 28 firms in Table 2 indicates that these firms are at the center of the whole corporate network.

TABLE 2

The 28 Corporations with the Most Connections Within the Corporate Community

Corporation	No. of Connections to Other Corporations	No. of Connections Within Inner 28
1. Chase Manhattan Bank	45	8
2. Wells Fargo Bank	41	2
3. American Express	40	9
4. Prudential Insurance	39	7
5. Sara Lee	39	8
6. Minnesota Mining & Manufacturing	37	7
7. General Motors	33	8
8. Kroger	33	5
9. Ashland Oil	32	3
10. Bank of America	32	1
11. CSX Railroad	32	2
12. Bell Atlantic Telephone	31	6
13. Coca-Cola	31	3
14. Procter and Gamble	31	8
15. Springs Industries	31	6
16. AMR	30	4
17. Mobil Oil	30	7
18. TRW	30	3
19. Xerox	30	4
20. Ameritech Telephone	29	5
21. Bell South Telephone	29	3
22. Union Pacific Railroad	29	6
23. Westinghouse Electric	29	4
24. Burlington Northern Santa Fe Railroad	28	2
25. Cummins Engine	28	5
26. Kellogg	28	6
27. Kmart	28	4
28. Time Warner	28	7

Source: Jeannette Glynn, *Who Knows Who 1997*, Detroit, MI, Gail Research Inc., 1997, p. 749.

Most social scientists agree that corporations have a strong basis for co-hesion, but there is disagreement about their relationship to the upper class. Some theorists state that members of the upper class used to dominate corporations but do not do so anymore because of the increase in the size of corporations, the need for highly trained and specialized executives, and the decline in family ownership. Thus, there is an upper class of rich families with one set of interests and a group of professional business executives with their own interests and power base. Members of the upper class have power based on wealth; corporate executives have organizational power.

Contrary to this purported division between owners and managers, there is strong evidence for an overlap in membership and interest between the upper class and the corporate community. The wealthiest and most co-hesive upper-class families often have "family offices" through which they can bring to bear the power of their stock ownership, sometimes placing their employees on boards of directors. Members of the upper class also control corporations through financial devices known as holding companies, which purchase a controlling interest in operating companies. More generally, members of the upper class own half of all corporate stock.[5]

Upper-class control of corporations can be seen in the overrepresentation of this class on boards of directors. Several studies have shown that members of the upper class sit on boards far more than can be accounted for by chance. They are especially likely to be part of the inner circle that has two or more directorships.[6] If we use "who governs" as a power indicator, it is clear that members of the upper class still control the corporate community. Thus, one can conclude that the upper class is rooted in the ownership and control of the corporations that constitute the corporate community. It can be said, therefore, that members of the upper class are a corporate rich who are involved in the business world as investors, directors, venture capitalists, bankers, corporate lawyers, and top executives.

It is true that many top corporate executives do not grow up in the upper class, but they are gradually socialized into that class and its values as they move up the corporate ladder. In fact, they are advanced because of their ability to fulfill upper-class goals of corporate expansion and profitability. In return, these rising managers are given the opportunity to buy corporate stock at below-market prices, are paid very high salaries, and are given other "perks" that allow them to join the upper class economically as well as socially. The end result is a strengthening of the power of the upper class.

► SHAPING THE POLITY

The upper class and the corporate community do not stand alone at the top of the power structure. They are supplemented by a wide range of nonprofit organizations that play an important role in framing debates over public policy and shaping public opinion. These organizations are often called nonpartisan or bipartisan because they are not identified with politics or with either of the major political parties. However, they are the real political party of the upper class because they ensure the stability of society and the compliance of the government.

Upper-class and corporate dominance of nonprofit organizations is revealed in the role of wealthy families in creating them and providing them with ongoing funding. However, dominance can be most readily demonstrated once again through studies of boards of directors, which have the ultimate control of these organizations, including the ability to hire and fire top executives. These studies show that members of the upper class are greatly overrepresented on the boards of these organizations and that nonprofit organizations share a large number of directors with the corporate community, particularly directors who are part of the inner circle.[7] In effect, most large nonprofit organizations are part of the corporate community (Table 3).

All the organizations in the nonprofit sector have a hand in creating the

TABLE 3

Organizations in the Policy-Formation Network with Numerous Connections to Major Corporations

Foundations	No. of Corporate Connections	Think Tanks	No. of Corporate Connections	Policy Groups	No. of Corporate Connections
Carnegie Corporation	29	Brookings Institution	48	Business Roundtable	134
Ford Foundation	18	American Enterprise Institute	37	Council on Foreign Relations	37
Sloan Foundation	18	Urban Institute	27		
Rockefeller Foundation	12				

framework of society and, hence, in shaping the political climate. Cultural and civic organizations set the standard for what is beautiful, important, and "classy." They guide our aspirations. Prestigious private universities play a large role in determining what is important to know, and they train most top-level professionals and experts. But it is foundations, think tanks, and policy-discussion organizations that have the most direct and important influence. Their ideas, criticisms, and policy suggestions go out to the general public through pamphlets, books, local discussion groups, mass media, public relations firms, and the public affairs departments of major corporations. Their materials reach the government through a variety of means. Let us look more closely at foundations, think tanks, and policy-discussion organizations to show how they function as a *policy-formation network*.

Foundations

Tax-free foundations receive money from wealthy families and corporations. Their primary purpose is to provide money for education, the arts, research, and policy discussion. They thus have the power to encourage ideas and researchers compatible with their values and goals. Support by major foundations often has an impact on the direction of research in agriculture, social science, and the health sciences. However, foundations also create policy projects on their own that are later adopted by the government. The Ford Foundation's "gray areas" demonstration project in several large cities in the late 1950s and early 1960s was the forerunner of the Johnson Administration's War on Poverty in 1964, for example. Its massive support for new research institutes in ecology provided one important basis for the environmental movement.[8]

Think Tanks

The role of *think tanks* is to suggest new policies for dealing with the problems that face the economy and the government. Using money from wealthy donors, corporations, and foundations, the several dozen think tanks in Washington, D.C., hire the experts produced by graduate departments at high-status universities. The ideas and proposals developed by these experts are disseminated through pamphlets, books, major magazines and newspapers, and, most important, the participation of these experts in the forums provided by policy-discussion organizations.

Policy-Discussion Organizations

Policy-discussion organizations are the hub of the policy-formation network. They bring together wealthy individuals, corporate executives, experts, and government officials for lectures, forums, meetings, and group discussions of issues ranging from the local to the international and from the economic to the political to the cultural. New ideas are tried out in weekly or monthly discussion groups, and differences of opinion are aired and subjected to compromise. These structured discussion groups usually begin with a presentation by invited experts, followed by questions and discussion involving all the participants. Such groups range in size from ten to fifty, with the usual group having fifteen to twenty-five members.

The many discussion groups within policy-discussion organizations have several functions that are not readily apparent. First, they help familiarize busy corporate leaders with policy issues far beyond their day-to-day business concerns. This allows executives to influence public opinion through the mass media and other outlets, argue with and influence experts, and accept appointments for government service. Second, policy-discussion organizations give members of the upper class and the corporate community an opportunity to determine which of their colleagues are the best natural leaders by watching them in the give-and-take of discussion groups. They can see which of their counterparts understand the issues quickly, offer their own ideas, facilitate discussions, and relate well to experts. These organizations thus serve as sorting and screening mechanisms for the emergence of new leadership for the corporate rich.

Third, these organizations present their participants to the media and the public as knowledgeable leaders who should be tapped for public service. They thus help turn wealthy individuals and corporate executives into national leaders. Finally, these organizations provide a forum in which members of the upper class and the corporate community can become friends with policy experts. This gives them a pool of experts from which they can draw advisers if they are asked to serve in government.

These organizations also serve two crucial functions for ambitious experts. First, presenting their ideas to these organizations gives them an opportunity to gain influence. Second, it gives them a chance to advance their careers.

The policy-planning network is not totally homogeneous. Reflecting differences within the corporate community, it has moderate-conservative and ultraconservative wings (Table 4). Moderate conservatives favor foreign aid and economic expansion overseas, whereas ultraconservatives tend to see foreign aid as a giveaway. Moderate conservatives generally accept the idea that governmental taxation and spending policies can be used to stimulate and stabilize the economy, whereas ultraconservatives insist that taxes

TABLE 4

Moderate Conservative and Ultraconservative Organizations in the Policy-Planning Network

Moderate Conservatives	Ultraconservatives
Foundations	
Carnegie Corporation	Bradley Foundation
Ford Foundation	Lilly Endowment
Rockefeller Foundation	Noble Foundation
Rockefeller Brothers Fund	Olin Foundation
Sloan Foundation	Smith Richardson Foundation
Think Tanks	
Aspen Institute	American Enterprise Institute
Brookings Institution	Heritage Foundation
Resources for the Future	Hoover Institution
Overseas Development Council	Hudson Institute
Urban Institute	Manhattan Institute

should be cut to the minimum and that government spending is basically evil. Moderate conservatives accept some social spending measures, or at least support them in the face of serious social disruption. Ultraconservatives consistently oppose welfare spending, claiming that it destroys moral fiber and saps individual initiative; they prefer to use arrest and detention when there is social unrest.

The reasons for these differences are not well understood. There is a tendency for moderate-conservative organizations to be directed by executives from the largest and most internationally oriented corporations, but there are numerous exceptions. Moreover, there are corporations that support policy organizations within both camps. However, for all their differences, leaders within the two clusters of policy organizations have a tendency to search for compromise because of their common membership in the upper class and the corporate community. Both groups have members in the main policy-discussion groups. Most important of all, both are connected to the central group in the network, the Business Roundtable, made up exclusively of chief executive officers from the very biggest banks and corporations (Figure 1).

The existence of the policy-planning network provides evidence for another form of power possessed by the wealthy few: expertise on social and political issues. This is an important complement to the economic power possessed by corporations.

► THE POWER ELITE

The *power elite* can be defined as the leadership group of the upper class. It consists of active working members of the upper class and high-level employees in profit-making and nonprofit institutions, which are controlled by members of the upper class through stock ownership, financial support, and

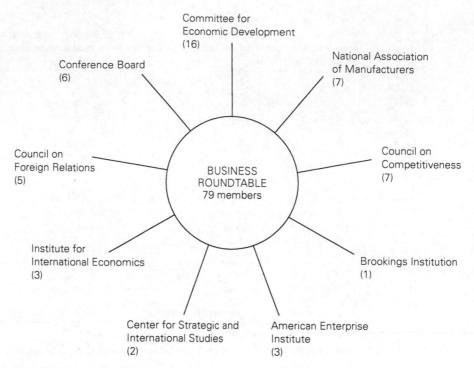

FIGURE 1

The number of shared directors between the Business Roundtable and other policy groups and think tanks. (*Updated from Val Burris, "Elite Policy-Planning Networks in the United States,"* Research in Politics and Society, *Vol. 4, 1992.*)

involvement on boards of directors. This does not mean that all members of the upper class are involved in governing. Some are more interested in social life, sports, or culture; their parties may provide a setting where members of the power elite mingle with celebrities, and sometimes they give money to political candidates, but that is as close as they come to political power. Conversely, not everyone in the power elite is a member of the upper class. Many are top-level employees who started their lives at the middle levels of the social ladder and are never fully assimilated into exclusive social circles. Figure 2 presents a visual representation of how the power elite is drawn from the overlapping circles of the upper class, the corporate community, and the policy-formation network.

The boardrooms of profit and nonprofit institutions are not only a major meeting ground for members of the power elite. They are also the place where the values and perspectives of the wealthy owners and the organizational needs of large-scale institutions are blended together. Upper-class directors ensure that their interests are reflected in the organizations they control, but the day-to-day managers of the organizations who also serve on the boards are able to harmonize class interests with organizational principles. This means that there is no inherent opposition between rival sociological theories that stress social class and class conflict on the one hand,

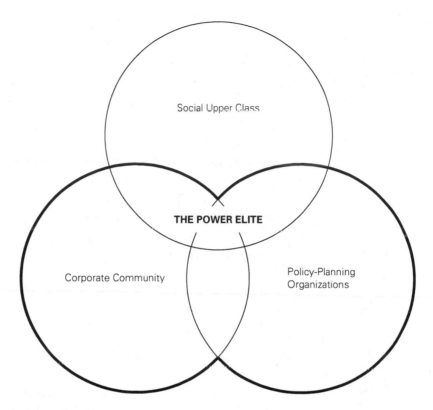

FIGURE 2
A multi-network view of the power elite, showing how it derives from three overlapping
networks, the social upper class, the corporate community, and the policy-planning network.
The power elite is defined by the thick lines.

and those that emphasize the importance of organizations and institutionalized ways of doing business on the other.

It is important to realize that not all experts on public policy are members of the power elite. People have to be high-level employees in institutions controlled by members of the upper class to be considered part of the
power elite. Receiving a fellowship from a foundation, spending a year at a
think tank, or giving advice to a policy-discussion organization does not
make a person a member of the power elite. Furthermore, many experts
never go near the policy-planning network. Instead, they concentrate on
teaching and research or work for groups in the liberal-labor coalition that
oppose the policies of the power elite. In short, experts and advisers are a
separate group just below the power elite in the pecking order.

We now turn to how the power elite dominates the federal government
in the interest of the upper class and the corporate community.

The Power Elite and Government

Members of the power elite involve themselves in the federal government
through three basic processes, each of which has a slightly different role in
ensuring access to the White House, Congress, and specific departments in

the executive branch. Although some of the same people are involved in all three processes, most leaders specialize in one or two of them. These three processes are:

1. The *interest-group process,* through which specific families, corporations, and industries realize their narrow and short-run interests regarding taxes, subsidies, and regulation in their dealings with congressional committees, regulatory bodies, and executive departments.
2. The *policy-making process,* through which the policies developed in the policy-formation network are brought to the White House and Congress.
3. The *candidate selection process,* through which members of the power elite influence elections by means of campaign donations to political candidates. This is the process called "politics" in the United States, but it is best thought of as a candidate selection process because the real substance of politics, deciding on new policies, happens in the policy-making process shaped by the power elite through the policy-formation network outlined in the previous section.

Domination of the federal government by the power elite can be seen most directly in the workings of corporate lobbyists, back-room super-lawyers, and trade associations that represent the interests of specific corporations or business sectors. This interest-group process is based on varying combinations of information, gifts, friendship, and promises of lucrative private jobs in the future. This is the aspect of business-government relations described by journalists and social scientists in exposés and case studies. While these studies show that the special interests usually have their way, the conflicts that sometimes erupt within this process, pitting one corporate sector against another, reinforce the image of widely shared and fragmented power, including the image of a divided corporate community. Moreover, the corporate rich do suffer some defeats in the interest-group process at the hands of liberals and labor. For example, laws that improved automobile safety standards were passed over auto industry objections, and higher standards for water cleanliness were opposed at first by the paper and chemical industries.

Policies that concern the corporate community as a whole are not the province of the interest-group process. Instead, such policies come from the network of foundations, think tanks, and policy-discussion organizations discussed earlier. Plans developed in the policy-planning network reach the federal government in a variety of ways. On the most general level, the network's reports, news releases, and interviews are read by elected officials and their staffs either in pamphlet form or in summary articles in the *Washington Post, New York Times,* and *Wall Street Journal.* Members of the policy-planning network also testify before the congressional committees and subcommittees that write legislation or prepare budgets. More directly, the leaders of these organizations advise specific departments of the executive branch on general policies, making them in effect unpaid temporary members of the government. They are also very prominent on the presidential commissions that are appointed to make recommendations on issues ranging from foreign policy to highway construction. Finally, they are appointed to government positions with a frequency far beyond what would be expected if the corporate community had no more power than any of its rivals. Several different studies have shown that top cabinet positions in both Republican and Democratic administrations are always held by members of the upper class and corporate executives who are leaders in policy-discussion organizations, and the Clinton Administration is an ideal example (Table 5).[9]

The general picture that emerges from these findings is that the highest levels of the executive branch are interlocked with the upper class and the corporate community through the movement of executives and corporate lawyers into and out of the government. Although the same person is not in governmental and corporate positions at the same time, there is enough continuity for the relationship to be described as one of revolving interlocks. Corporate leaders resign their directorships in profit-making and nonprofit organizations to serve in government for two or three years, then return to the corporate community or the policy-planning network. This system gives them temporary independence from the narrow concerns of their organizations and allows them to perform the more general roles they have learned in policy-discussion groups. They return to the private sector with useful personal contacts, new insights, and information on how to dominate the government.

TABLE 5

Important Members of the Clinton Administration Who Were Directors or Members of the Council on Foreign Relations Before Taking Office

Directors		
Name	**Dates CFR Director**	**Government Position**
Warren Christopher	1982–1991	Secretary of State, 1993–1997
William S. Cohen	1989–1996	Secretary of Defense, 1997–
Lloyd Cutler	1977–1979	Special Counsel to President, 1994–1995
Alan Greenspan	1982–1988	Chair, Federal Reserve Board, 1993–
Alice Rivlin	1989–1992	Director, Office of Management and Budget, 1995–1996
Donna Shalala	1992–1993	Secretary of Health and Human Services, 1993–
Strobe Talbott	1988–1993	Deputy Secretary of State, 1995–
Clifton Wharton, Jr.	1983–1992	Deputy Secretary of State, 1993–1994

Members	
Name	**Government Position**
Madeleine Albright	Secretary of State, 1997–
Les Aspin	Secretary of Defense, 1993–1995
Bruce Babbitt	Secretary of the Interior, 1993–
Henry Cisneros	Secretary of Housing and Urban Development, 1993–1996
John Deutch	Director, CIA, 1995–1996
Franklin Raines	Director, Office of Management and Budget, 1997–
Laura Tyson	Chair, Council of Economic Advisors, 1993–1997

As important as the interest-group and policy-planning processes are, they could not operate successfully without sympathetic business-oriented elected officials in the government who are selected through the candidate selection process that operates through the two major political parties. The two parties play a very small role in political education and policy formation; they have been limited to the function of filling offices.

The political system focuses on candidate selection to the relative exclusion of political education and policy formulation because there can be only two main parties as a result of the structure of the government and the nature of our electoral system. The fact that Americans select a President instead of a parliament and elect legislators from single-member geographic areas (states for the Senate, districts for the House) leads to a two-party system because in these winner-take-all elections a vote for a third party of the left or right is a vote for one's least desired choice.[10] A vote for a very liberal party instead of the Democrats, for example, helps the Republicans. Under these rules, the most sensible strategy for both Democrats and Republicans is to blur their policy differences and compete for voters with middle-of- the-road policy views or no policy views at all.

Contrary to what many social scientists claim, American political parties are not very responsive to voter preferences. Their candidates are fairly free to say one thing to win elections and then do another once they are in office. This contributes to confusion and apathy among the electorate and leads to campaigns in which there are no issues except images and personalities, even when the polls show that voters are concerned about certain policy issues. Voter preferences matter most in setting limits on power elite actions and in times of social turmoil like depressions and wars.

It is precisely because the candidate selection process is so personalized, and therefore dependent on name recognition, images, and emotional symbolism, that it can be dominated by members of the power elite through large campaign contributions. Playing the role of donors and money raisers, the same people who direct corporations and take part in the policy planning network have a crucial place in the careers of most politicians who advance beyond the local level. Their support is especially important in party primaries, where money is an even larger factor than it is in general elections.[11]

The American two-party system, therefore, results in elected officials who accept the policies advocated by the members of the power elite working in the interest-group and policy-planning processes. They are motivated by personal ambition far more than by political conviction. Still, some extremely conservative Republicans in Congress sometimes oppose power elite proposals, claiming that such policies are the work of Communists or pointy-headed intellectuals out to wreck the free enterprise system. Many liberal Democrats in Congress from blue-collar and university districts consistently oppose power elite policies as members of the liberal-labor coalition. However, both ultraconservatives and liberals are outnumbered by moderates in both parties, especially in key leadership positions in Congress. After many years in Congress, some liberals decide to "go along to get along."

Although members of the power elite are the most important financial backers of both parties, there are differences between the parties. The rival leaders have intraclass, ethnic, and regional differences, whereas rank-and-file Republicans and Democrats tend to have racial, religious, and interclass differences. The Republican Party is controlled by the wealthiest families of the upper class and the corporate community, who are largely Protestant. The Democratic Party, by contrast, is the party of the "fringes" of the upper class and the power elite. Although often called "the party of the common person," it was in fact the party of the southern segment of the upper class until very recently. The power of southern Democrats in the party and in Congress was secured in a variety of ways, the most important of which was the seniority system for selecting committee chairs in Congress. (By tradition, the person who has been on the committee longest becomes the chair, although the process has been subject to ratification by party members since the 1970s; seniority avoids conflict among members of the party.) Most importantly, the one-party system in the south and the exclusion of African Americans from the voting booth until the mid-1960s gave southern planters and merchants power at the national level out of all proportion to their wealth and numbers.[12] This shows that it is not necessarily the wealthiest people who rule; the nature of the political system also enters into the equation. However, the southern well-to-do were not poor; they were merely "less rich" than most of their northern counterparts.

The southerners dominated the Democratic Party in alliance with the "ethnic rich" in the north, meaning wealthy Jews and Catholics who were shunned or mistreated by rich Protestants. The businesses they owned were often local or smaller than those of Republican backers, and they usually were excluded from the social institutions of the upper class. These ethnic rich were the primary financial supporters of the infamous political machines (political organizations made up of government officials and paid precinct workers) that dominated Democratic politics in most large northern cities between 1880 and 1970.[13]

The alliance between the southern segment of the upper class and the northern ethnic rich usually was able to freeze out the policy initiatives of the party's liberal-labor coalition through its control of congressional committees, although there was a time (1940 to 1975) when labor unions had significant influence on the Democrats. When the machine Democrats sometimes sided with the liberals and labor, southern Democrats simply joined with northern Republicans to create a conservative voting bloc, in which a majority of southern Democrats and a majority of northern Republicans voted together against the northern Democrats. This conservative voting bloc usually formed around issues that reflect class conflict in the legislative arena: civil rights, union rights, social welfare, and business regulation. Most legislation on these issues weakens employers in the face of workers and their unions, which means that the conservative voting bloc was based on the shared interests of northern and southern employers. This alliance won far more often than it lost in the years between 1937, when it was formed, and the early 1990s, when it disappeared for the simple reason that most southerners had become Republicans.[14]

The Democratic party began to change in the 1990s. Southern whites completed their gradual shift to the Republican Party, which began when African Americans won the right to vote in the South in 1965 through the Civil Rights Movement and the Voting Rights Act. The Republican party is now the party of wealthy employers in both the north and the south. Thus, the Democratic Party is slowly becoming what many people always thought it to be—the party of liberals, minorities, workers, and the poor. There are now few Democrats in Congress who are as conservative as any Republican, a very great change from just a few years ago.[15]

Why Business Leaders Feel Powerless

Despite the evidence that the power elite has great influence over the federal government, many corporate leaders claim they are relatively powerless. From their perspective, Congress is more responsive to organized labor, environmentalists, and consumers. They also claim to be harassed by willful and arrogant bureaucrats. These negative feelings toward government are not a recent development, contrary to those who blame the New Deal and the social programs of the 1960s. A study of businesspeople's views in the nineteenth century found they believed political leaders to be "stupid" and "empty" people who went into politics only to earn a living, and a study of businesspeople's views during their most powerful decade until recently, the 1920s, found the same mistrust of government.[16]

The feelings of business leaders about their supposed lack of power cannot be taken seriously as a power indicator: feelings are one thing; the effects of one's actions are another. However, it is interesting to speculate as to why businesspeople complain about a government they dominate. First, complaining about the government puts government officials on the defensive and forces them to keep proving they are friendly to business. Second, businesspeople complain about government because very few civil servants are part of the upper class and the corporate community. The antigovernment ideology of the United States tends to keep members of the upper class out of government careers except in the State Department, and so the only contacts for members of the power elite tend to be at the very top of the government. There is thus uncertainty about how the middle levels will react to new situations and a fear that it is necessary to "ride herd on" or "rein in" potentially troublesome "bureaucrats."

There also seems to be an ideological aspect to business leaders' attitudes toward the government: a fear of the populist, democratic ideology that underlies the American political system. Since power is, in theory, in the hands of all the people, there is always the possibility that someday the majority will turn the government into the pluralist democracy it is said to be. In a real way, then, the great power of the upper class and the corporate community is culturally illegitimate and is, therefore, vigorously denied: It is acceptable to be rich, and even to brag about one's wealth a little, but not to be powerful or, worse, to flaunt that power.

The most important reason for the fear of popular control of the government lies in the primary power issue for business leaders: the domination of labor markets. The corporate rich fervently believe that their power and profits depend on a minimum of employee power and unionization. The issue is particularly important in terms of wage levels because labor costs are 60–70 percent of the overall costs for most profit and nonprofit organizations in the United States. Government can tip the balance of power to workers in four ways: (1) by providing legal support for unions, as first happened when the National Labor Relations Act was passed in 1935 at the height of social disruption during the Great Depression; (2) by hiring unemployed people to work for the government, a policy consistently favored in public opinion polls by a strong majority of Americans but vehemently opposed as destructive of economc freedom and growth by the power elite; (3) by providing more generous health, injury, old-age, and unemployment benefits to those who are otherwise forced to continue working; and (4) by restricting immigration, which decreases the number of people available to do low-wage work in the garment industry, farming, microchip assembly, and other similar business sectors.

Government is absolutely essential to the continuing domination of the United States by the corporate rich. Among many things, it enforces contracts, regulates markets, ensures the integrity of the credit system, controls the money supply, and looks out for the interests of American corporations that invest and sell in other countries. But it is also the greatest danger to control of employees and labor markets by business, and thus to profit margins. The result is vigilance by the corporate rich in the face of new government initiatives and a tendency to overreact with impassioned rhetoric at the slightest hint that government might be aiding ordinary Americans.

► COMMUNITY POWER

Not all power is wielded at the national level. To gain a full picture of who rules in the United States, it is necessary to understand the power structures that exist at the local level and see how they relate to the national power elite. Power at the local level is based on the ownership and control of land and buildings. A community power structure is essentially an aggregation of land-based interests that profit from increasingly intensive use of land. The typical way of intensifying land use is growth, which usually expresses itself in a constantly rising local population. A successful local power structure is able to attract the corporate plants and offices, defense contracts, federal and state buildings, and educational and research establishments that lead to an expanded work force and then to an expansion of retail and other commercial activity, extensive land and housing development, and increased financial activity. Because this chain of events is at the core of every developed locality, power analysts call the local power structure a *growth coalition*.[17]

Growth coalitions are local counterparts to the national power elite and have many interests in common with it. However, there also can be tensions between local and national power structures. For example, if corporations decide that the local business climate has not been made favorable by a growth coalition, they can pull up stakes and leave. There also can be conflicts between rival growth coalitions as they compete for investment from corporations, universities, and government agencies.

Because so many government decisions can affect land values and growth potential, leaders of the growth coalition are prime participants in local government. It is the most overrepresented group on local city councils and is also well represented on planning commissions, zoning boards, water boards, and downtown parking authorities. However, this direct involvement in government is usually not the first or only contact with government for the members of a growth coalition. These individuals often have served on the local chamber of commerce's committees and commissions concerned with growth, planning, roadways, and off-street parking. These committees are the local counterparts of policy-discussion organizations.

A growth coalition does not dominate local government without opposition. There is sometimes conflict between the coalition and specific neighborhoods. Neighborhoods are something to be used and enjoyed in the eyes of those who live in them, but they are sites of further development for the "highest and best use" of the land in the eyes of those who run the growth coalition. This conflict between use value and exchange value is a basic one in cities where the downtown interests try to expand into nearby neighborhoods. Sometimes the neighborhoods win these battles, especially when they are aided by organized environmentalists or supplemented by a university community that can marshal professorial expertise and student votes.

The Weaknesses of the Working Class

In many democratic countries, the *working class*, defined as all white-collar and blue-collar workers who earn a salary or a wage, has more social power than it does in the United States. This power is achieved primarily through labor unions and political parties. It is reflected in more egalitarian wealth and income distributions, a more equitable tax structure, more extensive public health services, and higher old-age and unemployment benefits.

How can the American working class be relatively powerless in a country that prides itself on a history of pluralism and free elections? There are several interacting historical reasons. First, the *primary producers* in the United States—those who work with their hands in factories and fields—are more seriously divided among themselves than is the case in most other countries. The deepest and most important of these divisions is between whites and African Americans. In the beginning, of course, African Americans had no social power because of their enslavement, but even after African Americans gained their freedom, prejudice in the white working class kept the two groups apart.

This black-white split in the working class is reinforced by conflicts between craft workers—also called skilled workers—and industrial workers— also called mass production or unskilled workers. In the late nineteenth century craft workers tried to keep their wages high by opposing the immigration of industrial workers into the country. Their sense of superiority as skilled workers was reinforced by the fact that they were of northern European, Protestant origin whereas the new industrial workers tended to be Catholics and Jews from eastern and southern Europe.[18] Some African Americans, along with other racial minorities, are now in the ranks of the industrial workers as well.

It would be difficult to overcome these longstanding historical divisions even if workers could develop their own political party, but they are unable to do so because of the way the electoral system greatly disadvantages third parties. As a result, workers have no place to go but to the Republicans or Democrats. In the late nineteenth and early twentieth centuries, craft workers sometimes supported the Democrats, while the immigrant industrial workers tended to support the Republicans, and most African Americans could not vote at all. Even when craft and industrial workers moved into the Democratic Party en masse in the 1930s, they could not control the party because of the traditional power of wealthy southern planters and merchants within it, reinforced by the voting alliance with northern Republicans on some issues discussed earlier as the conservative voting bloc.

Nor did workers have much luck organizing themselves through unions. Employers were able to call on the government to defeat organizing drives and strikes through both court injunctions and arrests. Not only did employers have great influence with politicians, but the American tradition of law, based on "laissez-faire," "individualistic," anti-government liberalism, was fiercely opposed to any restraint of trade or interference with private property. It was not until the 1930s that the liberal-labor coalition was able to pass the National Labor Relations Act guaranteeing workers the right to join a union and engage in collective bargaining. This advance was made possible by excluding the southern work force, that is, agricultural and seasonal labor, from coverage by the new laws. Further, the passage of this legislation had only a limited impact because the industrial unions were defeated almost completely in the south and southwest.[19] Unions thrived in a few major industries in the north after World War II, but their power was eroded beginning in the 1970s as the big corporations moved their factories to other countries, introduced labor-saving technology, or lost market share to European and Japanese companies. Corporate lawyers have rendered the National Labor Relations Act harmless to corporations through a series of legislative amendments and successful court cases.[20] Only 10 percent of private-sector workers are still in unions.

Given this history of internal division, political frustration, and union defeat, it is not surprising that American workers continue to accept the highly individualistic ideology that has characterized the United States since its founding. That is, they have not been able to develop the counter organizations that could create and disseminate a more communal, cooperative, and pro-government way of looking at the problems facing average Americans at home, school, and the workplace. This acceptance makes it even more difficult to organize workers around bread-and-butter issues. Therefore, they sometimes vote instead on the basis of social issues, racial resentments, or religious convictions. Those who are deeply religious, opposed to affirmative action, or opposed to gun control, sometimes vote for the avowedly anti-union and anti-government Republican Party.

Thus, it is important not to confuse freedom with social power. Since the 1960s there has been a great expansion in individual rights as a result of the civil rights, feminist, and lesbian-gay movements, but during that time the ratio of a top business executive's pay to a factory worker's pay increased from 41 to 1 to 93 to 1, and some chief executives now make tens of millions of dollars each year while most people's income has been stuck for years in the $20,000 to $50,000 a year range.[21] American workers can say and do what they want within very broad limits and their children can study hard in school and then join the well-off professional class as doctors, lawyers, architects, or engineers. However, most Americans have very little social power if they are not part of the power elite.

▶ CONCLUSION

The differentiation between a national corporate community based on the production of goods and services, on the one hand, and local growth coalitions based on land use, on the other, provides a subtle, less monolithic picture of power in the United States than power analysts painted in the past. At the same time, it shows that government in this country, at whatever level, is mostly dominated by business in one form or another. The liberal-labor coalition at the national level and the neighborhood-environmental-university coalitions at the local level are sometimes able to win delays or modifications on specific policies or projects, but so far they have not been able to alter the terms of the debate, elect very many of their own political representatives, or make either the income or wealth distribution less unequal through higher minimum wages, better benefits packages, and more progressive taxation they consistently advocate.

Whether we look at "who benefits," "who governs," or "who wins" as our power indicator, the power elite and the growth coalitions currently have the preponderance of power in the United States, and all present indications are that they will continue to do so. But power structures are not immutable. They do change, sometimes suddenly or dramatically, as the collapse of the Soviet Union and the transformation of South Africa most recently and dramatically demonstrate, but no one can predict when gradual underlying trends or unexpected breakdowns will lead to new power arrangements. No one predicted the Great Depression of the 1930s and the ensuing set of programs called the New Deal, for example. Nor did anyone predict the activist phase of the Civil Rights Movement in the early 1960s or the subsequent transformation of the Democratic Party in the south, making the entire party potentially open to the influence of the liberal-labor coalition for the first time in American history.

Due to the fall of the Soviet Union, Americans are now less concerned with foreign threats to their way of life. They have seen their incomes stagnate while the rich become even richer. Organized labor has become more involved in politics as it watches its position continue to be undermined. Minority groups, civil rights groups, women's groups, and environmentalists are working more closely with each other than they have for two decades. Whether these trends and changes will lead to a challenge to the power elite through a transformed Democratic Party, and whether such a challenge would have any success, is one of those imponderables that cannot be predicted even after careful study of structural and attitudinal changes by several generations of social scientists.

▶ ENDNOTES

1. Dennis Wrong, *Power: Its Forms, Bases, and Uses*, Chicago, University of Chicago Press, 1979, p. 2.
2. E. Digby Baltzell, *Philadelphia Gentlemen: The Making of a National Upper Class*, New York, The Free Press, 1958; G. William Domhoff, *The Higher Circles*, New York, Random House, 1970; G. William Domhoff, *Who Rules America?*, Mountain View, CA, Mayfield, 1998.
3. Edward Wolff, *Top Heavy*, New York, The New Press, 1996, p. 67.
4. Michael Useem, *The Inner Circle*, New York, Oxford University Press, 1984; Beth Mintz and Michael Schwartz, *The Power Structure of American Business*, Chicago, University of Chicago Press, 1985; Domhoff, *Who Rules America?*, op. cit., chap. 2.
5. Wolff, op. cit., p. 63.
6. Thomas R. Dye, *Who's Running America?*, Englewood Cliffs, NJ, Prentice-Hall, 1995, chap. 6; Useem, op. cit.
7. Dye, op. cit., chap. 9; Domhoff, *Who Rules America?*, op. cit., chap. 4; Harold Salzman and G. William Domhoff, "Nonprofit Organizations and the Corporate Community," *Social Science History* 7:203–216, 1983.
8. Alice O'Connor, "Community Action, Urban Reforms and the Fight Against

Poverty: The Ford Foundation's Gray Areas Program," *Journal of Urban History* 20: 586–626, 1996; Marshall Robinson, "The Ford Foundation: Sowing the Seeds of a Revolution," *Environment* 35: 10–20, 1993.

9. Philip Burch, *Elites in American History,* 3 vols., New York, Holmes and Meier, 1981–82; Beth Mintz, "The President's Cabinet, 1897–1972," *Insurgent Sociologist* 5: 131–148, 1975; Domhoff, *Who Rules America?,* op. cit., chap. 7.

10. Steven Rosenstone, Roy Behr, and Edward Lazarus, *Third Parties in America,* 2nd ed., Princeton, NJ, Princeton University Press, 1996.

11. Dan Clawson, Alan Neustadtl, and Denise Scott, *Money Talks: Corporate PACS and Political Influence,* New York, Basic Books, 1992; Herbert Alexander and Anthony Corrado, *Financing the 1992 Election,* Armonk, NY, M. E. Sharpe, Inc., 1995.

12. David M. Potter, *The South and the Concurrent Majority,* Baton Rouge, Louisiana State University Press, 1972; Mack Shelley, *The Permanent Majority,* Tuscaloosa, The University of Alabama Press, 1983.

13. G. William Domhoff, *The Power Elite and the State,* Hawthorne, NY, Aldine de Gruyter, 1990, chap. 9.

14. Aage Clausen, *How Congressmen Decide,* New York, St. Martin's Press, 1973; Barbara Sinclair, *Congressional Realignment, 1925–1978,* Austin, University of Texas Press, 1982.

15. Keith Poole and Howard Rosenthal, *Congress. A Political-Economic History of Roll Call Voting,* New York, Oxford University Press, 1997, pp. 229–232.

16. James W. Prothro, *The Dollar Decade,* Baton Rouge, Louisiana State University Press, 1954; Leonard Silk and David Vogel, *Ethics and Profits,* New York, Simon & Schuster, 1976.

17. John Logan and Harvey Molotch, *Urban Fortunes,* Berkeley, University of California Press, 1987.

18. Gwendolyn Mink, *Old Labor and New Immigrants in American Political Development, 1870–1925,* Ithaca, NY, Cornell University Press, 1986.

19. Michael Goldfield, *The Decline of Organized Labor in the United States,* Chicago, University of Chicago Press, 1987; Domhoff, *The Power Elite and the State,* op. cit., chap. 4.

20. James Gross, *Broken Promise: The Subversion of U.S. Labor Relations Policy, 1947–1994,* Philadelphia, Temple University Press, 1995.

21. Lawrence Mishel and Jared Bernstein, *The State of Working America, 1994–95,* Armonk, NY, M. E. Sharpe, Inc., 1994.

MODULE 28 | Poverty and Social Mobility

Approximately one out of every nine people in the United States lives below the poverty line established by the federal government. In 2007, no fewer than 37.2 million people were living in poverty. The economic boom of the 1990s passed these people by. A Bureau of the Census report shows that one in five households has trouble meeting basic needs, from paying the utility bills to buying dinner (Bauman 1999; DeNavas-Walt et al. 2009).

One contributor to the United States' high poverty rate has been the large number of workers employed at minimum wage. The federal government has raised the minimum wage over the past half century from 75 cents in 1950 to $6.55 in 2008 and $7.25 in 2009. But in terms of its real value adjusted for inflation, the minimum wage has frequently failed to keep pace with the cost of living.

Moreover, raising the minimum wage does not remedy other difficulties that low-wage workers encounter. A 2009 survey of workers in various low-wage occupations, such as apparel manufacturing, child care (see Module 15), and discount retailing, showed that these workers lose about 15 percent of the pay that is due them through employers' wage violations. Typically, employers limit workers' wages by pressuring them not to file for workers' compensation after on-the-job injuries, requiring them to work off the clock, and paying the straight hourly wage rate for overtime hours. Women are far more likely than men to be cheated in this way (Bernhardt et al. 2009).

Sociologists have long had an interest in the impact of substandard work on society, beginning with the writings of Karl Marx, Émile Durkheim, and Max Weber. Their interest increased with the global economic decline that began in 2008, which trapped many people in jobs they did not want or left them unemployed. The Research Today box considers recent sociological work on *precarious work*.

In this section, we'll consider just how social scientists define *poverty*. We'll also take a closer look at the people who fall into that category—including the working poor.

Studying Poverty

The efforts of sociologists and other social scientists to better understand poverty are complicated by the difficulty of defining it. This problem is evident even in government programs that conceive of poverty in either absolute or relative terms. **Absolute poverty** refers to a minimum level of subsistence that no family should be expected to live below.

One commonly used measure of absolute poverty is the federal government's *poverty line,* a money income figure that is adjusted annually to reflect the consumption requirements of families based on their size and composition. The poverty line serves as an official definition of which people are poor. In 2008, for example, any family of four (two adults and two children) with a combined income of $21,834 or less fell below the poverty line. This definition determines which individuals and families will be eligible for certain government benefits (DeNavas-Walt et al. 2009:43).

Although by absolute standards, poverty has declined in the United States, it remains higher than in many other industrial nations. As Figure 28-1 shows, a comparatively high proportion of U.S. households are poor, meaning that they are unable to purchase basic consumer goods. If anything, this cross-national comparison understates the extent of poverty in the United States, since U.S. residents are likely to pay more for housing, health care, child care, and education than residents of other countries, where such expenses are often subsidized (Smeeding 2008).

In contrast, **relative poverty** is a floating standard of deprivation by which people at the bottom of a society, whatever their lifestyles, are judged to be disadvantaged *in comparison with the nation as a whole.* Therefore, even if the poor of 2005 are better off in absolute terms than the poor of the 1930s or 1960s, they are still seen as deserving of special assistance. The Sociology in the Global Community box explores the difference between relative poverty in Appalachia and relative affluence in the Congo.

Debate has been growing over the accuracy of the federal government's measure of poverty, which has remained largely unchanged since 1963. If noncash benefits such as Medicare, Medicaid, tax credits, food stamps, public housing, and health care and other employer-provided fringe benefits were included, the reported poverty rate would be lower. On the other hand, if out-of-pocket medical expenses and mandatory work expenses for transportation and child care were included, the poverty rate would be higher. Although the current poverty measure does consider family size, it does not consider a household's location, whether in a relatively expensive city like New York or in a less expensive rural area. Nor does it consider whether a householder pays rent or a mortgage installment, lives at home or with someone else. To address some of these shortcomings, in 2010 the federal government launched a second statistic called the Supplemental Poverty Measure (SPM), which will be used to estimate economic hardship. The SPM is a relative poverty measure that is based on a broad range of changing household resources and expenses. It will be calculated beginning in late

FIGURE 28-1   **Poverty in Selected Countries**

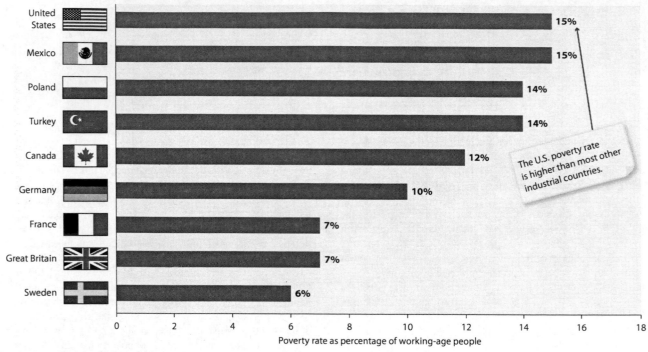

Note: Data are averages for mid-2000s, as reported in 2009. Poverty threshold is 50 percent of a nation's median household income.
Source: Organisation for Economic Co-operation and Development 2009a.

 Sociology in the Global Community

It's All Relative: Appalachian Poverty and Congolese Affluence

What does it mean to be well off? To be poor? To explore this question, the editors of the London-based publication *The Economist* compared the situations of two men living very different lives: an unemployed truck driver in the Appalachian Mountains and a physician in Congo.

Enos Banks makes his home in a forgotten pocket of rural poverty, described over 40 years ago in Michael Harrington's *The Other America*. Banks once worked for a coal-mining company, but a heart attack forced him to quit

> By U.S. standards, Kabamba's four-bedroom home, spacious compared to Banks's trailer, is overcrowded with 12 inhabitants.

his job. In his 60s, he lives in a trailer and gets by on a little more than $500 a month in supplemental security income (SSI). Because he owns a truck, he is not eligible for food stamps.

On the other side of the world, in the Democratic Republic of Congo, Mbwebwe Kabamba earns about $100 or $200 more per month than Enos Banks. Kabamba is a surgeon and head of the emergency room at a hospital in Kinshasa, the country's capital. His hospital salary is only $250 a month, but he supplements it by performing surgery on the side. In Congo, a similar income to that which impoverishes Enos Banks places Kabamba near the middle of his society's income distribution.

Though Kabamba may seem better off than Banks, especially given the Congo's lower cost of living, such is not the case. Kabamba supports a family of 12, while Banks supports only himself. By U.S. standards, Kabamba's four-bedroom home, spacious compared to Banks's trailer, is overcrowded with 12 inhabitants. And though Kabamba's home has a kitchen, it lacks running water, dependable electric service, and air-conditioning—services most Americans take for granted. Considered wealthy in his own country, Kabamba is worse off than a poor person in the United States.

Nevertheless, Banks's poverty is real; he occupies a position in the lowest quintile (see

Figure 27-1). In absolute terms defined by his own society, Kabamba is not poor, even though he is less well off than Enos Banks. Relative to most of the world's population, however, both men are doing well.

LET'S DISCUSS

1. Have you ever lived in or traveled to a foreign country where income and living standards were very different from those in the United States? If so, did the contrast give you a new perspective on poverty? What differences between the living standards in the two societies stand out in your mind?

2. If absolute measures of poverty, such as household income, are inconsistent from one country to the next, what other measures might give a clearer picture of people's relative well-being? Should the poverty level be the same everywhere in the world? Why or why not?

Sources: The Economist 2005f; Harrington 1962; Haub 2008.

Research Today

Precarious Work

In 2008 Jim Marshall, age 39, lost his job in Detroit's faltering auto industry. Figuring that job prospects had to be better elsewhere, he moved to Florida. But by May 2009 Jim was homeless, living in a tent city just north of St. Petersburg. "My parents always taught me to work hard in school, graduate high school, go to college, get a degree and you'll do fine. You'll do better than your parents' generation," Marshall says. "I did all those things. . . . For a while, I did have that good life, but nowadays that's not the reality" (Bazar 2009:A2).

Jim's story is all too common. He is one of the millions of Americans who have been reduced to doing **precarious work**—employment that is poorly paid and, from the worker's perspective, insecure and unprotected. People who engage in precarious work often cannot support a household, and they are vulnerable to falling into poverty.

Even before economists recognized the economic downturn in 2009, there was ample statistical evidence that precarious work was increasing, despite the fact that the unemployment rate remained steady. In his presidential address to the ASA, Arne L. Kalleberg offered the following five social indicators:

1. *A decline in the average length of time workers remain with an employer.* This trend has been especially noticeable among older White men, who in the past were protected by employers.

2. *An increase in long-term unemployment.* The proportion of workers who remained unemployed after six months rose in the 2000s, when the number of manufacturing jobs shrank and fewer new jobs were created.

3. *A decrease in job security.* Given the increase in long-term unemployment and the decrease in average time spent with an employer, workers became increasingly insecure about their ability to replace a lost job.

> To meet cyclical fluctuations in supply and demand, employers have turned more and more to nontraditional labor sources. Today, virtually any job can be outsourced, including accounting, legal, and military services.

4. *An increase in outsourcing and temporary work.* To meet cyclical fluctuations in supply and demand, employers have turned more and more to nontraditional labor sources. Today, virtually any job can be outsourced, including accounting, legal, and military services.

5. *A shift in risk from employers to employees.* Few companies offer traditional pensions anymore. Employees are being asked to shoulder at least part of the cost and risk, not only of their retirement investments, but of their health insurance plans.

Although precarious work is becoming more common, people differ in their vulnerability to it. Members of racial and ethnic minorities are more likely than others to be engaged in precarious work. Immigrants, including those who are in the United States legally, are also more likely than others to be precariously employed. Around the world—in the United States, other industrial countries, and developing nations—women are much more likely than men to do precarious work.

What can be done to revitalize labor markets so that fewer workers end up doing substandard work—or at least, that those who do will suffer less from it? Denmark is one country that has tried to deal with the problem. Although the government there cannot make jobs more secure, it does provide significant assistance to the unemployed. Help finding a job, significant income compensation (90 percent of a worker's previous wage for one year, without conditions), and subsidized education and training are all available to Danish workers who have lost their jobs.

LET'S DISCUSS

1. Has the trend toward increasing reliance on precarious work touched your family or friends? Has anyone you know been unemployed longer than six months? If so, did that person or persons belong to one or more of the groups that are particularly vulnerable to precarious work?

2. Looking forward to your own career, can you think of a strategy for avoiding precarious work, frequent job loss, and long-term unemployment?

Sources: Bazar 2009; Fudge and Owens 2006; Kalleberg 2009; McDowell et al. 2009; Somavia 2008; Westergaard-Nielsen 2008.

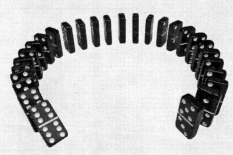

2011, but will not replace the poverty line in determining a household's eligibility for benefits (Blank 2008; Department of Commerce 2010).

Who Are the Poor?

Not only does the category of the poor defy any simple definition; it counters the common stereotypes about "poor people." For example, many people in the United States believe that the vast majority of the poor are able to work but will not. Yet many poor adults do work outside the home, although only a small portion of them work full-time throughout the year. In 2008, about 27 percent of all poor working adults worked full-time, compared to 66 percent of all adults. Of those poor adults who do not work, most are ill or disabled, or are occupied in maintaining a home (DeNavas-Walt et al. 2009:14).

Though many of the poor live in urban slums, a majority live outside those poverty-stricken areas. Poverty is no stranger in rural areas, from Appalachia to hard-hit farming regions to Native American reservations. Table 28-1 provides additional statistical information regarding low-income people in the United States.

Table 28-1   Who Are the Poor in the United States?

Group	Percentage of the Population of the United States	Percentage of the Poor of the United States
Age		
Under 18 years old	25%	35%
18 to 64 years old	62	56
65 years and older	13	9
Race-Ethnicity		
Whites (non-Hispanic)	65	43
Blacks	13	24
Hispanics	16	28
Asians and Pacific Islanders	4	4
Family Composition		
Married couples with male householders	75	40
Female householders	18	51

Source: Data for 2008, as reported by the Bureau of the Census; DeNavas-Walt et al. 2009:14.

Feminization of Poverty

Since World War II, an increasing proportion of the poor people of the United States have been women, many of whom are divorced or never-married mothers. In 1959, female householders accounted for 26 percent of the nation's poor; by 2008, that figure had risen to 51 percent (see Table 28-1). This alarming trend, known as the **feminization of poverty,** is evident not just in the United States but around the world.

About half of all women living in poverty in the United States are in transition, coping with an economic crisis caused by the departure, disability, or death of a husband. The other half tend to be economically dependent either on the welfare system or on friends and relatives living nearby. A major factor in the feminization of poverty has been the increase in families with women as single heads of the household (see Module 40). Conflict theorists and other observers trace the higher rates of poverty among women to three distinct factors: the difficulty in finding affordable child care, sexual harassment, and sex discrimination in the labor market.

The Underclass

In 2008, 43 percent of poor people in the United States were living in central cities. These highly visible urban residents are the focus of most government efforts to alleviate poverty. Yet according to many observers, the plight of the urban poor is growing worse, owing to the devastating interplay of inadequate education and limited employment prospects. Traditional employment opportunities in the industrial sector are largely closed to the unskilled poor. Past and present discrimination heightens these problems for those

low-income urban residents who are Black or Hispanic (DeNavas-Walt et al. 2009:14).

Along with other social scientists, sociologist William Julius Wilson (1980, 1987, 1996) and his colleagues (2004) have used the term **underclass** to describe the long-term poor who lack training and skills. According to an analysis of Census 2000 data, 7.9 million people live in high-poverty neighborhoods. About 30 percent of the population in these neighborhoods is Black, 29 percent Hispanic, and 24 percent White. In central cities, about 49 percent of the underclass is Black, 29 percent Hispanic, 17 percent White, and 5 percent "other" (Jargowsky and Yang 2006; O'Hare and Curry-White 1992).

Conflict theorists, among others, have expressed alarm at the portion of the nation's population living on this lower rung of the stratification ladder, and at society's reluctance to address the lack of economic opportunities for these people. Often, portraits of the underclass seem to blame the victims for their plight, while ignoring the other factors that push people into poverty.

Analyses of the poor in general reveal that they are not a static social class. The overall composition of the poor changes continually, because some individuals and families near the top edge of poverty move above the poverty level after a year or two, while others slip below it. Still, hundreds of thousands of people remain in poverty for many years at a time. Blacks and Latinos are more likely than Whites to be persistently poor. Both Latinos and Blacks are less likely than Whites to leave the welfare rolls as a result of welfare reform, discussed in the Social Policy section of this module (Jäntii 2009).

Explaining Poverty

Why is it that poverty pervades a nation of such vast wealth? Sociologist Herbert Gans (1995), who has applied functionalist analysis to the existence of poverty, argues that various segments of society actually *benefit* from the existence of the poor. Gans has identified a number of social, economic, and political functions that the poor perform for society:

- The presence of poor people means that society's dirty work—physically dirty or dangerous, dead-end and underpaid, undignified and menial jobs—will be performed at low cost.
- Poverty creates jobs for occupations and professions that serve the poor. It creates both legal employment (public health experts, welfare caseworkers) and illegal jobs (drug dealers, numbers runners).

Even if this single parent works her way up the chain of command, supporting her family will still be difficult.

- The identification and punishment of the poor as deviants upholds the legitimacy of conventional social norms and mainstream values regarding hard work, thrift, and honesty.

- Within a relatively hierarchical society, the existence of poor people guarantees the higher status of the rich. As psychologist William Ryan (1976) noted, affluent people may justify inequality (and gain a measure of satisfaction) by *blaming the victims* of poverty for their disadvantaged condition.

- Because of their lack of political power, the poor often absorb the costs of social change. Under the policy of deinstitutionalization, mental patients released from long-term hospitals have been transferred primarily to low-income communities and neighborhoods. Similarly, halfway houses for rehabilitated drug abusers, rejected by more affluent communities, often end up in poorer neighborhoods.

In Gans's view, then, poverty and the poor actually satisfy positive functions for many nonpoor groups in the United States.

● Life Chances

Max Weber saw class as being closely related to people's **life chances**—that is, their opportunities to provide themselves with material goods, positive living conditions, and favorable life experiences (Gerth and Mills 1958). Life chances are reflected in measures such as housing, education, and health. Occupying a higher social class in a society improves your life chances and brings greater access to social rewards. In contrast, people in the lower social classes are forced to devote a larger proportion of their limited resources to the necessities of life.

In times of danger, the affluent and powerful have a better chance of surviving than people of ordinary means. When the supposedly unsinkable British ocean liner *Titanic* hit an iceberg in 1912, it was not carrying enough lifeboats to accommodate all passengers. Plans had been made to evacuate only first- and second-class passengers. About 62 percent of the first-class passengers survived the disaster. Despite a rule that women and children would go first, about a third of those passengers were male. In contrast, only 25 percent of the third-class passengers survived. The first attempt to alert them to the need to abandon ship came well after other passengers had been notified (D. Butler 1998; Crouse 1999; Riding 1998).

Class position also affects people's vulnerability to natural disasters. When Hurricane Katrina hit the Gulf Coast of the United States in 2005, affluent and poor people alike became its victims. However, poor people who did not own automobiles (100,000 of them in New Orleans alone) were less able than others to evacuate in advance of the storm. The poor who survived its fury had no nest egg to draw on, and thus were more likely than others to accept relocation wherever social service agencies could place them—sometimes hundreds or thousands of miles from home. Those who were able to return are still dealing with the toxic debris left behind (Bullard and Wright 2009).

Class position affects people's vulnerability to natural disasters. Today, years after Hurricane Katrina forced the evacuation of New Orleans, many of the city's poor still have not returned home.

Some people have hoped that the Internet revolution would help to level the playing field by making information and markets uniformly available. Unfortunately, however, not everyone can get onto the information superhighway, so yet another aspect of social inequality has emerged—the **digital divide**. The poor, minorities, and those who live in rural communities and inner cities are not getting connected at home or at work. A recent government study found that despite falling computer prices, the Internet gap between the haves and have-nots has not narrowed. Although 74 percent of all people in the United States used the Internet in 2009, that group included 94 percent of people with incomes over $75,000 but 60 percent of people with incomes of less than $30,000. As wealthier people switch to high-speed Internet connections, they will be able to take advantage of even more sophisticated interactive services, and the digital divide will grow even wider (Pew Internet Project 2010).

Wealth, status, and power may not ensure happiness, but they certainly provide additional ways of coping with problems and disappointments. For this reason, the opportunity for advancement—for social mobility—is of special significance to those on the bottom of society. Most people want the rewards and privileges that are granted to high-ranking members of a culture. What can society do to increase their social mobility? One strategy is to offer financial aid to college students from low-income families, on the theory that education lifts people out of poverty. Yet such programs are not having as great an effect as their authors once hoped (the Sociology on Campus box).

 use your **sociological imagination**

Imagine a society in which there are no social classes—no differences in people's wealth, income, and life chances. What would such a society be like? Would it be stable, or would its social structure change over time?

Sociology on Campus

Social Class and Financial Aid

Today's young people have been dubbed Generation Y, but a more appropriate name for them could be Generation Debt. Every year, millions of prospective college students and their parents struggle through the intricate and time-consuming process of applying for financial aid. Originally, financial aid programs were intended to level the playing field—to allow qualified students from all walks of life to attend college, regardless of the cost. But have these programs fulfilled their promise?

In 2004, 40 percent of first-year students at major state universities came from families with incomes of more than $100,000 a year. In other words, close to half of all students

> Statistics that show the educational level in the United States rising overall obscure the widening gap between the advantaged and the less advantaged.

came from high-income families. This statistic should not be surprising, given the high cost of tuition, room, and board at state universities. For students from families with the lowest incomes, the cost can be prohibitive. Only 11 percent of children from the poorest families in the United States have earned college degrees, compared to 53 percent of children from families in the top fifth of the population. Those moderate-income students who do graduate, and even those who fail to complete their degrees, are often saddled with heavy postgraduate debt.

Community colleges, with their low tuition, are often regarded as a hedge against the high costs of higher education. Although these two-year commuter colleges may be cheaper than four-year residential schools, they are not inexpensive. In the academic year 2009–2010, the annual cost of attending community college was more than $14,000. For students at these schools, a greater proportion of their expenses goes to transportation and child care than for students who live on campus at four-year schools.

Besides the spiraling cost of an education, the widespread difficulty in paying for college stems from three trends. First, over the past few decades, colleges and universities have been moving away from making outright grants, such as scholarships, to deserving students, and toward low-interest student loans. Second, much of the assistance schools offer in the form of loans is not based strictly on need. Third, interest rates on federally guaranteed loans have risen steadily, increasing the burden of repayment.

These trends in financial aid for higher education are closely tied to trends in social inequality. As noted in Modules 27, over the past half century, rather than declining, inequality in income and wealth has actually increased. According to one analysis of U.S. economic trends over the past 30 years, this increase in wealth and income inequality has contributed to a modest increase in educational inequality, as measured by the number of years of formal schooling students achieve. In a variation on the truism that the rich tend to get richer while the poor get poorer, the rich are getting better educations and the poor are getting poorer educations. Statistics

PUMP & CIRCUMSTANCE.

that show the educational level in the United States rising overall obscure the widening gap between the advantaged and the less advantaged.

LET'S DISCUSS

1. How important is financial aid (grants, loans, work-study income) to you and your friends? Without these types of aid, would you be able to cover your college expenses?

2. Aside from a reduction in individual social mobility, what might be the long-term effects of the shortage of need-based financial aid? Relate your answer to the trend toward globalization.

Sources: Boushey 2005; Campbell et al. 2005; College Board 2009; Isaacs et al. 2008; Kamenetz 2006; Leonhardt 2004; Michals 2003; Trumbull 2006.

Social Mobility

In the movie *Maid in Manhattan*, Jennifer Lopez plays the lead in a modern-day Cinderella story, rising from the lowly status of chambermaid in a big-city hotel to a company supervisor and the girlfriend of a well-to-do politician. The ascent of a person from a poor background to a position of prestige, power, or financial reward is an example of social mobility. Formally defined, the term **social mobility** refers to the movement of individuals or groups from one position in a society's stratification system to another. But how significant—how frequent, how dramatic—is mobility in a class society such as the United States?

Open versus Closed Stratification Systems

Sociologists use the terms *open stratification system* and *closed stratification system* to indicate the degree of social mobility in a society. An **open system** implies that the position of each individual is influenced by his or her *achieved* status. Such a system encourages competition among members of society. The United States is moving toward this ideal type as the government attempts to reduce the barriers faced by women, racial and ethnic minorities, and people born in lower social classes. Even in the midst of the economic downturn of 2008–2009, nearly 80 percent of people in the United States felt they could get ahead (Economic Mobility Project 2009).

At the other extreme of social mobility is the **closed system,** which allows little or no possibility of individual social mobility. The slavery and caste systems of stratification are examples of closed systems. In such societies, social placement is based on *ascribed* statuses, such as race or family background, which cannot be changed.

Types of Social Mobility

An airline pilot who becomes a police officer moves from one social position to another of the same rank. Each occupation has the same prestige ranking: 60 on a scale ranging from a low of 0 to a high of 100 (see Table 27-1). Sociologists call this kind of movement **horizontal mobility.** However, if the pilot were to become a lawyer (prestige ranking of 75), he or she would experience **vertical mobility,** the movement of an individual from one social position to another of a different rank. Vertical mobility can also involve moving *downward* in a society's stratification system, as would be the case if the airline pilot became a bank teller (ranking of 43). Pitirim Sorokin ([1927] 1959) was the first sociologist to distinguish between horizontal and vertical mobility. Most sociological analysis, however, focuses on vertical rather than horizontal mobility.

One way of examining vertical social mobility is to contrast its two types, intergenerational and intragenerational mobility. **Intergenerational mobility** involves changes in the social position of children relative to their parents. Thus, a plumber whose father was a physician provides an example of downward intergenerational mobility. A film star whose parents were both factory workers illustrates upward intergenerational mobility. Because education contributes significantly to upward mobility, any barrier to the pursuit of advanced degrees can definitely limit intergenerational mobility (see the Sociology on Campus box; Isaacs 2007a; Isaacs et al. 2008; Sawhill and Morton 2007).

Figure 28-2 shows intergenerational mobility based on income. In 1978–1980, a national survey looked at the family income of 6,000 young people. Two decades later, in 1997–2003, researchers followed up on those young adults and their income. The results showed a strong stickiness in both the bottom and top quintiles, or fifths, of the income distribution. Just over 33 percent of those whose parents were in the bottom quintile and 37 percent of those who were in the top quintile remained in the same quintile as adults. Yet the study also showed mobility: almost 66 percent of those in the bottom quintile moved up, and over 60 percent of those at the top experienced downward mobility.

Among men born in the 1960s, this consistent intergenerational mobility resulted largely from economic growth. On average, these men earned more than their fathers did at the same age; their family incomes improved as well. However, the trend did not continue into the next generation. Currently, young men are earning less than their fathers did at the same age—about 12 percent less. Family incomes are slightly higher than in the

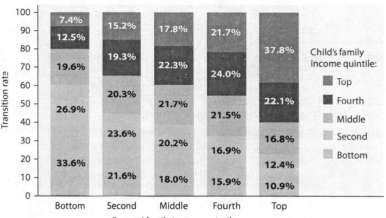

FIGURE 28-2   Intergenerational Income Mobility

Child's family income quintile:
- Top
- Fourth
- Middle
- Second
- Bottom

Source: Mazumder 2008:10.
Over a 25-year period, adult children often end up in the same income bracket as their parents. About 7 percent of those who begin in the bottom quintile reach the top quintile as adults; their story is one of rags to riches. About 11 percent of those who start in the top quintile fall to the bottom.

last generation, but only because women have moved into the paid labor force to supplement their husbands' earnings. With so few women left to join the labor force, most families will need to increase their wages to raise their incomes further (Sawhill and Haskins 2009).

Intragenerational mobility involves changes in social position within a person's adult life. A woman who begins work as a teacher's aide and eventually becomes superintendent of the school district experiences upward intragenerational mobility. A man who becomes a taxicab driver after his accounting firm goes bankrupt undergoes downward intragenerational mobility.

Social Mobility in the United States

The belief in upward mobility is an important value in our society. Does that mean that the United States is indeed the land of opportunity? Not unless such ascriptive characteristics as race, gender, and family background have ceased to be significant in determining one's future prospects. We can see the impact of these factors in the occupational structure.

Occupational Mobility   Two sociological studies conducted a decade apart offer insight into the degree of mobility in the nation's occupational structure (Blau and Duncan 1967; Featherman and Hauser 1978). Taken together, these investigations lead to several noteworthy conclusions. First, occupational mobility (both intergenerational and intragenerational) has been common among males. Approximately 60 to 70 percent of sons are employed in higher-ranked occupations than their fathers.

Second, although there is a great deal of mobility in the United States, much of it is minor. That is, people who reach an occupational level above or below that of their parents usually advance or fall back only one or two out of a possible eight occupational levels. Thus, the child of a laborer may become an artisan or a technician, but he or she is less likely to become a manager or professional. The odds against reaching the top are extremely high unless one begins from a relatively privileged position.

The Impact of Education   Another conclusion of both studies is that education plays a critical role in social mobility. The impact of formal schooling on adult status is even greater than that of family background (although as we have seen, family background influences the likelihood that one will receive higher education). Furthermore, education represents an important means of intergenerational mobility. A person who was born into a poor family but who graduates from college has a one in five chance of entering the top fifth of all income earners as an adult (Isaacs et al. 2008).

The impact of education on mobility has diminished somewhat in the past decade, however. An undergraduate degree—a BA or a BS—serves less as a guarantee of upward mobility now than it did in the past, simply because more and more entrants into the job market hold such a degree. Moreover, intergenerational mobility is declining, since there is no longer such a stark difference between generations. In earlier decades, many high school–educated parents successfully sent their children to college, but today's college students are increasingly likely to have college-educated parents (Sawhill and Morton 2007).

The Impact of Race and Ethnicity   Sociologists have long documented the fact that the class system is more rigid for African Americans than it is for members of other racial groups. African American men who have good jobs, for example, are less likely than White men to see their adult children attain the same status. The cumulative disadvantage of discrimination plays a significant role in the disparity between the two groups' experiences. Compared to White households, the relatively modest wealth of African American households means that adult African

Andrea Jung, chairman and chief executive officer of Avon Corporation since 1999, is one of the few women in the United States who have risen to the top of the corporate hierarchy. In 2008, Jung was elected to Apple's board of directors. Despite the passage of equal opportunity laws, occupational barriers still limit most women's social mobility.

If this lawyer were the son of a car mechanic, his rise to the upper-middle class would illustrate intergenerational mobility. If he had begun as a paralegal and worked his way up the occupational ladder, his career would illustrate intragenerational mobility.

American children are less likely than adult White children to receive financial support from their parents. Indeed, young African American couples are much more likely than young White couples to be assisting their parents—a sacrifice that hampers their social mobility (Favreault 2008).

Not surprisingly, African Americans are more likely than Whites to experience downward intergenerational mobility, and less likely to move up the social ladder. A study of the income data for people born between 1955 and 1970 shows that four in five Black children who began in the top quintile experienced downward mobility, compared to just two in five White children. Similarly, three in five White children who began in the bottom two quintiles experienced upward social mobility, compared to one in four Black children (Sharkey 2009).

The African American middle class has grown over the past few decades, due to economic expansion and the benefits of the civil rights movement of the 1960s. Yet many of these middle-class households have little savings, a fact that puts them in danger during times of crisis. We noted earlier that recession hits Black and Latino households harder than White households. Studies have consistently shown that downward mobility is significantly higher for Blacks than it is for Whites (Conley 2010; Oliver and Shapiro 2006, 2008; Sernau 2001; W. Wilson 1996).

The Latino population is not doing much better. The typical Hispanic has less than 10 percent of the wealth that a White person has. A 2008 study suggests that in recent years, Latinos have even lost ground. Their continuing immigration accounts for part of the disparity: most of the new arrivals are destitute. But even the wealthiest 5 percent of Latino households have only a third as much net worth as the top 5 percent of White households (Kochhar 2008).

The Impact of Gender   Studies of mobility, even more than those of class, have traditionally ignored the significance of gender, but some research findings are now available that explore the relationship between gender and mobility.

Women's employment opportunities are much more limited than men's (as Module 35 will show). Moreover, according to recent research, women whose skills far exceed the jobs offered them are more likely than men to withdraw entirely from the paid labor force. Their withdrawal violates an assumption common to traditional mobility studies: that most people will aspire to upward mobility and seek to make the most of their opportunities.

In contrast to men, women have a rather large range of clerical occupations open to them. But the modest salary ranges and few prospects for advancement in many of these positions limit the possibility of upward mobility. Self-employment as shopkeepers, entrepreneurs, independent professionals, and the like—an important road to upward mobility for men—is more difficult for women, who find it harder to secure the necessary financing. Although sons commonly follow in the footsteps of their fathers, women are unlikely to move into their fathers' positions. Consequently, gender remains an important factor in shaping social mobility. Women in the United States (and in other parts of the world) are especially likely to be trapped in poverty, unable to rise out of their low-income status (Beller 2009; Heilman 2001).

On the positive side, though today's women lag behind men in employment, their earnings have increased faster than their mothers' did at a comparable age, so that their incomes are substantially higher. The one glaring exception to this trend is the daughters of low-income parents. Because these women typically care for children—many as single parents—and sometimes for other relatives as well, their mobility is severely restricted (Isaacs 2007b).

social policy and Stratification

Rethinking Welfare in North America and Europe

In Pasadena, Denise Sims-Bowles, who has been out of work for more than two years, has sent 273 resumes to prospective employers. A victim of the deep economic recession that followed the stock market crash of 2008, she has more than two decades of experience as a white-collar worker, yet she cannot find an opening. She is not alone. At the end of 2009, about 40 percent of the nation's unemployed had been out of work for half a year or more.

In Tokyo, Atsushi Nakanishi lives in a coffin-sized cubicle that he rented after he lost his job. He, too, is not alone. When the global economic crisis hit Japan in 2009, millions of workers lost their jobs; many became homeless. To contain political unrest, the government has opened emergency shelters to house jobless workers.

In Middlebury, Indiana, Scott and Kelly Nichols confront a hard reality. Scott, once a well-paid blue-collar worker, and Kelly, an office clerk, have been out of work since the recreational vehicle industry collapsed, hit by high gas prices and tight credit. Now, nine months later, the Nichols can no longer afford the rent. They will move in with Kelly's mother, in her basement (Scherer 2010a; Schwartzman 2009; Tabuchi 2010).

These are the faces of people living on the edge—including women with children who are seeking to make a go of it amid changing social policies. Governments in all parts of the world are searching for the right solution to welfare: How much subsidy should they provide? How much responsibility should fall on the shoulders of the poor?

Understanding the Issue

In the 1990s, an intense debate took place in the United States over the issue of welfare. Welfare programs were costly, and concern was widespread (however unfounded) that welfare payments discouraged recipients from seeking jobs. Both Democrats and Republicans vowed to "end welfare as we know it."

In late 1996, in a historic shift in federal policy, Congress passed the Personal Responsibility and Work Opportunity

(continued)

Reconciliation Act, ending the long-standing federal guarantee of assistance to every poor family that meets eligibility requirements. The law set a lifetime limit of five years of welfare benefits, and required all able-bodied adults to work after receiving two years of benefits (although hardship exceptions were allowed). The federal government would give block grants to the states to use as they wished in assisting poor and needy residents, and it would permit states to experiment with ways to move people off welfare (Seccombe 2011).

A decade later, however, the severe economic downturn of 2008–2009 forced many more people into this shrunken safety net. By 2009, over 16 percent of all personal income in the United States was coming from Social Security, food stamps, and unemployment insurance. That was the highest percentage since the government began compiling such data in 1929. In the 1960s, the proportion of income coming from these sources was less than 8 percent (Bureau of Economic Analysis 2009).

Despite this increase in dependency, reliance on the government safety net still falls far short of that in Europe, even after recent cutbacks there. Available data indicate that in Great Britain, 87 percent of health expenditures are paid for by the government; in Sweden, 82 percent; in Canada, 70 percent; but in the United States, only 46 percent. In fact, most industrialized nations devote higher proportions of their expenditures to housing, social security, welfare, health care, and unemployment compensation than the United States does. As U.S. economist Dean Baker declared recently, "The increase in social spending is still relatively modest given the severity of the downturn. We're not France" (Cauchon 2009; World Bank 2009:98–100).

Applying Sociology

Many sociologists tend to view the debate over welfare reform in industrialized nations from a conflict perspective: the "haves" in positions of policymaking listen to the interests of other "haves," while the cries of the "have-nots" are drowned out. Critics of welfare reform believe that the nation's economic problems are unfairly blamed on welfare spending and the poor. From a conflict perspective, this backlash against welfare recipients reflects deep fears and hostility toward the nation's urban, predominantly African American and Hispanic underclass.

Those who are critical of the backlash note that "welfare scapegoating" conveniently ignores the lucrative federal handouts that go to *affluent* individuals and families. For example, while federal housing aid to the poor was cut drastically in the 1980s, tax deductions for mortgage interest and property taxes more than doubled.

Conflict theorists have noted an oft-ignored aspect of the welfare system, administrative sanctions. The law allows administrators to end welfare payments if clients fail to complete job-readiness classes, community work, or job searches. A great deal of discretion is used in applying sanctions. According to a recent study, Black clients are more likely to be sanctioned than White clients (Schram et al. 2009).

Those who take a conflict perspective also urge policymakers and the general public to look closely at **corporate welfare**—the tax breaks, bailouts, direct payments, and grants that the government gives to corporations—rather than looking closely at the comparatively small allowances being given to welfare mothers and their children. Yet any suggestion to curtail such corporate welfare brings a strong response from special-interest groups that are much more powerful than any coalition on behalf of the poor. One example of corporate welfare is the huge federal bailouts of distressed financial

In the deep economic recession that began in 2008, recent college graduates faced the most difficult job market of all. This young man vents his anger against the billion-dollar corporate bailouts that were supposed to get people back to work.

institutions in fall 2008 and of bankrupt automobile companies in 2009. Although the layout of hundreds of billions of dollars was vital to the nation's economic recovery, the measure received relatively little scrutiny from Congress. Just a few months later, however, when legislation was proposed to extend the safety net for laid-off workers—unemployment compensation, food stamps, subsidized child care, assistance to the homeless, disability support, and infant nutrition—it met with loud demands for the monitoring of expenditures (DeParle 2009; Piven and Cloward 1996).

Initiating Policy

The government likes to highlight welfare reform success stories. Though many people who once depended on tax dollars are now working and paying taxes themselves, it is much too soon to see if "workfare" will be successful. The new jobs that were generated by the booming economy of the late 1990s were an unrealistic test of the system. Prospects have faded for the hard-core jobless—people who are difficult to train or are encumbered by drug or alcohol abuse, physical disabilities, or child care needs—since the boom passed and the economy moved into recession (Jencks et al. 2006; M. Turner et al. 2007).

True, fewer people remain on the rolls since welfare reform was enacted in August 1996. By September 2009 just over 1.7 million families were still on the rolls, down 65 percent from a high of 5.1 million in 1994. But while those families that have left the rolls are modestly better off now, most of their breadwinners continue to hold low-paying, unskilled jobs. For them, the economic downturn that was well in place by 2009 made finding work tougher than ever. Of those adults who remain on welfare, nearly 60 percent are not in school or in welfare-to-work programs, as the law requires them to be. This group tends to face the greatest challenges—substance abuse, mental illness, or a criminal record. Finally, while the welfare rolls have declined, the number of people who receive Medicaid and food stamps has increased by 50 percent since 2000 (Health and Human Services Department 2010b; Handler 2009; R. Wolf 2006).

European governments have encountered many of the same citizen demands as in North America: keep our taxes low, even if it means reducing services to the poor. However, nations in eastern and central Europe have faced a special challenge since the end of communism. Though governments in those nations traditionally provided an impressive array of social services, they differed from capitalist systems in several important respects. First, the communist system was premised on full employment, so there was no need to provide unemployment insurance; social services focused on the old and the disabled. Second, subsidies for housing and even utilities played an important role. With new competition from the West and tight budgets, some of these countries are beginning to realize that universal coverage is no longer affordable and must be replaced with targeted programs. Even Sweden, despite its long history of social welfare programs, is feeling the pinch. Yet by any standard, the European safety net is still significantly better than that of the United States (Petrášová 2006; Walker and Thurow 2009).

Both in North America and in Europe, people are beginning to turn to private means to support themselves. For instance, they are investing money for their later years rather than depending on government social security programs. That solution works only if you have a job and can save money, however. Increasingly, people are seeing the gap between themselves and the affluent grow, with fewer government programs available to assist them. Solutions are frequently left to the private sector, while government policy initiatives at the national level all but disappear.

TAKE THE ISSUE WITH YOU

1. Do you personally know anyone who has had to depend on public assistance, such as food stamps? If so, what were the circumstances? Would you yourself need government assistance under such circumstances?
2. Do you think welfare recipients should be required to work? If so, what kind of support should they receive? Should any exceptions be granted to the work requirement?
3. Why do you think western and northern European countries have more generous welfare programs than the United States?

MODULE 28 | Recap and Review

Summary

Poverty is difficult to explain or define, although its effects are obvious and pervasive.

1. Many of those who live in poverty are full-time workers who struggle to support their families at minimum-wage jobs. The long-term poor—those who lack the training

and skills to lift themselves out of poverty—form an **underclass.**

2. Functionalists find that the poor satisfy positive functions for many of the nonpoor in the United States.

3. One's **life chances**—opportunities for obtaining material goods, positive living conditions, and favorable life experiences—are related to one's social class. Occupying a high social position improves a person's life chances.

4. **Social mobility** is more likely to be found in an **open system** that emphasizes achieved status than in a **closed system** that emphasizes ascribed status. Race, gender, and family background are important factors in social mobility.

5. Today, many governments are struggling with the question of how much tax revenue to spend on welfare programs. The trend in the United States is to put welfare recipients to work.

Thinking Critically

1. How do you identify areas of poverty in your own community or one nearby? Do you consider residents' achieved or ascribed characteristics?

2. How do people's life chances affect society as a whole?

3. Which factor—occupation, education, race and ethnicity, or gender—do you expect will have the greatest impact on your own social mobility? Explain.

Key Terms

Absolute poverty

Closed system

Corporate welfare

Digital divide

Feminization of poverty

Horizontal mobility

Intergenerational mobility

Intragenerational mobility

Life chances

Open system

Precarious work

Relative poverty

Social mobility

Underclass

Vertical mobility

14

Media and Consumption

looking AHEAD

What role do media play in your life, and how might this be changing as the **structure** of media changes?

How do you experience the **power** of media in contemporary society?

How has the growth of consumer **culture** changed your social life and your community?

On September 21, 2005, fifteen minutes into JetBlue Airways flight 292 from Burbank, California, to New York City, the captain announced a problem. A light on the instrument panel indicated that the front landing gear may not have retracted properly. After a flyover at a local airport to get visual confirmation, the pilots learned that not only was the front gear stuck in the down position, but the wheels were turned 90-degrees sideways. The plane, carrying 146 people, would have to make an emergency landing at the nearby Los Angeles airport.

To reduce the threat of an explosion upon landing, the plane burned off extra fuel by flying in circles for more than two hours. During that time, news of the flight's situation spread, and local television stations rushed camera crews to the airport to cover the developing story.

The seats on the JetBlue aircraft were equipped with DirecTV satellite television, providing thirty-six channels of news and entertainment. Row after row of seat-back television sets were tuned to the news coverage of the impending landing. In a moment made possible by modern media, passengers could watch their own fate developing live on television. They described this situation to reporters as "surreal" and "eerie" (Mooney 2005; Yu 2005).

Upon landing, the jet's front wheels burst into flames, but the plane stopped safely and no one was injured. As one passenger later reflected, "now instant celebrities, we were greeted by the mayor, hundreds of McDonald's cheeseburgers, and dozens of TV and print reporters. . . . The ratings for our show, we were told, had been stellar" (Laventhol 2005). Passengers can relive the tense moments any time they want; video clips of the landing are on YouTube. ▪

The JetBlue incident is just a tiny example of the pervasiveness of media in social life. Media have proliferated in many different forms throughout society and become accessible twenty-four hours a day, virtually anywhere, even on planes. Electronic media, especially, have saturated our lives, making vast quantities of text, sounds, and images available to us instantly—sometimes even images of our own impending fate. As in the JetBlue incident, in which the passengers were rewarded with a moment in the media spotlight and the chance to consume a brand-name fast-food treat, media coverage produces instant celebrities.

Usually, our media consumption is much more mundane than that experienced by the JetBlue passengers, but it is no less significant. We learn about our world, our society, and ourselves through the media's delivery of news and information and through its fictional depiction of social life. The media's role makes them profoundly influential in shaping our understanding of reality and therefore a central concern to anyone wanting to understand social life.

Much of the media content that surrounds us is produced and delivered by an enormous multifaceted industry that both sells media products to audiences and sells audiences to advertisers. Consequently, most media are inextricably linked to advertising and the promotion of consumption. This connection, too, has had a deep impact on social life, influencing how we spend our time and money as well as how we see ourselves and others.

As a major part of our daily lives, media play a crucial role in socialization and are a central part of contemporary culture. The structure of the media industry shapes, to a large degree, the content of popular media. Media content also reflects broader inequalities in contemporary society. Media help to promote consumerism, which reflects differences in economic power in society.

In this chapter we consider both media and consumption in contemporary society. We apply a sociological framework to understand media as a social institution, looking at the interactions among the media industry, media content, audiences, and technology within the broader social context. We then consider the role of consumption in society, examining how it is promoted and the consequences of a consumer culture.

A Sociological Approach to Media

Karl Marx, Max Weber, Emile Durkheim, and other early sociologists never saw television, imagined the Internet, or conceived of a tweet. When they were writing more than a century ago, media played a very different and much more limited role. But as the variety and significance of media have grown, me-

dia's impact on society has become a central topic of sociological study (Croteau, Hoynes and Milan 2011). We begin by defining important terms and describing key characteristics of media, both old and new.

What Are Media?

Media is the plural of the word *medium,* derived from the Latin word *medius,* meaning "middle." **Media** are *the various technological processes that enable communication between (and are in the "middle" of) the sender of a message and the receiver of that message.* Radio is a medium; film is a medium; print is a medium. Collectively, we refer to these as the media. "The media" can also popularly refer to the companies that produce media content, not just to the mechanisms that deliver the content. It is important to remember that media are sociologically significant because they enable and influence communication. Some media are useful primarily for individual communication between users who know each other, such as the traditional telephone. You know specifically whom you are trying to reach; you don't typically dial a number randomly. In contrast, **mass media** *reach a relatively large and mostly anonymous audience.* Unlike personal communication, the content of mass media is publicly available. People who record music, create television programs, make films, or construct web sites usually hope to reach large numbers of people without knowing specifically who they are. But, as we will see, the emergence of new forms of digital media has helped to blur boundaries between mass media and interpersonal communication.

Characteristics of Mass Media and New Media

The pre-Internet years, from the invention of the printing press in the fifteenth century through the late twentieth century, can be characterized as an era of traditional mass media—including books, newspapers and magazines, radio, film, and television. Traditional mass media typically have four key features:

1. **One-to-many communication.** Mass media allow communication to be delivered from one source to a large audience; they have a *one-to-many* orientation. Television, film, magazines, newspapers, and music are centrally produced and distributed to many viewers, readers, or listeners.

2. **Anonymous receivers.** Mass media messages generally have a known sender and are directed at a group of anonymous receivers. For example, when we read a book or watch a television program, the names of the author or producer are displayed prominently, whereas the book readers and television viewers are anonymous.

3. **One-way communication.** Traditional forms of mass media are not interactive; they typically enable *one-way* communication that does not permit direct feedback from audiences. For example, when we watch television or listen to a song on a CD, we can't use those media to respond directly to their creators.

4. ***Distinction between producers and audiences.*** In the traditional mass media landscape, a clear distinction exists between producers and audiences. Producers of mass media content are generally commercial media companies, whereas audiences are generally individual viewers, readers, or listeners.

New forms of media represent a significant break with traditional mass media. Digital media—including text, video, and audio content—can be stored as the 0s and 1s of computer code. Digital media content can be distributed through various media channels, including DVD, CD, or digital broadcast signal. The emergence of digital media made it easier and less expensive to copy and store media content. Digital media hardware and software—from desktop computers to digital video cameras and design programs to sound editing tools—opened up new opportunities for low-cost production of media, from newsletters and magazines to films and music.

Linking digital media to the Internet was the key to the development of the new media landscape. The Internet can deliver digital media content to a potentially wide audience on a growing number of devices, such as laptops, tablet computers, and various mobile devices from MP3 players to smartphones. The Internet opens up the possibility of a "many-to-many" web of communication in place of the "one-to-many" model of mass media. At the same time, it is more difficult to distinguish between individual and mass audiences online. People use the Internet for individual communication with individual known recipients (e-mail), small group communication (social networking sites), and forms of mass communication with an unlimited number of unknown recipients (web sites, blogs). This weakening of the boundaries between personal communication and mass communication has encouraged a shift from the term *mass media* to *media* in everyday language.

The idea of known senders and anonymous receivers does not accurately describe the online media environment. Media producers may remain anonymous when posting material on a blog or web site. At the same time, online audiences are not always anonymous; when registration is required to post comments on a web site, producers can know specific details about individual receivers. Even if you do not register, you still leave a digital trace (in the form of your computer's IP address). As a result, online advertisers can know far more about the identity and behavior of their target audience than they ever could in the age of traditional mass media.

In the Internet age, communication is potentially interactive, rather than being one-way. For example, visitors to a news web site can post comments on a news story, upload their own video, and communicate with one another through various user tools on the web site.

Finally, new media challenge the distinction between producers and audiences. More people have the capacity to create media than ever before, especially in wealthier nations. Individuals can build web sites and write their own blogs, post

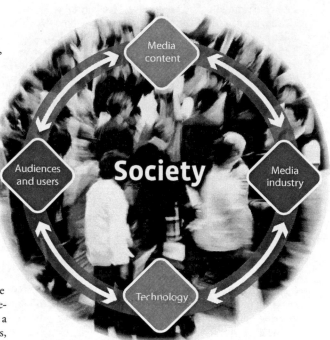

⬆ **FIGURE 14.1** | **SIMPLIFIED MODEL OF MEDIA AND SOCIETY**

This model of media and society illustrates the complex relationships among media content, media industries, audiences, and technology. A sociological approach to media highlights the bidirectional influence shown in this graphic. For example, the specific content of media messages can influence audiences by shaping how people think; at the same time, audience preferences can have a powerful influence on media content.

photos or songs online, and upload films to video-sharing sites. Instead of being an *audience* that merely receives media, more people today are media *users,* acting simultaneously as producer and consumer of media content (Bruns 2008; Ritzer and Jurgenson 2010).

Figure 14.1 illustrates the dynamics of media (Croteau, Hoynes, and Milan 2011). The model shows that the media content and the technology used to deliver it are influenced by the actions of two groups—the media industry and audiences or users. Each of these elements is influenced, in turn, by broad social forces—including cultural norms, legal standards, and regulatory practices of different societies.

The two-way arrows connecting the elements of the model indicate that interactions occur in both directions. Each element of the model exerts influence on and is affected by other elements. New technologies, for example, can influence how audiences use media, but the media industry decides how to apply new technologies and audiences ultimately choose whether or not to adopt them. We will look at each element of this media model, beginning with the media industry and the structural trends affecting it.

The Structure of Media

Why have "reality" programs and game shows come to dominate prime-time network television? Do portrayals of violence in media encourage real-world violence? Why does the news so often seem to focus on trivial or sensational stories? Such questions can be answered by looking at how the structure of media affects industry trends, media content, and the interaction of media with audiences.

Trends in the Media Industries

Formal organizations that make up the media industry produce and deliver the vast bulk of media products. As we saw in Chapter 4 with the case of news reporters, the structure of media organizations influences how media workers do their jobs, helping to shape work routines within hierarchical media organizations.

In addition to looking at relationships within media organizations, sociologists also analyze relationships among them. Examining four significant industry trends—company growth, integration, ownership concentration, and globalization—helps us to understand how the media industries operate and reveals how industry structure shapes the content of popular media and our experience of it (Croteau and Hoynes 2006).

GROWTH IN COMPANY SIZE Along with an overall growth in the size of the media industry, media corporations have grown bigger because of mergers and acquisitions. *Advertising Age* compiles an annual list of the 100 largest U.S. media corporations based on their advertising revenue. In 1980 the magazine identified the American Broadcasting Company (ABC) as the nation's largest media company, with about $5.7 billion in revenues (when adjusted for inflation to 2009 dollars). In 2009 the largest media company was Comcast, with $32.1 billion in revenues (Johnson 2010). The largest U.S. media company today is more than five times the size of the largest company in 1980.

This growth in scale has significant consequences because larger companies are more influential, have more resources at their disposal, and, as we will see, own a broader range of media content, all factors that help to give them considerable power in society.

Hierarchy and conflict within media organizations erupted in a dispute between television writers and the television networks in 2007. The writers wanted to be paid for the use of their work in new media contexts, such as the Internet. Media owners opposed such compensation, arguing that the financial outlook for these new uses of content was unclear. In response, the television writers' union went on strike.

INTEGRATION OF MEDIA COMPANIES Much of this growth in scale has occurred through integration of media companies. In **vertical integration,** *a media company owns the different stages of production and distribution of a single media form.* For instance, in the book industry one company might own paper mills, printing firms, publishers, and bookstores. **Horizontal integration** occurs *when a media company owns different forms of media.* An example would be a corporation that owns television stations, radio outlets, and newspapers. Figure 14.2 illustrates these two forms of integration; many large media conglomerates are both vertically and horizontally integrated.

Large integrated media corporations have distinct advantages. Horizontally integrated companies can create and promote products that are sold in different media forms: a comic book can be transformed into a television cartoon series, and then made into a movie with an accompanying video game. Each form of media helps to promote the other. Consider the 2009 blockbuster film *Avatar.* Its revenues from box office sales were just the tip of the iceberg. DVD/Blu-ray, a video game, on-demand viewing, action figures, and other *Avatar* merchandise provided a wide range of additional revenue sources.

thinking about power

Commercial media are typically produced by hierarchical organizations, where **power** is concentrated in high-level executive positions. Decisions about what to make and how to produce media most efficiently are largely top-down processes. How do you think this top-down process influences media content?

The Structure of Media

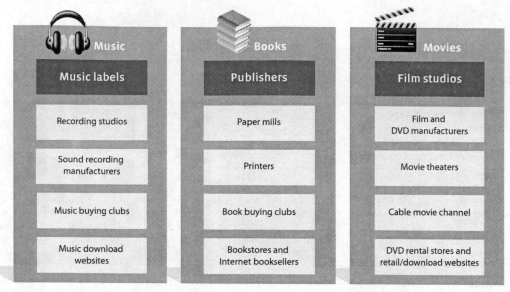

 FIGURE 14.2 | VERTICAL AND HORIZONTAL INTEGRATION OF MEDIA COMPANIES

With vertical integration, illustrated in each column, a media company owns different stages of production and distribution of a single media form. Horizontal integration, illustrated by the blue boxes, occurs when one media company owns different forms of media.

CORE CONCEPTS CHALLENGE

⊖ *How do media conglomerates gain forms of **power** from having each type of integration?*

CONCENTRATION OF OWNERSHIP As the media become increasingly integrated, ownership of media is becoming increasingly concentrated. Media **ownership concentration** occurs when *more media outlets come to be owned by a diminishing number of media corporations.* Ben Bagdikian (2004) has tracked ownership patterns over the years in various editions of his book, *The Media Monopoly.* When the first edition of his book was published in 1983, Bagdikian determined that fifty media firms controlled the majority of all media products used by U.S. audiences. By the 2004 edition of his book, he found that just five global conglomerates—Time Warner, Disney, News Corporation, Viacom, and Bertelsmann—"own most of the newspapers, magazines, book publishers, motion picture studios, and radio and television stations in the United States" (p. 3). These information and entertainment conglomerates produce and distribute media across a range of media platforms: print, broadcasting, film, and online.

The major media conglomerates have the potential to wield a great deal of political power. Media owners can promote a specific political agenda or support their candidacies for public office through their media holdings. Silvio Berlusconi leveraged his extensive media ownership of television and radio to become prime minister of Italy four times (1994, 2001, 2005, and 2008) (Ginsborg 2005). In the United States, media entrepreneur Michael Bloomberg built on the name recognition of his Bloomberg business media products in his successful New York City mayoral campaigns in 2001, 2005, and 2009. Point-

ing to the vast and far-reaching media portfolios of the major media conglomerates, Bagdikian (2004) argues that the largest media companies have "more communication power than was exercised by any despot or dictatorship in history" (p. 3).

⊕ As chairman of News Corporation, Australian-born Rupert Murdoch has been known for conservative politics, daring business moves, and "tabloid journalism." Critics argue that Murdoch has used his vast media empire (see Figure 14.3) to influence elections in several countries and to produce journalism and programming that highlights sensational crime stories and endless celebrity coverage. In 2011, a phone hacking scandal at one of his British tabloids had international repercussions.

News Corporation
Select Holdings, 2011

Television	Satellite	Cable		Film	Newspapers	Books	Internet
Fox Broadcasting Company	BSKyB (partial)	FOX News Channel	FOX Business Network	20th Century Fox	New York Post	Harper Collins	Hulu.com
Fox Sports	FOXTEL (partial)	FOX Sports Net	Fuel TV	Fox Searchlight Pictures	The Wall Street Journal	More than 30 publishing imprints, including 12 that produce children's books	Fox.com
Fox Television Stations (27 stations)	Sky Network Television Limited (partial)	FX	National Geographic Channel	Fox Studios LA	Cape Cod Media Group		FoxSports.com
		Fox Movie Channel	Speed	Blue Sky Studios	Houdson Valley Media Group	Zondervan (Christian Books)	Americanldol .com
20th Century Fox Television	Sky Italia	Big Ten Network	STAR	Shine Group	Seacoast Media Group		Milkround .com
				20th Century Fox Home Entertainment	South Coast Media Group		Scout.com
				20th Century Fox International	Southern Oregon Media Group		Many newspaper websites
					4 National newspapers in the UK		
					More than 140 news brands in Australia		

 FIGURE 14.3 │ **NEWS CORPORATION, SELECT HOLDINGS**

These are just some of the holdings of a single major media conglomerate, the News Corporation. *Sources:* News Corporation, and *Columbia Journalism Review.*

CORE CONCEPTS CHALLENGE

Do you think having such a vast portfolio of media holdings helps to give a single company too much **power** *in contemporary society? Explain.*

According to media scholar Herbert Schiller (1989), the major media conglomerates typically promote a "corporate voice" that is so pervasive most of us do not even think of it as a specifically corporate perspective. For example, news coverage of the 2008–2009 recession emphasized the perspectives of the business community, paying little attention to the views of everyday Americans (Project for Excellence in Journalism 2009).

GLOBALIZATION OF MEDIA CONGLOM-ERATES

To varying degrees, the major media conglomerates have become global entities, marketing their products worldwide. A single media conglomerate can own a vast array of media outlets that stretch around the globe. Consider News Corporation, best known for its Fox television network. News Corporation generates about half of its revenue from *outside* the United States (Wikinvest.com 2010). It owns satellite operations around the globe, as well as a variety of media that produce movies, television programs, magazines, newspapers, and books that are distributed around the world (see Figure 14.3).

The success of Hollywood movies was once measured by U.S. box office receipts alone. The *Sound of Music,* for ex-

ample, was a huge hit in the 1960s, earning more than $158 million in U.S. ticket sales (the equivalent of more than $1 billion in 2010 dollars). With the rise of integrated and globalized media conglomerates, however, the business model that studios use to make movies has changed. For example, *Avatar* made $760 million at the U.S. box office, but almost three times as much—more than $2 billion—in overseas ticket sales. To maximize their profit potential in markets outside the United States, major studios tend to look for films with content that will be well-received in other cultures. They reduce risk and maximize profit by following proven blockbuster formulas.

Media Content

The volume of media content is so vast that sociologists and other media scholars use several approaches to study it (McQuail 2005), including the following:

1. ***Compare content between two or more types of media.***
   How does news reported on television compare with that found in newspapers?

The Structure of Media

↪ Through a half-century of television, some of the best-known white, male, working-class television characters have shared strikingly similar stereotypical characteristics. Ralph Kramden (*The Honeymooners*, above), Archie Bunker (*All in the Family*, right), and Homer Simpson (*The Simpsons*, top right) are all generally lovable but ignorant and doltish.

2. ***Compare media depictions to social reality.*** How does the depiction of women in movies compare with their real-world roles in society?

3. ***Examine media content as an expression of broader cultural values and beliefs.*** How do music videos reflect contemporary values in the United States?

4. ***Evaluate the quality and performance of media based on certain criteria.*** How well did the news media perform in its coverage of the most recent election?

5. ***Examine the potential effects of media content on audiences.*** Do violent video games encourage real-world violence?

6. ***Study media content as a text, with its own structure, grammar, and syntax.*** How do entertainment "news" programs imitate the conventions of regular news broadcasts?

Because media play an important role in socialization, sociologists have been especially interested in how media content compares to social reality. Even content that is meant to be "just entertainment" and that does not claim to represent reality teaches us about our world. We use the example of class to illustrate this broader point.

IMAGES OF CLASS   Society in the United States, as portrayed in the media, is wealthier than it is in real life. Entertainment media—especially television, films, and magazines—disproportionately feature upper- and middle-class characters and underrepresent working-class and poor people. Doctors and lawyers are common, and even shows that portray police—a working-class occupation—tend to focus on better-educated and more highly paid detectives.

The most extensive study of class representation in entertainment television remains Richard Butsch's (2005) comprehensive analysis of more than 300 domestic-based situation comedies that aired between 1946 and 2000. Butsch found that only 14 percent of such programs featured blue-collar, clerical, or service workers as heads of the household. In contrast, more than two-thirds of these programs featured middle-class families. The portrayals of working-class life that did appear were usually unflattering stereotypes, showing the blue-collar workers as bungling, incompetent buffoons.

The media also typically depict labor unions, most of which represent working-class people, in stereotyped ways. William Puette (1992) analyzed representations of labor in television, film, and newspapers and found that unions were often portrayed as protecting unproductive, lazy, and insubordinate workers and as outmoded. In general, union leaders were portrayed as more likely to be corrupted by power than the more educated or cultured business and political leaders. Christopher Martin (2004) found that news coverage of labor disputes tends to favor management. The news media often treat labor strikes as stories about inconvenience to consumers rather than as struggles over economic justice, and they rarely communicate the source and substance of the conflict, accepting often-inaccurate claims from management as fact.

More broadly, news organizations orient their coverage to middle- and upper-class audiences, and provide extensive economic and business news aimed at investors and managers. Other "hard news" usually focuses on people in positions of power, notably politicians, professionals, and corporate managers. Working-class and poor people tend to be featured in crime stories (Croteau, Hoynes, and Carragee 1996; Heider 2004).

CLASS, ADVERTISING, AND MEDIA CONTENT

Media content is connected to the economic aspects of the media process. Back in the 1970s, the ABC television network produced a profile of its audiences for potential advertisers that it titled, "Some People Are More Valuable Than Others" (Wilson, Gutierrez, and Chao 2003, 27). This unusually frank title summarizes a basic reality of commercial media: content is produced to attract audiences that are desirable to advertisers. This insight can help us to understand the nature of much media content.

Most media firms operate in what is called a **dual product market,** in which *a company sells two completely different types of "products" to two completely different sets of buyers.* One buyer is the consumer audience, who purchase media products such as books, cable services, movies, and music CDs and downloads. The other buyer is the advertiser, who buys space or time in web and print ads, television and radio commercials, and other media platforms. Most media companies try to attract audiences so that they can sell advertising.

Dual product markets are important because the way they are structured determines who has the power to influence media content. For example, if a television program with modest ratings reaches a demographic group that advertisers want, it may be renewed, whereas a program with higher ratings but demographics less appealing to advertisers might be dropped. Higher income viewers are typically more appealing than low-income viewers because they are more likely to be able to afford many advertisers' products. In fact, for many forms of media, their customer is really the advertiser, not the audience. As a result, audiences may not get the media content they want simply because advertisers want something different.

Media content is also shaped by the desire of media companies not to offend their corporate sponsors. These sponsors have little interest in advertising in media with content critical of them (Herman and Chomsky 1988/2002). Media without corporate sponsors, such as documentary films and books, can afford to present a broader range of critical views.

Media content also reflects the broader social inequality in society. Studies exploring media depictions of race, gender, and sexual orientation have found plenty of stereotypes but have also shown that the images of various groups improve as those groups gain more power in society. For example, for decades racial minorities were either excluded from mainstream media or relegated to marginal roles (Wilson, Gutierrez, and Chao 2003). As racial discrimination was tempered and as people of color became a target of advertisers, racial minorities became a more regular staple of media content. The same is true for the increasing inclusion of lesbian and gay characters in television and film. For example, recent hit programs such as *Glee* and

HBO's critically acclaimed series *The Wire* was set on the gritty streets of Baltimore. Its predominantly African American cast portrayed a variety of characters, from drug addicts and dealers to high school students, police officers, and public officials, and the series also tackled major social issues. The character pictured here is a police officer whose complicated relationship with her lesbian domestic partner added another layer of diversity.

CORE CONCEPTS CHALLENGE

 What does The Wire *suggest about the potential for media to portray* cultural *diversity? Why do you think such images are so rare on television?*

Modern Family have won acclaim for including diverse characters. The Sociology Matters box on page 384 explores the efforts of one advocacy group to combat media stereotypes.

The Interaction of Audiences and Media

Do images of rail-thin models contribute to eating disorders? Do antismoking public service announcements have any impact? Since the advent of mass media, researchers have examined the interaction between media content and audiences, exploring how audiences use media as well as how they are influenced by them. As the findings have accumulated, researchers have come to see audiences as active participants in the media process rather than passive recipients of media messages.

ACTIVE AUDIENCES   **Active audiences** *make choices about how they use the media and actively interpret media content.* But how audiences use and interpret media varies depending on their social position and social characteristics, such as race, class, gender, age, and nationality. In a classic study, media scholars Jhally and Lewis (1992) studied how audiences interpreted the popular 1980s situation comedy, *The Cosby Show.* They found that white and black audiences liked the show for dramatically different reasons. Blacks appreciated the references to black culture and the positive portrayal of a *black* family. Whites, though, tended to see the show as evidence that

SOCIOLOGY Matters

Combating Media Stereotypes

MTV's reality show *Jersey Shore* was a hit in 2010, with millions of viewers and cast members who became minor celebrities. But the program was also the source of significant controversy for its regular use of the term *Guido*—widely regarded as an ethnic slur—to describe the cast members and its stereotypical depiction of Italian Americans as lazy, beer-guzzling, tan- and hair-obsessed beach bums.

For decades, sociologists have been documenting how the media often stereotype groups of people, helping to perpetuate racism, sexism, classism, and homophobia. Influenced by the evidence compiled by such research, numerous advocacy groups now track and combat media stereotypes, sometimes using the latest sociological studies. One such group is the Media Action Network for Asian Americans (MANAA). Among other activities, MANAA works "to advocate and provide reinforcement for fair, accurate, sensitive, and balanced depictions of persons of Asian Pacific descent in all facets of the media." As part of that effort, the group has compiled a list of common media stereotypes of Asians and the "stereotype-busters" that the media could employ to combat inaccuracies. Some of these are listed below:

Media Stereotype	Stereotype-Buster
Asian Americans as foreigners who cannot be assimilated.	Portraying Asians as an integral part of the United States. More portrayals of acculturated Asian Americans speaking *without* foreign accents.
Asian Americans restricted to clichéd occupations (for example, grocers, martial artists, laundry workers).	Asian Americans in diverse, mainstream occupations: doctors, lawyers, therapists, educators, U.S. soldiers, etc.
Asian racial features, names, accents, or mannerisms as inherently comic or sinister.	Asian names or racial features as no more unusual than those of Whites.
Asians relegated to supporting roles in projects with Asian or Asian American content.	More Asian and Asian American lead roles.
Asian male sexuality as negative or nonexistent.	More Asian men as positive romantic leads.
Asian women as "China dolls."	Asian women as self-confident and self-respecting, pleasing themselves as well as their loved ones.
Asian women as "dragon ladies."	Whenever villains are Asian, it's important that their villainy not be attributed to their ethnicity.
Asian Americans as the "model minority."	Asian characters with flaws and foibles, with whom audiences can empathize.
"Asian-ness" as an explanation for the magical or supernatural.	Asian cultures as no more or less magical than other cultures.

Source: Media Action Network for Asian Americans.

The efforts of researchers who document media stereotyping and activists who advocate for more accurate and diverse portrayal can help make a difference. Media scholar Jack Shaheen has studied film and television images of Arabs for more than three decades. He explains the formula for successfully challenging media stereotypes: "People worked together, until finally they managed to become filmmakers themselves, producing, directing, and appearing in courageous movies that elevated their humanity" (Shaheen 2009, 6).

think about it

1. *What would you include in a list of media stereotypes about college students? What "stereotype-buster" would you suggest for each?*
2. *What TV programs have perpetuated stereotypes? What shows have "busted" them?*

successful African Americans could be just like Whites; they liked the portrayal because it was *nonracial*. In a dynamic observed in many audience studies, *Cosby* audiences were active interpreters of media content, but those interpretations were influenced by their social positions.

Media audiences are also active when they engage in various forms of audience participation, such as calling in to talk radio shows and casting a vote on *American Idol*. In addition, some members of media audiences are actively involved in fan communities where they share opinions on media personalities and media content. They may attend events with other fans or participate in online fan forums. In the digital age, new forms of audience activity have developed, as viewers, listeners, readers, and players post reviews, analysis, and criticism on their own blogs, web sites, and Twitter accounts. Increasingly, audiences are active as both interpreters and producers of media in an evolving media environment (Napoli 2010).

MEDIA'S SOCIAL EFFECTS

Beginning in the 1940s, studies emphasized media's power to influence audiences. One theory, known as the hypodermic model of media influence, suggested that media could inject ideas into the public mind. Mass society theory argued that modern society has been marked by a decline in traditional social bonds, such as the family and neighborhood, leaving audiences susceptible to the influence of mass media.

Later studies, however, incorporated an appreciation for active audiences, leading to a more nuanced view of media effects. For example, **agenda-setting theory** *holds that media may not be able to tell people what to think, but they can significantly influence what people think about.* They do so through their emphasis (or silence) on various issues. This effect is especially true for the news media, but entertainment media, too, can raise or stifle awareness of specific social and political issues.

Through constant exposure, media can influence our view of reality. **Cultivation theory** *argues that by repeated and long-term exposure to the media's portrayal of the world (especially on television), people come to accept many of these depictions as reality.* Local broadcast news programs are notorious for emphasizing crime, fires, and accidents in their coverage. Such relentless media images inflame public anxiety and contribute to a "culture of fear," leading people in the United States to be "inordinately fearful of unlikely dangers" (Glassner 2009, xii). Over the long term, heavy viewers of such broadcasts are more likely than light or moderate viewers to believe that the world is a dangerous place, people cannot be trusted, and most people are selfishly looking out for themselves (Gerbner et al. 2008). In effect, by being exposed to constant images of danger and violence, people come to believe that this depiction accurately represents their community.

Media effects are difficult to prove definitively because we experience many influences at once in our complex social environment. Nevertheless, numerous studies using various methodologies have given us significant insight into the media's social influence.

The Explosive Growth of Media

Daneane Gallardo is located in Kitchener, Ontario, but she lives on the Internet. She coordinates web site development for a living, so she is online all day long. But her media use doesn't stop there. Reading the posts in her e-mail groups, exchanging instant messages, updating her blog—these take up more hours of her day. Her life is spent in the electronic cocoon of media. As she jokes, "If I didn't have to eat, pee, and have sex, probably I'd have no need for the 3-D world" (Hof 2005).

Media have become fully integrated into most waking moments of our daily lives. People in the United States spend more time producing and consuming media than any other single activity except breathing (Ransford 2005). Arguably no other change in contemporary life has been as far reaching and influential as the explosive growth of media.

Media Growth and Saturation

This media saturation has not only changed *what* we see and hear, but also *how* we interact with our world. As in Gallardo's case, more and more of our connection to the world is filtered through media, rather than generated through face-to-face personal contact. We often interact with our family and close friends through various communication media; some parents even wake up their school-age children via text message. Most of the music we hear is recorded rather than live. Increasingly, we learn about and discuss politics online rather than in our local communities. Students may contact professors via e-mail or even take entire courses online, rather than meet face-to-face. In whatever form, we spend increasing amounts of our life with media. Just ask yourself: how much time do you spend on Facebook?

How we use media varies, depending on the social context. Sometimes we focus closely on one form of media, as when we watch a movie in a theater. Other times, media are background to other activities, as when we drive with the radio on. Often, people use multiple forms of media simultaneously, such as listening to music while surfing the Internet. This multitasking makes it difficult for researchers to get a precise measure of media use.

The U.S. Census Bureau (2010i) reports that, in 2007, people in the United States used media an average of 9 hours and 35 minutes a day. This overall number counts simultaneous

Many people are surrounded by a number of media devices that enable multitasking. Fragmented attention to multiple media content has become a hallmark of contemporary life.

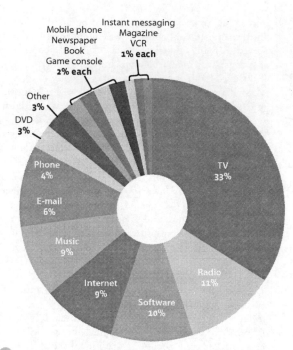

FIGURE 14.4 | BREAKDOWN OF AVERAGE DAILY MEDIA USE

This pie chart summarizes the results from the Middletown Media Studies II project, a study that tracked the different types of media people use on a typical day. *Source:* Holmes and Bloxham (2007).

media forms separately, and it does not count media use at work. However it is counted, time spent using media has grown significantly in recent years as more media, in more portable forms, have become available. Television continues to make up the bulk of media use, at an average of 4 hours and 25 minutes per person each day.

People dramatically underestimate the amount of time they spend with media (Papper, Holmes, and Popovich 2004). This tendency causes a problem for researchers who estimate media use based on surveys and individually kept records. To address this problem, some researchers followed nearly 400 individuals in Muncie, Indiana, for an entire day in 2005 to observe and record their media use at 15-second intervals. This approach enabled researchers to note whether individuals were using multiple forms of media simultaneously and whether they were carrying out other activities while they used media (Finberg 2005; Holmes and Bloxham 2007).

The study found that people used media an average of 8 hours and 41 minutes a day—about two-thirds of the time they were observed. During nearly a third of the time they spent with media, the research subjects used multiple forms of media simultaneously. Adding up the multitasking separately brought the total exposure to media to 12 hours and 2 minutes—significantly higher than the Census Bureau's estimate. As Figure 14.4 shows, television took up the largest share: just over 4 hours a day (33 percent). Overall, about 30 percent of the individuals' waking day was spent focused exclusively on using media. Another 39 percent of the time, they used media while engaged in some other activity.

The recent growth of media is due partly to the changing nature of media technology, which has made it possible for different forms of media to converge and has enabled the rise of portable media devices.

Media Convergence

Historically, different forms of media were marked by clear boundaries, and some still maintain distinct characteristics—for example, print newspapers do not have sound, and radio

has no images. But one of the most significant developments in recent years has been media **convergence,** *the merging of different media forms.* Digital technology that makes it easy to transfer information across different media platforms has accelerated this convergence. A digital image can easily be converted to print, television, the Internet, DVD, or a host of other media formats.

Individual types of media can also deliver multiple forms of media content. The Internet can be used for personal communication (e-mail) or for mass communication (web sites, e-blasts, and blogs). You can use it to send a message in the form of text, audio, or images. Even older forms of media, notably the telephone, have been reinvented as all-purpose media devices. Today's cell phones allow users to make personal calls, send text messages, listen to music, watch television, take photos and videos, and access the Internet, all while being completely portable.

User-Generated Content

Traditionally, formal organizations created mass media content. Today, however, **user-generated content** is *created by ordinary media users rather than by media organizations and is available to a potentially large audience.*

Users have always created media content. For decades, picture albums have housed family photos, home movies have starred wobbly toddlers, tapes have captured garage band performances, and yearbooks have immortalized high school seniors. Today, however, user-generated content can potentially reach a mass audience, not just family and friends. Ordinary YouTube stars, relatively unknown bands with a cult following, and podcasts aimed at a niche audience are all possible with today's media technology. More than ever, media-based information and entertainment that sidestep the media industry are available for potentially widespread distribution. Most will never develop a large audience, but some will.

Among the many forms of user-generated content are the following:

- Personal web sites created and controlled by an individual or a small group working together can serve as a platform for other media forms such as music recordings, blogs, photos, and videos.

- Some commercial web sites allow users to create or upload content. Examples include YouTube and Facebook, as well as book publishing sites such as CreateSpace and Lulu.

- Individuals can create user-generated content by manipulating existing content (often illegally) by sampling, altering, and recombining to make mash-ups, parodies, and other hybrid creations. For example, well-known music is sometimes remixed into new forms and distributed online, a process made famous early on by Danger Mouse's *Grey Album*, combining lyrics from Jay-Z's *Black Album* with samples from the Beatles' *White Album*.

- More broadly collaborative user-generated content, such as a *wiki*, a web site, or other online resource, allows users to add and edit content. No single user is responsible for the content on such sites. Wikipedia, the collaborative online encyclopedia, is the most well-known form of wiki media.

Regardless of the type, user-generated content is an alternative to the traditional industry-generated media experience.

User-generated content is not without costs, however. This unfiltered and unregulated media environment can include disturbing material. Racist hate groups, for example, have flourished on the Internet. Their web sites can help link far-flung individuals who share a racist ideology. Child pornography, bomb-making instructions, and other forms of potentially dangerous content can also flourish. Terrorists have made good use of encrypted e-mail communications, voice-over-Internet audio, and web sites. Such user-generated sites can feature political analyses; instructions on how to carry out violent attacks; and videos of incendiary speeches, attacks on U.S. soldiers, and even ghastly beheadings of kidnap victims. It is possible to post this content while maintaining anonymity (*The Economist* 2007).

Functions of Media

Reading this book gives you access to information. Watching a movie or listening to the radio can entertain you. Creating a web page on a social networking site can enable you to meet people and stay in touch with friends. Clearly, the many hours we spend with media serve different functions for us personally. The media serve similarly varied functions for society as a whole.

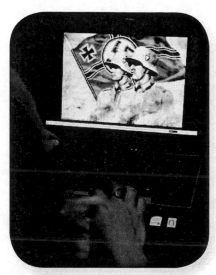

 Because the Internet is unfiltered, it can serve as a platform for user-generated content—like this YouTube video of a German neo-Nazi band—produced by groups that promote hate and violence.

CORE CONCEPTS CHALLENGE

How might hate groups take advantage of the Internet to build and sustain a racist **subculture**? How might the Internet be used to combat such efforts?

SOURCES OF INFORMATION Media serve as the storehouse and conduit for a society's accumulated knowledge and information, from the mundane to the profound. By examining media content, we can learn everything from the latest sports scores and celebrity sightings to vital medical information and the policy positions of political candidates. In recent years, media have made information more accessible more quickly than ever before. This development has transformed human society. Whereas information once was scant and difficult to obtain, a central challenge now is to make sense of the glut of information at our fingertips.

AGENTS OF SOCIALIZATION When a man was stopped for a traffic violation in Virginia, he tossed a box from his car window. The police discovered that the box contained sixty rocks of crack cocaine. The jury at the subsequent drug possession trial found the man "not guilty," largely because the box was never tested for fingerprints. This case was one of many in which juries have acquitted suspects on charges that, in the past, would have routinely resulted in guilty verdicts. Criminal prosecutors and police believe the primary reason for the rise in acquittals is that many jurors have watched a popular television police drama, *CSI: Crime Scene*

 S P O T L I G H T
on social theory

A **functionalist approach** emphasizes media's role in social integration through the construction of a national audience that shares a common culture. With so many media options available in the digital age, do you think media will continue to serve as a source of social integration in the United States?

Investigation, which highlights the extensive use of forensic evidence to solve crimes. They refer to jurors' increased and unrealistic expectation that detailed forensic evidence will be collected for all crimes as the "CSI effect" (Hooper 2005; Stockwell 2005).

The "CSI effect" is one example of how media can socialize us by telling stories and informing us about our culture and its norms. Even media content that is obviously "just entertainment" can influence how we interpret the world and alter how we see reality. The same is true for thousands of other aspects of social life that we learn about through the media filter. The media even provide models of appropriate behavior for the various social roles that are part of our lived experience, such as friend, parent, and citizen.

Our steady diet of media content informs and entertains us and, over time, influences how we come to understand ourselves, our society, and our world. Indeed, most of what we know about the world has reached us through the media. Media socialization can be especially influential for children. They have limited life experience and have not yet fully developed their own identity, and yet they are increasingly barraged with media messages on TV and the Internet. Children, in fact, spend more time with media than they do in the classroom, interacting with their parents, or engaged in physical activity (Rideout, Foehr, and Roberts 2010; Roberts, Foehr, and Rideout 2005). This constant media exposure shapes their understanding of the world.

PROMOTERS OF IDEOLOGY

The contest to control the media's messages—and thus its ideological influence—does not take place on an even playing field. Those with more power in society generally have greater access to the mainstream media to promote their ideas. That access is one reason why the issue of who owns and controls the media is such an important topic. User-generated content cannot compete with the deluge of media messages emanating from commercial media sources.

In discussing stratification in previous chapters, we defined ideology as a system of beliefs that justifies the existence of social inequality. But ideology also helps us to define, explain, and make value judgments about the world more broadly. The dominant ideology promotes the interests and reflects the worldview of the powerful. As we will see, the media's ideological function is not carried out by a single depiction in a newspaper or movie, but through the cumulative effect of exposure to many such depictions—and to the persistent absence of other depictions.

For example, U.S. news media typically take for granted the desirability of free markets, downplaying their negative features. They raise few questions about the growing economic inequality discussed in Chapter 9 or about the exploitation of workers in a global economy. Instead, the vast bulk of economic news coverage is actually "business" news, presented from the perspective of investors and managers, not labor representatives (Kollmeyer 2004). As we will see, much media content is linked to the promotion of consumption, with little regard for the social or environmental consequences of consumer culture. Even the recent uptick in environmental news coverage is often accompanied by the call for more consumption—this time of "green" products. The end result is coverage that explains the economic world from a particular perspective and treats this perspective as if it were the only reality.

As the media carry out their various functions, they are enmeshed in a variety of social relationships that make the media a key social institution. To understand media as an institution, we need to look at how power influences the media and is used by them.

Power and Media

Some scholars have heralded the media's compression of time and space as a new stage of human history. Canadian media theorist Marshall McLuhan (1911–1980) famously argued that the "medium is the message," meaning that the most significant feature of contemporary media is their technological capabilities rather than any particular content. McLuhan (1964) wrote that, with the rise of electronic media, "We have extended our central nervous system itself in a global embrace" (p. 19). He foresaw the rise of a "global village" in which media would bring people across the planet closer together.

The Effect of Social Inequality on Media Use

In the years since McLuhan wrote, global communication has become a reality, but it is tempered sharply by social inequality. The **digital divide** refers to *the gap between those who have the knowledge and resources needed to use digital information technology, especially computers and the Internet, and those who do not.* Class is the primary determinant of this digital divide. For example, in 2009 more than 94 percent of respondents from U.S. households with incomes of at least $100,000 had a broadband (high-speed) Internet connection at home, but only 36 percent of households with an income below $25,000 had such a connection (U.S. Department of Commerce 2010; see Figure 14.5).

The biggest digital divide exists between wealthy and poor nations. Comparable figures can be difficult to obtain, but as of 2010 the percentage of the population with Internet access (known as the "penetration rate") ranged from a high of 78.3 percent in North America to a low of 11.4 percent in Africa (see Map 14.1). Global media expansion has developed very unevenly, following preexisting lines of economic inequality.

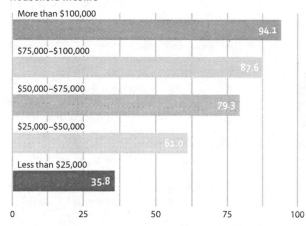

Household income

Percent of U.S. households with broadband

Income	%
More than $100,000	94.1
$75,000–$100,000	87.6
$50,000–$75,000	79.3
$25,000–$50,000	61.0
Less than $25,000	35.8

◀ **FIGURE 14.5 | THE U.S. DIGITAL DIVIDE, 2009**
Broadband Internet access increases with household income. Although the vast majority of higher income households have a high-speed connection, most low-income households do not. *Source:* U.S. Department of Commerce (2010).

Rather than being a "global village," the bulk of the world is still left out of the advances in media. To a large degree, the Internet is the preserve of the world's elites.

Inequities in media access vary by medium but include all forms of media. For example, television is far more prevalent than just a decade or so ago, but it is still rare in some poor and rural parts of the globe. As access to various forms of media expands to more of the earth's population, media's influence will continue to grow, playing an increasingly important role in social life. However, social inequality in the broader society will continue to create inequities in media access and use.

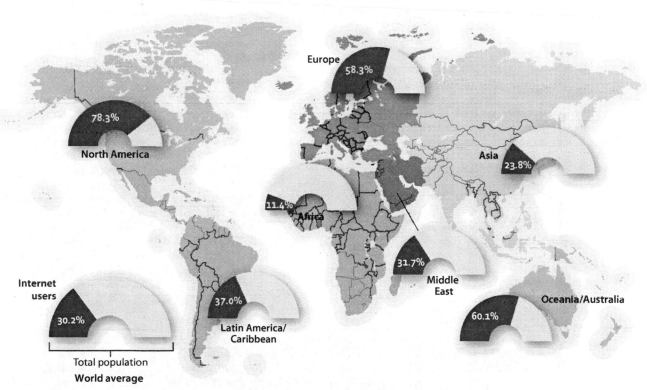

Europe 58.3%
North America 78.3%
Asia 23.8%
Africa 11.4%
Middle East 31.7%
Oceania/Australia 60.1%
Latin America/Caribbean 37.0%

Internet users 30.2%
Total population
World average

 MAP 14.1 | GLOBAL DIGITAL DIVIDE: INTERNET PENETRATION RATES, MARCH 2011
Much of the world still lacks access to the Internet. Whereas 77 percent of U.S. residents can log on to the Internet, only 11 percent of Africans are able to do so. Such dramatic discrepancies in Internet access help to sustain substantial inequality in information access and communication capacity, which can have political and economic consequences. *Source:* Internet World Stats (2011).

CORE CONCEPTS CHALLENGE

In what ways can access to the Internet be a source of **power**? *How might the "digital divide" help perpetuate global inequalities?*

Power and Media

Economic inequality across the globe results in the world's poorest being locked out of access to media technology. However, cell phones have become the "poor person's computer" in many developing countries, providing access to the Internet, banking services in rural areas without banks, and texting services that deliver health information, weather forecasts, political news, and more. Solar-powered cell phones are popular in areas with limited or no access to electricity.

Government Regulations

Governments across the globe regulate media. These regulations vary from society to society and are applied differently to different media. In the United States, for example, companies cannot advertise cigarettes on television, but they can buy cigarette ads in print media, and there are limits on the number of broadcast television stations that one company can own but not on the overall number of radio stations. Many regulations restrict activities of the media industry, but some require action. For example, drug companies are required to disclose possible side effects of their medications in ads.

Media companies typically welcome some regulations, such as copyright laws and licenses to use the public airwaves. These regulations protect their investments and give them exclusive control over their products. In some cases, media industries avoid formal regulation by policing themselves, as with the movie rating system initiated in 1968 by the movie industry.

Overall, the United States has relatively few media regulations. Some European countries have many more, especially on children's media. Some nations require that news, public affairs, religious, and children's programming run for thirty minutes before a commercial break. Others restrict the broadcast of violent programming during hours when children might be watching.

Global Media and Cultural Imperialism

In mid-May 2008, the movie *Iron Man* topped that week's U.S. box office revenue. At the same time, it was also the number one movie in nineteen other countries. The number two U.S. movie that week, *What Happens in Vegas,* was the top movie in twenty other countries (see boxofficemojo.com). This particular week's box office results were nothing special; it is common for U.S. movies to dominate theaters worldwide.

This U.S. domination of the global film box office is one example of **cultural imperialism,** *the tendency of media corporations from wealthier nations—especially the United States—to export so many of their media products that they come to dominate the local cultures of other, especially poorer, nations.* But films—especially big-budget Hollywood films—are somewhat unique in that they are so expensive to produce. India has a massive film industry of its own, widely known as Bollywood, and there is a large movie industry in Nigeria, often referred to as "Nollywood," but few other countries have the scale of capital investment in facilities necessary to produce big-budget films. The introduction of digital cameras and editing programs is lowering the costs of filmmaking, but the economic gap between wealthier and poorer nations remains enormous.

The gap is considerably smaller for other forms of media. It is relatively cheap to produce high-quality music recordings, for example. As a result, Western and American music faces much more competition from local recording artists (forcing MTV to include local artists in its programming outside the United States). Still, just four conglomerates—Sony (Japan), Universal (United States), Warner (United States), and EMI (United Kingdom)—account for about three-quarters of all music sales worldwide (Sabbagh 2008). Because of language differences, print media tend to be much more diverse and less likely to be dominated by U.S. media products. Nevertheless, the United States and other Western nations have unrivaled resources when it comes to promoting their media, making their impact on other societies a very real concern.

Some critics argue that media globalization will homogenize world culture and erode local cultures (Hamm and Smandych 2005; Schiller 1992). As television, movies, film, and music become globally mass-produced, cultures may begin to lose their distinctive elements. In response, some governments provide financial support to nurture a local alternative to imported foreign media. More than seventy countries participate in an International Network on Cultural Policy that seeks to "create an international environment that values diversity, creativity, accessibility and freedom" (International Network on Cultural Policy 2010).

thinking about structure

Government regulations have an impact on the **structure** of media in the United States and in other countries. In what situations, if any, do you think the government has the right to regulate media structure and content? Explain.

In Singapore, a country with a large Muslim minority, a woman in a traditional headscarf walks past a Western-style advertisement featuring women in revealing bathing suits. The clash between Western media content and the different cultural values found in many societies is part of the debate regarding cultural imperialism.

The Impact of Technology on Society

What effects might the nonstop advances in media technology have on our society? New media have many widely celebrated advantages, including increased connectivity, easier access to information, and a democratization of content creation. But a variety of analysts argue that new media technologies also have negative social consequences.

Traditional print media are generally read in a linear fashion, which is ideal for contemplation and rational thought. Books store a great deal of information. But the creation of books is a slow process, and access to the information in them is limited to those who are both literate and sufficiently disciplined to stay focused on an extended linear presentation.

In contrast, media developed since the mid-twentieth century—particularly television and online media—are immediate, easy to access, and often emotionally engaging. These media lead to a preoccupation with the immediate, as with "live" news and entertainment, constantly updated web sites, and instant messaging. They also use fast-changing images that evoke emotions, or hyperlinks that connect—but also fragment—bits of information.

The result of these new technologies is content that can be fast, fleeting, fragmented, and often insubstantial. Maggie Jackson (2008) argues that our embrace of new media has produced a sort of attention-deficit culture—characterized by constant stimulation, interruption, and multitasking—that provides little intellectual nutritional value. This culture un-

dermines our ability to focus, concentrate, and attend to the deeper and more substantive issues in life that are the bedrock of intimate social relationships, wisdom, and advances in culture.

Experimental evidence from neuroscience suggests that surfing the Internet develops different neural pathways in the brain than does reading a book. The constant stimulus that characterizes the contemporary media environment contributes to a decline in people's ability to focus, concentrate, and engage in serious thought (Carr 2010).

The ability of the Internet and mobile devices to connect people is typically celebrated as one of its greatest features. William Powers (2010) agrees but argues that wisdom, insight, and perspective are gained from being *disconnected;* by creating time and space for solitude and contemplative thought. A healthy and vibrant life in the digital age, he argues, needs to involve a balance between the advantages of connectivity and the benefits of solitude.

Some critics suggest that, despite the world of knowledge at their fingertips, the generation that has grown up with new media is less informed, less literate, and more self-absorbed than any that has preceded it (Bauerlein 2008; Twenge 2006). They point to the popularity of social networking as one source of the problem. The immediacy and personalized nature of social networking, these critics argue, emphasizes the value of newness and promotes an extreme focus on the self and an immediate network of friends. Information or news that isn't about this narrow world is often of little interest. The result is a worldview that promotes entitlement and self-centeredness, what Jean Twenge (2006) dubbed "Generation Me."

This all-encompassing world of fast, fragmented, fleeting images is a part of what some observers contend makes our postmodern period of history unique. Most famously, French scholar Jean Baudrillard (1988a) argued that in many ways we experience **hyperreality,** *the condition in which media depictions of the world replace the experience of the "real" world.* Increasingly, our lives are saturated by a near constant stream of media images that can create a reality all its own. A simple example of hyperreality is the familiar "photo opportunity"—an event created specifically for the purpose of being covered by the media. When the news becomes coverage of an event

⏴⏵ When Gannett launched *USA Today* in the early 1980s, it became the symbol of how electronic media were changing the newspaper business. The paper relied on bright colorful graphics, kept stories very short, and highlighted entertainment topics over more substantial news. The vending machines designed to sell the papers, with rounded corners and a pedestal format, resembled television sets.

created precisely for media coverage, media reality supplants the "real" world.

As Neil Postman (1985/2005) argues, electronic media have shifted the emphasis so dramatically from matters of substance to fleeting entertainment that we are in danger of "amusing ourselves to death." He and other observers (Downie and Kaiser 2003; Henry 2007) contend that this emphasis on immediate, engaging visuals has contributed significantly to a loss of substance in our media culture.

As media have come to permeate society, they have been accompanied by relentless messages promoting consumption. These messages have contributed to the rise of consumer culture, a defining characteristic of contemporary society.

Consumer Culture

Twenty-five-year-old Reema Patel thinks that "the first class in college should be about credit cards." That's because by the time she was twenty-one she had accumulated $28,000 in credit card debt and has been working hard to pay it off ever since. Like many college students, Reema was sucked into the trap of easy credit and the allure of consumer culture, spending much more than she should have on travel, shopping, and

partying. More than 80 percent of college students have at least one credit card, and the average number of cards per student is 4.6. Upon graduation the average college student carries $4,100 in credit card debt (Sallie Mae 2009).

Easy credit is just one feature of a broader consumer culture that incessantly promotes **consumption,** *the process of choosing, purchasing, and using goods.* A sociological approach to consumer culture emphasizes its economic, political, cultural, and social dimensions (Zukin and Maguire 2004). To sociologists, consumption

- Is structured by the economic institutions, political regulations, and social norms that help organize the production and sale of consumer goods
- Is promoted through advertising and the media
- Involves the values, beliefs, and behaviors of consumers who, beyond meeting basic needs, use consumption to form and express their identities

Humans have consumed basic goods—such as clothing, tools, and simple household goods—for centuries. But modern technological advances—especially the rise of industrialization and capitalism—fundamentally changed the nature and significance of consumption as a social process. (The Sociology Works box explores an applied sociologist's efforts to better understand consumers.)

The Rise of Consumer Culture

Consumer culture in the United States and Europe emerged in the late nineteenth and early twentieth centuries, enabled by several key developments:

- *Industrialization made it possible to produce an unprecedented quantity of goods.* Factories could mass produce a surplus of common personal and household items.

- *Mass production greatly reduced the cost of many items, making them affordable to a much larger number of people.* More people became consumers of manufactured goods rather than producers of their own items. Fewer clothes, for example, were made in the home as more were purchased in stores.

- *The immense capital investments needed to create mass manufacturing facilities gave rise to larger, more centralized business firms.* Eventually, the production and sale of most consumer goods shifted from craftsmen and small merchants to large corporations and retail chain stores.

- *Over time, competition to produce and sell goods more cheaply came to dominate much of the consumer market.* As part of this process, manufacturers introduced **planned obsolescence,** *the intentional design and manufacture of consumer goods so as to ensure a loss of utility in a relatively short period of time.* Products made cheaply could sell for less but would also break or become outdated more quickly, fueling another round of profitable consumption.

SOCIOLOGY WORKS

Hy Mariampolski and Consumer Research

Hy Mariampolski has been hired by the likes of Nissan, Clorox, Citibank, Microsoft, McDonald's, and dozens of other well-known corporations as well as numerous not-for-profits, such as Business for Social Responsibility, San Francisco Unified School District, Liberty Science Center, and the New Victory Theater, to better understand their customers. Like many sociologists who end up conducting consumer research studies, he sometimes faces criticism from academic colleagues who disdain his work as doing the bidding of corporate America, "the devil incarnate" (Rice 2007). Such are the contradictions involved when sociologists use their understanding of human behavior to assist clients in creating and selling their products.

With a Ph.D. in sociology, Mariampolski moved into consumer behavior studies after trying out work in an academic setting. Mariampolski and his spouse and business partner, Sharon Wolf, run a firm that specializes in qualitative data on how consumers use everyday products. Although the company, QualiData, uses focus groups and interviewing to learn about some consumer needs, it is best known for pioneering the use of ethnographic research in marketing.

Hy Mariampolski

This involves taking account of evolving cultural habits and observing consumers as they buy various brands and use products in their homes and workplaces. Mariampolski (2001, 2005) has written two books teaching these research methods. He also shares his tools and techniques and applies his academic training in workshops he conducts worldwide.

First-hand observations in natural settings can shed new light on how customers use products, on their frustrations with product design, and on how they may use products in ways that manufacturers never intended. Such insights help manufacturers design better products and market more effectively to consumers.

Mariampolski likes to think of himself as representing the "voice of the consumer," providing manufacturers with feedback on what people like and don't like. For example, one of his projects highlighted how working-class men avoid many pain relievers because they cause drowsiness, which can interfere with their ability to perform their jobs.

His firm was also involved in a variety of ad campaigns involving sexual health. He helped condom manufacturers find more "life-affirming" ways to advertise that encouraged consumers to integrate condoms into their "natural eroticism." "People are not necessarily motivated by ads threatening them with death," Mariampolski observed.

Mariampolski endorses the trend among consumers that demands more socially responsible business practices, such as caring about nutrition and the environment. Nevertheless, he sometimes gets criticized for "his enthusiastic endorsement of free-market capitalism" that runs counter to sociologists whose research documents the negative effects of consumer culture and corporate advertising. Mariampolski, though, is comfortable in his alliance with corporate America. "We help corporations implement their good intentions," he says. "We're not outside throwing bricks." (Rice 2007)

> "I use my [sociology] background and knowledge every day of the week when I explain to my clients how their products may have to be adapted for new or growing demographic categories, when I demonstrate how foundational ideas in societies undergo cross-cultural diffusion and drift and when I show them how technological changes stimulate modifications in social structures and beliefs."

think about it

1. *What do you think about sociologists using their knowledge and research techniques to help companies market their products effectively? What ethical issues, if any, might this form of research raise?*

2. *What insights might you gain from observational research that you might not learn from an interview or a focus group?*

■ *Excessive manufacturing capacity contributed to the rise of advertising as a way to promote more consumption.* Advertising also generated new kinds of consumer "needs" (Ewen 2001). As Stephanie Coontz (1992) notes, with the rise of consumer society, "The word consumption increasingly lost its earlier connotations of destroying, wasting, or using up, and came instead to refer in a positive way to the satisfying of human needs and desires" (p. 170).

Consumer Culture

Even when consumer culture was still in its infancy, it did not escape the notice of early sociologists. In the late nineteenth century, Karl Marx in particular considered the links between the changing methods of production and the new culture of consumption.

Alienated Labor and Commodity Fetishism

Have you ever experienced the satisfaction of doing it yourself—say, repairing a car, completing a craft project, or creating a web site? For Marx, work that we engage in to meet our human needs is, ideally, creative and satisfying. Growing food, building a home, or knitting a sweater are all inherently meaningful tasks that help to develop human potential. The rise of industrial capitalism, however, distorted our relationship to work so that it became separated from meeting basic needs. Rather than working for themselves to create useful things, wage laborers work at the discretion of employers for money to buy goods that will meet their needs. This system creates a distance between what we *do* (for money) and what we *use* (as consumers). One consequence of this distance, according to Marx, is **alienation,** *the separation and isolation of workers as a result of the structure of capitalist society.* Alienation under capitalism has several dimensions:

- *Workers are separated from their natural state as creative, autonomous beings.* They become largely interchangeable cogs in a productive machine.

- *Workers are separated from one another,* instead of working together toward a common good.

- *Workers are separated from what they produce.* Little or no connection exists between workers and the products of their labor, which are owned by their employers.

- *Workers are separated from the process of production.* For many, work is a meaningless, tedious activity with few, if any, intrinsic rewards.

Ironically, later researchers have found that the impersonal, isolating nature of work creates dissatisfaction and unhappiness that advertisers then exploit by encouraging consumption as a solution for this alienation. The beneficiaries of this system of production and consumption are capitalists, who gain, first, by exploiting workers—paying them less than the value of the goods they generate—and, second, by profiting from the sales of such goods back to workers.

When we no longer create or grow the goods we consume, the source of consumer products can seem obscure. Marx used the term **commodity fetishism** to describe *the failure of people to recognize the labor that created the value in the commodities they use.* In the study of primitive religions, *fetish* refers to objects that have magical powers. When we buy jeans or a

t-shirt, they seem to appear magically at the local mall with a price tag, entirely separate from the workers who made them. We generally do not think about the labor process involved in an item's creation: the likely low-paid workers—perhaps even child laborers—who made the item, the extensive markup added to the price to create profit, or the natural resources consumed in its production and transportation. This disconnect between production of goods and their consumption has become a feature of our consumer culture.

Consumption and Identity

Your great grandparents probably had identities that reflected where they were born and lived and worked, their religious beliefs, and their strong ties to a particular community. Your identity is no doubt still forming as a result perhaps of various moves, changing schools and peer groups, and living on your own and considering future career choices while you attend college. The nature of our identities reflects, in large part, the nature of our society.

As sociologist Peter Berger (1963) once put it, "[T]raditional societies assign definite and permanent identities to their members" (p. 48). In such societies, identity is often rooted firmly in the family and community, with rigid and permanent roles that are recognized widely. With the rise of modernity, radical economic, social, and political changes contributed to the creation of modern identities, partially freed from the influences of family and place. "In modern society," Berger notes, "identity itself is uncertain and in flux." Since our family of origin and place of birth do not necessarily determine our future, our sense of self does not develop automatically.

Today's postmodern era requires us to choose who we will become. We have more freedom to choose or construct our own social roles, decide where to live and what to do, and much more. A paramount question—one nearly unthinkable in traditional societies—becomes "Who do we want to be?"

In a highly commercial society, where nearly everything is a product for sale, what you buy and where you buy it can take on great importance as an affirmation of your identity. **Consumerism** is *an emphasis on shopping and the possession of material goods as the route to personal happiness.* Advertisers sell an identity through products, and individuals express their identity through the choices they make as consumers (or by their rejection of consumerism).

In his aptly titled book, *The Conquest of Cool,* cultural historian Thomas Frank (1997) showed how advertisers in the 1960s tapped into the popular culture of the day by promoting consumption as a type of creative self-expression. A variety of consumer products were touted as the choice of nonconformists, rebels, and the "hip," such as Volkswagen vans, Old Gold cigarettes, Polaroid cameras, and Suzuki motorcycles. Ads encouraged consumers to reject conformity—by following the

➔ Regardless of the product being sold or the audience being targeted, many advertisers sell their products by associating them with a particular image and lifestyle. Are these ads really about milk, MP3 players, watches, or big box stores?

ads' advice to buy a product. The result, of course, is conformity among all those who buy the product. The spectacle of major corporations selling mass consumption as a means of self-expression and individual rebellion—ironic though it may be—surfaces frequently in advertising campaigns. Apple Computer, for example, promoted the iPad "revolution" when it first released the new tablet computer in 2010. Its earlier "Think Different" Macintosh ad campaign featured rebels such as Mahatma Gandhi, John Lennon, and Martin Luther King, Jr.

Advertisers often promote their products to particular demographic groups, sometimes reinforcing differences based on gender, race, age, and class. Products not only do something, they *say* something about who we want to be and the group to which we belong. Far removed from Marx's notion that products meet human needs, today's consumer products are often about image and identity. This phenomenon is not entirely new. As we saw in Chapter 9, Thorstein Veblen explored the "conspicuous consumption" of the leisure class a century ago. However, this kind of consumption has expanded to include most of society. The brands we choose become infused with social meaning that go well beyond the practical use of the product. Prestigious commodities (such as cars, electronics, and clothes) are taken to be a reflection of our own social value (Baudrillard 1988b).

Promoting Consumption

Advertising is ubiquitous in contemporary society. Just think of the various places you've observed ads in the past week: On large highway billboards, on taxis and buses, at the airport, throughout your local mall, in the stalls in public restrooms, on a sticker on a piece of fruit—and in much of the media you consume. Advertising provides the primary source of revenue for most media. You don't have to pay for broadcast television and radio because advertisers foot the bill. The fees for cable television and print subscriptions are affordable because the majority of operating revenue typically comes from advertising. New media, such as Google and Facebook, have adopted the broadcast model—advertising-supported and free to users—for online sites. Most successful high-traffic web sites, from news and entertainment sites to medical advice and "how to" sites, are supported by advertisers willing to pay a premium for a targeted audience.

At its most basic level, advertising provides consumers with information about specific products and services. On the whole, however, advertising promotes more than just a particular product. As sociologist Michael Schudson (1986) has noted, advertising "fosters a consumer way of life" (p. 238).

A great deal of thought, money, and effort goes into encouraging people to be consumers. Advertisers must make people

SPORTS

ADVERTISING AND CHANGE

Until the mid-1980s, players in the National Hockey League skated on rinks with plain white ice and boards. When today's players take to the rink, they skate past countless commercial advertisements plastered on the boards and painted right into the ice on which they play. It is impossible to watch professional sports today without being forced to view the logos and other advertisements that cover and surround the playing surfaces and, sometimes, the players themselves. Even sports arenas and ballparks now carry the names of corporate sponsors and are designed to promote consumption.

unhappy with what they have and lead them to believe that a purchase will improve their condition. They cultivate dissatisfaction by encouraging consumers to feel insecure, bored, anxious, envious, or frustrated about the life they lead and then evoke an image or a lifestyle that consumers supposedly want to emulate, a process called "emotional obsolescence." The cycles of fashion, the new car models, the constant upgrades of media devices are all techniques designed to promote dissatisfaction with the older version of a product and plant the seed

of desire for the new product. This endless cycle of consumption, dissatisfaction, and consumption is an inherent part of consumer culture. Increasingly, advertisers are also exploiting the emotional vulnerabilities of children, as the Through a Sociological Lens box describes.

One problem for the advertising industry is that people generally do not like advertisements. As a result, the ad industry is constantly developing new ways to overcome audience resistance and promote consumption, including through advertising in public spaces, product integration, and stealth advertising.

PUBLIC SPACES AND CAPTIVE AUDIENCES

One way to overcome resistance to ads is simply to place them in public spaces that are difficult to avoid. In recent years, for example, ads have appeared on the exterior of airplanes, inside school classrooms, all around sports arenas, and just about everywhere on the Internet. Another strategy is to show ads in places where people are temporarily a captive audience: in elevators, taxicabs, airports, waiting rooms in doctors' offices, and rest rooms.

PRODUCT INTEGRATION

Today's television viewers can use their remote controls to change channels during commercials and fast forward past commercials in recorded programs. In response to audience resistance, advertisers in recent years have used the technique of **product placement,** in which *the product being advertised is integrated into media content,* making the ads unavoidable. For example, an entire episode of the television comedy *Arrested Development* was set in a Burger King restaurant. One report found that in a four-month period, Apple products—including Mac computers and iPods—were shown or mentioned over 250 times in television programs such as *The Office, 24,* and *CSI: NY* (Goo 2006).

Other media use product placement, as well. In movies, the car the hero drives, the computer the police detective uses, and the wristwatch the spy consults are all likely to be products provided to the movie producers and inserted into the film, sometimes for a fee. Movie producers keep costs down by using such free (or paid-for) props, advertisers get to associate their products with popular movie stars, and audiences experience a form of advertising that is woven seamlessly into the film.

Product placements show up regularly in just about every form of commercial media. Even many news programs incorporate advertising into their content. Companies distribute "video news releases" promoting their products that are broadcast by some local news programs, often without attribution. In addition, freelance "experts" appear on many local and national morning news shows offering reviews of new consumer products. Some of these experts are paid by advertisers for a positive mention of their products (Rainey 2010).

South Korean teen idol Lee Hyo Lee brought this form of advertising to its logical conclusion in her hit pop song "Anymotion." In the video for this song, Lee dances with Samsung's Anycall brand cell phone while she sings. The song, the video, even the choreographer were all paid for by Samsung, which crafted the lyrics to repeatedly include the word *any,*

THROUGH A SOCIOLOGICAL LENS

Examining the Commercialization of Childhood

More than ever before, advertisers are using the media to target society's most vulnerable members: children. Today's ad campaigns are much more sophisticated than in the past. For example, children in laboratories are studied for their reactions to various kinds of advertising; marketers even measure their eye movements and physiological responses. Children fill out marketing surveys in schools, and sponsored classroom materials sometimes include brand-name acknowledgments that serve as advertisements for youth-oriented products. Marketers also employ psychologists who help craft messages to exploit the emotional vulnerabilities of children, especially their feelings that they are "uncool," a "loser," or simply "left out" if they don't have the latest product. Children are even being hired for "stealth advertising" efforts (described later), for example, by participating in slumber parties sponsored by the research and marketing firm Girls Intelligence Agency, at which the children try to learn about and influence their friends' tastes and habits.

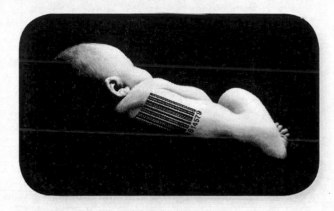

Once a tiny portion of the advertising industry, children's advertising has grown dramatically in the past few years as corporations have found ways to tap parents' wallets through their kids. This barrage of ad messages, says sociologist Juliet Schor, is literally making children sick, contributing to obesity and causing an array of health and psychological problems. Schor has used sociological inquiry to study the inside operations of advertising agencies that target children, and she has explored the effects of advertising on children. What she found is alarming.

Today's children are being inundated with many more ads than any other generation has ever experienced. In the 1970s, children watched an estimated fifty-five television commercials a day. By the 1990s this figure had doubled to 110 (or 40,000 a year), and it continues to increase. In 2006 the medical journal *Pediatrics* noted, with concern, that children see ads everywhere—on television, online, in magazines, and on billboards—and that the average child in the United States views more than 3,000 advertisements per day. In recent years, ads have become increasingly prevalent in other youth-oriented media, including video games and social networking web sites.

Children have a keen awareness of themselves as consumers and are often the first to try new technology. As Schor points out, "Children have become conduits from the consumer marketplace into the household, the link between advertisers and the family purse." As such, children drive many forms of household consumption, often by nagging parents until they give in or using their own allowance to purchase products. Advertisers understand this process and target children accordingly.

All this exposure to advertising, says Schor, has led to a public health crisis. An epidemic in childhood obesity can be traced, in part, to a sedentary lifestyle (often spent watching television and playing video games) coupled with the dramatic increase in the consumption of high-fat and high-sugar junk food (advertised on children's programs). More broadly, Schor's research suggests that the more children are caught up in the consumer culture, the more likely they are to suffer from depression, anxiety, lower self-esteem, and a variety of physical complaints brought on by emotional distress. The ability of advertising to promote dissatisfaction and envy can take a toll on young psyches.

Surveys show that four out of five Americans think there should be more restrictions on children's advertising, and nearly nine out of ten think that our consumer culture makes it more difficult to instill positive values in children. Even many of the marketers that Schor interviewed for her study knew something was wrong; they spontaneously expressed ambivalence and guilt about what their work was doing to children.

Sources: American Academy of Pediatrics (2006); Babb (2004); Center for the New American Dream, http://newdream.org; Schor (2004); Strasburger and Wilson (2002); Strasburger, Wilson, and Jordan (2009).

think about it

1. *What sorts of regulations, if any, do you think should be placed on advertising to children? Did your parents restrict your access to media? What steps would you take as a parent to help shield your children from the effects of advertising?*

2. *List all the consequences for children who are overly commercialized. Think about the psychic as well as the economic consequences. What might these children be missing in their lives?*

reminding listeners over and over again of their Anycall brand (Fowler 2005).

In all of these cases, the line between content and advertisement has been erased, a development that has angered some actors and writers. Their unions have protested these practices, saying they force actors to make product endorsements for which they are not compensated and writers to write ad copy rather than program content. They also argue that the practice is inherently deceptive (Waxman 2005).

STEALTH ADVERTISING Another increasingly common practice is stealth advertising. Sometimes called "guerilla marketing," **stealth advertising** is *the creation of covert advertising in everyday real-life situations*. For example, many advertisers take advantage of social networking sites and consumer review features of online retail sites to plant surreptitious advertising for their products. Advertisers hire employees to pose as ordinary users of these sites and praise the attributes of their employer's products by posting enthusiastic reviews. In one high-profile 2010 case, the Federal Trade Commission (2010) charged a public relations firm with posting game reviews at the iTunes store without disclosing that the firm was hired to promote the games.

Advertisers also hire people to promote their products subtly by, for example, going to bars and ordering a particular brand of beer, in effect becoming a walking advertisement. Camera companies have hired people to pose as tourists and ask passersby to take their picture in front of a popular landmark. As this innocuous exchange takes place, the "tourists" praise the virtues of their new camera, creating another stealth ad. Such advertising techniques, which rely on people's trust and good will, are deceptive and insert commercial motivations into everyday social interactions.

The Social Impact of Consumer Culture

What happens to a culture in which consumption becomes the center of social life and citizens are subject to an endless stream of advertising? We note some of the social implications in the sections that follow.

INEQUALITY AND CONSUMPTION Social and economic inequality is important to keep in mind when considering the impact of consumer culture. The affluence necessary for consumer spending is not distributed evenly, and large segments of the world's population still endure poverty and subsistence living. The transformation to consumer culture came first to the more affluent Western societies in the nineteenth and early twentieth centuries, and only recently to parts of the developing world that are now integrated into the global economy. After the fall of communism in 1989, Eastern Europe saw a dramatic expansion in consumer culture. China, too, has recently instituted major economic changes, enabling growth in consumer spending.

Using data to measure purchasing power, a United Nations study found that 85 percent of Americans were classified as active consumers, but only 28 percent of the world's population qualified for this classification (Gardner, Assadourian, and Sarin 2004). The vast majority of the world's population is un-

---

TABLE 14.1 | **THE COST OF LUXURY CONSUMER PRODUCTS VERSUS HUMAN NEEDS**

Luxury Consumer Products		Human Needs	
Product	**Annual Expenditure**	**Social or Economic Goal**	**Annual Investment Needed to Achieve Goal**
Makeup (global)	$18 billion	Reproductive health care for all women	$12 billion
Pet food in the United States and Europe	$17 billion	Elimination of hunger and malnutrition	$19 billion
Perfumes (global)	$15 billion	Universal literacy	$5 billion
Ocean cruises (global)	$14 billion	Clean drinking water for all	$10 billion
Ice cream in Europe	$11 billion	Immunizing every child	$1.3 billion

 The table lists examples of the annual expenditure on luxury consumer items compared to the estimated annual expenditures needed to achieve key social and economic goals. As the authors who assembled the table note, the list debunks the idea that "many of the unmet basic needs of the world's poor are too costly to address" (Gardner, Assadourian, and Sarin 2004, 10).

CORE CONCEPTS CHALLENGE

What does the list in Table 14.1 suggest about the hidden costs of consumer culture?

American fast-food restaurants line a street in Shenzhen, China. Consumer cultures of this sort, once limited to affluent Western countries, have now expanded to some developing nations. But U.S.-style levels of consumption cannot be sustained globally; the planet simply does not contain sufficient resources.

able to participate in consumer culture because of their starkly limited resources. Those who are active consumers face some sobering choices about how they direct their wealth. Table 14.1 compares the annual expenditure on luxury items versus what might have been accomplished had those resources been allocated to more basic human needs.

DEBT AND DISSATISFACTION As we saw in Chapter 12, Marx regarded religion as an "opiate" that gave temporary, but ultimately false, comfort to people suffering from society's injustices. Since the middle of the twentieth century, critical theorists have suggested that consumerism fills a similar role in modern society (Adorno and Horkheimer 1944/2000). Shopping is often touted as an escape from the drudgeries of daily life. "Treating yourself," "living for the weekend," and "splurging" because "you are worth it" are all popular notions that encourage guilt-free consumption. However, the fleeting comfort of consumption is often coupled with the accumulation of burdensome debt, producing more stress and anxiety in a person's life. Consumption and working to pay for it become a cyclical way of life (Schor 1999).

As far back as Durkheim, sociologists have understood that satisfaction in life comes from understanding and staying within limits and boundaries. Insofar as advertising and consumer culture encourage boundless desires that can never be

SPOTLIGHT
on social theory

Marx and contemporary **conflict theorists** emphasize the inability of consumption ultimately to offer satisfaction. Has consumption helped give you a sense of satisfaction? Who has benefited from your participation in consumer culture?

satisfied, they can be a source of social instability and can undermine human happiness.

Excessive consumption cannot substitute for addressing the underlying social conditions that create unhappiness. Since the cycle of consumption is at bottom based on perpetual dissatisfaction (Ewen 2001), any comforting effects are likely to be temporary, leaving deep-seated troublesome issues unchanged. What is more likely to produce happiness and satisfaction? Scholars point to rewarding interpersonal relationships, meaningful employment, outlets for creative self-expression, and gratifying civic and community participation (Kasser 2003; Lane 1994).

COMMODIFICATION **Commodification** is *the process of transforming all things into a product to be bought and sold.* Social relationships that used to be based on, and promoted by, mutual aid and trust are often just commercial transactions today. For example, a variety of goods and services that were once produced and shared among family and friends—such as yard work, pet sitting, home repairs, and childcare—are now more likely to be paid services. Today we even shop for mates on the Internet.

Religious holidays and communal festivals that once promoted social solidarity are now celebrations of consumption. Beginning with "Black Friday's" middle-of-the-night sales immediately following Thanksgiving, we count the shopping days left until Christmas. Birthdays, Mother's Day and Father's Day, Valentine's Day, and other events are marked by the obligatory mass-produced greeting card and the purchase of a consumer item. Big sales are associated with President's Day, Labor Day, and Memorial Day. The newest civic holiday, the Super Bowl, is as notable for the unveiling of new advertisements as for the game played on the field. Shopping has been transformed from a necessary chore to America's favorite pastime.

With commodification, monetary terms increasingly measure social life. If carried to an extreme, such a development can undermine the social trust necessary for a healthy society. A society in which everything—and everyone—has a price is one in which emptiness and alienation are likely to thrive (Dunn 2000; Slater 1999).

Consumer Culture

ENVIRONMENTAL DEGRADATION   Finally, the spread of the culture of consumption around the globe has taken a toll on the environment. For decades, affluent nations, especially the United States, have consumed the Earth's resources at a vastly disproportionate level. With about 5 percent of the Earth's population, Americans consume about 25 percent of the world's resources. Now, billions of residents of developing nations are seeing improvements in their standards of living and are themselves becoming consumers. For some, consumer culture is a step up from the grinding pain of poverty.

The more widespread availability of basic, affordable consumer goods has been a major positive development.

The overall expansion of consumer culture, however, has resulted in environmental destruction on a massive, unprecedented, and unsustainable scale—including slashed and burned forests, polluted air and water, toxic landfills, crippling carbon dioxide emission, holes in the atmosphere's protective ozone layer, and wholesale climate change. We explore some of these effects in Chapter 15.

In Transition

TARGETING CONSUMERS IN THE DIGITAL AGE

The Internet has taken advertising to a whole new level because it is the only medium that allows advertisers to track the activity of potential consumers (Story 2008), providing information about users' interests and habits.

In a 2010 investigative report about what it called "the business of spying on Internet users," the *Wall Street Journal* discovered that the "tracking of consumers has grown both far more pervasive and far more intrusive than is realized by all but a handful of people in the vanguard of the industry" (Angwin 2010). For example, the top fifty web sites in the United States each installed, on average, sixty-four different pieces of tracking technology on a visitor's computer—typically without giving users any warning. The top fifty youth sites installed a total of more than 4,000 tracking tools on users' computers. These new tracking tools are the foundation for a new promotional approach known as **behavioral targeting,** *advertising sent to online users based on their earlier Internet activities.*

The most well-known form of online tracking involves the installation of cookies. Many web sites install a tracking number, known as a cookie, on your computer when you visit the sites. Cookies initially facilitated online shopping by allowing consumers to place items in a virtual shopping cart until they checked out. Their use has since been expanded to link all of a consumer's online activity, including the sites you visit, the items you buy, and any personal information you supply. You may have noticed, for example, that on a visit to Amazon.com, the site recommends items related to your previous browsing. Cookies also help web sites to store important personal information such as your name, address, and payment preferences. This information can help users learn about new products that might match their interests and can make online shopping fast and easy.

In recent years, however, cookies have been installed primarily by companies that specialize in tracking and recording users' online activity and selling this information to advertisers. These companies pay web sites to permit them to install tracking tools on the computers of visitors to the site. In addition, tracking tools are sometimes hidden in banner ads or free downloadable apps, games, and ring tones.

By piecing together bits of information you leave behind as you browse the Internet, advertisers can anticipate your likely interests and pitch products to you based on your past online activity. Records of your searches on Google or other sites, the products you have viewed, the articles you have read, the zip code you entered to get local weather, your Facebook or MySpace likes and dislikes—all these pieces of information can be assembled to create a sophisticated consumer profile that allows marketers to create a targeted online consumer experience, steering you to advertisements tailor-made to your specific interests.

The principles of behavioral targeting are also visible in political campaigns. By mining data about your online activities, campaigns can customize the information you receive about a candidate. In this way, the campaign can personalize the candidate's message and target it to you based on your demographic and consumer profile. Different citizens can literally be getting different messages from the same candidate (Howard 2005; Panagopoulos 2009).

thinking about culture
As consumer **culture** spreads throughout the globe, environmental pollution is spreading, as well. What aspects of U.S. consumer culture might create these problems?

Research suggests there is substantial public concern about online tracking. One comprehensive national survey found that two-thirds of Internet users in the United States do not want to receive targeted advertising. Asked about the prospect of receiving targeted online ads based on their *offline* consumer activity, more than 85 percent of respondents indicated their disapproval (Turow et al. 2009).

Public opposition to behavioral targeting is connected to broader concerns about online privacy. For example, the practice of "scraping" involves copying material from online forums, career-oriented web sites, and social networking sites, on which users often discuss and post information about various aspects of their lives, from school, work, and relationships to health, exercise, and hobbies (Angwin and Stecklow 2010). In some cases, scrapers construct individual user profiles that connect people's online screen names to their real names, which they sell to advertisers, employers, and other web sites. Online scrapers also sell so-called "listening services," in which they report to clients what people are saying about a specific topic or product. Facebook and other social networking sites, which include personal information that users post voluntarily, are particularly valuable sources for information scrapers.

In the face of the growing sophistication of behavioral targeting and other data gathering techniques, consumer advocates have called for government regulations. The Federal Trade Commission proposed a "do not track" option in 2010, which would permit users to opt out of all tracking tools. In response, online data trackers and advertisers have come up with their own proposals to head off potential regulation. A group of online tracking companies started a service called the Open Data Partnership in 2011, which allows consumers to view and edit data that have been collected on them but does not permit users to opt out of tracking altogether (Steel 2010). In early 2011 Google and Mozilla announced software for their browsers that would allow consumers to opt out permanently. Whether the tracking companies would honor the opt-out requests is another worrisome question (*New York Times* 2011a).

The debate about online advertising techniques is sure to continue throughout the decade, as citizens and policymakers sort through the various arguments about consumer privacy and efficient marketing. In this new era of customized consumption, sociologists are likely to pay careful attention to the power associated with information tracking and the cultural consequences of the proliferation of personalized advertising (and political) messages.

THINKING SOCIOLOGICALLY ABOUT . . .

Media and Consumption

culture
- Media reflect and promote cultural norms.
- Consumption has become central to our culture and is used to help form social identities.

structure
- The structure of the media industry shapes the content of popular media.
- Media organizations must operate within the structural constraints imposed by their legal, political, economic, and cultural environments.
- The widespread presence of advertising helps to structure consumer society.

power
- Major media ownership is highly concentrated; those who control the media wield considerable power in society.
- Consumerism is linked to inequality and reflects disparities in economic power in society.

In Transition

REVIEW, REFLECT, AND APPLY

Looking Back

1. As a social institution, media involve the interaction of several key elements: the media industry, media content, audiences, technology, and the broader social context.

2. The media industry has been expanding, integrating, and globalizing, while its ownership has become more concentrated.

3. Media content often reflects the broader social inequalities in society, sometimes perpetuating them through the socialization process.

4. Audiences consist of active readers, viewers, and listeners who make choices about their media use and interpret media content, often based on their social position. But extensive and long-term exposure to media does have an impact on audiences, influencing what they think about and how they view the world.

5. Converging media forms, technological advances, and the rise in user-generated content have been major contributors to the explosive growth of media.

6. Whatever their form, media act as sources of information, agents of socialization, and as a means for those in power to promote ideology.

7. The rise in electronic media technology in postmodern life is a significant change from modernity's reliance on print, introducing new ways of thinking about and seeing the world.

8. The rise of consumer culture was accompanied by an increase in advertising delivered through various media. Advertising has become a ubiquitous force, and advertisers use a variety of techniques to influence our identities and promote consumption.

9. Consumer culture has had a significant social impact on how we live, work, and value our lives. It has also been a key factor in the escalation of environmental degradation.

Critical Thinking: Questions and Activities

1. In what ways and for how long do you use media in a typical day? Keep a log for one or two days, noting every use of media. How would you summarize the role that media play in your life? How do you think your lifelong exposure to media has influenced how you understand the world? How does the influence of media extend beyond *what* you know to include *how* you relate to the social world?

2. If someone relied exclusively on popular media portrayals to understand the life of a college student today, would they get a reasonably accurate picture of your real-world experiences in college? What does this say about the role of media in teaching about aspects of the world we don't experience first-hand?

3. Note your exposure to advertising for one day. What techniques did advertisers use to get your attention? Is there any part of your life that is free from brand names, logos, and ads?

4. Would you agree to have a corporate advertiser pay for your wedding ceremony in exchange for incorporating the corporation's logo into the event (for example, printed on invitations and napkins, displayed on a banner at the reception, announced as part of the ceremony)? Why or why not? What issues does this "product placement" raise about the appropriate limits for advertising?

5. In what ways do you participate in consumer culture? Do you have any concerns about the role of consumption in your life?

Key Terms

active audiences (p. 383) audiences that make choices about how they use the media and actively interpret media content.

agenda-setting theory (p. 385) a theory that holds that media may not be able to tell people what to think but can significantly influence what people think about.

alienation (p. 394) the separation and isolation of workers as a result of the structure of capitalist society.

behavioral targeting (p. 400) advertising sent to online users based on their earlier Internet activities.

commodification (p. 399) the process of transforming all things into a product to be bought and sold.

commodity fetishism (p. 394) consumers' failure to recognize the labor that created the value in the commodities they use.

consumerism (p. 394) an emphasis on shopping and the possession of material goods as the route to personal happiness.

consumption (p. 392) the process of choosing, purchasing, and using goods.

convergence (p. 386) the merging of different media forms.

cultivation theory (p. 385) a theory that argues that, by repeated and long-term exposure to the media's portrayal of the world (especially on television), people come to accept many of these depictions as reality.

cultural imperialism (p. 390) the tendency of media corporations from wealthier nations—especially the United States—to export so many of their media products that they come to dominate the local cultures of other, especially poorer, nations.

digital divide (p. 388) the gap between those who have the knowledge and resources needed to use digital information

technology, especially computers and the Internet, and those who do not.

dual product markets (p. 383) the situation that occurs when a company sells two completely different types of "products" to two completely different sets of buyers.

horizontal integration (p. 379) what occurs when a media company owns different forms of media.

hyperreality (p. 391) the condition in which media depictions of the world replace the experience of the "real" world.

mass media (p. 377) communications that reach a relatively large and mostly anonymous audience.

media (p. 377) the various technological processes that enable communication between (and are in the "middle" of) the sender of a message and the receiver of that message.

ownership concentration (p. 380) what occurs when more media outlets come to be owned by a diminishing number of media corporations.

planned obsolescence (p. 392) the intentional design and manufacture of consumer goods so as to ensure a loss of utility in a relatively short period of time.

product placement (p. 396) the integration into media content of a product that is being advertised.

stealth advertising (p. 398) the creation of covert advertising in everyday real-life situations.

user-generated content (p. 386) content that is created by ordinary media users, rather than by media organizations, and that is available to a potentially large audience.

vertical integration (p. 379) what occurs when a media company owns the different stages of production and distribution of a single media form.

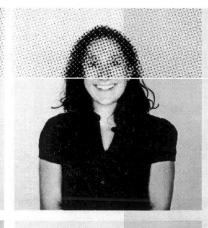

10

Race and Ethnicity

looking AHEAD

How does culture define your race?

How do individuals and institutional structures perpetuate racial and ethnic inequality?

How do majority and minority groups reflect inequalities in power?

In the summer of 2010, Diana Martinez, an eighteen-year-old student and the Mexican-born daughter of undocumented immigrants, stood quietly in a cap and gown—symbolizing her academic status—while a Washington, D.C., police officer handcuffed her. She and other undocumented students were being arrested for disorderly conduct for participating in a sit-in coordinated by United We Dream, a coalition of immigrant youth groups. The demonstrators were calling for the passage of legislation that would allow immigrant children who served in the military or completed college to qualify for U.S. citizenship, thus fulfilling a lifelong dream (Bahrampour 2010).

The nation's undocumented immigrants typically avoid the public spotlight, always aware that their illegal status could lead to arrest and deportation. In publicly announcing their undocumented status, Martinez and her fellow demonstrators were thus doing what would have been unthinkable to their parents. Their act of defiance in pursuit of citizenship might be a sign of things to come.

Immigration—and especially unauthorized immigration—divides people in the United States, especially along ethnic lines. One poll found that whereas 62 percent of non-Hispanics thought illegal immigration was a "serious crime," only 24 percent of Hispanics did. The same poll found that 60 percent of non-Hispanics felt that illegal immigrants were mostly a drain on society, whereas only 21 percent of Hispanics thought so (AP-Univision 2010).

Frustration with the federal government's failure to control illegal immigration has led some states and localities to act on their own. A controversial law passed in Arizona in 2010, for example, made it a state crime to be in the country illegally, required legal immigrants to carry paperwork proving their status, and instructed Arizona police to question anyone they "reasonably suspect" of being undocumented. Some supporters of immigration restrictions have links to racist organizations (Potok 2007), but most argue that their concerns have nothing to do with race or ethnicity and reflect only a desire to curb *illegal* immigration. In fact, according to one poll, along with an overwhelming percentage of Hispanics (86 percent), a majority of non-Hispanics (56 percent) support providing a legal way for undocumented immigrants to become U.S. citizens (AP-Univision 2010). That is the outcome for which Diana Martinez is hoping. ■

Debates about immigration and citizenship are as old as the country itself. Even before the United States existed, the arrival of Europeans in a land already populated by many native societies sparked conflict between people of different races and ethnicities. As we will see, neither race nor ethnicity is rooted in biological fact; both are cultural creations. But these cultural ideas have real-world consequences; they affect patterns of action—social structure—and they contribute to persistent inequalities in power and resources among racial and ethnic groups. In many ways, the social history of the United States is intertwined with the history of ideas about race and ethnicity, including debates about who is entitled to citizenship and equal rights.

Today, whether or not we realize it, whether or not we want them to be, race and ethnicity are parts of our identity, influencing our lives and the way people interact with us. To better understand ourselves and our increasingly diverse society, we need to grapple with the impact that race and ethnicity have had on our history and the role they continue to play today.

The Role of Culture: Inventing Ethnicity and Race

Many societies, including the United States, classify people in terms of *race* and *ethnicity*. **Ethnicity** refers to a *shared cultural heritage, often deriving from a common ancestry and homeland.* That cultural heritage can include, among other things, common language, traditions, customs, symbols, and distinctive foods and music. Ethnicities are social constructions that exist only to the extent that people embrace them or have them imposed by others. People are constantly reinventing and redefining ethnic identities, which can make them fluid and murky.

In the United States, the ethnic label *Hispanic* applies to people who come from Spanish-speaking countries or whose ancestors did. Many people who fit that description, however, reject the label because it lumps many cultures together. Instead, some people prefer the term *Latino* (male) or *Latina* (female) to specify a heritage from Latin America. Many prefer to identify with their specific ancestry as, for example, Mexican Americans (or Chicanos), Puerto Ricans, Cuban Americans, or Colombians. Similarly, some people of European ancestry in the United States identify with their ethnic roots, for example, calling themselves Polish Americans or Italian Americans. Others identify themselves as simply *American*, in the process creating yet another ethnicity.

In contrast to ethnicity, a **race** is *a category of people widely perceived as sharing socially significant physical characteristics such as skin color.* Ethnicity can be confused with race, since the two can overlap. For example, in the United States, many people mistakenly think of Hispanic as a "race" equivalent to "white," "black," or "Asian." In fact, the homelands from which Hispanics come are inhabited by people of Native American, African, European, and Asian origin. As a result, Hispanics may be of any race, though most identify as white.

Race as a Social Construction

If you walk into a room full of people, you can usually tell just by looking who is white, Asian, or black. Isn't race, then, a biological reality? Although it is based on physical characteristics and thus reflects biological variation, race, like ethnicity, is a social construction (Mukhopadhyay, Henze, and Moses 2007). Races exist only to the extent that people use physical characteristics to assign one another to social categories, but those categories do not represent biologically meaningful divisions in the human species.

For example, most important biological differences among people—differences that affect health, longevity, susceptibility to disease, and so on—are invisible and do not play any role in the definition of racial categories. These differences include things like blood types or the presence of genetic markers that predispose people to certain diseases. In addition, people are arbitrarily selective in the visible physical characteristics they do use to define racial categories. In the United States, for example, they largely ignore eye color and hair color when making racial distinctions, focusing instead on skin color (see the top photos on p. 254). Finally, no clear dividing line distinguishes one racial group from another. Physical variation occurs along a continuum, making it impossible to categorize humans neatly into a few distinct racial categories. (See the photo collage on the bottom of p. 254.) For example, much more physical variation exists among Whites than exists between Whites and any other racial category; some people classified as white even have darker skin than some people classified as black.

In short, when it comes to race, we don't see many physical differences that matter, we ignore many differences we can see, and we classify people into supposedly sharply bounded categories when in fact the members of those categories have continuously overlapping physical characteristics.

People make racial distinctions in part by paying attention selectively to some physical variations while largely ignoring others. Why are the different skin tones in these men more socially significant than their different hair color? What does this selective attention suggest about the arbitrary nature of race?

In reality, there is only a single human race with no subcategories or subspecies. All humans share a common ancestral lineage that evolved in Africa about 100,000–200,000 years ago (Mukhopadhyay, Henze, and Moses 2007). As a result, no biological feature or cluster of features clearly distinguishes one category of humans racially from any other. To understand what this common origin means in terms of the socially constructed nature of race, consider the physical feature most closely identified with racial differences in the United States: skin color.

Skin color is determined mostly by varying amounts of a pigment called melanin. Humans are vulnerable to the harmful effects of intense sunlight, which include an increased probability of having a child with birth defects for women and reduced fertility for men. Melanin—and the dark skin associated with it—protects against these adverse effects, but it also reduces the skin's ability to produce the essential nutrient vitamin D from sunlight. As a result, dark skin provides an evolutionary advantage in sunlight-intense tropical environments, whereas lighter skin provides an evolutionary advantage in re-

Human physical variation is too subtle and diverse to be captured accurately by a handful of racial or ethnic classifications.

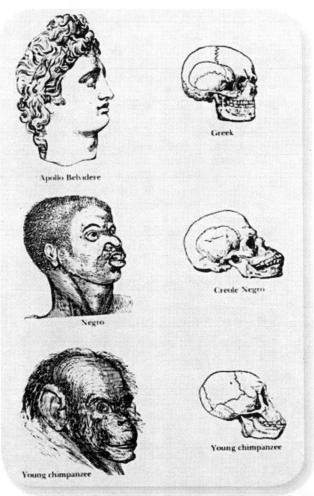

⬆⬇ **MAP 10.1 | GLOBAL DISTRIBUTION OF SKIN TONE**

Skin tone is roughly distributed along the earth's latitudes so that, for example, people in parts of Mexico, northern Africa, and portions of China all share similar skin tones, even though they are commonly classified as belonging to different racial groups. *Source:* Jablonski and Chaplin (2002).

gions of less intense sunlight (Jablonski and Chaplin 2002). As humans across many generations migrated and adapted to different geographic regions, they developed a range of skin tones that vary more or less continuously from dark to light between regions of intense sunlight and those of less intense sunlight (Map 10.1) (Jablonski and Chaplin 2002).

In addition, skin tone is not consistently connected to other physical features such as hair type or nose shape. Dark- or light-skinned people can have all types of hair, noses, and other physical attributes. Skin tone, in other words, is not a fixed biological attribute of any one race. To understand how it became linked with race in the popular imagination, we have to look to social factors—cultural beliefs, social structures, and power relationships—not to biology.

Pseudo-Science and Race

The term *race* took on its popular contemporary connotations in the eighteenth century, when European scientists began systematically to name and classify the plants and animals of the natural world. When they turned their attention to humanity, however, ethnocentric assumptions of European superiority reduced their efforts to pseudo-science (Smedley 2007).

For example, the Swedish naturalist Carolus Linnaeus (1707–1778), who laid the foundation for the biological classification system still in use today, invented four subspecies of

⬇ Early pseudo-scientific classification schemes perpetuated racist beliefs. This image is from an 1857 book titled *Indigenous Races of the Earth* by physician Josiah Nott and Egyptologist George Gliddon. It suggests white biological superiority, with Blacks somewhere in between Whites and chimpanzees.

The Role of Culture: Inventing Ethnicity and Race

Homo sapiens, attributing to each not only physical traits but also judgmental character traits. White-skinned *Europeanus,* described as creative and governed by laws, was at the top. The other three were copper-skinned *Americanus,* described as stubborn, easily angered, and governed by customs; sallow-skinned (yellowish) *Asiaticus,* described as greedy and governed by opinions; and dark-skinned *Africanus,* described as lazy, negligent, and governed only by impulse (Smedley 2007). This classification laid the groundwork for "scientific" justifications of **racism,** *the belief that one race is inherently superior to another.*

Later writers developed variations on this sort of racist classification system. These schemes often contradicted each other, proposing a widely varying number of "races," each based on different physical types and accompanying social characteristics. Whites, for example, were often divided into subgroups that purported to reflect the superiority of northern Europeans—labeled in various schemes as "Teutonic" or "Nordic"—over such other Whites as "Celtics," "Semitics," and "Mediterraneans" (Smedley 2007).

From today's perspective, the rationale used to justify these racial classification systems seems arbitrary and even bizarre. For example, in the nineteenth century, German anatomist and anthropologist Johann Blumenbach (1752–1840), apparently after admiring the symmetry of a particularly well-preserved skull from the Caucasus Mountains (located between Russia and Turkey), concluded that it must have been Caucasians whom God had created in his own image. Other races, he decided, had degenerated physically and morally from God's vision because they had moved and adapted to new environments. Thus, religion and folk belief, couched in pseudo-scientific language, combined to give us the term *Caucasian,* still in common use as a synonym for "White" (Mukhopadhyay, Henze, and Moses 2007).

These arbitrary and conflicting classification systems went hand in hand with a belief in **racial essentialism**—*the idea that supposedly natural and immutable differences separated the races.* Whites who created the classification systems lived in societies with the power to enforce these ideas. Cultural notions of racial essentialism were used to justify white supremacy, slavery, and the European colonial domination of other peoples.

Race and Ethnicity Over Time and Across Cultures

Because races and ethnicities are cultural creations rather than biological facts, the definition and significance of racial and ethnic groups varies from culture to culture and changes over time. In nineteenth-century China, people drew distinctions based on body hair rather than skin tone. To them, extensive facial hair marked European missionaries as uncivilized barbarians (Mukhopadhyay, Henze, and Moses 2007). In many parts of the world, ethnicity is more important than race; people are much more concerned about one another's tribe, clan, or ethnic affiliation than about skin color or other physical characteristics (Cornell and Hartmann 2007).

In countries where race does matter, definitions of race—and the standards for assigning people to one race or another—vary enormously. In the United States, sexual encounters between white owners and black slaves were common, and in the nineteenth century people of mixed race were often called "Mulattos." In the early twentieth century, however, Whites began changing state laws so that racial categories became mutually exclusive, and in the case of mixed ancestry, the Black status prevailed. For example, Virginia passed the "Racial Integrity Act" in 1924 mandating that all newborns be classified as either white or colored, with colored including those with *any* black or Native American ancestry. During the first half of the twentieth century, versions of this so-called one-drop rule—one drop of black blood makes a person black—were adopted by state legislatures throughout much of the South and Midwest (Murray 1997).

In recent years, however, the United States has returned to acknowledging mixed-race status. Since 2000, the U.S. Census

8. **Is Person 1 of Hispanic, Latino, or Spanish origin?**
- [ ] **No**, not of Hispanic, Latino, or Spanish origin
- [ ] Yes, Mexican, Mexican Am., Chicano
- [ ] Yes, Puerto Rican
- [ ] Yes, Cuban
- [ ] Yes, another Hispanic, Latino, or Spanish origin — *Print origin, for example, Argentinean, Colombian, Dominican, Nicaraguan, Salvadoran, Spaniard, and so on.* ↗

9. **What is Person 1's race?**   Mark **X** one or more boxes.
- [ ] White
- [ ] Black, African Am., or Negro
- [ ] American Indian or Alaska Native — *Print name of enrolled or principal tribe.* ↗

- [ ] Asian Indian
- [ ] Chinese
- [ ] Filipino
- [ ] Japanese
- [ ] Korean
- [ ] Vietnamese
- [ ] Native Hawaiian
- [ ] Guamanian or Chamorro
- [ ] Samoan
- [ ] Other Asian — *Print race, for example, Hmong, Laotian, Thai, Pakistani, Cambodian, and so on.* ↗
- [ ] Other Pacific Islander — *Print race, for example, Fijian, Tongan, and so on.* ↗

- [ ] Some other race — *Print race.* ↗

⬆ FIGURE 10.1 | RACE, ETHNICITY, AND THE U.S. CENSUS
The U.S. Census includes questions about race and Hispanic origin. The categories included in these questions reflect the unique social history of the United States. *Source:* U.S. Census Bureau.

Bureau (2011c, 2011e) has allowed people the option of indicating a mixed racial heritage, and by 2010 more than 9 million people—about 3 percent of the population—reported being of two or more races (see Figure 10.1). Some people with mixed-race backgrounds, though, still choose to identify with a single race. When President Obama filled out his 2010 census form, he identified himself only as black, although his mother was white (Roberts and Baker 2010).

The countries of Latin America and the Caribbean have long had a variety of categories for people of mixed descent—including mixtures of European, African, and Indian—and physical appearance carries much less social significance in the region than it does in the United States. For example, the legacy of slavery in Brazil endured in the ranking of people by racial cat-

egory. However, in Brazil these categories were never codified legally. In addition, intermarriage and sexual relations among indigenous peoples, Africans, and Europeans were much more commonly accepted than in the United States. Brazilians now have dozens of racial categories based on differences in a variety of physical features, including hair, lips, eyes, and noses, as well as skin color. As a result, siblings from the same family can fall into different racial categories. Also, in Brazil the presence of any white ancestor helps to determine a person's classification, and over half of Brazilians fall into the broad category of "white" (which is broken down into many smaller subcategories). However, many white Brazilians would be perceived as black if they traveled to the United States (Kephart 2003). For a look at various systems of racial and ethnic classification, see Figure 10.2.

Australia 2001 Census

Are you of Aboriginal or Torres Strait Islander origin?
If you are of both Aboriginal and Torres Strait Islander origin, mark both 'Yes' boxes.

☐ No
☐ Yes, Aboriginal
☐ Yes, Torres Strait Islander

What is your ancestry? Provide more than one if necessary.

☐ English
☐ Irish
☐ Italian
☐ German
☐ Greek
☐ Chinese
☐ Australian
☐ Other

England 2001 Census

What is your ethnic group?
A) White
☐ British
☐ Irish
☐ Any other white background

B) Mixed
☐ White and Black Caribbean
☐ White and Black African
☐ White and Asian
☐ Any other Mixed background

C) Asian or Asian British
☐ Indian
☐ Pakistani
☐ Bangleshi
☐ Any other Asian background

D) Black or Black British
☐ Caribbean
☐ African
☐ Any other black background

E) Chinese/other ethnic group
☐ Chinese
☐ Any other

Brazil 2000 Census

Choose your race:
☐ White - branca
☐ Black - peta
☐ Yellow - amaréta
☐ Brown - parda
☐ Native, aboriginal - indigena
☐ Undeclared

Bulgaria 2001 Census

What is your ethnic group?
☐ Bulgarian
☐ Turkish
☐ Gypsies
☐ Other

Canada 2001 Census

Are you an aboriginal person, that is, North American Indian, Métis or Inuit (Eskimo)? If "Yes", check the box(es) that describe(s) you now.

☐ No, > Continue with the next question
☐ Yes, North American Indian
☐ Yes, Métis
☐ Yes, Inuit (Eskimo)

Are you a member of an Indian Band/First Nation?
☐ No
☐ Yes, member of an Indian Band/First Nation

Are you a Treaty Indian or a Registered Indian as defined by the Indian Act of Canada?
☐ No
☐ Yes, Treaty Indian or a Registered Indian

Mexico 2000 Census

Are you Náhuatl, Mayan, Zapoteco, Mixteco or of another indigenous group?
☐ Yes
☐ No

South Africa 2001 Census

How would you describe yourself in terms of population group?

☐ Black African
☐ Coloured
☐ Indian or Asian
☐ White
☐ Other

FIGURE 10.2 | RACE AND ETHNICITY ACROSS CULTURES
Because race and ethnicity are social constructions, they vary by culture. Different countries use different classification systems in their census collection. If you moved to another country, your race or ethnicity might change. *Source:* American Anthropological Association (2011).

The Role of Culture: Inventing Ethnicity and Race

Minority and Majority Groups

In any given society, people often think of its members who are of different races and ethnicities in terms of majority and minority groups. A **minority group** is *a collection of people who suffer disadvantages and have less power because of identifiable physical or cultural characteristics.* In contrast, a **majority group** is *a collection of people who enjoy privileges and have more access to power because of identifiable physical or cultural characteristics.* Sociologists do not use these terms in a literal sense. A minority group need not be an actual minority of the population, and a majority group need not be an actual majority. In South Africa under the white supremacist apartheid regime, for example, the black population held the minority status even though they far outnumbered Whites.

Although the status of individual members of a minority can vary widely, *as a group,* compared to the majority group, minorities tend to have lower incomes, less education, less political influence, and poorer health. Conversely, individual members of a majority group may not wield great power or have access to great resources, but, *as a group,* majorities dominate society. In addition to greater resources, the majority group also has the power to create and enforce the labels used to designate minority groups.

Members of minority groups tend to be conscious of their status and aware of the hurdles and barriers they face in society. To navigate a majority-dominated society successfully, they must learn how the majority group operates. In contrast, majority-group members often take their status for granted and are unaware of their relative privilege. They typically do not need to learn about minority cultures to be successful within a society their group dominates.

Patterns of Majority-Minority Interaction

The relationship between majority and minority groups in a society can range from benign to destructive. In some cases, members of a minority group might find acceptance and equal standing with the majority group, whereas in other situations a minority group may be subjected to widespread prejudice and discrimination. To have **prejudice** means *to "pre-judge" someone or some group negatively based on inadequate information.* These judgments are often based on **stereotypes,** *exaggerated, distorted, or untrue generalizations about categories of people that do not acknowledge individual variation.* Stereotypes can be either negative or positive; examples of positive stereotypes are the Asian math whiz and the African American sports star. Prejudice is limited to beliefs and attitudes that individuals hold but may not act on. When prejudice is joined to action, however, it leads to **discrimination,** *unequal treatment that gives advantages to one group of people over another without justifiable cause.*

The patterns of interaction among majority and minority groups can take a variety of forms, sometimes straddling more than one category. In a society that embraces **pluralism,** *dis-*

RACE · AND · CHANGE

For many years, white people were the assumed norm when manufacturers created "flesh"-colored products such as adhesive bandages. Today, reflecting changes in the culture, manufacturers are more likely to recognize a diversity of skin tones, as with these "multicultural" crayons.

Structure and Power Among Racial and Ethnic Groups

By identifying certain cultural or physical traits as socially significant, people create a social reality that influences how they behave with one another. In other words, "seeing" others in terms of race, ethnicity, and other social categories (such as religion, age, and sexual orientation) can affect how we act toward them and help to legitimize social inequality based on those categories. Let's look at some of these dynamics.

tinct ethnic and racial groups coexist on equal terms and have equal social standing. Members of these groups recognize and maintain their differences, but the differences have no significant impact on anyone's political, social, or economic standing. Switzerland is a successful pluralistic society. The Swiss Confederation—Switzerland's official name—unites four cultures, each with its own regions and its own official language: German, French, Italian, or Romansch (based on Latin).

Amalgamation is *the process by which a majority and a minority group blend or mix to form a new group.* This is typically accomplished through intermarriage over the course of several generations. For example, Mexican society today is primarily an amalgamation of Indian and Spanish cultures that have blended to create what is now a distinctly Mexican identity.

Assimilation is *the process by which members of a minority group come to adopt the culture of the majority group.* As we will see, the experience of many white European ethnic groups in the United States has been one of assimilation; ethnic groups largely abandoned their distinct cultures and were absorbed into the nation's dominant culture. The assimilation experience is often partially voluntary, as minority group members emulate the dominant culture, and partially coerced as majority-group members require others to conform to their cultural expectations.

Segregation involves *keeping distinct social groups physically and socially separate and unequal.* In the United States, segregation is most associated with the oppression of African Americans, especially in the South after the Civil War and before the civil rights movement.

Genocide is *the systematic killing of a group of people, based on their race, ethnicity, nationality, or religion.* Typically, genocide involves a majority group seeking to exterminate a minority group. The deliberate killing of Jews and others by the Nazi regime in Germany and other European countries during World War II is the most infamous example of genocide, but not the first and, unfortunately, not the last (Kiernan 2007).

Minority Group Responses to Discrimination

Minority groups can respond to majority-group domination in a variety of ways:

■ **Withdrawal** involves physically escaping the worst oppression. As we will see, the Great Migration of African Americans out of the South to the North and Midwest in the early and mid-twentieth century is one example of this strategy. Other examples include the formation of racial and ethnic enclaves in urban areas: places with names like Germantown, Little Italy, and Chinatown.

■ **Passing** involves blending in with the dominant group. White ethnics in the United States often changed their

names on arrival to better blend into the dominant Anglo-Saxon culture. Germans with the name "Schmidt" would change it to "Smith," for example. Today many recent immigrants from Vietnam, China, India, and elsewhere similarly adopt names that are more familiar to native-born Americans and easier for them to spell and pronounce. Passing can also occur when people in a minority group take advantage of physical similarities to the members of the majority group, as when light-skinned Blacks conceal their race or even change their hair to appear more "white."

■ **Code-switching**—a term coined by sociologist Elijah Anderson (1999)—refers to the strategy of complying with the social expectations of the majority by creating a "front-stage" self-presentation while maintaining a different more comfortable and authentic "back-stage" identity. Code-switching may involve dressing "white" or using "white" English at work or school, while retaining a more comfortable mother tongue, ethnic slang, and ethnic dress at home.

■ **Resistance** involves actively asserting oneself—either individually or collectively—in defiance of majority discrimination. The many civil rights struggles that have characterized U.S. history are examples of this strategy.

The Origins of Racial and Ethnic Diversity in the United States

In the United States, ideas about race and ethnicity are rooted in the country's history—the European conquest of native peoples, the immigration of Europeans, the enslavement of Africans, and the recruitment of Asian laborers.

Native Peoples

In 1492, before Europeans established their first permanent settlements in the Western Hemisphere, an estimated 50 million people lived in North and South America, about 5 million of them in what is today the United States and Canada (Taylor 2001). When Europeans arrived, the Aztec capital of Tenochtitlán had a quarter of a million inhabitants—five times the size of London at the time (Gonzalez 2000). Native peoples formed hundreds of different societies with unique languages, religions, forms of government, and cultural traditions. These ranged from the Inuit, who lived in nomadic bands in what is today the Canadian Arctic, to the powerful urban civilizations of the Aztec and Maya in what is today Mexico and the Inca in what is today Peru.

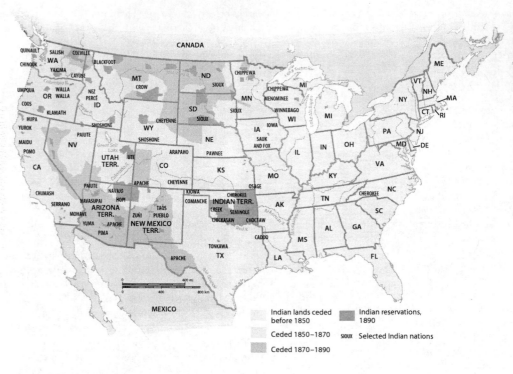

MAP 10.2 | NATIVE AMERICAN LOSS OF TERRITORY FROM BEFORE 1850 TO 1890

By 1890, conquest and expansion had confined most of the Native American population to a series of reservations, transforming North America from a land controlled by dozens of different native societies to one dominated by white European Americans. *Source:* Davidson et al. (2011).

Indian lands ceded before 1850

Ceded 1850–1870

Ceded 1870–1890

Indian reservations, 1890

SIOUX Selected Indian nations

The European invasion that began with Christopher Columbus's first voyage in 1492 had a devastating effect on native peoples. At any given place, within a decade after contact with Europeans, the native population typically fell to about half its precontact numbers, and within fifty years to just one tenth (Taylor 2001). Most of this devastation was caused by disease. The native peoples had no immunity to the many infections the Europeans brought with them, including smallpox, measles, tuberculosis, and the bubonic plague, and they succumbed to them in huge numbers. Like many European settlers, early Massachusetts founder John Winthrop interpreted the widespread deaths as a sign that God was "making room" for the colonists and "hath hereby cleared our title to this place" (in Takaki 2008, 40).

Of those who survived disease, many were killed as European powers, vying for control of the Americas, steadily dispossessed native peoples of their land and autonomy. By just before the American Revolution in 1776, the British and French controlled much of what became the United States and Canada. The Spanish were the dominant power in what is now the southwestern United States, Mexico, and much of Latin and South America, whereas the Portuguese controlled what is now Brazil.

After it achieved independence from Britain, the United States continued to subjugate and uproot the native populations of North America as it expanded westward. Its tactics included political deception, blatant treaty violations, forcible removal, and military conquest. By 1890, the country's Native American population had been reduced to less than 250,000 (Gibson and Jung 2002) who were confined largely to reserva-

tions that represented only a tiny fraction of the lands their ancestors had once occupied (Map 10.2). The U.S. government, which managed these reservations, sometimes seized Native American children and sent them to boarding schools where they were taught English and encouraged to adopt Christianity and abandon their own language and culture.

Native peoples struggled to maintain their cultural identity despite this invasion, and they have had an enduring and continuing impact on post-conquest societies, especially in places with the densest precontact populations, such as Mexico, Guatemala, Ecuador, Peru, and Bolivia.

Hispanics or Latinos

In the first half of the 1500s, various Spanish explorers traveled through what is today the southern half of the United States, claiming the region for Spain as they went. These expeditions—which took place decades before the 1607 founding of the first British colony at Jamestown, Virginia—gave names to many geographical features in the United States and established some of its earliest European settlements, including St. Augustine in Florida and Santa Fe in New Mexico (Gonzalez 2000).

Spanish control of areas that became Mexico, Puerto Rico, Cuba, and other nations of Central and South America laid the foundation for ethnic combinations that we now define as Hispanic or Latino.

MEXICAN AMERICANS Mexican Americans are the largest Latino group in the United States, partly because when Mexico gained its independence from Spain in 1821, it

One way to dominate a population is to eradicate its culture. Native American boarding schools, typically run by Christian missionaries, taught native children to adopt European ways of life and abandon their own language, religion, traditions, and styles of dress.

as African Americans. They were excluded from many restaurants and other public facilities, and their children attended segregated schools intended to prepare them to be farm workers, not to help them get ahead. White-controlled courts also rejected the titles many Mexican Americans held to land, thus helping Anglos gain control of most of the Southwest. Deprived of land, many Mexican Americans worked for Anglos in mining, railroad construction, and ranching and farming, earning lower wages than their white counterparts (Montejano 1987). Both stoking and exploiting this racial and ethnic conflict, employers were able to blunt efforts by Mexican Americans and other workers to organize unions and strike for better conditions (Roediger 1999).

Some Mexican citizens, meanwhile, fled the political turmoil of the 1910 Mexican Revolution and headed north across the U.S. border in search of security and work. But then, when work dried up during the Great Depression of the 1930s, 400,000 Mexicans—including many U.S.-born citizens—were sent back to Mexico, sometimes forcibly. Just a few years later, though, labor shortages that followed the outbreak of World War II prompted the U.S. government to recruit 200,000 Mexican laborers to work temporarily in the United States through the *bracero* program (from *brazos* for arms). Since then, agriculture in the Southwest has remained dependent on the labor of migrant Mexican and Mexican-American farm workers. The low pay and difficult conditions of this work sparked many labor disputes, which increased in the 1960s and 1970s with the rise of the United Farm Workers union led by César Chávez and Dolores Huerta.

PUERTO RICANS Puerto Ricans, the second largest Latino group in the United States, are also linked to U.S. expansion. The United States invaded and occupied Puerto Rico during the Spanish-American War of 1898, transforming the island from a Spanish colony to a U.S. colony. In the ensuing decades, U.S. sugar companies acquired vast tracts of land on the island, displacing small growers and prompting sometimes violent labor clashes. Many agricultural workers fled to the U.S. mainland in search of better opportunities. In 1917, Puerto Ricans became U.S. citizens and, in 1947, Puerto Rico became a commonwealth with the right to elect its own

included what are today the states of Texas, New Mexico, Arizona, California, Nevada, Utah, and part of Colorado. In the 1820s, thousands of white U.S. citizens illegally crossed the Mexican border into the sparsely populated region of Téjas—present-day Texas. By 1835, U.S. citizens in the region outnumbered Mexicans by five to one. A year later they launched an insurrection that ended with the creation of the Republic of Texas. Its president, Sam Houston, declared in his inaugural address that the newly created republic reflected "glory on the Anglo-Saxon race" (Montejano 1987; Takaki 2008, 158).

In 1845 the United States annexed Texas, and an ensuing border dispute provided the justification for the Mexican-American War (1846–1848). By the end of the war, the United States seized nearly half of Mexico, including what is now California and the U.S. southwest, fulfilling the common belief in Manifest Destiny, which asserted that white Americans had a divinely ordained right and duty to occupy the continent from coast to coast (Horsman 1981).

The Treaty of Guadalupe Hidalgo that concluded the war in 1848 granted U.S. citizenship to about 80,000 formerly Mexican citizens who now found themselves living within the United States. Overnight, they had become, as Mexican American leader Pablo de la Guerra, later put it, "foreigners in their own land" (Takaki 2008, 165). In California, the discovery of gold that same year triggered a massive influx of Anglos—white English speakers—making Mexican Americans a minority there. Ironically, the newly arrived Whites often saw the native Mexicans as "foreign" competitors for their land claims.

As they gained political power, Anglos began changing the laws already biased in favor of Whites to give themselves further advantages at the expense of the native Mexican population, creating a de facto racial caste system. Throughout the Southwest, Mexican Americans faced the same segregation

The Origins of Racial and Ethnic Diversity in the United States

THROUGH A SOCIOLOGICAL LENS

Understanding Whiteness

In a classic essay, Peggy McIntosh (1988) notes that Whites are often taught to recognize the disadvantages that minorities face but not the advantages they enjoy as Whites. She describes some of the dozens of ways that she benefits from white privilege in her daily life. When she shops, for example, she doesn't experience the suspicion and harassment to which minorities are often subjected. Minorities are often judged individually as if they represented their entire community: If they excel, they are a credit to the community; if they behave questionably, it's because of the deficiencies of their community. As a white person, McIntosh does not bear this burden. Cumulatively, these and similar advantages constitute an "invisible package of unearned assets," as McIntosh calls it, that reflects the dominant position of the white majority in the United States.

McIntosh's essay is one example of the study of whiteness. People often think of race in terms of minorities. But white majorities in the European colonies created the modern idea of "race" during the eighteenth century, and to understand "race" we must understand whiteness and its connection to power and inequality.

Although he is best known for writing about the condition of black Americans, African American sociologist and activist W.E.B. Du Bois (1935/1998) recognized the importance of whiteness a century ago. Although American society as a whole was divided by class, he noted, the working class was divided further along racial lines. White workers might be poorly paid, but they were "compensated in part by a sort of public and psychological wage. They were given public deference and titles of courtesy because they were white" (p. 700). They, like white people of all classes, could attend public functions and enjoy public parks. They were served by a white police force, by a court system staffed by white

jurists, and by white elected officials, and they had access to the best schools, which were reserved for them. Ironically, however, by embracing these race-based privileges, white workers lost the opportunity to organize with black workers to improve conditions for all of them.

Du Bois was writing at a very different moment in history than ours, of course, but sociologists have used his basic sociological insights to inform their current analysis of race, particularly on the nature of whiteness (Rothenberg 2004). Sociologists engaged in "whiteness studies" examine both the historical roots and the contemporary processes associated with whiteness and white privilege. The questions they explore (some of which are discussed in this chapter) include: How did diverse ethnic groups once considered fundamentally different become lumped together as "Whites"? How have the U.S. political, legal, and economic systems been structured to give advantages to Whites? Does white privilege endure, and, if so, what forms does it take? How can Whites help to combat racism and its legacy?

The point is not to blame today's Whites for the history of racial injustice. Instead, whiteness studies help us better understand that history of injustice, to recognize its continuing legacy today, and to use those insights to work toward a more just society.

think about it

1. Has your education about race included consideration of what it means to be "white?"

2. How does the study of whiteness illustrate the sociological insight that power is a social relationship?

---

governor. Although it otherwise remains subject to U.S. law, it has only a nonvoting delegate to Congress and its residents cannot vote for president. Puerto Ricans are divided about the island's future political status. Some support the current arrangement, some favor gaining U.S. statehood, and some advocate independence (Takaki 2008).

CUBAN AMERICANS The Spanish colony of Cuba, unlike Puerto Rico, gained formal independence after the Spanish-American War. However, it remained subject to U.S. military and economic intervention and suffered from political instability. In 1959, Fidel Castro led a revolution to overthrow the Cuban dictator Fulgencio Batista and instituted radical economic reform, eventually aligning his nation with the Soviet Union and communist bloc nations. Castro's reforms were popular among many of the country's poor, but not among the more affluent middle and upper classes, many of whom fled to

the United States, forming the core of today's Cuban American community.

WASPs and White Ethnic Groups

The colonies founded by Great Britain on the east coast of North America were what became the early United States, and for many years the descendents of colonial-era immigrants from Great Britain—White Anglo-Saxon Protestants, or WASPS—were the country's most powerful ethnic group. Other white ethnic groups arrived in large numbers during the nineteenth and twentieth centuries.

WHITE ANGLO-SAXON PROTESTANTS The WASP label combines race, ethnicity, and religion. It refers mostly to people of English ancestry but also includes those

of Scottish and Welsh ancestry. It excludes Whites from other parts of Europe as well as Catholics and Jews. (The Through a Sociological Lens box explores the study of whiteness.)

WASPs were not a single unified group. Religious rivalries and class divisions made life better for some than for others. However, as the first immigrants to what was to become the United States, WASPs were able to develop and control the country's emerging government, business, and religious institutions. They thus amassed enormous power and avoided the sorts of discrimination that later immigrants would have to overcome. In the early years of the United States, WASPs typically believed in white racial superiority—often calling themselves the Anglo-Saxon race—and created laws to exclude non-Whites from the new nation.

The monopoly on power that WASPs maintained through much of U.S. history loosened considerably by the middle of the twentieth century. The influence of this group endures, however, on much of U.S. culture, most noticeably in the use of English as the country's dominant language and the standing of Protestant Christianity as the country's largest religious affiliation.

WHITE ETHNIC GROUPS The first major wave of European immigrants who were not WASPs arrived in the early and mid-nineteenth century. After their English landlords evicted them to make way for more grazing lands for cattle and sheep, many impoverished Irish tenant farmers were left dependent on potatoes for survival. When blight devastated the potato crop in Ireland in 1845, hundreds of thousands of Irish tenant farmers fled to the United States. At around the same time, large numbers of Germans arrived, as well.

Many WASPs at first denied these and other European newcomers equal racial standing with themselves, referring to them instead as "Celtic" (Irish, Welsh, Scots), "Alpine" (German, Norwegian, Swedish, and other central European), and "Mediterranean" (Italian, Spanish, Greek, and other southern European). But as the new groups gained some power, they rejected these separate designations and claimed the mantle of racial superiority together with WASPs as part of a broadened "white" race (Mukhopadhyay, Henze, and Moses 2007).

The history of the Irish in America illustrates this process (Ignatiev 1996). The Irish had white skin, but they were Catholic, not Protestant, and many spoke Gaelic (Irish) rather than English. As a result, many WASPs considered the Irish a different race and discriminated against them as they did against black people, though never subjecting the Irish to the systematic legal discrimination Blacks faced. Often poor and unskilled, the Irish commonly lived in the same neighborhoods as free Blacks in northern cities and were often referred to as "white Negroes." Common stereotypes portrayed them as happy, lazy, and stupid with a penchant for drink, dance, and music—stereotypes that were also associated with Blacks.

In time, the Irish learned English and took steps to differentiate themselves from black people, establishing their own

Along with Italians, Jews, Greeks, and others, Irish immigrants were among those not considered "white" in the nineteenth century and subject to discrimination. Common complaints were that new immigrants didn't speak English, had unfamiliar religious beliefs, had strange cultural practices, had too many children, engaged in crime and excessive drinking, and took away jobs from established Americans. How do such criticisms compare to today's discussions about immigration?

churches and schools and forming their own social organizations. Although they had earlier supported the abolition of slavery, they gained political power by associating themselves with the Democratic Party, which at that time supported slavery. As a result, the Irish eventually came to be perceived as "Whites" in American society—an option not available to darker-skinned people of African or Asian descent.

The second—and largest—wave of white ethnic immigrants arrived between 1890 and 1924. During that span, 20 million people came to the United States, most of them from southern and eastern Europe, including Italians, Poles, and Jews. Driven by poverty or political repression and drawn by the demand for labor in a rapidly industrializing United States, they were often met with resentment, prejudice, discrimination in housing and employment, and, sometimes, outright violence (Daniels 1997).

The Origins of Racial and Ethnic Diversity in the United States

thinking about culture
Can you think of ways in which the WASP influence on **culture** has affected you? Consider common words you use, values you have, and the history you were taught in school.

Anti-immigrant sentiment increased after World War I (1914–1918), resulting in the Immigration Act of 1924. This law slashed total immigration to 150,000 a year (excepting immigration from the Western Hemisphere) and dramatically reduced the percentage of foreign-born people in the United States for the next forty years. The legislation effectively ended Asian immigration because it prohibited immigration by "aliens ineligible to citizenship" and naturalization was limited to Whites only. It also slashed immigration from southern and eastern Europe through a severely restrictive quota system (Daniels 1997).

African Americans

Unique among the diverse racial and ethnic groups that make up the U.S. population, most African Americans are descended from people forcibly removed from their homeland, sent here against their will, and subjected to a lifetime of coerced labor. This experience is reflected in the distinctively North American idea of race that European colonists created to justify an economic system based on the slave labor of Africans. Before the American experience, slavery existed mostly independent of race. Greeks and Romans kept slaves with pale skin just like themselves, while some dark-skinned Africans captured and enslaved dark-skinned members of other African tribes. In what became the United States, however, a new notion of race was invented piecemeal, over a series of decades, and eventually used to justify a race-based slave system that was the foundation of the agricultural economy of the day, especially in the American South (Johnson and Smith 1999; Smedley 2007). This process so influenced the uniquely American notions of race—and the interaction between race and class in the United States—that it warrants close attention.

INDENTURED SERVITUDE Race-based slavery emerged only after a labor system based on white indentured servitude failed. When English colonists settled the region that later became the United States, they needed workers to build settlements and raise crops. Especially during the early and mid-1600s, colonists relied primarily on the labor of indentured servants. These poor Whites, mostly Britons and Germans, contracted to work for a period of four to seven years in exchange for trans-Atlantic passage and sometimes "freedom dues"—which might include food, clothes, a gun, and, most important, land—upon completion of their contract. Some came voluntarily; others—including homeless children, convicts, beggars, and others considered by British officials to be social undesirables—were shipped forcibly. The work was brutal and the conditions harsh, and many indentured servants died before gaining their freedom. In many ways, they were essentially slaves: they were bought and sold

as property, served at the whim of their employers, and were often chained and beaten. Unlike slaves, however, they suffered only temporary servitude; slavery was lifelong (Jordan and Walsh 2008).

Indentured servitude declined eventually, however. As word of the harsh conditions spread, fewer people volunteered to indenture themselves. Unrest grew among indentured servants who had been cheated of their freedom dues, and in 1676, white and black servants joined black slaves in Bacon's Rebellion in Virginia, frightening wealthy colonial officials. To maintain their authority, powerful Whites used race to keep poor Whites from joining forces with poor Blacks and slaves (Johnson and Smith 1999; Horton and Horton 2005).

SLAVERY AS AN ECONOMIC INSTITUTION
In the early 1600s, Africans were only a small part of the colonial work force. At first, many were treated similarly to white indentured servants. They lived with white servants; had similar legal rights, including the right to sign contracts; and were even able to travel to some extent. As the supply of indentured servants dwindled, however, white planters began to rely increasingly on the labor of black African slaves.

The enslaved Africans were the victims of an economic system that linked England, West Africa, and England's American colonies in a three-stage pattern of trade. In the first stage, English goods were shipped to West Africa and traded for Africans who had been kidnapped by fellow Africans and sold to European slavers. Packed into ships under horrific conditions, up to 20 million captives suffered the second stage, the infamous middle passage from Africa to the Americas that only half would survive. In the Americas, they were exchanged for raw materials such as tobacco, rice, and cotton. Finally, the raw materials were shipped to England and exchanged for finished goods, beginning the cycle again (Johnson and Smith 1999; Horton and Horton 2006).

THE RACIALIZATION OF SLAVERY As the importance of slave labor grew, the ideology justifying it changed. At first, colonists claimed that as non-Christians, Africans were unworthy of freedom. In a few cases, African slaves successfully sued for their freedom after converting to Christianity. By the end of the 1600s, however, with slaves increasingly converting to Christianity, religious differences no longer provided a convincing rationale for enslaving Africans and their descendants (Johnson and Smith 1999; Horton and Horton 2006). Instead, Whites now drew on pseudo-science and, ironically, biblical scripture to claim that black Africans were a different and inferior human subspecies fit only to serve the superior white race (Smedley 2007).

At the same time, wealthy Southern landowners used their political clout to strip slaves of any legal rights and to define

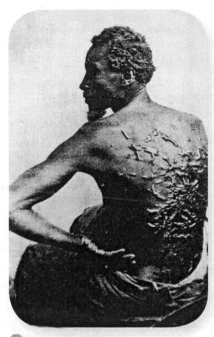

⬆ This man's back shows the scars left from brutal whippings he received as a slave in the American South.

⬆ This idealized image of George Washington, painted in 1853, shows the nation's first president on his Mount Vernon plantation among his slaves. Like other large landowners of the time, Washington depended on slave labor to run his home and to generate his wealth by working his plantation.

CORE CONCEPTS CHALLENGE

↪ *What cultural beliefs about the nature of slavery does this painting promote? Who do you think is the intended audience for a picture like this?*

slave status legally in racial terms. In 1705 the Virginia Assembly for the first time passed laws designating slaves as property. Slave rebellions in the following years provoked increasingly restrictive laws, including laws making it illegal for slaves to learn to read (Johnson and Smith 1999; Horton and Horton 2006).

SLAVERY AND AFFLUENCE   Race-based slavery, justified by an ideology that viewed Africans as less than human, underlay the growing wealth of the new colonial elites and not just in the South. Members of a white planter aristocracy owned large estates and benefitted directly from the labor of their many slaves. George Washington, among the wealthiest colonists of his day, owned more than 300 slaves. But even the northern colonies—not directly dependent on plantation agriculture—benefited from slavery. Merchants, shipbuilders, metal smiths, rum distillers, sawmill operators, and many others all profited directly or indirectly from the slave trade (Johnson and Smith 1999; Horton and Horton 2006).

Slaves lived under varied conditions, but their labor was always coerced, and the coercion was backed by force, often applied barbarically. White masters also often took it as their prerogative to rape their female slaves, and the offspring of these encounters were legally slaves at birth. Slaves resisted their oppression in various ways, from avoiding work, to escaping, to joining rebellions (Johnson and Smith 1999; Horton and Horton 2006).

SLAVERY'S LEGACY   While Thomas Jefferson was writing "All men are created equal" in the Declaration of Independence, a slave in the next room was on call to attend to his every need. In 1776, some Whites recognized that slavery was unjust and spoke out against it, but they were few. Slavery persisted for nearly a hundred years in the newly independent United States until it was outlawed by the Thirteenth Amendment to the U.S. Constitution in the wake of the Civil War (1861–1865). The legacy of slavery endured, however, with the imposition of legalized (*de jure*) racial segregation in the South and segregation in fact (*de facto*), if not by law, in much of the rest of the country. Under the South's so-called Jim Crow laws, all aspects of life, including housing, employment, education, and political participation, were structured along racial lines, ensuring that Blacks and Whites would remain separate and unequal.

Racial segregation was enforced through violence and terror. Between 1882 and 1968, for example, white mobs lynched and killed an estimated 4,742 Blacks (and many members of other ethnic minorities, as well) (Allen et al. 2000). During the Great Migration of the early and middle twentieth century, many African Americans—some two million by 1930—fled the repressive South in search of economic opportunity in the urban North (Takiki 2008).

African Americans had long challenged their subordinate status under Jim Crow, and in the 1950s these efforts coalesced and intensified in the civil rights movement. By the mid-1960s,

A group of white people in Indiana pose proudly for a photo after a lynching in 1930. Lynchings of this sort, often of alleged criminals, were conducted in broad daylight with the consent of local authorities. Some were treated as community events with a carnival atmosphere. Photos like this one—sometimes including children—were regularly taken to commemorate the occasion, and copies of these gruesome pictures were then sold as postcards.

this landmark movement had succeeded in dismantling legal segregation and begun to significantly change the country's entrenched culture of racism.

Asian Americans

The experiences of African slaves in the plantation economy were unique. However, throughout U.S. history, race and ethnicity have been used repeatedly to divide workers for the benefit of the powerful. Early Asian Americans experienced this phenomenon as well.

CHINESE AMERICANS
Early Chinese immigrants to the United States fled the violence of Britain's "Opium Wars," political turmoil resulting from peasant rebellions, and harsh economic conditions. The hope of finding possible riches in the California Gold Rush of 1849 motivated the earliest Chinese to immigrate. More came between 1863 and 1869—recruited to displace higher-paid Irish workers—to build the transcontinental railroad, a massive, sometimes brutally dangerous, labor-intensive project. After the railroad was completed, some Chinese workers moved to cities, most notably San Francisco, while others played a prominent role in California's emerging agricultural economy (Takaki 2008).

A group gathers behind the barbed wire fence of an internment camp in California around 1942. Camps like these kept Japanese Americans confined for the duration of World War II.

The Chinese were particularly vulnerable to discrimination because, as non-Whites, they were ineligible for U.S. citizenship. California, for example, targeted them with a special tax on foreign miners who were not going to become citizens. Over the years, white workers grew increasingly resentful of Chinese workers, often blaming them for taking their jobs and driving down wages. In the 1870s, Irish American politician Dennis Kearney rose to prominence in California with the slogan "The Chinese must go!" and led violent attacks on Chinese workers. In the early 1890s, unemployed white workers rioted throughout California, beating and sometimes shooting Chinese immigrants and shipping them out of town in freight cars in what the Chinese would come to call the "driving out" (Takaki 2008). Anti-Chinese feeling culminated in the Chinese Exclusion Act of 1882—the first U.S. law to prohibit immigration on the basis of a specific nationality—effectively ending Chinese immigration for a decade (Takaki 2008).

In the face of this hostility, Chinese immigrants already in the country often had to develop their own businesses and rely on their own community for support. Chinese laundries—which were inexpensive to start up—became a staple of many western cities, and urban "Chinatowns" emerged as the center of Chinese social and economic life.

JAPANESE, KOREAN, AND FILIPINO AMERICANS
Japanese, Koreans, and Filipinos have distinct cultures and sometimes conflicting histories, but they share some common experiences in the United States. In the late nineteenth and early twentieth centuries, some 200,000 Japanese, along with others from countries including China, Korea, and the Philippines, were recruited to work on sugar-cane plantations in Hawaii, which was annexed as a U.S. territory

in 1898. Plantation owners expected that this ethnic diversity would keep their workforce divided and vulnerable to exploitation. In 1919, however, the workers united in a successful strike and formed the Hawaii Laborers' Association, Hawaii's first interethnic union (Jung 2006, Takaki 2008). From Hawaii, some Japanese, Korean, and Filipino immigrants went on to the mainland, most of them to work on farms in California. The Asian Exclusion Act, part of the Immigration Act of 1924, however, brought Asian immigration to a virtual stop.

In what was perhaps the most dramatically racist act against an Asian group in the country's history, the U.S. government interned nearly 120,000 Japanese Americans—two-thirds of them U.S. born—for the duration of World War II. In the wake of Japan's attack on Pearl Harbor in December 1941, the government uprooted entire families and sent them to camps in often remote and desolate areas of the country. Although the United States was at war with Germany and Italy as well as Japan, no such measures were taken against white Americans with German or Italian ancestry. In 1988 the U.S. government paid survivors of the camps $20,000 each in reparations and apologized for what it called a "grave injustice," admitting that the internments were done "without adequate security reasons" and "were motivated largely by racial prejudice, wartime hysteria, and a failure of political leadership" [Public Law 100-383 (1988)].

Diversity Today

As a result of the civil rights movement and immigration, U.S. society is one of the most racially and ethnically diverse societies in the world.

The Civil Rights Revolution

During the 1950s and 1960s, the struggle for social justice known as the civil rights movement succeeded in dismantling legal discrimination for the first time in U.S. history and fostered a culture of tolerance that made racial and ethnic prejudice broadly unacceptable. Sometimes working through interracial and interethnic coalitions, previously marginalized groups celebrated their distinct cultures, gained some political power, and challenged discriminatory practices. Changes in immigration law that Congress enacted in the 1960s contributed further to the new diversity that has marked the United States ever since.

Racial and Ethnic Groups Today

Although the United States as a whole is diverse, that diversity varies significantly from region to region. According to the U.S. Census Bureau (2009a), different ancestries predominate in each of the four major regions of the country. In the Northeast, Irish ancestry is the most common (17 percent), whereas African American ancestry is most common in the South

TABLE 10.1	SUMMARY OF MAJOR RACIAL AND ETHNIC GROUPS IN THE UNITED STATES, 2010	

Racial/Ethnic Group	Percentage Within Population
White (any ethnicity)	72.4%
Non-Hispanic white	63.7
Latino/Hispanic (any race)	16.3
Black or African American	12.6
Asian	4.8
American Indian or Alaska Native	0.9
Native Hawaiian and Pacific Islander	0.2

Source: U.S. Census Bureau (2011c, 2011e, 2010h).

(19 percent), German in the Midwest (29.3 percent), and Mexican in the West (23.4 percent).

WHITE AMERICANS At 72.4 percent of the population, white people of many different ancestries continue to be by far the largest racial group in U.S. society. Non-Hispanic Whites account for 63.7 percent of the population (see Table 10.1). Whites are found in substantial numbers throughout the country, with especially heavy concentrations in parts of the Midwest and northern New England. In 2010, only Hawaii, New Mexico, California, and Texas (as well as the District of Columbia) were "majority minority" states with a non-Hispanic white population of less than 50 percent. In contrast, about half of the states were at least 75 percent white and non-Hispanic (U.S. Census Bureau 2011c, 2011e).

HISPANICS OR LATINOS Latinos are the largest and fastest-growing minority group in the United States. Numbering 50.5 million in 2010, they make up 16.3 percent of the U.S. population and are expected to be nearly one-quarter of the U.S. population by 2050. Nearly 53 percent identify themselves as white only, 2.5 percent as black or African American only, and 6 percent as two or more races; and 36.7 percent report being of "some other race," likely treating Hispanic as a racial rather than ethnic category (U.S. Census Bureau 2011c, 2011e). Latinos are concentrated in the Southwest and West (reflecting the annexation of these areas from Mexico), in Florida (where Cuban Americans are concentrated), and in the New York metropolitan area.

AFRICAN AMERICANS African Americans number nearly 39 million. At about 12.6 percent of the U.S. population, they are the nation's largest racial minority. Most African Americans live in the South, but they are also a major presence in cities of the northeast and northern Midwest. In addition, recent immigrants are diversifying the African American

Diversity Today

community, especially in major metropolitan areas. In 2007, nearly 8 percent of those who reported their race as only black were foreign born, compared with just 1 percent in 1960 (U.S. Census Bureau 2011c, 2011e, 2010h).

ASIAN AMERICANS Asian Americans today account for 4.8 percent of the population in the United States. Chinese, Indian, and Filipinos are today's largest Asian subgroups. Those in the second largest subgroup—from India— are relatively recent arrivals. Filipinos are the third largest subgroup. In addition, many Koreans and Vietnamese immigrated to the United States in the wake of the Korean War and the Vietnam War. Asian Americans are mostly located on the West coast, in major Hawaiian urban centers, and in the New York region (U.S. Census Bureau 2011c, 2011e).

Asian Americans are found at every class level, but on average they have both higher incomes and more education than members of other racial and ethnic groups, including Whites. As a result, they are often perceived to be a "model minority," a label that overlooks the diversity within the Asian community and disregards the discrimination Asians have endured during much of American history. It can also place unfair pressure on Asian youth to live up to a stereotypical ideal.

NATIVE AMERICANS In 2010, 1.7 percent of the U.S. population (over 5.2 million people) reported their race as American Indian or Alaska Native, either alone (0.9 percent) or in combination with another race (0.7). Of these, 3.1 million identified as exclusively Native American and the rest identified as multiracial (U.S. Census Bureau 2011c, 2011e). As with other groups, most native peoples identify with a particular tribal heritage—such as Cherokee, Iroquois, or Navajo—more than with such generic, outsider-imposed terms as "Indian," "Native Peoples," or "Native American."

Not until the passage of the Indian Citizenship Act of 1924 were Native Americans granted the unlimited right to American citizenship. Before then, they had only limited access to citizenship that usually required them to give up tribal membership. Citizens or not, poverty and bleak prospects drove many to move away from reservations and into the white-dominated society. In the 1960s and 1970s, though, Native Americans organized to revive their traditional cultures and gain wider recognition of the injustices committed against them. In 1976 the Supreme Court ruled that states do not have the right to regulate activities on Indian reservations, opening the way for the establishment of the casinos and other gambling operations that have provided economic opportunity for some tribes.

ARAB AMERICANS The Arab world consists of more than twenty culturally varied Arabic-speaking countries. As a result, Arab Americans are a diverse ethnic group whose members, like those of other ethnic groups, often identify more with their specific ancestral homelands than with a broader ethnic label. The three largest Arab American subgroups are those who report ancestry from Lebanon (30 percent), Egypt (11.7 percent), and Syria (9.5 percent) (U.S. Census Bureau 2009a). Often highly educated, Arab Americans hold both bachelor's and graduate degrees at nearly double the rate of Americans as a whole, and their median household income is slightly higher than the U.S. national median (Arab American Institute 2010).

In the United States, many people confuse the ethnic label "Arab" with the religious label "Muslim." In fact, more than 80 percent of the world's Muslims live *outside* the Arab world, mostly in sub-Saharan Africa, Southeast Asia, and the Far East. Furthermore, one out of ten people in the Arab world is not Muslim (Kayyali 2007). Among Arab Americans, between 50 percent and 63 percent are Christian, whereas between 24 percent and 50 percent are Muslim (Kayyali). Just 0.55 percent of the U.S. population, or about 1.7 million people, claim Arab ancestry (U.S. Census Bureau 2009a). However, because many Christians with Arab ancestry do not self-identify as Arabs, the actual number of Arab Americans may be much higher, perhaps 3.5 million (Arab American Institute 2010).

The earliest Arab immigrants, mostly Lebanese Christians, began arriving in the 1880s. Among more recent immigrants, Muslims predominate. In a striking example of the social construction of race, in 1915, George Dow, a Syrian immigrant living in segregated South Carolina, successfully argued in court that Syrians were white and therefore eligible for citizenship under the existing immigration laws, which limited citizenship to "free white persons" (Naff 1985). The U.S. Census Bureau ever since has counted Arab Americans as white. However, some Arab Americans petitioned the Census Bureau, unsuccessfully, to make "Arab" a separate racial category on the 2010 census (Ashmawey 2010).

Since the September 11, 2001, attacks by Muslim extremists, many Arab Americans, particularly Muslims, have found themselves demonized and subjected to discrimination and violence. Half of American Muslims report that it has been more difficult to be Muslim in the United States since the attacks (Pew Research Center 2007).

Immigration in the Post–Civil Rights Era

In the post–civil rights era, two developments coincided to produce a significant change in immigration patterns. First, global migration increased dramatically, with people from poorer countries seeking economic opportunity in the world's wealthy countries. Second, the Immigration and Nationality Act of 1965, passed in the midst of the civil rights revolution,

Percentage of foreign-born population by region of origin

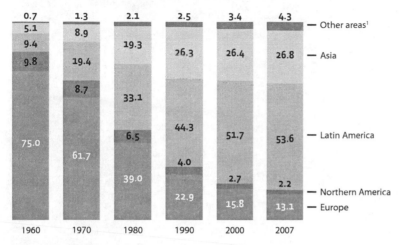

	1960	1970	1980	1990	2000	2007	
Other areas[1]	0.7	1.3	2.1	2.5	3.4	4.3	— Other areas[1]
Asia	5.1 / 9.4 / 9.8	8.9 / 19.4	19.3	26.3	26.4	26.8	— Asia
Latin America	75.0	61.7	8.7 / 33.1 / 6.5	44.3	51.7	53.6	— Latin America
Northern America			4.0 / 39.0		2.7	2.2	— Northern America
Europe				22.9	15.8	13.1	— Europe

[1] Other areas include Africa and Oceania.

FIGURE 10.3 | FOREIGN-BORN POPULATION SINCE 1960

Changes in immigration law enacted in the 1960s eliminated preferences for European immigrants, contributing to a shift toward greater immigration from Latin American and Asian countries. *Source:* U.S. Census Bureau (2010h).

eliminated the discriminatory national quotas that had favored immigrants from northern and western Europe. Instead, the act put in place a system that favored family members of U.S. citizens, skilled workers, and political refugees. New immigrants started arriving from more regions than before, and as a result, the percentage of foreign-born people in the United States from Latin America and Asia, especially, increased significantly, whereas the percentage of foreign-born people from Europe declined (see Figure 10.3).

Significantly, the 1965 legislation allowed naturalized immigrants to sponsor an unlimited number of family members as new immigrants. Once naturalized, these family members could in turn sponsor more family members, a process sometimes called "chain immigration." An unintended consequence of this provision was to increase overall immigration to unprecedented levels, raising the foreign born as a percentage of the country's population to levels approaching those of the 1920s (see Figure 10.4). By 2008, about one out of eight people in the United States was born elsewhere. Because recent immigrants tend to have a higher birthrate than native-born Americans, the result will significantly affect the racial and ethnic composition of the United States in the coming decades (Lee and Bean 2004). (The Sociology Works box on page 270 explores a sociology major's work with immigrant tenants.)

Transnational Migrants

Unlike earlier immigrants, who often sought to assimilate into the dominant society and typically had limited contact with their homelands, many of today's immigrants are **transnational migrants** who *retain strong personal, cultural, and economic ties to both their country of birth and their newly*

The increase in unauthorized immigration has generated considerable controversy.

CORE CONCEPTS CHALLENGE

Some people advocate limiting immigration, stricter enforcement of immigration laws, and a clampdown on the borders. Others argue for continuing high levels of legal immigration and contend that unauthorized immigrants should have more access to citizenship. What role do **culture** *and* **power** *play in these conflicts?*

Diversity Today

SOCIOLOGY WORKS

Mikey Velarde and Community Organizing

When Mikey Velarde began college, he intended to study cognitive science. He had no idea that a few years later he would be helping to organize a tenants' meeting in New York City's East Harlem as part of his new job as a community organizer. But, motivated by a growing desire to understand—and challenge—racial and ethnic inequalities, Velarde switched from cognitive science to a major in sociology. He graduated with a bachelor's degree and now works primarily with immigrant tenants to help them secure dignified housing in the face of plans for urban development that threaten to displace low-income residents. Velarde has learned a broad array of skills as he works to support local community activists in myriad ways. He knocks on doors to build support networks and to staff meetings of the local tenant association; he organizes community protests; he corresponds with journalists; and he conducts research on housing code violations.

Velarde helps to organize local tenants' associations and to support the development of local leaders within these organizations. He sees the formation of these community-based organizations serving a dual purpose: they contribute to a broader social justice movement and help to deliver specific, immediate benefits to local tenants.

As an undergraduate, Velarde took a range of sociology courses that emphasized questions about the relationship between power and inequality with a specific focus on the experiences and perspectives of oppressed groups. These classes deepened and broadened his knowledge of the dynamic intersection of race, class, gender, sexuality, and nationality in contemporary U.S. society.

Just about every day Velarde is reminded of the relevance of sociology to his work and the lives of the people he serves. He recalls, for example, how, during a discussion at a community meeting, tenants began to grasp the connections among racial inequality, poor housing conditions, and city policies. The fragile housing situation in their neighborhood, they concluded, was more than an isolated phenomenon, but rather an expression of

structural relationships that kept them disadvantaged.

Overall, Velarde concludes, the most valuable thing he gained from his undergraduate education was the sociological perspective. "The best and most basic tool sociology has given me is, as Mills put it, a 'sociological imagination'." Ultimately, he says, sociology "has given me a language to critique and contest unjust social arrangements. I am reminded even in the most difficult times that these very arrangements are within the reach of social actors."

Mikey Velarde

For community organizer Mikey Velarde, sociology encourages hope in the capacity of human beings to recognize—and challenge—injustice.

Velarde has combined his personal experience as a Chicano from El Paso, Texas with the insights he gained from sociology to cultivate a sociological imagination that he brings to bear on his efforts to help the residents of East Harlem improve their lives. He urges others to similarly bring the sociological imagination to bear on their own goals and circumstances. His advice? "Connect to the material from your own social location and life experience."

> "Ultimately, he says, sociology 'has given me a language to critique and contest unjust social arrangements'."

think about it

1. *What relationship does Mikey Velarde see between sociology and his work in East Harlem?*

2. *How does the sociological perspective encourage Velarde's optimism about our capacity to challenge injustice?*

---

adopted home (Gibson 1988; Portes and Rumbaut 2001). Many recent immigrants have access to inexpensive telephone and Internet services that can provide instantaneous communication with family at home. They can travel to their homeland more easily and can stay abreast of home country news and entertainment on satellite television and the Internet. Transnational migrants often make *remittances*—money transfers to relatives back home—which make up a significant share of

the national economies of most Central American countries, the Philippines, Pakistan, Egypt, and other nations (Vertovec 2009). Recognizing these trends, some countries—such as the Philippines—make it easy for migrants to retain their citizenship even as they become citizens in their new homeland. These emerging models of citizenship are likely to become more common, promoting economic advancement and social integration without full cultural accommodation.

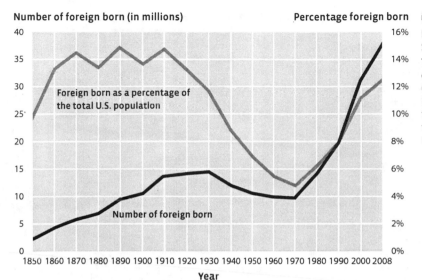

Number of foreign born (in millions)   Percentage foreign born

FIGURE 10.4 | FOREIGN-BORN POPULATION WITHIN THE UNITED STATES, 1850 TO 2008
The *number* of people in the United States born elsewhere has reached unprecedented levels (purple line, left axis), but the *percentage* of the U.S. population that is foreign born is still less today than it was in the late 1800s and early 1900s (orange line, right axis). Source: U.S. Census Bureau (2010h).

Unauthorized Immigration

The surge in immigration that began in the 1960s has been followed by a political backlash similar to the one that followed the earlier surge that began in the late nineteenth century. As before, critics worry that increasing the number of immigrants from different cultures will potentially "disunite" the country (Schlesinger 1998). Unlike before, however, the focus of today's backlash is unauthorized immigrants.

Because these immigrants are by definition "unauthorized" (they are also called "illegal" or "undocumented"), determining their exact number is impossible. The Department of Homeland Security estimates that 10.8 million of them were in the United States in 2010—about a million fewer than three years earlier, a decrease that is likely due to the downturn in the economy. Over 60 percent entered the United States before 2000, and nearly two-thirds (62 percent) are from Mexico. Nearly half live in California (24 percent), Texas (16 percent), or Florida (7 percent) (Hoefer, Rytina, and Baker 2011). They are employed mostly in agriculture, construction, and service occupations.

Several factors have contributed to the increase in undocumented immigrants. First, many Mexicans were recruited as legal temporary workers under the *bracero* program that began in the 1940s. When the program ended in 1964, many stayed in the United States without documentation (Durand, Massey, and Zenteno 2001). Second, the North American Free Trade Agreement (NAFTA) took effect in 1994, eliminating barriers to cross-border trade and investment and undermining broad sectors of the Mexican economy. In particular, many small-scale Mexican farms failed in the face of competition from government-subsidized U.S. agricultural products. As a result, displaced Mexican workers sought opportunities in the United States (Portes 2002). Finally, U.S. employers play a significant role in recruiting immigrant laborers, including undocu-

mented workers, especially in agricultural and meat processing facilities (Rodriguez 2004).

Culture, Structure, and Power: Explaining Ethnic and Racial Inequality

Why has U.S. history been so marked by racial and ethnic inequality? And why has inequality persisted, as we will see, in a society in which discrimination is outlawed? To answer these questions we need to look through the lens of sociological theories about culture, structure, and power at both the legacy of past racial discrimination as well as the new forms of discrimination that have emerged since the civil rights era. These theories address the attitudes and behavior of individuals as well as processes that take place within institutions and society as a whole.

Enduring Inequality

Since the civil rights era, minority groups in the United States have made remarkable progress, but most continue to experience discrimination.

■ *Housing.* Numerous studies show that racial discrimination is a significant factor in the continuing stark racial and ethnic segregation of the nation's neighborhoods (Squires,

Friedman and Saidat 2002; U.S. Department of Housing and Urban Development 2005).

■ **Education.** Although their achievement is comparable in the early school years, Blacks lag behind Whites on many education measures by the time they reach middle school. Teachers in black-majority districts have less experience and are more likely to be teaching outside their area of expertise than are teachers in white-majority districts (Jones 2007). Similar gaps affect other minorities, as well.

■ **Health care.** Racial minorities and Hispanics tend to receive a lower standard of health care than do non-Hispanic Whites, even after controlling for key factors such as income and insurance (Institute of Medicine 2003).

■ **Media.** Stereotypical portrayals of racial and ethnic minorities have a long history in the media and are not entirely a relic of the past (Entman and Rojecki 2001; Gray 2004).

■ **Economics.** Blacks and Hispanics are about three times more likely to be poor than are non-Hispanic Whites. The median income for non-Hispanic white households is about 40 percent greater than it is for black households and about 30 percent greater than for Hispanic households. Blacks have only about one-tenth the wealth of Whites (U.S. Census Bureau 2010f; Oliver and Shapiro 2006).

In these and many other ways, racial and ethnic inequality continues to characterize U.S. society, as shown in Figure 10.5.

The Legacy of Past Discrimination: The Black-White Wealth Gap

Imagine a long-distance foot race in which some competitors are shackled with leg irons at the start, while others can run freely. Partway through the race, a judge instructs the runners to stop where they are and orders the leg irons removed. The race then continues, but even though all competitors are now allowed to run freely, the gap between frontrunners and those who had been shackled continues to affect the outcome.

This analogy reflects the dilemma facing society in dealing with the legacy of racism. Sociological research shows that people's life chances are affected dramatically by the families into which they are born. So even those who have not experienced discriminatory practices directly can still indirectly inherit either the privileges or disadvantages they create. One of the clearest examples of this legacy is the black-white wealth gap.

As we saw in Chapter 9, income refers to money a person receives over a set period of time. Wealth, though, is what people own, including savings, real estate, stocks and bonds, and other investments. The median income of Blacks is about

Median family income (in thousands of dollars)

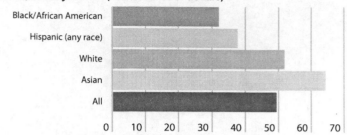

Percentage living in poverty

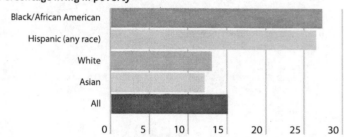

Percentage of those aged 25 or older with at least a 4-year college degree

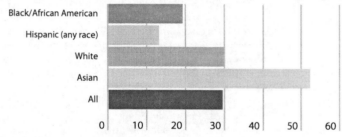

FIGURE 10.5 | RACIAL AND ETHNIC INEQUALITY

A half-century after the civil rights movement, a number of measures indicate the persistence of racial and ethnic inequality in the United States today. Source: U.S. Census Bureau (2011a, 2011d, 2011e).

CORE CONCEPTS CHALLENGE

How do the group disparities illustrated here reflect the relationship of race and ethnicity to American social structure?

60 percent that of Whites, but the median wealth of Blacks is only about 10 percent that of Whites. Even when we compare only college graduates, Whites have four times as much wealth as Blacks (Oliver and Shapiro 2006).

The massive gap in wealth reflects the persistence of past inequalities from generation to generation. Imagine two young people, both hired fresh out of college to work for the same company at exactly the same salary. Their incomes are equal. However, if only one of them comes from a family with some financial assets, her wealth may be significantly higher. Her parents might have paid for her college education and car and may help pay for a first house, thus reducing or eliminating her mortgage payments. Upon her parents' death, she may inherit real estate, stocks, or other financial investments, allowing her to pass on similar advantages to her children. The other young graduate, enjoying none of these advantages, has more limited options despite his equal salary.

The sort of cumulative, intergenerational impact of wealth inequality illustrated by this example affects everyone, regardless of race. Even though most Whites are not wealthy—and some Blacks have considerable wealth—Whites have never had to face the race-specific barriers created by what sociologists Melvin Oliver and Thomas Shapiro (2006) call the **racialization of the state,** *the implementation of government and private-sector policies that discriminated against minorities and provided Whites with numerous advantages.* These policies included the following:

- The legalization and enforcement of slavery
- Laws that barred Blacks and other minorities from owning property
- Local ordinances that barred Blacks from entering certain occupations
- Regulations that prevented Blacks from selling to Whites, making it nearly impossible for Blacks to compete with white-owned businesses
- Segregated and unequal schooling that ensured unequal opportunities in the job market based on race
- Biased federal home loan programs that steered money to the rapidly growing white suburbs after World War II
- Biased bank loan practices that required black applicants to meet more stringent mortgage criteria than white applicants and continued long after the end of legal segregation

Although these circumstances no longer exist, they made it far more difficult for Blacks than Whites to accumulate wealth and pass it on to their children, a legacy whose impact continues to be felt today.

One lesson of contemporary research, then, is that racial and ethnic inequality continues today because the discrimination of the past still matters. One attempt to overcome this legacy involves **affirmative action,** *a variety of policies and programs that aim to avoid discrimination and redress past discrimination through the active recruitment of qualified minorities for jobs, promotions, and educational opportunities.* One debate over affirmative action is explored in the Sociology Matters box on page 274.

Individual Attitudes and Behaviors: Prejudice and Discrimination

Social-psychological theories that focus on individual attitudes and behaviors can help us understand how people come to adopt their views about inequality. As we noted in Chapter 7, people often define themselves as a member of an *in-group* and feel negatively toward members of an *out-group*. Racism creates an in-out group distinction based on a usually negative stereotype. According to the Thomas theorem (also discussed in Chapter 7), social characteristics that are defined as real have real consequences. Thus a widely accepted stereotype can become the basis for prejudicial attitudes toward the members of an out group.

Stereotypes and prejudice are limited to beliefs and attitudes, but discrimination, as we have seen, involves actions and behaviors (Pettigrew and Taylor 2000). Racial discrimination, for example, involves actions that help maintain the domination of one race over others based on the dominant group's belief in the subordinate group's inferiority (Wilson 1973). As such, discrimination is generally limited to those who have the power to act in ways that hinder others. Those who are relatively powerless may have prejudices of their own, but they generally lack the resources or ability to turn those prejudices into effective discriminatory action. In this sense, discrimination can be thought of as prejudice plus power.

Institutional Discrimination: Structural Barriers to Equality

Individuals can discriminate— for example, a small business owner might refuse to hire members of a different racial or ethnic group. However, racial and ethnic inequality is typically produced and reinforced through institutional discrimination, not just individual action. **Institutional discrimination** *results from the structural organization, policies, and procedures of social institutions such as the government, businesses, and schools.* Institutional discrimination is especially powerful, since it affects large numbers of people. It is especially difficult to change, since it is not associated with any one individual but rather is a generalized feature of an institutional bureaucracy.

In some cases, institutional discrimination is intentional, as with Jim Crow laws in the pre–civil rights era South. In many cases, though, policies and practices that are not themselves overtly or intentionally discriminatory can have a discriminatory impact. For example, the hiring practices of many workplaces rely heavily on informal word-of-mouth communication. When those workplaces are nearly all white, the result can be institutional discrimination toward racial and ethnic minorities who do not have access to these informal channels of communication.

Theories of Prejudice and Discrimination: Culture and Group Interests

Sociological explanations for prejudice and discrimination tend to fall into one of two theoretical traditions, those emphasizing culture and those emphasizing group interests. Much

Culture, Structure, and Power: Explaining Ethnic and Racial Inequality

---

thinking about structure

The **structure** of an organization can contribute to institutional discrimination. How can an institution's structure help prevent discrimination?

SOCIOLOGY Matters

Race, Class, and the Affirmative Action Debate on Campus

If education is to serve as a fair mechanism for individual social mobility, it must be equally accessible to all qualified students. Historically, college and university administrators limited or barred the admission of racial and ethnic minorities while giving wealthy white children of alumni preferential treatment (Kahlenberg 2010a; Karabel 2005; Stevens 2007). Since the 1960s, race-based affirmative action has been used to help overcome the effects of this discrimination and promote more racially diverse campuses. In recent years, however, court decisions have limited race-based affirmative action, and some states have prohibited its use altogether. Meanwhile, some scholars and policymakers have been using sociological insights to suggest new ways to maintain diversity and promote fair access to higher education.

One major sociological criticism of race-based affirmative action programs is that they are blind to the way race intersects with class to affect who benefits from them. Perhaps the most comprehensive study of the subject suggests that the greatest beneficiaries are minorities from middle- and upper-class backgrounds (Bowen and Bok 1998). The programs can also benefit recent minority immigrants, even though they have not suffered the effects of American racism's historical legacy. Meanwhile, affirmative action provides no benefit to poor and working-class Whites disadvantaged by attending weak schools in low-income school districts.

Consequently, some analysts argue for a shift from race-based to class-based affirmative action, thereby assisting students to overcome educational disadvantages, regardless of race (Kahlenberg 1997, 2010b). They argue that well-designed class-based programs will continue to benefit racial and ethnic minorities because minorities are disproportionately represented among the poor and working class. At the same time, however, class-based programs would also benefit white students of modest means, thus overcoming the political objection faced by race-based programs that they unfairly exclude disadvantaged Whites.

If they are to be fair, however, class-based affirmative action programs must take into account the sociological insight that the

wealth gap between races is much greater than the income gap. Relying solely on family income as a measure of class would likely harm some racial and ethnic minorities because it would mask the effect of this legacy of racial discrimination. One possible solution would be to define class broadly enough to capture factors beyond income that can influence early educational quality, such as school-district income levels, parents' education level, and family wealth.

Sociologists have also pointed out that one of the principal tools colleges use to evaluate students for admission—scores on standardized tests such as the SAT and ACT—is inherently unfair. The tests are supposed to be an unbiased measure of a student's individual ability, but they turn out to be weak predictors of later academic success. Competitive colleges nonetheless rely heavily on them, giving the appearance that admission decisions are based solely on merit. In fact, these tests give an advantage to affluent students who typically score higher than less affluent students, thanks to well-funded schools, expensive test-taking tutoring, and a home environment that promotes college-related cultural capital. In fact, some sociologists argue that overemphasis on standardized test scores, to the neglect of other indicators of ability such as class ranking, is precisely what puts both racial minorities and lower-income students of all races at a disadvantage. If such tests were a less important part of the decision, the admissions gap between the races and classes would be greatly reduced (Alon 2009; Alon and Tienda 2007).

In the coming years, sociological insights about race and class will continue to help inform the debate over affirmative action and contribute to the development of policies that try to create a fairer system of higher education.

think about it

1. *Overall, do you think affirmative action based on race has been useful? Why or why not?*

2. *Do you agree with advocates who now suggest shifting to class-based affirmative action? Why or why not?*

---

sociological work on the subject, however, combines elements of each approach.

LEARNING PREJUDICE THROUGH CULTURE
Cultural explanations focus on the way familiarity breeds comfort whereas unfamiliarity often produces anxiety or fear. Our socialization has made it easy for us to interact with people who look and behave like us because they are familiar and predictable. By contrast, interacting with people who look different or whose behavior is unfamiliar and therefore unpredictable, can make us uncomfortable.

As children grow up, their socialization often encourages them to form attachments with those in their own group, people like themselves, while often learning negative stereotypes about out-group members, people less like themselves. Some research suggests that youngsters learn stereotypes and develop prejudices as early as age three, often before fully comprehending their meaning or significance (Aboud 1988). Later in life, the mass media can perpetuate negative stereotypes with entertainment that presents such stock characters as the Asian martial-arts expert, the black criminal, the Arab terrorist, or the exotic Asian sex symbol (Wilson, Gutierrez, and Chao 2003).

According to Gordon Allport's (1954) *contact hypothesis*, contact between members of different groups will reduce prejudice *if* the contact is sustained, involves groups with equal status who share common goals, and is sanctioned by authorities. Those are difficult conditions to meet, but college campuses often qualify. For example, one study found that white students randomly assigned a minority roommate had more contact and were more comfortable with members of other races than white students who were assigned a white roommate (Boisjoly et al. 2006). However, without a structure to encourage interaction, diversity on campus does not necessarily translate into increased interracial or interethnic contact.

DISCRIMINATING TO GAIN ADVANTAGE

Group-interest explanations of prejudice and discrimination focus on the way groups compete with one another for scarce and valuable resources such as jobs or desirable housing. Such competition can lead to conflict and to discrimination by one group against another as a means of gaining an advantage over them. As we saw, discrimination often seems to increase in difficult economic periods as competition for scarce resources increases.

Split labor market theory *argues that ethnic and racial conflicts often emerge when two racial or ethnic groups compete for the same jobs.* According to this theory, employers, higher-paid workers, and lower-paid workers form three groups with separate and competing interests (Bonacich 1972, 1976; Gordon, Edwards, and Reich 1982). Employers recruit lower-paid workers to maximize their profits, thereby creating conflict between higher-paid workers and the lower-paid workers who are replacing them. As we have seen, employers often encouraged immigration as a source of inexpensive labor, sometimes stoking racial and ethnic divisions among workers to prevent them from organizing for better wages and working conditions. In the short term, discrimination against minorities also served the interest of higher-paid workers—often Whites, in the context of American history—because it prevented minorities from competing with them for desirable jobs. In the long term, however, these divisions weakened the negotiating power of all workers.

More generally, members of one group can see those of another as a threat, especially when facing difficult circumstances. A **scapegoat** is *an individual or a group of people falsely blamed for a negative situation.* When people are frustrated by their inability to overcome difficulties, they sometimes seek simplistic explanations for their troubles in the form of a scapegoat. In the wake of World War I, for example, Germany faced enormously complex economic and political difficulties, but the Nazis scapegoated Jews and other minorities, blaming them for all the nation's problems. In the United States, Blacks, Irish, Jews, communists, immigrants, and Muslims, among many others, have all been targeted as scapegoats at different times (Hardisty 1999).

Discrimination in the Post–Civil Rights Era: Hidden, Implicit, and Color-Blind

Continuing racial and ethnic inequality in the post–civil rights era has prompted sociologists to conduct new research and develop new theories to explain how discrimination operates in a society in which it is often illegal and covert (Quillian 2006).

HIDDEN PREJUDICE Robert Merton (1949) recognized long ago that people who were not prejudiced could engage in discriminatory behaviors to conform to biased social norms. Some Whites in the segregated South, for example, acquiesced to the dominant culture even though they personally rejected its racist assumptions. Similarly prejudiced people may keep silent about their attitudes when the dominant norms condemn them but still engage in discriminatory behavior. Indeed, recent research suggests that, in some cases, norms promoting racial and ethnic equality in the post–civil rights era have not eliminated racism but rather have driven it underground, transforming overt prejudices into covert ones.

For example, some people refrain from racist talk or action in public but give vent to racial or ethnic stereotypes when among friends and family. In one study, over a thousand students from a variety of colleges and universities kept journals recording their social interactions for several weeks during the 2002–2003 academic year (Picca and Feagin 2007). The journals of the more than 600 white students in the study showed them to be nearly always polite to their black peers, avoiding racially offensive language in public "front-stage" situations. However, in "back-stage," white-only settings, students reported the frequent use of the word "nigger" and other racial epithets to refer to Blacks. Some students reported feeling uncomfortable about the racist language but lacked the courage to object. In their journals, the white students also commonly referred to Blacks in terms of racial

SPOTLIGHT on social theory

Split labor market theory is in the tradition of *conflict theory.* Have you worked in or seen a workplace in which higher-paid workers and lower-paid workers were divided along ethnic or racial lines?

SPOTLIGHT on social theory

As part of the symbolic *interactionist* tradition, **dramaturgical theory** draws attention to the differences between front-stage and back-stage behaviors. Are research findings that racist back-stage behavior is relatively common among college students, whereas front-stage behavior is noticeably free of such actions, consistent with your own experiences?

Culture, Structure, and Power: Explaining Ethnic and Racial Inequality

---

thinking about power

People in authority have often used scapegoats as a means of gaining or maintaining their **power** over others. Can you think of an example of the use of this tactic, from your own life or from recent history?

stereotypes, describing them as lazy, criminally inclined, and oversexed. The results suggest that, even fifty years after the civil rights movement, these stereotypes and prejudices remain deeply entrenched and widely prevalent.

Hidden prejudices can also lead people who deny they are motivated by any personal prejudice to engage in discriminatory practices. White employers, for example, may justify their acknowledged reluctance to hire Blacks by citing the prevalence of crime in black communities. Ironically, some managers admit to steering clear of hiring Blacks precisely because of the public sanctions against racial discrimination: they fear a discrimination lawsuit if an African American employee needs to be fired (Wilson 1997).

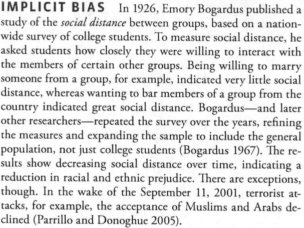

IMPLICIT BIAS In 1926, Emory Bogardus published a study of the *social distance* between groups, based on a nationwide survey of college students. To measure social distance, he asked students how closely they were willing to interact with the members of certain other groups. Being willing to marry someone from a group, for example, indicated very little social distance, whereas wanting to bar members of a group from the country indicated great social distance. Bogardus—and later other researchers—repeated the survey over the years, refining the measures and expanding the sample to include the general population, not just college students (Bogardus 1967). The results show decreasing social distance over time, indicating a reduction in racial and ethnic prejudice. There are exceptions, though. In the wake of the September 11, 2001, terrorist attacks, for example, the acceptance of Muslims and Arabs declined (Parrillo and Donoghue 2005).

As researchers learn more about how the brain works, however, they are finding that some biases may be more implicit—existing at the subconscious level—than overt and at a conscious level where they can be measured in surveys. Recent research suggests that we learn prejudices at a deep, unconscious level and respond to people with lightning-fast assessments that are beyond rational evaluation (Vedantam 2005). In our conscious activities, we can control our behaviors and overcome implicit biases, but this restraint is cognitively challenging and requires additional effort (Richeson et al. 2003). At the unconscious level, we may be acting on well-known stereotypes and deeply held prejudices.

Social psychologist Mahzarin Banaji and her colleagues have devised a series of implicit association tests (IAT) that measure unconscious biases by tapping into fast, unexamined responses. (You can take some of these tests yourself online at https://implicit.harvard.edu.) These researchers have found that most respondents show an unconscious preference for people like themselves, regardless of their stated beliefs. Even when people who feel and say they are not biased are tested, in

most cases the results indicate they actually have unconscious biases based on race, ethnicity, sexual orientation, and class as well as other categories. These tests have their critics (Blanton and Jaccard 2008), but, if confirmed by further research, they may demonstrate that implicit bias is one source of enduring prejudice and discrimination in contemporary society.

Racial discrimination persists in many areas of social life, whether because of prejudice, hidden racism, or implicit bias. One method sociologists use to measure discrimination is the *field audit* (Quillian 2006). In typical field audits, researchers pair people from different races or ethnic groups who are otherwise similar on all characteristics that might affect the study's outcome. They then send each member of the pair into social situations in which they may encounter discrimination, such as renting an apartment or applying for a job. Using this method repeatedly, researchers have documented persistent racial discrimination in housing (Turner and Ross 2005) and hiring (Altonji and Blank 1999). One study even found discrimination based on no more than the name on otherwise comparable resumes mailed in response to ads for jobs. Resumes for people with white-sounding names, such as Emily and Greg, were 50 percent more likely to get a callback than were those for people with black-sounding names, such as Lakisha and Jamal (Bertrand and Mullainathan 2004). Another study found that employers were much more likely to hire a white person with a criminal record than a black person with a criminal record (Pager 2003). Yet another study found that doctors recommended different treatments for people of different races who came to them with identical symptoms (Shulman et al. 1999).

THE NEW RACISM Sociologists often refer to today's persistent racism as *the new racism,* and they describe its dynamics with a variety of approaches that have a variety of labels, including "symbolic racism" (Kinder and Sanders 1996), "laissez-faire racism" (Bobo, Kluegel, and Smith 1997), "color-blind racism" (Bonilla Silva 2001, 2009), and "modern racism" (McConahay 1986). Although their analyses vary somewhat, these approaches agree on two points:

- Prejudice and discrimination persist in contemporary social life.

- The ways in which prejudice and discrimination manifest themselves have changed in the post–civil rights era.

For example, in a significant shift from earlier attitudes, many Americans today advocate race neutrality and a "color-blind" society. But ideas that once might have been progressive and antiracist can reinforce existing racial inequality in a different historical era. **Color-blind racism** is *the promotion of race neutrality when it actually helps to maintain existing racial and* *ethnic inequality.* It reveals itself in the rejection of efforts to reduce racial and ethnic inequality on the grounds that those efforts violate a color-blind approach to society and may even constitute reverse racism.

Some who advocate color-blind policies are likely using race neutrality as a cover for prejudiced views, understanding that overt racism is no longer acceptable in our society. However, color-blind approaches are not inherently prejudicial, and some advocates of this view genuinely believe that race neutrality is the best route to racial justice. The result is a complex mix of racial and nonracial beliefs that in combination—intentionally or not—can help perpetuate racial inequality.

How do those who believe that racism is no longer a significant hurdle in our supposedly post-racial society explain the continuing inequality among racial and ethnic groups in U.S. society? Some simply deny that inequality and discrimination exist, despite the vast body of social science research showing that it does. Some point to cultural differences to account for this variation and, in particular, to the success of Asian Americans as evidence that racial and ethnic discrimination no longer holds back social advancement. Some have argued that enduring racial inequality simply reflects the natural outcome of competition between groups with inherently differ-

ent abilities. Richard Herrnstein and Charles Murray (1996), for instance, claimed that differences in scores on intelligence tests (IQ scores) reflect innate and unchangeable differences between the races. Critics have pointed out the inadequacies of such studies, which ignore the impact of environment on IQ scores (Fischer et al. 1996). They argue that efforts to measure differences in intelligence are repackaged racist ideas that hark back to the ugly history of racist pseudo-science.

Critics of color-blind policies argue that to pretend that race no longer matters is to overlook the legacy of racism and the persistence of prejudice and discrimination. As U.S. Supreme Court Justice Harry Blackmun famously said in defending the use of affirmative action, "In order to get beyond racism, we must first take account of race."

In the nineteenth century, a civil war led to the end of slavery in the United States. In the twentieth century, the civil rights movement led to the end of racial segregation and legal discrimination. In both cases, social change came only after intense controversy and prolonged conflict. Just as those struggles were contentious in their day, so too are the efforts to understand inequality and advance racial and ethnic justice in a post–civil rights society.

In Transition

MULTIRACIAL AND MULTIETHNIC IDENTITIES

As part of his stand-up act a few years ago, comedian Chris Rock would raise a question about the success of golf great Tiger Woods and popular rapper Eminem. "What's happening in America," he would ask in astonishment, "when the best golfer is black and the best rapper is white?" This line always got a laugh, but it also exposes enduring racial stereotypes. Tiger Woods's father had a mix of African American, Chinese, and Native American ancestry, and his mother had a mix of Thai, Chinese, and Dutch. Yet in the United States, Tiger Woods is still often seen simply as black.

Woods's complex ancestry highlights the growth of multiracial and multiethnic identities. As marriages across racial and ethnic lines increase, people with these new identities are likely to play a larger role in tomorrow's world. It has long been common for people to identify with multiple ethnicities, saying, for example "I'm Irish on my father's side and Russian on my mother's." Today, however, multiethnic identities include an ever-larger range of ethnicities from all parts of the world.

As immigration and intermarriage increase, so do the number of people with multiracial identities. At least one in every twenty Americans under the age of eighteen is now multiracial, and some analysts expect that proportion to rise to one in five by 2050 (Lee and Bean 2004). In the 2010 census, 9 million Americans (3 percent of the population) identified themselves as being of two or more races, although this number is an undercount since those who answer "multiracial" are classified as "some other race" (U.S. Census Bureau 2011c, 2011e). In addition, cultural norms still encourage people in the United States to identify with only one race. For example, in the 2010 census, only 7.4 percent of Blacks indicated they had a multiracial background, even though the U.S. Census Bureau estimates that at least 75 percent of black Americans have a multiracial ancestry. As multiracial identities become more socially accepted, however, we are likely to see a significant increase in the percentage of people who embrace them, the latest development in our evolving conception of race and ethnicity.

Percent

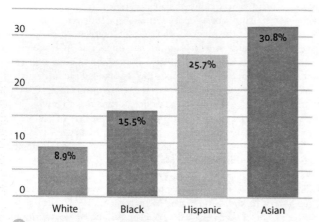

FIGURE 10.6 | **INTERMARRIAGE RATES OF NEWLYWEDS, 2008**
Asians are the most likely to marry someone of a different race or ethnicity. Whites are the least likely to do so. *Note.* "Newlyweds" refers to people who got married in the 12 months before the survey. All groups (other than Hispanic) are non-Hispanic single races. *Source:* Passel, Wang, and Taylor, 2010

seven marriages in the United States unites either people of different races or Hispanics and non-Hispanics, a rate that has doubled between 1980 and 2008 and increased sixfold since 1960 (Passel, Wang, and Taylor 2010). (See Figure 10.6.)

Only one in nine Whites is in an interracial or interethnic marriage. In contrast, nearly a third of Asian Americans and a quarter of Hispanics are married to someone of another race or ethnicity, usually non-Hispanic Whites. More than two-thirds of Native Americans marry someone who is not Native American (Lee and Bean 2004). Intermarriage by Whites has doubled since 1980 and tripled for Blacks but has remained fairly steady for Hispanics and Asians, probably because a growing number of Asians and Hispanics are available as potential partners as their percentages of the population increase (Passel, Wang, and Taylor 2010). Intermarriage rates also vary by gender within racial and ethnic groups. Among Whites and Hispanics, intermarriage rates are about equal for men and women. However, the intermarriage rate for black men (22 percent) is more than twice as high as it is for black women (8.9 percent), whereas Asian women (39.5 percent) intermarry at twice the rate of Asian men (19.5 percent). Younger people and native-born adults are more likely to marry outside their racial or ethnic group than are older people and immigrants, suggesting intermarriage will likely increase in the coming years as the taboo against it fades and recent immigrants become more established (Passel, Wang, and Taylor 2010).

As the trend toward intermarriage continues, it promises to alter the nature of racial and ethnic relations in the United States, making it easier for members of minority groups to cross boundaries in employment, housing, and marriage. Perhaps it will even diminish the social significance of racial and ethnic categories altogether.

Rising intermarriage is one sign that the boundaries between some racial and ethnic groups have become less rigid. Intermarriage between members of different white ethnic groups was rare a hundred years ago but is now so common that only about 20 percent of Whites have a spouse with the same ethnicity, and such unions are no longer even categorized as interethnic (Lee and Bean 2004). Interracial marriage was still outlawed in fifteen states when the Supreme Court declared such statutes unconstitutional in 1967. Today, though, about one out of

THINKING SOCIOLOGICALLY ABOUT . . .

Race and Ethnicity

culture

- Race and ethnicity are social constructs whose definitions change over time and vary across cultures.
- Social norms about race and ethnicity—both racist and antiracist—are learned through the process of socialization.

structure

- Interpretations of race and ethnicity influence patterns of social interaction.
- The policies and practices of social institutions can both reflect racist beliefs and perpetuate racial and ethnic inequality.
- Groups, from slaves to the activists of the civil rights movement and later, have resisted racial discrimination, sometimes producing long-lasting changes in the social structure.

power

- Racial and ethnic inequality reflects differences in power within society.
- Powerful groups have historically justified their privileges on the basis of their supposed racial or ethnic superiority.
- The post–civil rights era has seen both enduring racial and ethnic inequality as well as new relations of power, reflecting the increasing diversity of society.

REVIEW, REFLECT, AND APPLY

Looking Back

1. Race is not a biological reality, but rather a social construct whose origin lies in eighteenth- and nineteenth-century pseudo-science. Ethnicity is also a social construct that, like race, has been interpreted differently in different cultures and in various historical periods.

2. Grouping people into different races and ethnicities sets up majority-minority group dynamics that become a part of the social structure and reflect inequalities in power.

3. The social history of the United States resulted in unique ideas and practices concerning race and ethnicity. In particular, Whites used ideas about race and racial superiority to justify slavery and adopt laws that enshrined racial inequality.

4. Native societies were decimated by the arrival of European colonizers. Spanish colonists, the ancestors of today's Hispanics, took control of what is now the southwestern United States. White Anglo-Saxon Protestants settled primarily on the east coast and rapidly expanded their landholdings westward. African slaves were imported in growing numbers as labor for an agrarian economy. In the nineteenth century, Asian laborers—especially Chinese—were recruited to work on railroads and in other industries.

5. Rising immigration from throughout Europe in the nineteenth and early twentieth centuries increased ethnic diversity. Some groups—including Jews, the Irish, and Italians—were not considered "white" until they gradually assimilated.

6. The civil rights movement helped transform society, making racial and ethnic discrimination illegal and promoting tolerance. One consequence was a change in immigration laws that opened the way to new diversity. Recent immigrants, who come mostly from Asia and Latin America rather than Europe, are substantially changing the racial and ethnic makeup of the country.

7. Despite the gains of the civil rights movement, racial and ethnic inequalities endure, reflecting racism's historical legacy as well as contemporary practices. Racial prejudice and discrimination operate at different levels of social life, involving individual attitudes and behaviors and the structural barriers created by institutions. Prejudice and discrimination can be fueled by cultural differences or by the pursuit of group interests. In a post–civil rights society, prejudice and discrimination can be hidden, implicit, or produced by support for color-blind policies.

8. One consequence of our increasing diversity is the growth of multiethnic and multiracial identities, in part the result of an increase in interracial marriage.

Critical Thinking: Questions and Activities

1. A friend asks, "Are you blind? Of course race exists!" Explain to your friend why race is, in fact, a social construction, rather than a biological fact.

2. How did you first learn about race and ethnicity? Did this early socialization include the perpetuation of stereotypes? Explain. What socializing forces later influenced your understanding of these issues?

3. Is the social history of race and ethnicity in the United States summarized here consistent with what you learned in high school? If not, how is it different?

4. How do you think changing demographics in the United States will influence other aspects of life fifty years from now?

5. Do you think racial attitudes today among people under age thirty differ significantly from those held by older people? Why or why not? (How could you find out for sure?) What factors do you think contributed to this situation?

Key Terms

affirmative action (p. 273) a variety of policies and programs that aim to avoid discrimination and redress past discrimination through the active recruitment of qualified minorities for jobs, promotions, and educational opportunities.

amalgamation (p. 259) the process by which a majority and a minority group blend or mix to form a new group.

assimilation (p. 259) the process by which members of a minority group come to adopt the culture of the majority group.

color-blind racism (p. 276) a form of bias in which the promotion of race neutrality helps to maintain existing racial and ethnic inequality.

discrimination (p. 258) unequal treatment that gives advantages to one group of people over another without justifiable cause.

ethnicity (p. 253) shared cultural heritage often deriving from a common ancestry and homeland.

genocide (p. 259) the systematic killing of a group of people, based on their race, ethnicity, nationality, or religion.

institutional discrimination (p. 273) unequal treatment that results from the structural organization, policies, and procedures of social institutions such as the government, businesses, and schools.

majority group (p. 258) a collection of people who enjoy privileges and have more access to power because of identifiable physical or cultural characteristics.

minority group (p. 258) a collection of people who suffer disadvantages and have less power because of identifiable physical or cultural characteristics.

pluralism (p. 258) a situation in which distinct ethnic and racial groups coexist on equal terms and have equal social standing.

prejudice (p. 258) to "pre-judge" someone or some group negatively based on inadequate information.

race (p. 253) a category of people widely perceived as sharing socially significant physical characteristics such as skin color.

racial essentialism (p. 256) the idea that supposedly natural and immutable differences separate the races.

racialization of the state (p. 273) the implementation of government and private-sector policies that discriminated against minorities and provided Whites with numerous advantages.

racism (p. 256) the belief that one race is inherently superior to another.

scapegoat (p. 275) an individual or a group of people falsely blamed for a negative situation.

segregation (p. 259) keeping distinct social groups physically and socially separate and unequal.

split labor market theory (p. 275) the theory that ethnic and racial conflicts often emerge when two racial or ethnic groups compete for the same jobs.

stereotypes (p. 258) exaggerated, distorted, or untrue generalizations about categories of people that do not acknowledge individual variation.

transnational migrants (p. 269) immigrants who retain strong personal, cultural, and economic ties to both their country of birth and their newly adopted home.

MODULE 39 | Global View of the Family

Among Tibetans, a woman may be married simultaneously to more than one man, usually brothers. This system allows sons to share the limited amount of good land. Among the Betsileo of Madagascar, a man has multiple wives, each one living in a different village where he cultivates rice. Wherever he has the best rice field, that wife is considered his first or senior wife. Among the Yanomami of Brazil and Venezuela, it is considered proper to have sexual relations with your opposite-sex cousins if they are the children of your mother's brother or your father's sister. But if your opposite-sex cousins are the children of your mother's sister or your father's brother, the same practice is considered to be incest (Haviland et al. 2008; Kottak 2011).

Universal Principles

As these examples illustrate, there are many variations in the family from culture to culture. Yet the family as a social institution exists in all cultures. A **family** can be defined as a set of people related by blood, marriage or some other agreed-on relationship, or adoption, who share the primary responsibility for reproduction and caring for members of society. Moreover, certain general principles concerning its composition, kinship patterns, and authority patterns are universal.

Composition: What Is the Family?

If we were to take our information on what a family is from what we see on television, we might come up with some very strange scenarios. The media do not always present a realistic view of the family. Moreover, many people still think of the family in very narrow terms—as a married couple and their unmarried children living together, like the family in the old *Cosby Show*. However, this is but one type of family, what sociologists refer to as a **nuclear family.** The term *nuclear family* is well chosen, since this type of family serves as the nucleus, or core, on which larger family groups are built.

Most people in the United States see the nuclear family as the preferred family arrangement. Yet by 2000, only about a third of the nation's family households fit this model. The proportion of households in the United States that is composed of married couples with children at home has decreased steadily over the past 40 years and is expected to continue shrinking. At the same time, the number of single-parent households has increased (Figure 39-1).

A family in which relatives—such as grandparents, aunts, or uncles—live in the same home as parents and their children is known as an **extended family.** Although not common, such living arrangements do exist in the United States. The structure of the extended family offers certain advantages over that of the

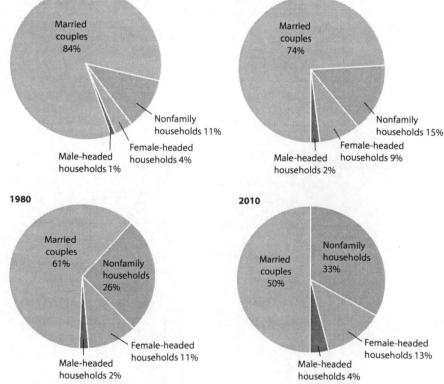

FIGURE 39-1 **U.S. Households by Family Type, 1940–2010**

1940
Married couples 84%
Nonfamily households 11%
Female-headed households 4%
Male-headed households 1%

1960
Married couples 74%
Nonfamily households 15%
Female-headed households 9%
Male-headed households 2%

1980
Married couples 61%
Nonfamily households 26%
Female-headed households 11%
Male-headed households 2%

2010
Married couples 50%
Nonfamily households 33%
Female-headed households 13%
Male-headed households 4%

Note: Nonfamily households include women and men living alone or exclusively with people to whom they are not related, as in a college dormitory, homeless shelter, or military base.
Sources: Author's estimate based on Bureau of the Census 1996; Jason Fields 2004; see also McFalls 2003:23.

nuclear family. Crises such as death, divorce, and illness put less strain on family members, since more people can provide assistance and emotional support. In addition, the extended family constitutes a larger economic unit than the nuclear family. If the family is engaged in a common enterprise—a farm or a small business—the additional family members may represent the difference between prosperity and failure.

In considering these different family types, we have limited ourselves to the form of marriage that is characteristic of the United States—monogamy. The term **monogamy** describes a form of marriage in which one woman and one man are married only to each other. Some observers, noting the high rate of divorce in the United States, have suggested that "serial monogamy" is a more accurate description of the form marriage takes in this country. In **serial monogamy,** a person may have several spouses in his or her lifetime, but only one spouse at a time.

Some cultures allow an individual to have several husbands or wives simultaneously. This form of marriage is known as **polygamy.** In fact, most societies throughout the world, past and present, have preferred polygamy to monogamy. Anthropologist George Murdock (1949, 1957) sampled 565 societies and found that in more than 80 percent, some type of polygamy was the preferred form. While polygamy declined steadily through most of the 20th century, in at least five countries in Africa 20 percent of men still have polygamous marriages (Population Reference Bureau 1996).

There are two basic types of polygamy. According to Murdock, the most common—endorsed by the majority of cultures he sampled—is **polygyny.** Polygyny refers to the marriage of a man to more than one woman at the same time. The wives are often sisters, who are expected to hold similar values and have already had experience sharing a household. In polygynous societies, relatively few men actually have multiple spouses. Most individuals live in monogamous families; having multiple wives is viewed as a mark of status.

The other principal variation of polygamy is **polyandry,** in which a woman may have more than one husband at the same time. Such is the case in the culture of the Nyinba, described in Sociology in the Global Community. Polyandry, however, is exceedingly rare today, though it is accepted in some extremely poor societies. Like many other societies, polyandrous cultures devalue the social worth of women (Zeitzen 2008).

Kinship Patterns: To Whom Are We Related?

Many of us can trace our roots by looking at a family tree or by listening to elderly family members talk about their lives—and about the lives of ancestors who died long before we were born. Yet a person's lineage is more than simply a personal history; it also reflects societal patterns that govern descent. In every culture, children encounter relatives to whom they are expected to show an emotional attachment. The state of being related to others is called **kinship.** Kinship is culturally learned, however, and is not totally determined by biological or marital ties. For example, adoption creates a kinship tie that is legally acknowledged and socially accepted.

The family and the kin group are not necessarily one and the same. Whereas the family is a household unit, kin do not always live together or function as a collective body on a daily basis. Kin groups include aunts, uncles, cousins, in-laws, and so forth. In a society such as the United States, the kinship group may come together only rarely, for a wedding or funeral. However, kinship ties frequently create obligations and responsibilities. We may feel compelled to assist our kin, and we may feel free to call on them for many types of aid, including loans and babysitting.

How do we identify kinship groups? The principle of descent assigns people to kinship groups according to their relationship to a mother or father. There are three primary ways of determining descent. The United States follows the system of **bilateral descent,** which means that both sides of a person's family are regarded as equally important. For example, no higher value is given to the brothers of one's father than to the brothers of one's mother.

Most societies—according to George Murdock, 64 percent—give preference to one side of the family or the other in tracing descent. In **patrilineal** (from the Latin *pater,* "father") **descent,** only the father's relatives are significant in terms of property, inheritance, and emotional ties. Conversely, in societies that favor **matrilineal** (from the Latin *mater,* "mother") **descent,** only the mother's relatives are significant.

New forms of reproductive technology will necessitate a new way of looking at kinship. Today, a combination of biological and social processes can "create" a family member, requiring that more distinctions be made about who is related to whom.

 use your **sociological imagination**

In your family, which relatives do you have a significant relationship with? Which do you hardly ever see?

Authority Patterns: Who Rules?

Imagine that you have recently married and must begin to make decisions about the future of your new family. You and your spouse face many questions. Where will you live? How will you furnish your home? Who will do the cooking, the shopping, the cleaning? Whose friends will be invited to dinner? Each time a decision must be made, an issue is raised: Who has the power to make the decision? In simple terms, who rules the family? Conflict theorists examine these questions in the context of traditional gender stratification, under which men have held a dominant position over women.

Societies vary in the way power is distributed within the family. A society that expects males to dominate in all family decision making is termed a **patriarchy.** In patriarchal societies, such as Iran, the eldest male often wields the greatest power, although wives are expected to be treated with respect and kindness. An Iranian woman's status is typically defined by her relationship to a male relative, usually as a wife or daughter. In many patriarchal societies, women find it more difficult to obtain a divorce than a man does. In contrast, in a **matriarchy,**

Sociology in the Global Community

One Wife, Many Husbands: The Nyinba

The Nyinba culture of Nepal and Tibet is an agrarian society located in the remote valleys of the Himalaya Mountains, more than 9,000 feet above sea level. Despite the Nyinba's isolation, they have been closely studied. Scholars from around the world have traveled to the Himalayas to observe this people, one of the few remaining cultures on earth to practice polyandry.

In the physically challenging environment of the Himalayas, polyandry seems to work well. Because the land and climate make it difficult to sustain crops, farming is labor-intensive: many Nyinba laborers must work the fields to support a single family. Thus, a typical marriage involving three brothers and one wife provides the necessary adult male laborers, yet minimizes the number of offspring—a necessity in a place where the food supply is limited.

While an outsider might suppose that Nyinba women dominate their families, in fact authority and inheritance rest on the husband or son. The birth of a son is celebrated, while the birth of a daughter, regardless of who might be the father, brings disappointment. Paternity appears to be a nonissue in this culture, since households are shared by brothers from the same family. The literal head of the household is the oldest brother,

A Nyinba family threshing buckwheat in the field. At left is the wife; in the center, one of her five husbands (with raised mallet); at right, her mother-in-law.

> Favoritism toward a particular husband is frowned on by the Nyinba. Thus, it is the wife's responsibility to see that each husband shares time with her in a rotational fashion.

who typically chooses a wife from outside his extended family.

Favoritism toward a particular husband is frowned on by the Nyinba. Thus, it is the wife's responsibility to see that each husband shares time with her in a rotational fashion. Often, over the morning meal, she will indicate which husband will sleep with her that night. To avoid any confusion, the chosen husband will place his shoes outside her bedroom door.

As in any society (for example, the United States), not all Nyinba households conform to the social norm. If a family has only one son, he must of necessity marry monogamously—an unfortunate outcome in this society. If a wife is unable to have children, a second wife, typically her sister or cousin, may be welcomed into the marriage.

LET'S DISCUSS

1. Why would a monogamous marriage be considered an unfortunate one in the Nyinba culture?

2. What might be some other ways for a society to handle the physical constraints of life in a mountainous terrain?

Sources: N. Levine 1988; Stockard 2002; Zeitzen 2008.

women have greater authority than men. Matriarchies, which are very uncommon, emerged among Native American tribal societies and in nations in which men were absent for long periods because of warfare or food-gathering expeditions (Farr 1999).

In a third type of authority pattern, the **egalitarian family,** spouses are regarded as equals. That does not mean, however, that all decisions are shared in such families. Wives may hold authority in some spheres, husbands in others. Many sociologists believe the egalitarian family has begun to replace the patriarchal family as the social norm in the United States.

Sociological Perspectives on the Family

Do we really need the family? A century ago, Friedrich Engels ([1884] 1959), a colleague of Karl Marx, described the family as the ultimate source of social inequality because of its role in the transfer of power, property, and privilege. More recently, conflict theorists have argued that the family contributes to societal injustice, denies women opportunities that are extended to men,

Although spouses in an egalitarian family may not share all their decisions, they regard themselves as equals. This pattern of authority is becoming more common in the United States.

4. **Regulation of sexual behavior.** Sexual norms are subject to change both over time (for instance, in the customs for dating) and across cultures (compare strict Saudi Arabia to the more permissive Denmark). However, whatever the time period or cultural values of a society, standards of sexual behavior are most clearly defined within the family circle.

5. **Affection and companionship.** Ideally, the family provides members with warm and intimate relationships, helping them to feel satisfied and secure. Of course, a family member may find such rewards outside the family—from peers, in school, at work—and may even perceive the home as an unpleasant or abusive setting. Nevertheless, we expect our relatives to understand us, to care for us, and to be there for us when we need them.

6. **Provision of social status.** We inherit a social position because of the family background and reputation of our parents and siblings. The family presents the newborn child with an ascribed status based on race and ethnicity that helps to determine his or her place within society's stratification system. Moreover, family resources affect children's ability to pursue certain opportunities, such as higher education.

Traditionally, the family has fulfilled a number of other functions, such as providing religious training, education, and recreational outlets. But Ogburn argued that other social institutions have gradually assumed many of those functions. Education once took place at the family fireside; now it is the responsibility of professionals working in schools and colleges. Even the family's traditional recreational function has been transferred to outside groups such as Little Leagues, athletic clubs, and Internet chat rooms.

and limits freedom in sexual expression and mate selection. In contrast, the functionalist view focuses on the ways in which the family gratifies the needs of its members and contributes to social stability. The interactionist view considers the intimate, face-to-face relationships that occur in the family. And the feminist approach examines the role of the wife and mother, especially in the absence of an adult male.

Functionalist View

The family performs six paramount functions, first outlined more than 70 years ago by sociologist William F. Ogburn (Ogburn and Tibbits 1934):

1. **Reproduction.** For a society to maintain itself, it must replace dying members. In this sense, the family contributes to human survival through its function of reproduction.

2. **Protection.** In all cultures, the family assumes the ultimate responsibility for the protection and upbringing of children.

3. **Socialization.** Parents and other kin monitor a child's behavior and transmit the norms, values, and language of their culture to the child.

Conflict View

Conflict theorists view the family not as a contributor to social stability, but as a reflection of the inequality in wealth and power that is found within the larger society. Feminist and conflict theorists note that the family has traditionally legitimized and perpetuated male dominance. Throughout most of human history—and in a wide range of societies—husbands have exercised overwhelming power and authority within the family. Not until the first wave of contemporary feminism in the United States, in the mid-1800s, was there a substantial challenge to the historic status of wives and children as the legal property of husbands.

While the egalitarian family has become a more common pattern in the United States in recent decades—owing in good part to the activism of feminists beginning in the late 1960s and early 1970s—male dominance over the family has hardly

disappeared. Sociologists have found that while married men are increasing their involvement in child care, their wives still perform a disproportionate amount of it. Furthermore, for every stay-at-home dad there are 38 stay-at-home moms. And unfortunately, many husbands reinforce their power and control over wives and children through acts of domestic violence (Jason Fields 2004:11–12; Garcia-Moreno et al. 2005; Sayer et al. 2004).

Conflict theorists also view the family as an economic unit that contributes to societal injustice. The family is the basis for transferring power, property, and privilege from one generation to the next. Although the United States is widely viewed as a land of opportunity, social mobility is restricted in important ways. Children inherit the privileged or less-than-privileged social and economic status of their parents (and in some cases, of earlier generations as well). The social class of parents significantly influences children's socialization experiences and the degree of protection they receive. Thus, the socioeconomic status of a child's family will have a marked influence on his or her nutrition, health care, housing, educational opportunities, and, in many respects, life chances as an adult. For this reason, conflict theorists argue that the family helps to maintain inequality.

Interactionist View

Interactionists focus on the micro level of family and other intimate relationships. They are interested in how individuals interact with one another, whether they are cohabiting partners or longtime married couples. For example, in a study of both Black and White two-parent households, researchers found that when fathers are more involved with their children (reading to them, helping them with homework, or restricting their television viewing), the children have fewer behavior problems, get along better with others, and are more responsible (Mosley and Thomson 1995).

Another interactionist study might examine the role of the stepparent. The increased number of single parents who remarry has sparked an interest in those who are helping to raise other people's children. Studies have found that stepmothers are more likely than stepfathers to accept the blame for bad relations with their stepchildren. Interactionists theorize that stepfathers (like most fathers) may simply be unaccustomed to interacting directly with children when the mother isn't there (Bray and Kelly 1999; F. Furstenberg and Cherlin 1991).

Feminist View

Because "women's work" has traditionally focused on family life, feminist sociologists have taken a strong interest in the family as a social institution. As we saw in Module 34, research on gender roles in child care and household chores has been extensive. Sociologists have looked particularly closely at how women's work outside the home impacts their child care and housework—duties Arlie Hochschild (1989, 1990, 2005) has referred to as the "second shift." Today, researchers recognize that, for many women, the second shift includes the care of aging parents as well.

Feminist theorists have urged social scientists and social agencies to rethink the notion that families in which no adult male

Interactionists are particularly interested in the ways in which parents relate to each other and to their children. The close and loving relationship illustrated here is one of the foundations of a strong family.

is present are automatically a cause for concern, or even dysfunctional. They have also contributed to research on single women, single-parent households, and lesbian couples. In the case of single mothers, researchers have focused on the resiliency of many such households, despite economic stress. According to Velma McBride Murray and her colleagues (2001) at the University of Georgia, such studies show that among African Americans, single mothers draw heavily on kinfolk for material resources, parenting advice, and social support. Considering feminist research on the family as a whole, one researcher concluded that the family is the "source of women's strength" (V. Taylor et al. 2009).

Finally, feminists who take the interactionist perspective stress the need to investigate neglected topics in family studies. For instance, in a growing number of dual-income households, the wife earns a higher income than the husband. In 2005, a study of 58 married couples revealed that 26 percent of the wives earned more than their husbands. In 1981, the proportion was just 16 percent. Yet beyond individual case studies, little research has been done on how these families may differ from those in which the husband is the major breadwinner (Wills and Risman 2006).

Table 39-1 summarizes the four major theoretical perspectives on the family.

Table **39-1**　**Sociological Perspectives on the Family**

Theoretical Perspective	Emphasis
Functionalist	The family as a contributor to social stability Roles of family members
Conflict	The family as a perpetuator of inequality Transmission of poverty or wealth across generations
Interactionist	Relationships among family members
Feminist	The family as a perpetuator of gender roles Female-headed households

summing up

MODULE 39 | Recap and Review

Summary

The family, in its many forms, is present in all human cultures.

1. Families vary from culture to culture and even within the same culture.

2. The structure of the **extended family** can offer certain advantages over that of the **nuclear family.**

3. Societies determine **kinship** by descent from both parents (**bilateral descent**), from the father only (**patrilineal descent**), or from the mother only (**matrilineal descent**).

4. Sociologists do not agree on whether the **egalitarian family** has replaced the patriarchal family in the United States.

5. William F. Ogburn outlined six basic functions of the family: reproduction, protection, socialization, regulation of sexual behavior, companionship, and the provision of social status.

6. Conflict theorists argue that male dominance of the family contributes to societal injustice and denies women opportunities. Interactionists focus on how individuals interact within the family and other intimate relationships. Feminists stress the need to broaden research on the family. Like conflict theorists, they see the family's role in socializing children as the primary source of sexism.

Thinking Critically

1. From a woman's point of view, what are the economic advantages and disadvantages of monogamous, polygamous, and polyandrous families? What are the advantages and disadvantages of each of these family situations for men?

2. How would functionalist, conflict, interactionist, and feminist theorists explain a polygamous family structure?

Key Terms

Bilateral descent

Egalitarian family

Extended family

Family

Kinship

Matriarchy

Matrilineal descent

Monogamy

Nuclear family

Patriarchy

Patrilineal descent

Polyandry

Polygamy

Polygyny

Serial monogamy

MODULE 40 | Marriage and Family

Currently, over 95 percent of all men and women in the United States marry at least once during their lifetimes. Historically, the most consistent aspect of family life in this country has been the high rate of marriage. In fact, despite the high rate of divorce, there are some indications of a miniboom in marriages of late.

In this module, we will examine various aspects of love, marriage, and parenthood in the United States and contrast them with cross-cultural examples. Though we're used to thinking of romance and mate selection as strictly a matter of individual preference, sociological analysis tells us that social institutions and distinctive cultural norms and values also play an important role.

Courtship and Mate Selection

In the past, most couples met their partners through family, friends, or their neighborhood or workplace. Today, however, many couples meet on the Internet. According to a national survey done in 2010, the Internet is second only to friends as a source of romantic partners—ahead of family, workplace, and neighborhood. Significantly, online networking is just as important to mate-seekers in their 40s and 50s as to those under age 30. It is especially important to gays and lesbians, given the limited number of meeting places available to them: 61 percent of same-sex couples meet online, compared to 23 percent of heterosexual couples (Rosenfeld 2010).

Internet romance is only the latest courtship practice. In the central Asian nation of Uzbekistan and many other traditional cultures, courtship is defined largely through the interaction of two sets of parents, who arrange marriages for their children. Typically, a young Uzbekistani woman will be socialized to eagerly anticipate her marriage to a man whom she has met only once, when he is presented to her family at the time of the final inspection of her dowry. In the United States, in contrast, courtship is conducted primarily by individuals who have a romantic interest in each other. In our culture, courtship often requires these individuals to rely heavily on intricate games, gestures, and signals. Despite such differences, courtship—whether in the United States, Uzbekistan, or elsewhere—is influenced by the norms and values of the larger society (Carol J. Williams 1995).

One unmistakable trend in mate selection is that the process appears to be taking longer today than in the past. A variety of factors, including concerns about financial security and personal independence, has contributed to this delay in marriage. Most people are now well into their 20s before they marry, both in the United States and in other countries (Figure 40-1).

Aspects of Mate Selection

Many societies have explicit or unstated rules that define potential mates as acceptable or unacceptable. These norms can be distinguished in terms of endogamy and exogamy. **Endogamy** (from the Greek *endon*, "within") specifies the groups within which a spouse must be found and prohibits marriage with others. For example, in the United States, many people are expected to marry within their racial, ethnic, or religious group, and are strongly discouraged or even prohibited from marrying outside the group. Endogamy is intended to reinforce the cohesiveness

trend|spotting

Cougars on the Rise

Typically, people choose someone of the same age as a romantic partner. In the most common deviation from this pattern, the husband is older than the wife. Yet today, the number of marriages that involve a much older woman—at least 10 years older—is growing. In fact, there is at least one online dating service that is dedicated to matching older women, dubbed "cougars," with younger men. According to sociologist Andrew Beveridge, although this type of couple represents only 1.3 percent of all marriages, that percentage is double that of 1960.

A similar trend can be seen among dating couples. According to an AARP survey, 20 percent of single women ages 40 to 69 said they were dating or had recently dated a man who was at least five years younger. And an informal tally by one dating service, published in the *New York Times*, indicates a rapid increase in the percentage of women over 40 who want to date men much younger than they are.

Professor Sandra L. Caron of the University of Maine has studied the reasons for this new trend. She notes that unlike many younger women, mature women are self-sufficient and don't need to look for an older, better educated man to support them. She finds that, in general, women who marry much younger men have happy marriages, although they may be insecure about their ages. That insecurity is probably misplaced. University of Washington sociologist Pepper Schwartz says she thinks young men are attracted to older women who are sexually free and don't make the demands that younger women do. As men become more accustomed to the idea of women earning more money than they do, the social barriers between young men and older women begin to melt away.

FIGURE 40-1 Median Age at First Marriage in Eight Countries

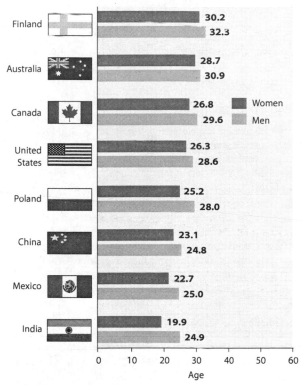

Country	Women	Men
Finland	30.2	32.3
Australia	28.7	30.9
Canada	26.8	29.6
United States	26.3	28.6
Poland	25.2	28.0
China	23.1	24.8
Mexico	22.7	25.0
India	19.9	24.9

Age (0, 10, 20, 30, 40, 50, 60)

Source: United Nations Statistics Division 2008.

Think about It

Why do people marry earlier in India than in Finland?

Although most interracial couples are not as visible as Seal and Heidi Klum, such unions are becoming increasingly common and accepted. They are also blurring the definitions of race. Will the children of these couples be considered Black or White? Why do you think so?

of the group by suggesting to the young that they should marry someone "of their own kind."

In contrast, **exogamy** (from the Greek *exo,* "outside") requires mate selection outside certain groups, usually one's own family or certain kinfolk. The **incest taboo,** a social norm common to virtually all societies, prohibits sexual relationships between certain culturally specified relatives. For those of us in the United States, this taboo means that we must marry outside the nuclear family. We cannot marry our siblings, and in most states we cannot marry our first cousins.

Endogamous restrictions may be seen as preferences for one group over another. In the United States, such preferences are most obvious in racial barriers. Until the 1960s, some states outlawed interracial marriage. Nevertheless, the number of marriages between African Americans and Whites in the United States has increased more than nine times in recent decades, jumping from 51,000 in 1960 to 481,000 in 2009. Marriage across ethnic lines is even greater among Hispanics: 35 percent of all married Hispanics have a non-Hispanic spouse. But while

these examples of racial exogamy are noteworthy, endogamy is still the social norm in the United States (Bureau of the Census 1998, 2009a:54).

Another factor that influences the selection of a marriage partner is **homogamy,** the conscious or unconscious tendency to select a mate with personal characteristics similar to one's own. The "like marries like" rule can be seen in couples with similar personalities and cultural interests. However, mate selection is unpredictable. Though some people may follow the homogamous pattern, others observe the "opposites attract" rule: one person is dependent and submissive—almost childishly so—while the other is dominant and controlling.

Recently, the concept of homogamy has been incorporated into the process of seeking a date or marital partner online. The Internet dating site eHarmony, which claims to be the first to use a "scientific approach" to matching people based on a variety of abilities and interests, says that it "facilitates" 46 marriages a day. Sociologist Pepper Schwartz, who works as a consultant for the competing site PerfectMatch.com, has developed a 48-question survey that covers everything from prospective mates' decision-making style to their degree of impulsivity (Gottlieb 2006; Kalmijn 1998).

The Love Relationship

Today's generation of college students seems more likely to hook up or cruise in large packs than to engage in the romantic dating relationships of their parents and grandparents. Still, at some point in their adult lives, the great majority of today's students will meet someone they love and enter into a long-term relationship that focuses on creating a family.

Parents in the United States tend to value love highly as a rationale for marriage, so they encourage their children to develop intimate relationships based on love and affection. Songs, films, books, magazines, television shows, and even cartoons and comic books reinforce the theme of love. At the same time, our society expects parents and peers to help a person confine his or her search for a mate to "socially acceptable" members of the opposite sex.

Though most people in the United States take the importance of falling in love for granted, the coupling of love and marriage is by no means a cultural universal. Many of the world's cultures give priority in mate selection to factors other than romantic feelings. In societies with *arranged marriages* engineered by parents or religious authorities, economic considerations play a significant role. The newly married couple is expected to develop a feeling of love *after* the legal union is formalized, if at all.

Even where arranged marriage is the norm, new media technologies have changed the mating game. Today, when young people exchange phone numbers, a flurry of short text messages is more likely to follow than a series of extended phone conversations. In India, where most young people defer to their parents' wishes when they marry, much of this text messaging is recreational. Still, it can test the limits of traditional dating norms, by reducing the formality of social interactions between men and women (Giridharadas 2008).

In some societies, neither the parents nor the bride has a say in whom she marries. Since at least the 12th century, men in the central Asian nation of Kyrgyzstan have literally kidnapped their future wives from the street in a custom known as *ala kachuu*, which translates roughly as "grab and run." In its most benign form, this custom is a kind of elopement in which the man whisks off his girlfriend. Men do it to avoid the bride-price that parents often demand in return for their consent. But, as of 2005, one-third of the brides in Kyrgyzstan had been abducted against their will. Many of them—perhaps 80 percent—eventually assent to the kidnapping, often at their parents' urging. For these women, romantic love does not precede marriage, though love may well develop over time (Craig Smith 2005).

 use your **sociological imagination**

Your parents and/or a matchmaker are going to arrange a marriage for you. What kind of mate will they select? Will your chances of having a successful marriage be better or worse than if you selected your own mate?

Variations in Family Life and Intimate Relationships

Within the United States, social class, race, and ethnicity create variations in family life. Studying these variations will give us a more sophisticated understanding of contemporary family styles in our country.

Social Class Differences

Various studies have documented the differences in family organization among social classes in the United States. In the upper class, the emphasis is on lineage and maintenance of family position. If you are in the upper class, you are not simply a member of a nuclear family but rather a member of a larger family tradition (think of the Rockefellers or the Kennedys). As a result, upper-class families are quite concerned about what they see as proper training for children.

Lower-class families do not often have the luxury of worrying about the "family name"; they must first struggle to pay their bills and survive the crises often associated with a life of poverty. Such families are more likely to have only one parent at home, which creates special challenges in child care and financial management. Children from lower-class families typically assume adult responsibilities—including marriage and parenthood—at an earlier age than children from affluent homes. In part, that is because they may lack the money needed to remain in school.

Social class differences in family life are less striking today than they once were. In the past, family specialists agreed that the contrasts in child-rearing practices were pronounced. Lower-class families were found to be more authoritarian in rearing children and more inclined to use physical punishment. Middle-class families were more permissive and more restrained in punishing their children. And compared to lower-class families, middle-class families tended to schedule more of their children's time, or even to overstructure it. However, these differences may have narrowed as more and more families from all social classes turned to the same books, magazines, and even television talk shows for advice on rearing children (Kronstadt and Favreault 2008; Luster et al. 1989).

Among the poor, women often play a significant role in the economic support of the family. Men may earn low wages, may be unemployed, or may be entirely absent from the family. In 2008, 29 percent of all families headed by women with no husband present fell below the government poverty line. In comparison, the poverty rate for married couples was only 5.5 percent. The disproportionate representation of female-headed households among the poor is a persistent and growing trend, referred to by sociologists as the *feminization of poverty* (see Module 28; DeNavas-Walt et al. 2009:14).

Many racial and ethnic groups appear to have distinctive family characteristics. However, racial and class factors are often closely related. In examining family life among racial and ethnic minorities, keep in mind that certain patterns may result from class as well as cultural factors.

Racial and Ethnic Differences

The subordinate status of racial and ethnic minorities in the United States profoundly affects their family lives. For example, the lower incomes of African Americans, Native Americans, most Hispanic groups, and selected Asian American groups make creating and maintaining successful marital unions a difficult task. The economic restructuring of the past 60 years, described by sociologist William Julius Wilson (1996, 2009) and others, has especially affected people living in inner cities and desolate rural areas, such as reservations. Furthermore, the immigration policy of the United States has complicated the successful relocation of intact families from Asia and Latin America.

The African American family suffers from many negative and inaccurate stereotypes. It is true that, in a significantly higher proportion of Black than White families, no husband is present in the home (Figure 40-2). Yet Black single mothers often belong to stable, functioning kin networks, which mitigate the pressures of sexism and racism. Members of these networks—predominantly female kin such as mothers, grandmothers, and aunts—ease financial strains by sharing goods and services. In addition to these strong kinship bonds, Black family life has emphasized deep religious commitment and high aspirations for achievement (DuBois [1909] 1970; F. Furstenberg 2007).

Like African Americans, Native Americans draw on family ties to cushion many of the hardships they face. On the Navajo reservation, for example, teenage parenthood is not regarded as the crisis that it is elsewhere in the United States. The Navajo trace their descent matrilineally. Traditionally, couples reside with the wife's family after marriage, allowing the grandparents to help with the child rearing. While the Navajo do not approve of teenage parenthood, the deep emotional commitment of their extended families provides a warm home environment for children, even when no father is present or involved (Dalla and Gamble 2001).

Sociologists also have taken note of differences in family patterns among other racial and ethnic groups. For example, Mexican American men have been described as exhibiting a sense of virility, personal worth, and pride in their maleness that is called **machismo.** Mexican Americans are also described as being more familistic than many other subcultures. **Familism** refers to pride in the extended family, expressed through the maintenance of close ties and strong obligations to kinfolk outside the immediate family. Traditionally, Mexican Americans have placed proximity to their extended families above other needs and desires.

Although familism is often seen as a positive cultural attribute, it may also have negative consequences. Sociologists who have studied the relatively low college application rates of Hispanic students have found they have a strong desire to stay at home. Even the children of college-educated parents express this preference, which diminishes the likelihood of their getting a four-year degree and dramatically reduces the possibility that they will apply to a selective college (Desmond and Turley 2009).

These family patterns are changing, however, in response to changes in Latinos' social class standing, educational achievements, and occupations. Like other Americans, career-oriented Latinos in search of a mate but short on spare time are turning to Internet sites. As Latinos and other groups assimilate into the

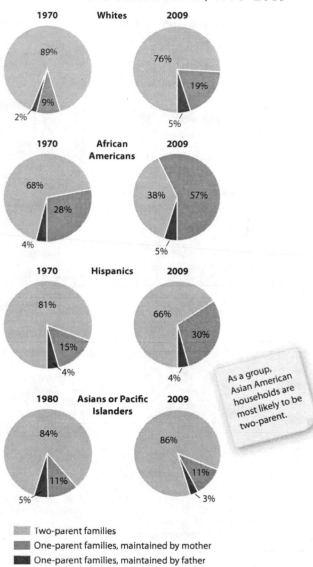

FIGURE 40-2 **Rise of Single-Parent Families in the United States, 1970–2009**

Two-parent families
One-parent families, maintained by mother
One-parent families, maintained by father

As a group, Asian American households are most likely to be two-parent.

Note: Families are groups with children under 18. Early data for Asian Americans are for 1980. Hispanics can be of any race. Not included are unrelated people living together with no children present. All data exclude the 11 percent of children in nonparental households. *Sources:* Bureau of the Census 2008a:56, 2010b:Table EG10.

dominant culture of the United States, their family lives take on both the positive and negative characteristics associated with White households (Landale and Oropesa 2007).

Child-Rearing Patterns

The Nayars of southern India acknowledge the biological role of fathers, but the mother's eldest brother is responsible for her children. In contrast, uncles play only a peripheral role in child care

Sociology in the Global Community

Family Life, Italian Style: Thirty-Something and Living with Mom

Bamboccioni—adult children who live with their parents—are no longer socially unacceptable in Italy. In fact, they're not even unusual. In December 2009, the Italian government released new data showing that 40 percent of Italian men between ages 30 and 34 live with their parents. So do 20 percent of Italian women in this age bracket. Among those a little older, ages 35 to 39, 17.5 percent of men and 9.3 percent of women live with their parents.

This state of affairs is not a recent phenomenon. What is new is that 80 percent of these adult children say they cannot afford to leave their parents' homes. Salaries in Italy are low but rents are high, so these not-so-young adults linger on with mama and papa. As one of them, a 30-year-old biologist, put it, "We are the €1,000-per-month generation—who can afford spending more than €800 for an apartment?"

> About 40 percent of *bamboccioni* live with their parents not because of financial need, but because they enjoy the company.

The amount of time Italians take to graduate from college also contributes to the trend. Many are still studying for their degree in their late 20s. As in the United States, most find that living alone before graduation is financially impossible.

About 40 percent of *bamboccioni* live with their parents not because of financial need,

but because they enjoy the company. Others feel responsible for their aging parents. Among the women ages 35 to 40, more than half feel it is a duty. Sociologist Giampiero dalla Zuanna says their commitment to the family means the elderly in Italy are much more likely to remain in their own homes than those in northern Europe, many of whom must move to retirement communities.

The pattern of adult children staying home with their parents is not unique to Italy. In North America and throughout Europe, young people are feeling the impact of the recent economic downturn. Many are delaying childbearing until their job prospects improve.

One relatively unnoticed factor that is contributing to the trend is parents' greater

longevity. Today, more parents survive long enough for their children to become adults, and remain healthy enough to maintain a home for them.

LET'S DISCUSS

1. Do you or someone you know live at home with parents? If so, do you see the situation as similar to that of the *bamboccioni*?

2. In the United States, what other factors might contribute to adult children choosing to live with their parents?

Sources: Haub and Kent 2009; Momigliana 2010; S. Roberts 2010.

---

in the United States. Caring for children is a universal function of the family, yet the ways in which different societies assign this function to family members can vary significantly. Even within the United States, child-rearing patterns are varied. We'll take a look here at parenthood and grandparenthood, adoption, dual-income families, single-parent families, and stepfamilies.

Parenthood and Grandparenthood

The socialization of children is essential to the maintenance of any culture. Consequently, parenthood is one of the most important (and most demanding) social roles in the United States. Sociologist Alice Rossi (1968, 1984) has identified four factors that complicate the transition to parenthood and the role of

socialization. First, there is little anticipatory socialization for the social role of caregiver. The normal school curriculum gives scant attention to the subjects most relevant to successful family life, such as child care and home maintenance. Second, only limited learning occurs during the period of pregnancy itself. Third, the transition to parenthood is quite abrupt. Unlike adolescence, it is not prolonged; unlike the transition to work, the duties of caregiving cannot be taken on gradually. Finally, in Rossi's view, our society lacks clear and helpful guidelines for successful parenthood. There is little consensus on how parents can produce happy and well-adjusted offspring—or even on what it means to be well-adjusted. For these reasons, socialization for parenthood involves difficult challenges for most men and women in the United States.

One recent development in family life in the United States has been the extension of parenthood, as single adult children continue to live at home or return home after college. In 2009, 33 percent of men and 22 percent of women in their 20s lived with their parents. Some of these adult children were still pursuing an education, but in many instances, financial difficulties lay at the heart of these living arrangements. While rents and real estate prices have skyrocketed, salaries for younger workers have not kept pace, and many find themselves unable to afford their own homes. (This problem, along with the trend toward adult children living with their parents, is not unique to the United States: see the Sociology in the Global Community box above.) Moreover, with many marriages now ending in divorce—most commonly in the first seven years of marriage—divorced sons and daughters often return to live with their parents, sometimes with their own children (Bureau of the Census 2010b:Table A2).

Is this living arrangement a positive development for family members? Social scientists have just begun to examine the phenomenon, sometimes called the "boomerang generation" or the "full-nest syndrome" in the popular press. One survey in Virginia seemed to show that neither the parents nor their adult children were happy about continuing to live together. The children often felt resentful and isolated, but the parents suffered too: learning to live without children in the home is an essential stage of adult life and may even be a significant turning point for a marriage (*Berkeley Wellness Letter* 1990; Mogelonsky 1996).

In some homes, the full nest holds grandchildren. In 2009, 7 million children, or 9 percent of all children in the United States, lived in a household with a grandparent. In about a third of these homes, no parent was present to assume responsibility for the youngsters. Special difficulties are inherent in such relationships, including legal custodial concerns, financial issues, and emotional problems for adults and youths alike. It is not surprising that support groups such as Grandparents as Parents have emerged to provide assistance (Bureau of the Census 2010b:Table C4).

Adoption

In a legal sense, **adoption** is a "process that allows for the transfer of the legal rights, responsibilities, and privileges of parenthood" to a new legal parent or parents (E. Cole 1985:638). In many cases, these rights are transferred from a biological parent or parents (often called birth parents) to an adoptive parent or parents. At any given time, about 2 million adults in the United States are raising adopted children (Jo Jones 2009).

Viewed from a functionalist perspective, government has a strong interest in encouraging adoption. Policymakers, in fact, have both a humanitarian and a financial stake in the process. In theory, adoption offers a stable family environment for children who otherwise might not receive satisfactory care. Moreover, government data show that unwed mothers who keep their babies tend to be of lower socioeconomic status and often require public assistance to support their children. The government can lower its social welfare expenses, then, if children are transferred to

When nine-year-old Blake Brunson shows up for a basketball game, so do his *eight* grandparents—the result of his parents' remarriages. Blended families can be very supportive to children, but what message do they send to them on the permanency of marriage?

economically self-sufficient families. From an interactionist perspective, however, adoption may require a child to adjust to a very different family environment and parental approach to child rearing.

About 4 percent of all people in the United States are adopted, about half of whom were adopted by persons not related to them at birth. There are two legal methods of adopting an unrelated person: the adoption may be arranged through a licensed agency, or in some states it may be arranged through a private agreement sanctioned by the courts. Adopted children may come from the United States or from abroad. In 2009 over 12,700 children entered the United States as the adopted children of U.S. citizens. Figure 40-3 shows how the countries of origin have changed over time. International adoptions began to decline in 2004 after a long and steady increase. Recently China, the source for about one-fourth of overseas adoptions, tightened the rules for foreign adoptions, effectively reducing their number. Applicants for adoption who are single, obese, or older than 50 are now automatically disqualified.

The 2010 earthquake in Haiti drew attention to the foreign perspective on international adoptions, which is not always positive. When well-meaning people from the United States arrived in Haiti to rescue alleged orphans and arrange for their adoption in other countries, government officials objected. Some of the children, it turned out, were not orphans; their parents were simply too poor to care for them. For the governments of overstressed developing nations, adoption can be both a solution and a problem.

Adoption is controversial, not only abroad, but at home. In some cases, those who adopt children are not married. In 1995, an important court decision in New York held that a couple does not need to be married to adopt a child. Under this ruling, unmarried heterosexual couples, lesbian couples, and gay couples can all adopt children in New York. Today, most states permit gay and lesbian couples to adopt. Florida is the only state that explicitly forbids it; five others (Arkansas, Michigan, Mississippi, Nebraska, and Utah) prohibit couples who are not legally married from adopting (National Gay and Lesbian Task Force 2008).

FIGURE 40-3   **Foreign-Born Adoptees by Top 10 Countries of Origin, 1989 and 2009**

	1989	Country	Rank	Country	2009	
	3,544	S. Korea	1	China	3,001	
	736	Colombia	2	Ethiopia	2,277	
	648	India	3	Russia	1,586	
	465	Philippines	4	S. Korea	1,080	
	253	Chile	5	Guatemala	756	
	252	Paraguay	6	Ukraine	610	
	222	Peru	7	Vietnam	481	
	202	Guatemala	8	Haiti	330	
	201	China	9	India	297	
	131	Honduras	10	Kazakhstan	295	

Total 6,654

Total 14,862

4,000 3,500 3,000 2,500 2,000 1,500 1,000 500 0   0 500 1,000 1,500 2,000 2,500 3,000 3,500 4,000

Number of children   Number of children

Source: Department of State 2001, 2010.

Think about It

Why did so many foreign-born adopted children come from these countries in particular? Why did the children's countries of origin change so much from 1989 to 2009?

For every child who is adopted, many more remain the wards of state-sponsored child protective services. At any given time, around half a million children in the United States are living in foster care. Every year, about 58,000 of them are adopted; another 123,600 are eligible and waiting to be adopted (Department of Health and Human Services 2010a).

Dual-Income Families

The idea of a family consisting of a wage-earning husband and a wife who stays at home has largely given way to the dual-income household. Among married people between ages 25 and 34, 96 percent of the men and 69 percent of the women were in the labor force in 2007 (Bureau of the Census 2008a:375).

Miles Harvey reads to his children via Skype. Harvey, who is happily married, lives 900 miles from his family in Chicago. He accepted a job in New Orleans for economic reasons.

Why has there been such a rise in the number of dual-income couples? A major factor is economic need, coupled with a desire by both men *and* women to pursue their careers. Evidence of this trend can be found in the rise in the number of married couples living apart for reasons other than marital discord. The 3.6 million couples who now live apart represent 1 out of every 33 marriages. More than half of them live farther than 100 miles apart, and half of those live 1,000 or more miles apart. Of course, couples living apart are nothing new; men have worked at transient jobs for generations as soldiers, truck drivers, or traveling salesmen. Now, however, the woman's job is often the one that creates the separation. The existence of such household arrangements reflects an acceptance of the egalitarian family type (Holmes 2009; Silverman 2009).

 use your **sociological imagination**

What personal experience do you have with child rearing by grandparents, adoption, or dual-income families? Describe what you observed using sociological concepts.

Single-Parent Families

The 2004 *American Idol* winner Fantasia Barrino's song "Baby Mama" offers a tribute to young single mothers—a subject she knows about. Barrino was 17 when she became pregnant with her daughter. Though critics charged that the song sends the wrong message to teenage girls, Barrino says it is not about encouraging teens to have sex. Rather, she sees the song as an anthem for young mothers courageously trying to raise their children alone (Cherlin 2006).

In recent decades, the stigma attached to unwed mothers and other single parents has significantly diminished. **Single-parent families,** in which only one parent is present to care for the children, can hardly be viewed as a rarity in the United States. In 2009, a single parent headed about 24 percent of White families with children under 18, 34 percent of Hispanic families with children, and 62 percent of African American families with children (see Figure 40-2).

Interestingly, since 1995 the greatest increase in unwed motherhood has occurred among women in their 20s and 30s. This age group still constitutes a smaller proportion of unwed mothers than teens. In 2007, however, 45 percent of births to women in their 20s were to unmarried women (Ventura 2009).

The lives of single parents and their children are not inevitably more difficult than life in a traditional nuclear family. It is as inaccurate to assume that a single-parent family is necessarily deprived as it is to assume that a two-parent family is always secure and happy. Nevertheless, life in a single-parent family can be extremely stressful, in both economic and emotional terms. A family headed by a single mother faces especially difficult problems when the mother is a teenager.

Why might low-income teenage women wish to have children and face the obvious financial difficulties of motherhood? Viewed from an interactionist perspective, these women tend to have low self-esteem and limited options; a child may provide a sense of motivation and purpose for a teenager whose economic worth in our society is limited at best. Given the barriers that many young women face because of their gender, race, ethnicity, and class, many teenagers may believe they have little to lose and much to gain by having a child.

According to a widely held stereotype, "unwed mothers" and "babies having babies" in the United States are predominantly African American. However, this view is not entirely accurate. African Americans account for a disproportionate

 use your **sociological imagination**

What special challenges have you witnessed in stepfamilies? What about advantages they may experience? Describe what you observed using sociological concepts.

Most households in the United States do not consist of two parents living with their unmarried children.

share of births to unmarried women and teenagers, but the majority of all babies born to unmarried teenage mothers are born to White adolescents. Moreover, since 1980, birthrates among Black teenagers have generally declined (J. Martin et al. 2009).

Although 84 percent of single parents in the United States are mothers, the number of households headed by single fathers more than quadrupled from 1987 to 2008. Though single mothers often develop social networks, single fathers are typically more isolated. In addition, they must deal with schools and social service agencies that are more accustomed to women as custodial parents (Bureau of the Census 1994, 2009a:58).

Stepfamilies

Approximately 45 percent of all people in the United States will marry, divorce, and then remarry. The rising rates of divorce and remarriage have led to a noticeable increase in stepfamily relationships.

The exact nature of blended families has social significance for adults and children alike. Certainly resocialization is required when an adult becomes a stepparent or a child becomes a stepchild and stepsibling. Moreover, an important distinction must be made between first-time stepfamilies and households where there have been repeated divorces, breakups, or changes in custodial arrangements.

In evaluating the rise of stepfamilies, some observers have assumed that children would benefit from remarriage because they would be gaining a second custodial parent, and would potentially enjoy greater economic security. However, after reviewing many studies of stepfamilies, sociologist Andrew J. Cherlin (2008a:800) concluded that "the well-being of children in stepfamilies is no better, on average, than the well-being of children in divorced, single-parent households."

Stepparents can play valuable and unique roles in their stepchildren's lives, but their involvement does not guarantee an improvement in family life. In fact, standards may decline. Studies suggest that children raised in families with stepmothers are likely to have less health care, education, and money spent on their food than children raised by biological mothers. The measures are also negative for children raised by stepfathers, but only half as negative as in the case of stepmothers. These results don't mean that stepmothers are "evil"—it may be that the stepmother holds back out of concern for seeming too intrusive, or she relies mistakenly on the biological father to carry out parental duties (Schmeeckle 2007; Schmeeckle et al. 2006).

MODULE 40 | Recap and Review

Summary

People select mates in a variety of ways: in some societies, marriages are arranged, while in others, people select their own mates.

1. Some societies require mates to be chosen within a certain group (**endogamy**) or outside certain groups (**exogamy**). Consciously or unconsciously, many people look for a mate with similar personal characteristics (**homogamy**).
2. In the United States, family life varies with social class, race, and ethnicity.
3. Currently, in the majority of all married couples in the United States, both husband and wife work outside the home.
4. **Single-parent families** account for an increasing proportion of U.S. families.

Thinking Critically

1. How do both cultural and socioeconomic factors contribute to the following trends: later age of first marriage, the increasing number of extended-family households, and the "boomerang generation"?
2. Explain mate selection from the functionalist and interactionist perspectives.

Key Terms

Adoption
Endogamy
Exogamy
Familism
Homogamy
Incest taboo
Machismo
Single-parent family

MODULE 41 | Alternatives to Traditional Families

Divorce

In the United States, the pattern of family life includes commitments both to marriage and to self-expression and personal growth. Needless to say, the tension between those competing commitments can undermine a marriage, working against the establishment of a lasting relationship. This approach to family life is distinctive to the United States. In some nations, such as Italy, the culture strongly supports marriage and discourages divorce. In others, such as Sweden, people treat marriage the same way as cohabitation, and both arrangements are just as lasting (Cherlin 2009).

Statistical Trends in Divorce

Just how common is divorce? Surprisingly, this is not a simple question; divorce statistics are difficult to interpret. The media frequently report that one out of every two marriages ends in divorce, but that figure is misleading. It is based on a comparison of all divorces that occur in a single year (regardless of when the couples were married) with the number of new marriages in the same year.

In many countries, divorce began to increase in the late 1960s but then leveled off; since the late 1980s, it has declined by 30 percent (Figure 41-1, shows the pattern in the United States). This trend is due partly to the aging of the baby boomer population and the corresponding decline in the proportion of people of marriageable age. But it also indicates an increase in marital stability in recent years (Coontz 2006).

Getting divorced obviously does not sour people on marriage. About 63 percent of all divorced people in the United States have remarried. Women are less likely than men to remarry because many retain custody of their children after a divorce, which complicates a new adult relationship (Bianchi and Spain 1996; Saad 2004).

Some people regard the nation's high rate of remarriage as an endorsement of the institution of marriage, but it does lead to the new challenges of a kin network composed of both current and prior marital relationships. Such networks can be particularly complex if children are involved or if an ex-spouse remarries.

Factors Associated with Divorce

Perhaps the most important factor in the increase in divorce over the past hundred years has been the greater social *acceptance* of divorce. It is no longer considered necessary to endure an unhappy marriage. More important, various religious denominations have relaxed their negative attitudes toward divorce, so that most religious leaders no longer treat it as a sin.

The growing acceptance of divorce is a worldwide phenomenon. A decade ago, Sunoo, South Korea's foremost matchmaking service, had no divorced clients. Few Koreans divorced; those who did felt social pressure to resign themselves to the single life. But in one recent seven-year period, South Korea's divorce rate doubled. Today, 15 percent of Sunoo's membership are divorced (Onishi 2003; United Nations Statistics Division 2009:Table 23).

In the United States, several factors have contributed to the growing social acceptance of divorce:

- Most states have adopted more liberal divorce laws in the past three decades. No-fault divorce laws, which allow a couple to end their marriage without fault on either side (by specifying adultery, for instance), accounted for an initial surge in the divorce rate after they were introduced in the 1970s, but appear to have had little effect beyond that.

- Divorce has become a more practical option in newly formed families, since families tend to have fewer children now than in the past.

- A general increase in family incomes, coupled with the availability of free legal aid to some poor people, has meant that more couples can afford costly divorce proceedings.

- As society provides greater opportunities for women, more and more wives are becoming less dependent on their husbands, both economically and emotionally. They may feel more able to leave a marriage if it seems hopeless.

What about the stress of separation caused by military duty? Forced transfer overseas, the tension of war, new duties at home, and anxiety over a spouse's return might seem a recipe for marital failure. The Research Today box considers military marriages' vulnerability while the husband or wife is away at war.

Impact of Divorce on Children

Divorce is traumatic for all involved, but it has special meaning for the more than 1 million children whose parents divorce each year. Of course, for some of these children, divorce signals the welcome end to a very dysfunctional relationship. Perhaps that is why a national study that tracked 6,332 children both before and after their parents' divorce found that their behavior did not suffer from the marital breakups. Other studies have shown greater unhappiness among children who live amidst parental conflict than among children whose parents are divorced. Still, it would be simplistic to assume that children are automatically better off following the breakup of their parents' marriage. The interests of the parents do not necessarily serve children well (Zi 2007).

FIGURE 41-1 **Trends in Marriage and Divorce in the United States, 1920–2009**

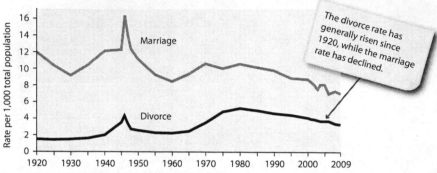

Sources: Bureau of the Census 1975:64; *National Vital Statistics Reports* 2010.

The divorce rate has generally risen since 1920, while the marriage rate has declined.

● Diverse Lifestyles

Marriage is no longer the presumed route from adolescence to adulthood. In fact, it has lost much of its social significance as a rite of passage. The nation's marriage rate has declined since 1960 because people are postponing marriage until later in life, and because more couples, including same-sex couples, are deciding to form partnerships without marriage.

MAPPING LIFE NATIONWIDE

FIGURE 41-2 **Unmarried-Couple Households by State**

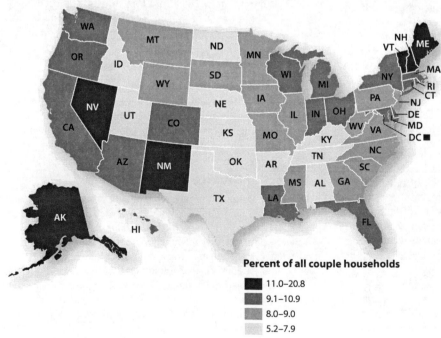

Percent of all couple households

- 11.0–20.8
- 9.1–10.9
- 8.0–9.0
- 5.2–7.9

Note: Data are for 2000 and include both opposite-sex and same-sex partners. U.S. average is 9.1 percent.
Source: Simmons and O'Connell 2003:4.

Cohabitation

In the United States, testing the marital waters by living together before making a commitment is a common practice among marriage-wary 20- and 30-somethings. The tremendous increase in the number of male–female couples who choose to live together without marrying, a practice called **cohabitation,** is one of the most dramatic trends of recent years.

About half of all *currently* married couples in the United States say that they lived together before marriage. This percentage is likely to increase. The number of unmarried-couple households in the United States rose 600 percent in the 1960s and increased another 72 percent between 1990 and 2000. Presently over 8 percent of opposite-sex couples are unmarried. Cohabitation is more common among African Americans and American Indians than among other racial and ethnic groups; it is least common among Asian Americans. Figure 41-2 shows regional variations in cohabitation (Peterson 2003; Simmons and O'Connell 2003).

In much of Europe, cohabitation is so common that the general sentiment seems to be "Love, yes; marriage, maybe." In Iceland, 62 percent of all children are born to single mothers; in France, Great Britain, and Norway, about 40 percent. Government policies in these countries make few legal distinctions between married and unmarried couples or households. Perhaps as a result, partnerships between cohabiting adults are not necessarily brief or lacking in commitment. Children born to a cohabiting couple in Sweden, for example, are less likely than children born to a cohabiting couple in the United States to see their parents break up (Cherlin 2009; Lyall 2002; M. Moore 2006).

People commonly associate cohabitation with younger couples. But according to a study done in Los Angeles, working couples are almost twice as likely to cohabit as college students. And census data show that in 2003, 45 percent of unmarried couples had one or more children present in the household. These cohabitants are more like spouses than dating partners. Moreover, in contrast to the common perception that people who cohabit have never been married,

Research Today

Divorce and Military Deployment

Whenever soldiers talk about the hardships of foreign deployment, separation from their families and the toll on their marital relationships are the main topic. Too often, military couples marry just before a deployment, following a brief romance. Then, when they are suddenly separated, the relationship begins to fall apart. To keep wives from worrying or to reduce their own homesickness, many soldiers avoid calling home. Those couples who do communicate by phone, letter, or e-mail often argue; some talk about divorce. Impulsively, a soldier may throw his wedding ring away. A wife struggling to manage on her own may empty the family's bank account.

Yet many couples make heroic efforts to hold together despite the hardship. Those who are left home continue to care for their families, coping with life as a single parent and comforting children who miss their father or mother. They will themselves to overcome loneliness and anxiety. For these couples, every new deployment is a challenge; being apart doesn't get easier as they get older.

On balance, does overseas deployment affect the divorce rate among military couples? Current research delivers a mixed message. One long-term study published recently indicates that the longer the deployment, the lower the risk of divorce. Studies of soldiers who served in the Vietnam War and the 1991 Persian Gulf War came to the same conclusion. Yet 2009 data show that the current divorce rate among those in the military is 3.6 percent a year—slightly higher than the national rate of 3.4 percent. Furthermore, 23 percent of soldiers stationed in Iraq in 2009 say they plan to divorce or separate after returning home, compared to 12 percent in 2003.

There were other negative findings of the study. Female service members were found to be twice as likely as male service members to end their marriages. Moreover, enlisted service members were more likely than officers to end their marriages. This second disparity may be due to the fact that officers tend to be older than enlisted personnel, and older couples are less likely than younger couples to divorce.

Studies of the impact of overseas deployment on couples' children have not been reassuring. In 2007, an Army-funded study found that the rate of child neglect among military families was almost four times higher when husbands were deployed than when they were home. Physical abuse of children in those

Welcome home! Military families reunite after a long, anxious separation.

cases was nearly twice as high when husbands were away. Given these findings, one can only hope that support programs for families separated by war will be strengthened.

How can we explain the resiliency of some service members' marriages in the face of war? Although wartime separation is undeniably stressful for couples, the researchers speculated that it might also benefit them, perhaps through higher earnings (combat pay) or the potential for career advancement. Moreover, many couples reported finding meaning and fulfillment in the deployment, which they saw as an important service to the nation. Finally, the spouses who are left behind are not totally isolated. The military provides strong social support, along with health care, child care, and housing subsidies. All these forms of

> 23 percent of soldiers stationed in Iraq in 2009 say they plan to divorce or separate after returning home.

support offer some protection from the impact of stress.

There is a need for further research on this topic. The information that researchers have covers only the short term and pertains only to those soldiers who remained in the military. Could the long-term impact on military couples be more telling? Could the outcome be different for those who leave the military soon after a war? And might soldiers consider marriage more carefully than the average person, knowing that their futures are uncertain? As with even the most detailed research, this study's conclusions raise new questions for scientific investigation.

LET'S DISCUSS

1. Do you know any married couples who have been separated by military deployment overseas? If so, how did they cope? What was the effect on their children?

2. Can you think of some other reasons why military marriages might survive the strain of war as well as they do?

Sources: Block 2009; Bowman 2009; D. Gibbs et al. 2007; Karney and Crown 2007; Krauss 1993; T. Perry 2007; Priest 2008; RAND 2007; A. Stone and Bello 2009; Wheller 2009; Zoroya 2009.

researchers report that about half of all people involved in cohabitation in the United States have been previously married. Cohabitation serves as a temporary or permanent alternative to matrimony for many men and women who have experienced their own or their parents' divorces (Jason Fields 2004; Popenoe and Whitehead 1999).

Periodically, legislators attempt to bolster the desirability of a lifelong commitment to marriage. In 2002, President George W. Bush backed funding for an initiative to promote marriage among those who receive public assistance. Under the Healthy Marriage Initiative, the federal government created a resource center that promoted marriage-related programs. Critics charged that the effort was underfunded or an inappropriate mission for the federal government. Still, the Obama administration has indicated a desire to continue the initiative, although the worsening economy may jeopardize its funding (Jayson 2009).

Remaining Single

Looking at TV programs today, you would be justified in thinking that most households are composed of singles. Although that is not the case, it is true that more and more people in the United States are postponing entry into a first marriage. Over one out of three households with children in the United States is a single-parent household. Even so, fewer than 4 percent of women and men in the United States are likely to remain single throughout their lives (Bureau of the Census 2008a).

The trend toward maintaining a single lifestyle for a longer period is related to the growing economic independence of young people. This trend is especially significant for women. Freed from financial needs, women don't necessarily need to marry to enjoy a satisfying life. Divorce, late marriage, and longevity also figure into this trend.

There are many reasons why a person may choose not to marry. Some singles do not want to limit their sexual intimacy to one lifetime partner. Some men and women do not want to become highly dependent on any one person—and do not want anyone depending heavily on them. In a society that values individuality and self-fulfillment, the single lifestyle can offer certain freedoms that married couples may not enjoy. Even divorced parents may not feel the need to remarry. Sociologist Andrew J. Cherlin (2009) contends that a single parent who connects with other adults, such as grandparents, to form a solid, supportive relationship for child rearing should not feel compelled to re-partner.

Nevertheless, remaining single represents a clear departure from societal expectations; indeed, it has been likened to "being single on Noah's Ark." A single adult must confront the inaccurate view that he or she is always lonely, is a workaholic, or is immature. These stereotypes help to support the traditional assumption in the United States and most other societies that to be truly happy and fulfilled, a person must get married and raise a family. To counter these societal expectations, singles have formed numerous support groups (Hertz 2006; Lundquist 2006).

Marriage without Children

There has been a modest increase in childlessness in the United States. According to census data, about 16 to 17 percent of women will now complete their childbearing years without having borne any children, compared to 10 percent in 1980. As many as 20 percent of women in their 30s expect to remain childless (Biddlecom and Martin 2006).

Childlessness within marriage has generally been viewed as a problem that can be solved through such means as adoption and artificial insemination. More and more couples today, however, choose to not have children and regard themselves as child-free rather than childless. They do not believe that having children automatically follows from marriage, nor do they feel that reproduction is the duty of all married couples. Childless couples have formed support groups (with names like No Kidding) and set up Web sites.

Economic considerations have contributed to this shift in attitudes; having children has become quite expensive. According to a government estimate made for 2008, the average middle-class family will spend $221,190 to feed, clothe, and shelter a child from birth to age 18. If the child attends college, that amount could double, depending on the college chosen. In 1960, parents spent only 2 percent of their income on child care and education; now they spend 16 percent, reflecting the rising dependence on nonfamily child care (see the Social Policy section in Module 15). Aware of the financial pressures, some couples are weighing the advantages of a child-free marriage (Lino and Carlson 2009).

Childless couples are beginning to question current practices in the workplace. While applauding employers' efforts to provide child care and flexible work schedules, some nevertheless express concern about tolerance of employees who leave early to take children to doctors, ball games, or after-school classes. As more dual-career couples enter the paid labor force and struggle to balance career and familial responsibilities, conflicts with employees who have no children may increase (Biddlecom and Martin 2006).

 use your **sociological imagination**

What would happen to our society if many more married couples suddenly decided to not have children? How would society change if cohabitation and/or singlehood became the norm?

Lesbian and Gay Relationships

Twenty-one-year-old Parke, a junior in college, grew up in a stable, loving family. A self-described fiscal conservative, he credits his parents with instilling in him a strong work ethic. Sound like an average child of an average family? The only break with traditional expectations in this case is that Parke is the son of a lesbian couple (P. Brown 2004).

The lifestyles of lesbians and gay men are varied. Some live in long-term, monogamous relationships; others live alone or with roommates. Some remain in "empty-shell" heterosexual marriages and do not publicly acknowledge their homosexuality. Others live with children from a former marriage or with adopted children. Based on election exit polls, researchers for the National Health and Social Life Survey and the Voter News Service estimate that 2 to 5 percent of the adult population identify themselves as either gay or lesbian. An analysis of the 2000 Census shows a minimum of at least 600,000 gay households, and a gay and lesbian adult population approaching 10 million (E. Laumann et al. 1994b:293; David M. Smith and Gates 2001).

Gay and lesbian couples face discrimination on both a personal and a legal level. Their inability to marry denies them many rights that married couples take for granted, from the ability to make decisions for an incapacitated partner to the right to receive government benefits to dependents, such as Social Security payments. Though gay couples consider themselves families just like the straight couples who live down the street, they are often treated as if they are not.

Precisely because of such inequities, many gay and lesbian couples are now demanding the right to marry. In the Social Policy section that follows, we will examine the highly controversial issue of gay marriage.

 use your **sociological imagination**

Which of the four different lifestyles described in this module do you think would be most and least acceptable to your friends? Why?

social policy and the Family

Gay Marriage

In the United States, attitudes toward marriage are complex. As always, society and popular culture suggest that a young man or woman should find the perfect mate, settle down and marry, have children, and live happily ever after. But young people are also bombarded by messages implying the frequency of adultery and the acceptability of divorce. In this atmosphere, the idea of same-sex marriage strikes some people as only the latest of many attacks on traditional marriage. To others, it seems an overdue acknowledgment of the formal relationships that faithful, monogamous gay couples have long maintained.

Understanding the Issue

What has made gay marriage the focus of national attention? Events in two states brought the issue to the forefront. In 1999, Vermont gave gay couples the legal benefits of marriage through civil union, but stopped short of calling the arrangement a marriage. Then, in 2003, the Massachusetts Supreme Court ruled 4–3 that under the state's constitution, gay couples have the right to marry—a ruling the U.S. Supreme Court has refused to review. Now, with gay married couples in this state passing their 5th anniversaries and approaching their 10th, scholars are beginning to study their experiences compared to those of opposite-sex couples.

Recently, national surveys of attitudes toward gay marriage in the United States have shown an almost even split among the public. A 2009 survey showed that 53 percent oppose allowing gay men and lesbians to marry. However, 57 percent favor allowing them to enter legal unions—arrangements that give gay couples many of the same rights as marriage (E. Kelley and Bazar 2010).

(continued)

MAPPING LIFE NATIONWIDE

FIGURE 41-3 **Gay Marriage by State**

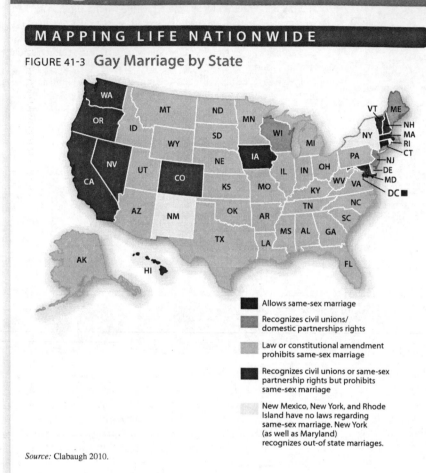

- Allows same-sex marriage
- Recognizes civil unions/ domestic partnerships rights
- Law or constitutional amendment prohibits same-sex marriage
- Recognizes civil unions or same-sex partnership rights but prohibits same-sex marriage
- New Mexico, New York, and Rhode Island have no laws regarding same-sex marriage. New York (as well as Maryland) recognizes out-of-state marriages.

Source: Clabaugh 2010.

Applying Sociology

Functionalists have traditionally seen marriage as a social institution that is closely tied to human reproduction. Same-sex marriage would at first appear not to fit that arrangement. But many same-sex couples are entrusted with the socialization of young children, whether or not their relationship is recognized by the state. Functionalists also wonder whether religious views toward marriage can be ignored. The courts have focused on civil marriage, but religious views are hardly irrelevant, even in a country like the United States, which observes a separation between religion and the state. Indeed, religious teachings have led even some staunch supporters of gay rights to oppose same-sex marriage on spiritual grounds.

Conflict theorists have charged that denial of the right to marry reinforces the second-class status of gays and lesbians. Some have compared the ban against gay marriage to past policies that until 1967 banned interracial marriage in 32 states. Figure 41-3 illustrates the different ways same-sex partnerships are treated today in different states.

Interactionists generally avoid the policy question and focus instead on the nature of same-sex households. They ask many of the same questions about gay partner relations and child rearing that they ask about conventional couples. Of course, much less research has been done on same-sex households than on other families, but the studies published to date raise the same issues as those that apply to conventional married couples, plus a few more. For gay couples, the support or opposition of family, co-workers, and friends looms large (Dundas and Kaufman 2000; Dunne 2000).

Initiating Policy

The United States is not the first nation to consider this issue. Recognition of same-sex partnerships is common in Europe, including legal recognition of same-sex marriage in Belgium, the Netherlands, Norway, Portugal, Spain, and Sweden. Today, as many as 8 percent of all marriages in the Netherlands are same-sex. The trend is toward recognition in North America as well, since gay couples can marry legally in Canada.

Many nations strongly oppose such measures, however. For example, when Kofi Annan, then secretary general of the United Nations (UN), proposed extending the benefits that married UN employees receive to employees' same-sex partners in 2004, so many countries rose in protest that he reneged. Annan decided that such benefits would extend only to those UN employees whose member nations extend the same benefits to their citizens (Cowell 2005; Maggie Farley 2004; Wines 2005).

In the United States, many local jurisdictions have passed legislation allowing for the registration of domestic partnerships, and have extended employee benefits to those relationships. Under such policies, a **domestic partnership** may be defined as two unrelated adults who share a mutually caring relationship, reside together, and agree to be jointly responsible for their dependents, basic living expenses, and other common necessities. Domestic partnership benefits can apply to couples' inheritance, parenting, pensions, taxation, housing, immigration, workplace fringe benefits, and health care. Even though the most passionate support for domestic partnership legislation has come from lesbian and gay activists, the majority of those eligible for such benefits would be cohabiting heterosexual couples.

In the United States, marriage has traditionally been under the jurisdiction of state lawmakers. But recently, pressure has been mounting for national legislation. The Defense of Marriage Act, passed in 1996, provided that no state is obliged to recognize same-sex marriages performed in another state. However, some legal scholars doubt that the law could withstand a constitutional challenge, since it violates a provision in the Constitution that requires states to recognize one another's laws. In 2003, therefore, opponents of gay marriage proposed a constitutional amendment that would limit marriage to heterosexual couples. The measure was introduced in the Senate in 2006, but failed to receive sufficient support to come to a vote.

Within the United States, state courts in California, Iowa, and Massachusetts have ruled that there is no state law that precludes same-sex marriage. In California, 18,000 same-sex couples were married before voters amended the state constitution to prohibit such marriages in the future. As of mid-2010, the District of Columbia and five states (Connecticut, Iowa, Massachusetts, New Hampshire, and Vermont) were issuing marriage licenses to same-sex couples. In August 2010, a federal court weighed in for the first time on gay marriage, ruling that California's ban on same-sex marriage was unconstitutional. Ultimately the Supreme Court will consider the issue. Gay rights activists claim their movement is gathering momentum, but opponents argue that their high-profile actions have galvanized conservatives who wish to define marriage as the union of one man and one woman.

TAKE THE ISSUE WITH YOU

1. If marriage is good for heterosexual couples and their families, why isn't it good for homosexual couples and their families?

2. How can interactionist studies of gay couples and their families inform policymakers who are dealing with the issue of gay marriage? Give a specific example.

3. Who are the stakeholders in the debate over gay marriage, and what do they stand to gain or lose? Whose interest do you think is most important?

MODULE 41 | Recap and Review

Summary

Divorce and alternatives to traditional marriage such as cohabitation now represent common choices of family style.

1. Among the factors that contribute to the rising divorce rate in the United States are greater social acceptance of divorce and the liberalization of divorce laws in many states.

2. More and more people are living together without marrying, a practice known as **cohabitation.** People are also staying single longer, and some married couples are deciding not to have children.

3. The gay marriage movement, which would confer equal rights on gay and lesbian couples and their dependents, is strongly apposed by conservative religious and political groups.

Thinking Critically

1. In a society that maximizes the welfare of all family members, how easy should it be for couples to divorce? How easy should it be to get married?

2. How is romantic cohabitation similar to marriage? How is it different? Could gay and lesbian couples achieve all the benefits of marriage without actually marrying?

Key Terms

Cohabitation

Domestic partnership